THE RIVER RUNS BLACK

THE RIVER RUNS BLACK

THE ENVIRONMENTAL CHALLENGE TO CHINA'S FUTURE
Second Edition

ELIZABETH C. ECONOMY

A COUNCIL ON FOREIGN RELATIONS BOOK

CORNELL UNIVERSITY PRESS
ITHACA & LONDON

Copyright © 2004, 2010 by Cornell University

All rights reserved. Except for brief quotations in a review, this book, or parts thereof, must not be reproduced in any form without permission in writing from the publisher. For information, address Cornell University Press, Sage House, 512 East State Street, Ithaca, New York 14850.

First edition published 2004 by Cornell University Press. Second edition 2010.

Printed in the United States of America

Library of Congress Cataloging-in-Publication Data

Economy, Elizabeth, 1962–
  The river runs black : the environmental challenge to China's future / Elizabeth C. Economy.
    p. cm.
  2nd ed.
  "A Council on Foreign Relations book."
  Includes bibliographical references and index.
  ISBN 978-0-8014-4924-6 (cloth : alk. paper)
  ISBN 978-0-8014-7613-6 (pbk. : alk. paper)
    1. Environmental policy—China. 2. Economic development—Environmental aspects. 3. China—Economic conditions. I. Title.

  HC430.E5E36 2010
  333.70951—dc22

                                                            2010018970

Cornell University Press strives to use environmentally responsible suppliers and materials to the fullest extent possible in the publishing of its books. Such materials include vegetable-based, low-VOC inks and acid-free papers that are re-cycled, totally chlorine-free, or partly composed of nonwood fibers. For further information, visit our website at www.cornellpress.cornell.edu.

Cloth printing 10 9 8 7 6 5 4 3 2 1
Paperback printing 10 9 8 7 6 5 4 3 2 1

To my family

CONTENTS

ACKNOWLEDGMENTS

For nearly three decades, I, along with the rest of the world, have watched as the Chinese people have transformed their country from a poverty-stricken nation into an economic powerhouse. Equally striking, however, has been the terrible price China's environment has paid for this impressive transformation. Today, the environment is exacting its own toll on the Chinese people, impinging on continued economic development, forcing large-scale migration, and inflicting significant harm on the public's health. When *The River Runs Black* was first published in 2004, these issues were still well below the radar of many in and outside China. In the six years since, events such as the Beijing Olympics and issues such as climate change have made China's environmental challenges a household concern. The result has been an explosion of interest and activity surrounding the challenge of how China can more effectively integrate economic development and environmental protection. Senior Chinese officials, business leaders, and civil society are all engaged in transforming the way their country does business. This second edition of *The River Runs Black* captures this new dynamism: Beijing's drive for green technology, the growing activism of the Chinese people, and the innovative efforts of Chinese planners and their international partners to establish eco-cities throughout the country. Still, powerful political and economic forces within China's system continue to impede change. This book illuminates not only the exciting changes but also the continuing challenges to realizing real progress in China's environmental effort. They are challenges that neither the Chinese people nor the rest of the world can afford to ignore.

For the past fifteen years, I have been a Fellow at the Council on Foreign Relations. During this time, I have benefited immeasurably from the support and guidance of the former Council president Leslie Gelb and the current president, Richard Haass. Both have challenged me to be better, without ever impinging on my freedom to set my own research agenda. They, together with the Council's director of studies James Lindsay, have also created a dynamic community of Fellows at the Council, and my work has benefited in every way from my interaction with these talented scholars. Adam Segal has been particularly generous in taking time from his own research to challenge me and my ideas throughout the process of writing and revising this work.

Many Chinese environmentalists, scientists, and officials have been extraordinarily patient in helping me navigate the world of China's environmental politics and have shared their expertise with me for more than fifteen years. Many have become close friends, and, while they remain unnamed, I owe them a special debt of gratitude.

Throughout my tenure at the Council, I have also been blessed by an outstanding group of research associates and interns. In the process of producing this second edition, I have relied above all on the first-rate research abilities, good humor, and unflagging patience of my research associate Jaeah Lee and intern Sarah McGrath. They have spent countless hours delving deeply into Chinese statistical materials and helping me to see a forest from within all the trees. Sarah Miller and Paull Randt also provided important research assistance at an earlier stage of this edition. Nancy Yao, Vanessa Guest, Eric Aldrich, and Laura Geller all contributed significantly to the first edition.

I thank Roger Haydon at Cornell University Press for his enthusiasm for my manuscript and willingness to move quickly to bring it to fruition. Jonathan Hall provided excellent support for the first edition once it was published. Their continued encouragement has made the process of revisiting and rethinking my first work a pleasure.

No amount of counsel and guidance, however, could substitute for the support and love of my family. For that, I thank my parents, James and Anastasia, and siblings, Peter, Katherine, and Melissa. Together, they created a loving and intellectually stimulating family in which to grow up. I am most fortunate now to have another wonderful home with my husband, David Wah, and our three children, Alexander, Nicholas, and Eleni. They make every day an adventure.

Elizabeth C. Economy

New York City

THE RIVER RUNS BLACK

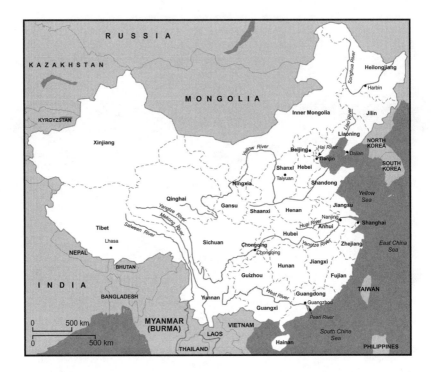

CHAPTER ONE

THE DEATH OF THE HUAI RIVER

In late July 2001, the fertile Huai River Valley—China's breadbasket—was the site of an environmental disaster. Heavy rains flooded the river's tributaries, flushing more than 38 billion gallons of highly polluted water into the Huai.[1] Downstream, in Anhui Province, the river water was thick with garbage, yellow foam, and dead fish.[2] Although the authorities quickly proclaimed the situation under control, the incident represented a stunning failure for China's leadership. Only seven months earlier, the government had proclaimed its success in cleaning up the Huai. A six-year campaign to rid the region of polluting factories that dumped their wastewater into the river had ostensibly raised the quality of the water in the river and its more than one hundred tributaries to the point that people could once again fish, irrigate their crops, and even drink from the river.

The story of the Huai River over the past five decades epitomizes the saga of environmental change in China. It's a paradoxical tale, one that holds out the promise of significant change in the future, while exposing the failures of China's current environmental practices, many of which are rooted in centuries-old traditions.

The Huai River Valley, including Anhui, Jiangsu, Shandong, and Henan Provinces, is a fertile region in eastern China. It is roughly the size of England with a population of over 150 million people, all of whom depend on the Huai for their water supply. The river originates in Henan's Tongbai Mountain and flows east for over six hundred miles through Henan, Anhui, and Jiangsu Provinces before flowing into the Yangtze River.

The Huai River Valley is a relatively prosperous region, with average per capita incomes in 2007 ranging from about $950 in Anhui to almost $1,680 in Jiangsu.[3] Long known for its rich supply of grain, cotton, oil, and fish, the river basin has over the past twenty-five years become home to tens of thousands of small factories. Paper and pulp mills, chemical factories, and dyeing and tanning plants, employing anywhere from ten to several thousand people, have sprouted all along the banks of the river and its tributaries, driving much of the economic dynamism of the region and the nation. They have also freely dumped their waste into the river, making the Huai China's fourth most polluted river system.[4]

The Huai River boasts a dramatic and tumultuous history. In 1950, disastrous flooding prompted Mao Zedong to create the Huai River Basin Commission. As part of Mao's campaign to control rivers, the Commission commandeered tens of millions of Chinese to construct no fewer than 195 dams along the Huai.[5] In August 1975, two of the largest dams, Shimantan and Banqiao, collapsed, killing an estimated 230,000 people.[6]

The dams have also contributed to the numerous pollution disasters that have plagued the Huai River for more than two decades. Local officials upstream have repeatedly opened the sluice gates of the dams, releasing polluted water that has poisoned crops and fish downstream thereby ruining local farms and fisheries. The problem is compounded by the roughly four thousand reservoirs constructed along the river, which limit the river's capacity to dilute the pollutants.[7] In many stretches of the river, the water is unfit for drinking.

Despite relatively high average annual rainfall of thirty-four inches, many parts of the river basin are also prone to drought,[8] worsening the concentration of pollutants. Along some parts of the river, people have long recorded higher than normal rates of cancer and birth defects. According to one estimate, the death rate along one stretch of the main river is one third above the provincial average, and the cancer rates are twice the provincial average.[9] A report on the region in the late 1990s also notes that "for years no boy from [certain villages in] the Huai River area has been healthy enough to pass the physical examination required to enter the army."[10]

The Chinese leadership has not been unaware of the river's growing pollution. After the first pollution disaster in 1974, the Chinese leadership in Beijing established the Huai River Valley Bureau of Water Resources Protection and the Huai River Conservancy Commission of the Ministry of Water Resources. These offices had no funding and no real authority, however, and as the region developed economically, the environment deteriorated rapidly. As one official from China's central environmental agency, the National Environmental Protection Agency (NEPA) described the situation, "Economic development had just occurred blindly."[11] In 1988, Beijing established a central government agency, the Leading Group on Water Resources Protection for the Huai River Basin, raising the profile of the problem at least bureaucratically. But by 1990, to cut costs and realize greater profits, fewer than half of the factories in the valley were operating their waste disposal systems, and only 25 percent of treated wastewater met state standards. Sensing impending disaster, the Bureau of Water Resources Protection pressed local officials to close down or retrofit some of the most egregious polluters. Some were closed, but others quickly opened in their stead.[12]

Moreover, the four provinces dependent on the Huai were incapable of coordinating a policy to address the problem. By 1993, the director of the Bureau of Water Resources Protection was complaining to no avail about the rising number of interprovincial disputes over the Huai and the lack of any authority capable of resolving them. In May 1994, Beijing responded—at last—to the warnings of the local environmental officials and, perhaps, to the growing social unrest in the region.[13] The country's top environmental oversight body, the State Environmental Protection Commission (SEPC), under the auspices of the State Council, convened a meeting in Anhui Province to discuss the problem of provincial cooperation on environmental issues. But the meeting produced no tangible change in policy or practice.

Just two months later, a number of factories along the Huai emptied their waste tanks directly into the river, producing a toxic mix of ammonia and nitrogen compounds, potassium permanganate, and phenols, contaminating the middle and lower reaches of the river. The water turned black, and factories were forced to close down. Fisheries were destroyed, almost 26 million pounds of fish were killed, and thousands of people were treated for dysentery, diarrhea, and vomiting.[14] In the immediate aftermath, local authorities in one town (Bengbu, Anhui) released polluted water that had been pent up by their local dam. During the following two weeks, more than 52 billion gallons of polluted river water were released. As the media flocked to the scene, local officials attempted to hide the extent of the disaster; in response, villagers pelted the officials with eggs.[15]

The central leadership immediately dispatched an investigation team, headed by Song Jian, the highly respected chairman of the SEPC. During the team's visit, a peasant offered Song a glass of the river water to drink. After sipping from the cup, Song invited the provincial and local officials to finish the glass, informing them simultaneously that if they did not clean up the river, they would be fired.[16] Some action followed. Reportedly nearly one thousand factories were closed down or relocated; others received a three-year grace period until 1997 to improve their environmental practices. Premier Li Peng announced a two-stage campaign: first, to halt all industrial waste pollution by 1997; and second, to have the river run clear by 2000.

To accomplish these goals, the State Council established an interministerial subcommission including the Ministry of Water Resources, the State Planning Commission, and the Ministry of Finance, among others.[17] Then director of NEPA Xie Zhenhua announced specific steps to improve the situation: nineteen industrial firms in four provinces were given specific targets to meet. In 1996, hundreds of polluting factories along the Huai were closed.

Yet the imperative of economic development continued to overwhelm environmental concerns. As Cang Yuxiang, a member of NEPA's Pollution Control Division, reported in 1997:

> They [local industries and regions] pay attention only to short-term interests to the detriment of the long-term, or their own area to the detriment of the entire river basin and, disregarding the harm done

to others, allow large amounts of waste water to flow to other areas. . . . Towns and villages continue to blindly build small paper mills, dye works, tanneries, and chemical plants with crude equipment, despite the government already having temporarily closed down some such 5,000 factories during the cleanup process. . . . Most of the water in the river system is rated at levels 4 and 5 (on a scale ranging from 1 to 5, the higher numbers indicating greater pollution) with some of the tributaries even failing to meet the number five standards and in the dry season basically becoming wastewater sewers.[18]

There were additional reports that the equipment from the shuttered enterprises was being sold to other factories,[19] and the U.S. Embassy reported that within two years, 40 percent of the closed factories had reopened.

Still, the government pressed on with the second stage of its campaign. On January 1, 1998, the Chinese leadership launched the three-year Zero Hour Operation (*Lingdian Xingdong*) to clean up the Huai River. In short order, local officials closed down 35 factories and halted production at an additional 198 plants.[20] Yet researchers at the Chinese Academy of Social Sciences Rural Development Institute voiced their doubts concerning the future efficacy of the campaign:

It is very unlikely that very serious regional pollution can be solved through the Zero Hour Operation. . . . Before the Zero Hour Operation arrives, many polluters will suspend discharging waste until the NEPA finishes its examinations. . . . The situation is unlikely to be reversed in the near future. It is difficult for the state to collect pollution discharge fees from small and scattered factories. They don't produce any proper accounts and no one can be sure about their finances.[21]

In discussing the problem, one of China's leading environmentalists at the time reported on the tactics used by factories along the Huai for avoiding closure. He commented that some of the small paper and pulp mills banded together to form large plants in order to evade government regulations on the size of the factories; other factories closed down during the day but operated at night. Moreover, local governments, fearful of economic loss, exerted enormous pressure on environmental protection officials not to pursue the campaign aggressively. The Chinese investigative television program *Newsprobe* paid two visits to the region in 2000, first to report on the efforts to clean up the river and then to assess their success. Not surprisingly, during the second visit, *Newsprobe* discovered that many factories that should have been closed were still operating.[22]

Reports of problems multiplied. In January 1998, just after the initial Zero Hour push, the water in Xiuzhou, an industrial city downstream from one of the Huai's tributaries, turned black, the fish died, and the residents were without running water for two weeks. (A few days earlier, the government had announced that the Huai was well on its way to "environmental resurrection.")[23] One resident complained to a foreign journalist, "The water here is always polluted. It's really serious. We can't even wash our clothes in this water. And when we tried to give it to the pigs, the pigs refused to eat for a couple of days."[24]

A second especially egregious case of continued pollution of the Huai involved Fuyang in Anhui Province, whose wastewater flows into the Huai. In 1999, Fuyang was designated one of China's ten "Clean Industry Cities." Yet in May 2000, ten residents of Fuyang collapsed along the city's main sewage outlet known as the Seven-Li Trench. Six of the ten died from exposure to the contaminated water. While the Fuyang government had already spent almost $600,000 on a system of sluice gates designed to control the flow of wastewater, they refused to spend the $30 million needed to clean up the wastewater that flowed through the gates into the Huai, arguing that attacking the problem aggressively would require the closure of much of the city's industrial base.[25] The residents of Fuyang were well aware of the dangers of the polluted water; when the sluice gate emptying waste from the city's main industrial area was open, the water turned black and a foul smell and haze emanated from it. Although the local villagers had complained publicly about the Seven-Li Trench, their complaints probably died with unsympathetic local officials. A television news team that reported on Fuyang in 1999, for example, edited a farmer's criticism to sound like praise. It emerged that Fuyang's designation as a "Clean Industry City" was the result of a deception common to many cities: Local factory officials were always warned before environmental inspectors arrived, and they ensured that their factories passed the inspections by shutting off waste outlets and flushing systems with clean running water.[26]

Fuyang now faces severe water shortages. The local groundwater is so polluted that the city has been forced to dig wells deeper and deeper, causing severe subsidence. According to one report, "[U]nderground water [is now] completely drained."[27]

In 1999 and 2000, the Huai ran dry for the first time in twenty years.[28] Shipping came to a halt as boats were left "high and dry in the mud."[29] In Hongze Lake downstream, residents "witnessed the ghostly walls of Sizhou, a city submerged by floods some 300 years ago, emerging into the light."[30] The local economy was hit hard with crops ruined and thousands of tons of fish dead.

Despite such reports, in January 2001, Xie Zhenhua, then the head of China's State Environmental Protection Administration (called the National Environmental Protection Agency until March 1998 and the Ministry of Environmental Protection since March 2008), stepped forward to claim that the water quality on the Huai River had reached the national III standard—suitable for drinking and fishing—and that 70 percent of the major tributaries had reached IV—suitable for industry and agriculture.[31] The *People's Daily*, China's foremost government newspaper, claimed that the kind of cleanup that had taken other countries twenty years to accomplish had been achieved by the Chinese in just a few years.

In the past, such assertions might have passed unchallenged. No more. On January 18, the *Worker's Daily* printed a front-page article asserting that the government's campaign had failed. Su Kiasheng, professor at Huainan Industrial College and vice-chairman of Anhui's People's Political Consultative Conference, a reform-oriented advisory body within the provincial government, claimed that the water was still seriously polluted and far from achieving the State Council's standards. Su also asserted that the discharge of pollutants in 2000 was actually double the government's targets and that the water quality of the Huai in Anhui was V—unsuitable even for irrigation: "To meet the State Council's targets, some provinces gave false figures and made false reports to the central government. As a matter of fact, the pollution has not changed much, although some of the smaller factories have been ordered to halt production." Su further pointed out that according to the government's plan there were to be fifty-two water-treatment plants along the river; instead there were only six, with a few more under construction.[32]

As surprising as Su's willingness to challenge the official line was the willingness of the *Worker's Daily*, as well as the Shanghai bureau of the *People's Daily*, to publish articles in support of Su's story. Moreover, a letter to the editor pointing out the discrepancy between the *People's Daily* and the *Worker's Daily* was published in a third newspaper, *China Youth Daily*.[33]

Su's analysis was soon borne out. In summer 2001, torrential rains caused yet another pollution crisis on the Huai, pushing 144 million cubic meters (38 billion gallons) of polluted water, which had been stored behind water locks in the upper reaches of the river, downstream, killing fish and plant life and threatening drinking water. The central government reacted quickly, ordering one hundred polluting firms to slow down or stop production and sending an inspection team to the region.[34] In 2002, the World Bank also signed on to assist in the development of several municipal and enterprise wastewater treatment plants in Anhui and Shandong Provinces to reduce water pollution in the Huai River Basin.[35]

And in 2003, a photographer, Huo Daishan, established a nongovernmental organization (NGO), Huai River Defenders, to track and publicize the devastating health impacts of the river's pollution. Huo had lost both his mother and one of his close friends to cancer. He has gained widespread admiration among many villagers who live along the river for the work his group has done, and he has brought about significant change in the wastewater treatment processes of some factories. Yet local officials often try to limit his activities out of concern that their reputations will be harmed.[36]

This lack of local commitment is the primary source of the continuing pollution challenges of the Huai, which is sometimes referred to as the most polluted river in the country. The Ministry of Environmental Protection reported in 2008 that over 60 percent of the Huai River's water was grade IV or worse—unsuitable for drinking, fishing, or, in the worst case, industry and agriculture.[37] The Ministry also noted that the capacity of the urban wastewater treatment plants was about 2.7 billion tons; the annual average waste, however, was 4.4 billion tons. Only 40 percent of the planned wastewater treatment plants had been built, and three of the four provinces along the Huai— Henan, Anhui, and Jiangsu—had failed to meet their targets for wastewater treatment. Only Shandong Province had met its goals.[38]

The costs of pollution to the Huai region will only increase. Cleanup costs are now estimated at more than $100 billion, and the number is rising.[39] The region is bracing for a huge, expensive river diversion project to bring water from the Yangtze to the Huai, a project that officials hope will be largely complete by 2014. As for the economic toll of illness and death, it is incalculable.

Beyond the Huai

Sadly, the saga of the Huai River Valley is typical of today's China. Throughout the country, centuries of rampant, sometimes willful destruction of the environment have produced environmental disasters.

- *Flooding.* In 1998, the Yangtze River flooded, killing more than three thousand people, destroying five million homes, and inundating fifty-two million acres of land. The economic losses were estimated at more than $20 billion. The culprit: two decades of rampant deforestation and destruction of wetlands.

- *Desertification.* Desert and highly degraded land, already covering one-quarter of the country, continues to spread, with the pace of desertification having doubled since the 1970s. Efforts to stem the advance of the desert through afforestation and development of grassland have had limited success. Today, dust storms originating in China traverse around the globe in a matter of days, shrouding skies from Beijing to Los Angeles, and dumping polluted particles into the Pacific Ocean.

- *Water scarcity*. Water scarcity born of changing ecosystems, sky-rocketing demand, increasing pollution, and few conservation efforts is having a profound impact on China's social and economic situation. As a result, factories are closing, tens of millions of people are leaving their land, public health is endangered, and the government faces a future of expensive river diversion and pollution remediation projects, even in areas once rich in water resources.

- *Dwindling forest resources*. China's forest resources rank among the lowest in the world. Demand for furniture, chopsticks, and paper has driven an increasingly profitable, environmentally devastating illegal logging trade abroad. China is now the world's largest importer of timber, the largest producer of paper and cardboard, and the largest exporter of furniture. Loss of biodiversity, climatic change, desertification, and soil erosion are all on the rise as a result.

- *Population growth*. Underpinning much of China's resource degradation has been the continued pressure of a burgeoning population. China's top leader until March 2003, Jiang Zemin, called the country's population size his biggest problem, particularly in the countryside, where many routinely defy the coercive one-child policy. Even if the 2005 official census is accurate, China's 1.3 billion people exceed by more than 300 million the goal set by China's leaders 15 years earlier. Yet in July 2009, Shanghai's family planning director Xie Lingli launched a campaign to encourage couples to have a second child, responding to concerns over the city's aging population and future labor shortages.[40]

At first glance, China's story appears to be a classic tale of economic development run amok: As China has moved to a market economy, freeing its economic actors to make money and exploit the country's natural resources without penalty, it now confronts an environmental crisis. Such an explanation fits squarely within the logic of thinkers such as Karl Polanyi, who predicted that the unfettered market would yield only negative consequences for the environment.[41] Others have argued convincingly, too, that China's large population and rapidly increasing integration into the international economy help explain why China now confronts such a substantial array of environmental challenges.[42] Yet, equally potent arguments are offered by others to suggest that economic development, population, and trade benefit a country's environment. Both sides of these long-standing debates over the relationship between economic development, population, and trade, on the one hand, and the environment, on the other, provide important clues for understanding China's environmental trajectory.

The Broader Debates

Whether economic development provides opportunities or challenges for environmental protection provokes sharp debate. Some believe that development is necessarily harmful to the environment, demanding the extraction and consumption of natural resources, such as timber, minerals, oil, and water. Studies of developing countries in Southeast Asia, including Malaysia, Indonesia, and the Philippines, offer some striking examples of how such exploitation of natural resources has contributed to devastating levels of deforestation, soil erosion, and desertification.[43] Proponents of this line of thought also point out that levels of pollution rise as economic development proceeds. Economist Asayehgn Desta, for example, notes that in China, the development of rural areas has contributed to alarming levels of municipal waste and pollution from increased pesticide and fertilizer use.[44] Underlying the problem, according to many theorists within this school of thought (such as Polanyi), is that the market does not properly account for either the use or the abuse of environmental and natural resources. So, as the market and economy continue to develop, this accounting failure becomes magnified and environmental problems increase.[45]

Others, however, counter that economic development brings important transformations within society that enhance environmental protection, through value change, technological progress, and improved state capacity. As political scientist Ronald Inglehart has discovered through decades of survey research, as incomes grow and poverty is reduced, educational standards rise and values such as environmental protection become more prevalent within society such that demands for a better environment grow.[46] Opinion polls in

China suggest the country may well be on a similar trajectory. In addition, economic development contributes to broader changes within the economy that can have a positive impact on the environment, such as growing access to technology that is environmentally friendly. As noted international economist Jagdish Bhagwati has argued, economic growth provides governments with the ability to tax and raise resources for a variety of social welfare goods, including environmental protection.[47]

This is not an either–or debate. Geographer Vaclav Smil suggests a middle ground for China: "There are no solutions within China's economic, technical, and manpower reach that could halt and reverse these degradative trends—not only during the 1990s but also during the first decade of the new century." At the same time, he notes that technical innovation, among other policy strategies, can reduce the future rates of China's environmental impacts from economic development.[48]

A second, related debate focuses on whether trade and foreign investment exert a negative or positive impact on a country's environmental situation. One commonly heard line of thought is that the comparative advantage in global trade for developing countries lies in the exploitation of their resources; therefore the impact on the environment is likely to be negative. In addition, trade, like the domestic market, does not take into account environmental costs and therefore further impedes a country's ability to protect the environment.[49] Moreover, competition for foreign investment may lead countries to specialize in pollution-intensive industries,[50] providing opportunities for other countries to offload their most polluting industries. As Yok-shiu Lee and Alvin So argue in their study of environmental movements in Asia, many multinationals transfer "substandard industrial plants and hazardous production processes" to Southeast Asia to avoid the health and pollution standards of their home countries. They note: "To a great extent, most of these trade- and investment-induced environmental degradation and pollution problems in Southeast Asia can be traced to multinational corporations that are either exploiting raw materials in or have shifted their industrial production operations to the region."[51] Finally, while some analysts acknowledge that trade-created wealth allows for social conditions to improve, they further point out that national governments will try to protect national industries. This in turn will contribute to inefficiencies in domestic production with negative environmental impacts.[52]

Yet, others have argued equally vociferously that economic development and integration into the international economy positively affect environmental protection. As Jose Furtado and Tamara Belt suggest, trade stimulates economic growth, optimizes efficiency of resource use, increases the standard of living and thus the demand for environmental services, and results in more funding of institutions for environmental protection.[53] Similarly, as John Audley argues in his study *Green Politics and Global Trade*, free trade simultaneously contributes to domestic economic growth, which will alleviate poverty and allow governments to spend more protecting the environment, and provides greater access to environmental technologies and less polluting industries.[54]

The third broad debate—perhaps the most contentious one—concerns how population affects the environment. It is encapsulated well by John Carey in his article, "Will Saving People Save Our Planet?":

> In particular, the question of just how much population control is necessary for sustainable development provokes a very nasty debate. On [one] side are the Malthusian pessimists like Stanford's Paul Ehrlich, who see teeming people as a malignant cancer that will grow to kill its planetary host. Unless the population bomb is defused, they say, no amount of development can save our priceless natural heritage. Nonsense, scoff the technological Panglossians, such as Ester Boserup, a Danish specialist in international development. They believe the additional people simply drive the engine of progress faster, raising standards of living for everyone. What keeps the disputes boiling is that plenty of evidence supports both positions.[55]

As Desta elaborates on the Malthusian perspective, "One consequence of population growth is the need for more land both for cultivation and for residential construction, leading to an increase in environmental deterioration. Similarly, population growth can lead to the decrease of per capita agricultural land, soil productivity, and a decline in nonrenewable resources such as coal, oil, and metal ores."[56] Many Chinese analysts, too, are among the strongest supporters of the necessity of controlling population to protect the environment:[57] "The Chinese population has long become [*sic*] a pressure on the resources in China. The overload, the excessive exploitation of the resources and the borrowing of the portion of resources due to the future generation have constituted a constant threat to the material base for the survival and development of the Chinese nation."[58]

Others, however, compellingly argue the benefits of population growth for the environment; namely, that population growth can drive technological progress either because of resource scarcity[59] or because population growth means more people to "drive the engine of progress faster"[60] and increases the chance that scientists will make discoveries that will improve the human condition in the long run.[61]

As Carey's comments indicate, these debates are kept alive because evidence exists to support both sides of each debate. As such, they do not provide a road map for understanding China's environmental trajectory. Instead, they offer some guidance in understanding both the environmental challenges and opportunities that China confronts as it develops economically, integrates into the international economy, and negotiates a burgeoning population.

Important, too, is what these debates do not address. In their purest form, they resist a discussion of the role of political institutions and politics in shaping a country's environmental and developmental pathway. But as many others have noted, excluding the political variable in these debates misstates the problem.[62] As China's story unfolds, politics—in a variety of forms—emerge as critical:

- Who are the key actors and what is their relative power?
- How are resources allocated to environmental protection?
- How is environmental policy formulated and implemented?
- What incentives do or do not exist for government, business, and society in China to advance goals of environmental protection?

Answering these questions helps explain why and under what circumstances factors such as economic development, population growth, and foreign trade and investment exert a positive or negative impact on China's environment. They are the key to understanding how China has arrived at its current environmental challenge and what this challenge portends for the country's future.

The Contemporary Political and Economic Context

As we will see, China's current environmental situation is the result not only of policy choices made today but also of attitudes, approaches, and institutions that have evolved over centuries. Yet, today, China's environmental practices are overwhelmingly shaped by the dramatic process of economic and political reform that has been transforming the country since the late 1970s.

The China inherited by Deng Xiaoping and his supporters thirty years ago reflected decades, if not centuries, of political and economic upheaval. Over two thousand years, dynasties rose and fell, typically amid great turmoil. China's first experiment with a republican form of government, beginning in 1912, soon fell victim to both internal and external challenges to its legitimacy. More than three decades of turmoil, civil war, and Japanese military aggression ensued, and General Chiang Kai-shek's efforts to unify China under his own brutal and corrupt leadership during this time ultimately collapsed at the hands of Mao Zedong and China's communists in 1949.

Mao moved quickly to establish an extensive, functioning bureaucracy and centrally planned economy modeled generally on that of the Soviet Union. Yet his pursuit of "continuous revolution" wreaked havoc on China's political and economic system. He instigated mass campaigns, such as the anti-rightist campaign and the Cultural Revolution, to root out those perceived to be not sufficiently revolutionary in their thinking; his quest for a communist utopia led to the Great Leap Forward, with its wildly unrealistic targets for steel and grain output. Together, these campaigns isolated China from the rest of the world and left tens of millions of Chinese dead or imprisoned and the Chinese economy in shambles.

By the time of Mao's death in 1976, the Chinese leadership had just begun the process of recovery. In 1971, the leadership took the first steps toward rejoining the international community by claiming the China seat in the United Nations (UN) from Taiwan and reestablishing relations with the United States, among other measures. In 1975, Premier Zhou Enlai enunciated the Four Modernizations (agriculture, industry, science and technology, and military) to revitalize China's economy and society.

With attainment of the Four Modernizations as their overarching objective, Deng Xiaoping and his supporters initiated a wholesale reform of the country's economic and political system. In the early 1980s, they began to relax the tight state control that, in one way or another, had defined China's economic and political situation since 1950.[63]

In the economic realm, this signaled the beginning of a transition from a state-directed, command economy to a more market-based economy. Beijing devolved significant economic authority to provincial and local officials, removing political constraints on their economic activities and diminishing Beijing's own ability to influence the development and outcome of these activities. China also began to invite participation from the international community in China's economic development through foreign direct investment and trade. By the mid- to late 1990s, the state had begun in earnest to dismantle the system of state-owned enterprises that had been the foundation of the urban economy, to encourage the expansion of private and cooperative ventures, and to energize the rural economy through the development of smaller-scale township and village enterprises.

In the political sphere, a similar transformation of institutions and authority took place, marked by four distinct processes of reform: (1) the highly personalized system of governance was transformed into a more institutionalized system with a codified system of laws; (2) significant political authority was devolved from central to local officials; (3) China embraced technological assistance, policy advice, and financial support from the international community; and, perhaps most dramatic, (4) as the government retreated from the market, it also retreated from its traditional role as social welfare provider, encouraging private, nonstate actors to fill the gap in areas such as education, medical care, and environmental protection.

China's reforms have significantly diminished the role of the state and encouraged newfound reliance on the market and the private sector to meet the economic and social welfare needs of society. They have also introduced new actors, institutions, and ideas into the political system. At the same time, as discussed below, the reforms have reinforced some of China's traditional policy attitudes and methods, sometimes in surprising ways. China's current environmental challenges, as well as its approach to environmental protection, reflect this rich, sometimes complicated mix of deeply rooted links to the past and dynamic new pressures and opportunities of today.

A Legacy of Devastation

The roots of China's current environmental crisis run deep. Through the centuries, the relentless drive of China's leaders to amass power, consolidate territory, develop the economy, and support a burgeoning population led to the plundering of forests and mineral resources, poorly conceived river diversion and water management projects, and intensive farming that degraded the land. As chapter 2 describes, this exploitation of natural resources, in turn, contributed significantly to the wars, famines, and natural disasters that plagued China through the centuries. The result was a continuous cycle of economic development, environmental degradation, social dislocation, turmoil, and often violent political change.

Furthermore, China lacked any compelling ethos of conservation. Rather, attitudes, institutions, and policies evolved from traditional folk understandings and philosophical thought, such as Confucianism, which most often promoted man's need to use nature for his own benefit.

As a result, little effort was made to develop institutions to protect the environment. China's leaders from the emperors to Mao Zedong relied on a highly personal system of moral suasion with few environmental regulations and no codified environmental laws. During the Qing dynasty, great effort was expended to develop a system of detailed laws, but it was not sustained after the dynasty fell. China's system of environmental protection was also highly decentralized, relying on individual regional and local officials to safeguard the environment within their jurisdiction.

China's leadership typically approached the environment through frequent campaigns and mass mobilization efforts for large-scale infrastructure projects, such as dams or river diversions that wreaked havoc with local ecosystems and were undertaken with little consideration for the actual environmental and scientific factors necessary to achieve success. The campaign to clean up the Huai River, in which the central government set unrealistic targets for pollution control and failed to follow through with appropriate incentives or disincentives for local government officials and businesses to change their behavior, is emblematic of how deeply rooted the campaign mentality remains in China's political culture (as discussed in chapters 4 through 6).

History therefore offered little environmental wisdom to China's post-Mao reformers. As economic reform took hold, China experienced dramatic average annual growth rates exceeding 8 percent, the elevation of hundreds of millions of Chinese out of poverty, and, eventually, the transformation of China into a global economic powerhouse. No effort, however, was made to account for the costs reform levied on the environment, and natural resources remained priced far below their replacement costs in order to encourage continued rapid economic development. China's leaders were well aware that they were trading environmental health for economic growth. The maxim "First development, then environment," was a common refrain throughout the 1980s and much of the 1990s.

Chapter 3 illustrates the enormous toll the reform period has taken on the environment. Rates of air and water pollution have skyrocketed. By 2006, China had become home to twenty of the thirty most polluted cities in the world and remains so today.[64] Acid rain now affects about one-third of China's territory, including approximately one-third of its farmland. More than 75 percent of the water in rivers flowing through China's urban areas is unsuitable for drinking or fishing. About one-quarter of China's land is severely degraded due to desertification, soil erosion, and salinization, and this area is expanding at a rate roughly equal to the size of New Jersey every year.[65] The leadership has also begun to witness the broader social and economic costs of its environmental failure. Over the next decade or two, Beijing anticipates the migration of 30–40 million Chinese—some voluntary, many forced—as a result of depleted or degraded resources. At the same time, a McKinsey & Company report from March 2009 estimates that China will urbanize more than 350 million people by 2025.[66] The economic costs of environmental degradation and pollution are also dramatic. By some estimates, they are already the equivalent of 8–12 percent of China's annual gross domestic product (GDP).

In addition, pollution-related illnesses are soaring. There have been serious outbreaks of waterborne disease, as well as long-term health problems in riverside communities reflected in rising rates of spontaneous abortion, birth defects, and premature death. Air pollution alone, primarily from coal burning, is responsible for 600,000 to 700,000 premature deaths per year.[67]

Perhaps most threatening to the Chinese leaders, protests over polluted water, damaged crops, air pollution, and forced resettlement contribute to the increasingly pervasive social unrest already confronting them. Top leaders have commented on the danger that environmental protest poses to the authority of the Communist Party and the stability of the state, noting that such protests topped 50,000 in 2005.

At the same time, China's leaders are grappling with the legacy of the past as population and national security concerns continue to shape environmental practices. While an aggressive family planning effort has cut the birthrate in half, there are wide regional discrepancies, with important economic and environmental implications. And, even as national security concerns over issues such as civil war have diminished, others have emerged. In the mid-1990s, declining grain yields and growing reliance on international grain markets prompted concerns over China's food security, resulting in yet another massive land reclamation and grain-growing campaign to ensure grain self-sufficiency. In the late 1990s the Chinese leadership turned its attention to China's west, where it confronted—and still confronts—a combination of discontent among minority populations and lack of economic development. In response, China's leaders initiated a massive economic development campaign to raise the standard of living and to secure China's borders from separatist movements—at great risk to the environment.

Yet, China's reforms have also changed the political landscape for environmental protection in more positive ways. As chapter 4 describes, spurred on by both environmentally concerned Chinese officials and the country's participation in the 1972 United Nations Conference on the Human Environment, China's leaders began the long, slow process of developing a formal environmental protection apparatus both at the central and local levels in the 1970s and 1980s. At the same time, they began to build a legal infrastructure for environmental protection, drafting increasingly sophisticated laws, signing on to international environmental agreements, and, beginning in the 1990s, training lawyers and judges on issues of environmental law.

Still, challenges remain. Beijing has not sufficiently empowered its environmental protection infrastructure to meet the vast array of environmental challenges. The Ministry of Environmental Protection and local environmental protection bureaus remain weak and underfunded, often incapable not only of advancing their interests in the face of more powerful development-oriented bureaucracies but also of utilizing the nascent legal infrastructure to protect the environment.

Moreover, devolution of authority to local officials, which contributed to such dramatic economic development in many regions of the country, has produced a patchwork of environmental protection. Some regions have moved aggressively to respond to environmental challenges, while others, as in the Huai Valley, have been far slower to develop the necessary policies and implementation capacity.

Some of the difficulty rests in the nature of the political economy at the local level. Local government officials often have close ties with local business leaders and indeed may be part-owners in local factories. It is difficult to police polluting factories that are at least partly owned by the local government and directly contribute to the wealth of local officials. Moreover, local environmental bureaus are embedded within the bureaucratic infrastructure of the local governments; enormous pressure may be brought to bear on local environmental protection bureaus by officials concerned with maintaining high levels of economic growth no matter the environmental costs. In some respects, this devolution of authority perpetuates a form of the same traditional, personalistic system of environmental protection that characterized Imperial China and produced wide regional variation in environmental protection.

In addition, in the 1990s, as the Chinese leadership gradually withdrew from its responsibility to meet all the social welfare needs of the population, including health, education, and environmental protection, it welcomed greater public participation in environmental protection. As chapter 5 explores, China's leaders have allowed the establishment of genuine NGOs, encouraged aggressive media attention to environmental issues, and sanctioned independent legal activities to protect the environment, partly to compensate for the weakness of its formal environmental protection apparatus. Grassroots NGOs have sprung up in many regions of the country to address issues as varied as the fate of the Tibetan antelope, the deterioration of China's largest freshwater lakes, and mounting urban refuse. And nonprofit legal centers have emerged to wage class action warfare on behalf of farmers and others whose livelihood and health have suffered from pollution from local factories.

The media have played a crucial role, directing a harsh public spotlight on enterprises that refuse to respect environmental laws, investigating the accuracy of government accounts of environmental cleanup campaigns, and exposing large-scale abuses of the environment such as rampant logging. In this way, the Chinese leadership hopes to fill the growing gap between the people's desire to improve the environment and the government's capacity or will to do so.

The scientist Su Kiasheng and the media that challenged the government's story concerning the water quality of the Huai River reflect the potential of society to become more vocal in its demands for a cleaner environment and to bring a new level of accountability to the Chinese government's environmental policies and proclamations, and perhaps even to the entire Chinese political system.

China's leaders have also looked abroad for inspiration and assistance. Chapter 6 describes how China has eagerly gobbled up technical and financial help from international institutions, as well as other countries. The international community has supported China in virtually every aspect of its environmental protection work—the development of a legal system, monitoring systems for air pollution, exploring energy alternatives to coal, and so on.

Yet, deepening integration with international actors carries with it a set of unpredictable challenges. Involvement by the international community brings not only financial assistance and technical expertise but also an array of political and social considerations that often diverge from the interests of many within the Chinese government. Infrastructure projects involving massive forced resettlement or programs involving minority populations, for example, often alarm international donors and focus unwanted international attention on China's human rights record. China's weak incentive system and enforcement apparatus for environmental protection also often thwart effective cooperation. Corruption siphons off money and goodwill from both donors and intended recipients.

Inviting such participation from both domestic and international actors outside the government is also an enormous gamble in other respects. Chapter 7 offers examples from outside China that show, once unleashed, such independent social forces may be very difficult to contain. In the former Soviet Union and Eastern Bloc countries, intelligentsia, including writers, scholars, scientists, and other professionals, as well as college students, used environmental protection as a cover for the sharing of broader grievances, and environmental NGOs served as a "school of independence for an infant civil society," as well as a training ground for liberally minded individuals to become "activist citizens" and "alternative elites." Many environmental NGOs in these countries allied with other social interest groups to focus more directly on revolutionizing the political system.

Similarly, in the less dramatic cases of China's Asia Pacific neighbors, environmental NGOs have been consistently at the forefront of political change. In advancing the cause of environmental protection, they have exposed the institutionalized corruption and lack of accountability of the entire system of governance. In countries such as South Korea, the Philippines, and Thailand, during the 1970s and 1980s, environmental activists became closely linked with the democracy activists who agitated for broader political reform. In these instances, environmental issues did not serve directly as a catalyst for regime change but did permanently enlarge the political space for social action. Already, several of China's leading environmental activists leave no doubt as to their desired outcome: not only the greening of China but also further reform of the country's political system.

Thus, China's path to its current environmental crisis and its environmental future depend significantly on how not only the central government but also local officials, citizens, and the international community manage the environmental legacy of the past and elect to respond to the challenges and opportunities that reform presents for environmental protection today. Chapter 8 explores three scenarios outlining how the choices they make will shape China's future environment and have broader implications for the country's social, economic, and political future.

Assessing the Trends

Looking back over the period since China began its process of reform, trends in environmental pollution and degradation alone would suggest that the reform process has contributed to a significant deterioration in China's environmental situation. Yet, scratch beneath the surface and an additional, more useful set of observations concerning China's current and future environmental challenges emerges.

First, while the reform period marks a break in both the nature of the environmental challenges that China confronts and the opportunities it has to respond to them, important continuities remain from centuries-old practices and ideas concerning environmental protection. In some respects, the reforms reinforce these traditional approaches to environmental protection: maintaining a campaign mentality, relying on local officials for core aspects of environmental protection, and viewing the environment as an issue of national security.

Second, the Chinese government has made dramatic strides in developing institutions and a legal system to protect the environment, but the nature of Chinese politics, including endemic corruption and a lack of transparency, often renders the system dysfunctional.

Third, within China, there is extraordinary variability in environmental pollution and degradation statistics. As others have discovered looking at issues as varied as agriculture, automobiles, and technology, the decentralized nature of the state and decades of devolution of power to local officials virtually ensure that policy choices will be made and implemented differently from one region to the next.[68]

In a few select regions of the country, the reform process has already produced dramatic new benefits for China's environment and society. Still, in many others, it has contributed to a slide deeper into environmental crisis. Those regions in which reform has produced a positive environmental outcome, where pollution and environmental degradation are being aggressively and effectively addressed, share some common features: (1) the top local official supports or is perceived by other local officials to support environmental protection goals; (2) there is a strong level of environmental support provided by the international community and/or Beijing; and (3) the domestic resources available to local leaders to address environmental challenges are significant. The losers, in turn, are those regions with much weaker links to the international environment and development community; whose leaders are still overwhelmingly concerned with economic development and perceive the environment as a costly luxury; and, often, whose local resources to invest in environmental protection are far less than those in other parts of the country.

Finally, as the interplay of political and economic reform exerts an impact on China's environment, it becomes clear that the environment then too comes back to influence the reform process in critical ways. Most clearly, environmental degradation and pollution constrain economic growth, contribute to large-scale migration, harm public health, and engender social unrest. Moreover, there is the potential, already evident in nascent form, for the environment to serve as a locus for broader political discontent and further political reforms, as it did in some of the former republics of the Soviet Union and in some countries in Asia and Eastern Europe.

China's Rising Star: Implications for China and the World

In the first decade of the twenty-first century, China's leadership can claim much to celebrate. Sixty years of leadership by the Communist Party have brought unparalleled economic growth and well-being for the Chinese people, the expansion of Chinese influence throughout the Asia Pacific and beyond, and the return to Chinese control of Hong Kong and Macao. Only Taiwan remains to fulfill Beijing's dream of a Greater China. China's rise to major player status on the world stage was confirmed as the country completed negotiations to join the World Trade Organization in 2001, held the 2008 Olympics in Beijing, and has become the second largest economy and the largest exporting nation in the world.

But these successes come at a heavy price. Ignored for decades, even centuries, China's environmental problems now have the potential to bring the country to its knees economically. Estimates of the costs of environmental pollution and degradation range from 8–12 percent of GDP annually. Moreover, pollution and resource scarcity have become major sources of social unrest, massive migration, and public health problems throughout the country.

How China's leadership balances its desire for continued economic growth with growing social and political pressures to improve its environmental protection has profound implications for the world beyond China. Resolution of the world's most pressing global environmental challenges, such as climate change, ozone depletion, and biodiversity loss requires the full commitment and cooperation of China, one of the world's largest contributors to these environmental problems. Regionally, China's economic development contributes to problems of transboundary air pollution, fisheries depletion, and management of international water resources such as the Mekong River. China's influence is also being felt widely throughout the developing world as tens of thousands of Chinese companies "go out" (*zou chu qu*), or invest in and develop natural resources abroad to fuel the country's economic growth, often incurring serious environmental problems in the process.

Beyond this lies the fundamental question of the future of China's political and economic system and its orientation toward the rest of the world. The authority and legitimacy of the Communist Party depend on how well China's leaders provide for the basic needs of their people and improve their standard of living. Fundamental to the state's capacity to meet this challenge is the environment. Access to resources for household and industrial consumption, improvements in public health, and continued economic growth are all predicated on Beijing's ability to slow or reverse the forces of environmental pollution and degradation. Thus, the environment will be the arena in which many of the crucial battles for China's future will be waged.

A LEGACY OF EXPLOITATION

The environmental challenges China faces today result not from decades but from centuries of abuse of the country's natural resources. Nation building, war, and economic development have all exerted unrelenting pressure on land, water, and forest resources over the country's history. As early as the seventh century, China's population also began to take a toll on the environment. Through the centuries, in turn, exploitation of the environment contributed to the cycles of war, famine, and natural disasters that plagued China and hastened the disintegration of one dynasty after the next.

Underpinning China's current environmental challenge, moreover, is a deeply rooted cultural tradition that accords little value to some of the core elements of effective environmental governance: independent scientific inquiry, a transparent political system, and accountable leadership. As historians of science in China have described, Chinese culture, rooted in Confucianism and later reinforced by Marxism-Leninism, hampered the development of modern scientific rationalism.[1] Chinese scholars' concern with preserving doctrinal orthodoxy also constrained their ability to question freely. The harsh punishments meted out to those who challenged the prevailing dogma also severely inhibited "personal responsibility, initiative, and risk-taking."[2] Furthermore, the imagery and doctrine of Confucianism have prompted exploitation rather than conservation of nature's resources.

Of course, China is not alone in its wanton environmental practices and the devastation they have wrought. As Derek Wall notes in his history of environmentalism,

> Numerous ancient societies have collapsed because of environmental degradation. The builders of Avebury and Stonehenge seem likely to have caused massive deforestation, leading to soil erosion, climatic change and probable famine. The Mayan pyramid builders may have caused their own demise in a similar fashion. Over-zealous irrigation schemes that drew salt into the soil hastened the collapse of Sumerian society and possibly that of the Indus valley.[3]

A century ago, the United States was grappling with many of the same problems that currently confront China: rapid deforestation in the midwestern states, water scarcity in the west, soil erosion and dust storms in the nation's heartland, and loss of fish and wildlife.[4] These challenges sparked a number of grand-scale public and private initiatives to conserve the land, water, and forest resources, as well as the biodiversity, of the country.[5]

But what sets China today apart from the United States of a century ago, and from other countries currently at the same level of economic development, is the scale of the environmental degradation it confronts and the magnitude of the social, political, and economic challenges this degradation has engendered. No other country confronts the gargantuan task of meeting the needs of almost a quarter of the world's population on a land mass roughly the size of the United States.

The Environmental Tradition

The search through history for a cultural tradition of environmentalism in China yields a rich trove of artistic and literary references to the importance and beauty of nature. Chinese painting and poetry are replete with images depicting man's reverence for the natural environment. In Chinese painting, for example, respect for nature is reflected in the "smallness" of man relative to that of mountains, rivers, and trees.[6] Artists refrained from positioning people at the center of their paintings in order to counter the notion of man at the center of the universe.[7] Throughout history, wilderness symbolized sanctuary and refuge from the political strife of the times.[8] Mountains were especially symbolic in the major philosophies and religions of China as places where one could restore one's energy as well as one's understanding of the "good and the true."[9] Even buildings were sited to ensure harmony "with the local currents of the cosmic breath."[10] The great Chinese philosopher Confucius, for example, observed, "The wise find joy in water; the benevolent find joy in mountains."[11] This evidence of a deep appreciation for nature in ancient Chinese art and literature has prompted some environmental historians to suggest that China's environmental tradition was dominated by a respect for nature.[12]

Indeed, as early as the Western Zhou dynasty (1115–1079 B.C.E.),[13] the official elite demonstrated an appreciation for the need to protect China's environment. According to "Rite of Zhou: Regional Officer," local governors were responsible for protecting rivers, mountains, forests, birds, and other animals.[14] Several centuries later, Guan Zhong, the prime minister of the Qi State (?–645 B.C.E.) in the Spring and Autumn period of the Eastern Zhou dynasty, espoused values and practices that respected the relationship between humans, development, and environment. He advised the people to utilize the forest and the fisheries, but only to a "reasonable extent."[15] He also cautioned people "not to raise too many cattle on the grassland, lest it fail to recover from over exploitation; and not to plant crops too close together, otherwise the fertility of the soil would be insufficient."[16]

In contrast, Chinese folktales more often portrayed nature as a force to be overcome and utilized for human purposes. In one myth, for example, the great archer Hou Yi encounters ten suns burning so brightly that they threaten life on earth. He bravely shoots down all but one of the suns, thereby preserving earth and earning the elixir of life from the Queen Mother of the West.[17] Another story recalls the triumph of the Great Emperor Yu, who, seven thousand years ago, held back the floods of the Yellow River by dredging the waterways. His success gave rise to the belief that if people adjust their actions to circumstances, they can conquer nature's scourges, just as "Dayu [the Great Emperor Yu] regulating rivers"[18] did.

China's environmental tradition was also influenced heavily by the leading schools of early Chinese thought: Confucianism, Taoism, and Legalism. Buddhism, while not Chinese in origin, was also influential. Each school embraced earlier notions of man's relationship to nature as expressed in art, literature, and practice, and each brought to these ideals and practice its own perspective. In turn, these philosophies influenced Chinese authorities, elite and popular attitudes, and the overall ordering of Chinese society in ways both distinctive and important for the natural environment. Yet, as China historian Charles Hucker notes, while these schools of thought had "different points of view and emphases . . . , they were not mutually exclusive. Confucianism focuses on man in his social and political relationships, Taoism on man's status in the larger cosmic sphere, and Legalism on state administration."[19]

The Philosophical Underpinnings

To a significant extent, each of the major Chinese approaches to organizing social relations within the broader cosmos was rooted in earlier practices of the Western Zhou dynasty, which established principles regarding the human relationship to the cosmos that the great philosophers and statesmen of later dynasties would build on and modify. The Zhou believed that the cosmos was ruled by an all-powerful heaven (*tian*), which in turn entrusted one man, the King of Zhou or the son of heaven (*tian zi*), with responsibility for managing "all under Heaven." The Chinese world was to be united under this ruler, whose mandate was to govern with the counsel of wise advisers and bring peace and order to his domain.[20]

During the Spring and Autumn period of the Eastern Zhou (722–481 B.C.E.), the emperor was expected to respect the environment: "People who are of ruling quality but are not able to respectfully preserve the forests, rivers, and marshes are not appropriate to become rulers." And "In spring, if the government does not prohibit (cutting) then hundreds will not grow. In summer if the government does not prohibit (cutting) then the crops will not succeed."[21]

Confucianism

Confucius' vision of social organization emphasized the importance of morality, propriety, and social harmony.[22] Confucius imputed morality not only to people but also to the cosmos. He made the linkage thus: The universe and mankind are governed by an impersonal but willful heaven (*tian*); heaven wills that men be happy and orderly in accord with the cosmic harmony (*Tao*);[23] and an "ethical and virtuous life is the appropriate human contribution to the cosmic harmony."[24] The cornerstone of his philosophy was the "five fundamental relationships": parent to child, husband to wife, elder sibling to junior sibling, elder friend to junior friend, and ruler to subject. As long as the first subject in each pair provided the proper example for the second, harmony and freedom from conflict were assured.[25] A leader thus established order by being a moral exemplar, and government as a whole operated by example rather than by law.[26]

Nature occupied its own space in this filial ordering. The Confucian scholars Mencius and Zi Si (Tzu-Ssu), while developing the idea that humankind and nature were inseparable (*tian ren he yi*), also suggested that *tian*, encompassing the sky, God, and nature, was superior to humans, and that only raising the level of human morality could enable us to understand the objective laws of nature.[27] Xunzi (Hsün-tzu), the Chinese philosopher of the Warring States period (403–221 B.C.E.), however, conceived of humans and nature as occupying two different worlds, and he argued that nature would not change its objective laws because of human will: "*Tian* would not stop the coming of winter because of my hatred to coldness. *Di* [the earth] would not stop being broad because of my hatred to broadness."[28] At the same time, he articulated a belief in the human ability to meet nature's challenges and control it for human needs.[29] He developed the notions of "*Zhi tianming er yungzhi*" (master nature for use) and "*Ying shi er shi zhi*" (follow the law of

the seasons in agriculture).[30] He believed that by appreciating nature's laws, man could overcome nature's superiority and use it for
his benefit.[31]

During the Qin (221–207 B.C.E.) and Han (202 B.C.E.–220 C.E.) dynasties, philosophers continued to refine their understanding of the
interaction among the divine, natural, and human worlds.[32] Qin
scholars and philosophers, under the tutelage of Lu Buwei (Lü Pu-
wei), prime minister of the First Emperor of the Qin, produced the
comprehensive work *The Spring and Autumn of Mr. Lü* (*Lü-shih
ch'un-ch'iu*),[33] which established the emperor (*tianzi*)[34] as the intermediary among the three worlds.

Nature possessed a godlike ability to wreak havoc or bring bounty
as punishment or reward for humans' behavior. As the spiritual and
temporal leader of all mankind, the emperor was responsible for ensuring that every phase of human activity proceeded properly and
remained in harmony with the workings of the other two orders.[35]
Emperors took this responsibility seriously. According to one tale,
during the Shang dynasty (1766?–1122? B.C.E.), for example, "Emperor Shangtang decided to sacrifice himself after his country had
suffered drought for seven years. At the moment he lit the firewood
to burn himself, *tian* was moved and rained to put out the fire. The
drought was then relieved."[36]

Scholars did not merely content themselves with abstract philosophical ideals, however. Mencius, for example, counseled King Hui
of Liang: "Plant your crops according to the changes of season, you
will have more food than you want; limit the size of the holes in
your net, you will have more fish than you want; bide your time to
fell the trees, you will have more fuelwood than you want."[37]

Thus, in the Confucian conception, the world was governed by a
triad of heaven, which was the "creative force with an effective will";
earth, which was to "bring forth what Heaven generated, and to support and nourish"; and mankind in the middle.[38] Earth had the critical role of providing for man's benefit. In practical terms, "it was up
to man to invest toil and ingenuity in realizing Earth's potential,
thereby bringing forth the means of mankind's sustenance, and creating an admirable material civilization fit to awe barbarians. The
state justified its existence by leading society in this endeavor."[39]

Historian Rhoads Murphey elaborates:

In this classic agrarian society, the Chinese saw the land and the agricultural system which made it yield as the *summum bonum*, both materially and symbolically, the source of all value and of all virtue. The bulk of imperial administration was devoted to its care, directly or indirectly, and agriculture was the support of state and society probably to a greater degree than in any other civilized tradition since ancient Egypt. The emperor's most important ceremonial function was the yearly rites at the Temple of Heaven in the capital, where he ploughed a ritual furrow and interceded with heaven for good harvests . . . most of the gentry-literati . . . supported a deep respect, even a reverence, for a natural order conceived as grander than man and more to be admired. Admittedly this frequently had didactic overtones: a man should respect and admire nature as he must respect and admire his human superiors, specifically his parents and the official hierarchy which was symbolically viewed in surrogate parental terms. The proper attitude in both cases was filial. To question or attack nature was to contradict a broader natural order, sometimes labelled "heaven" (tian), and hence was potentially disturbing to the profoundly hierarchical social order of traditional China.[40]

Taoism

In contrast to the highly structured, morality-based system of Confucius and his disciples, the Taoist credo was "Let Nature take its course! Be yourself! Relax and enjoy life!"[41] As Hucker comments,

Taoism is a lyrical, mystical, but by no means irrational advocacy of individualism, quietism, and spontaneity in union with Nature (tao). . . . Nature is conceived as all-encompassing, as an impersonal, purposeless cosmos in which everything has its natural place and function; it is what it is for no reason other than that it is what it is, and can only be distorted and misunderstood when it is defined, labeled, or evaluated by standards such as good and bad that do not exist in nature.[42]

Taoism embraced a life of simplicity; man should live as close to nature as possible and do nothing with regard to organizing or managing affairs of state.[43] As Laozi (Lao-tzu) argued in *Dao De Jing* (*Tao-te Ching*): If it was a man's "lot" in the "natural scheme of things" to be a ruler, then he should keep the people "rustic and simple"—"fill their bellies and empty their minds, strengthen their muscles and weaken their wills."[44] As Ray Huang points out, the taoists' "acceptance of cosmic unity and readiness to return to primitive simplicity were reinforced by their resistance to the curtailment of freedom, either through enticement or through cohesion [*sic*]. Taoism, therefore, gave comfort to pantheism, romanticism, and not the least anarchism. Those sentiments, however, provided no immediate cure for the current political turmoil except to turn wise men into recluses."[45] Such a philosophy might protect the environment, but it would also delay economic development.[46]

Neo-Confucianism

The writings of later neo-Confucian scholars such as Zhang Zai (Chang Tsai; 1020–1077 C.E.) and Wang Fuzhi (Wang Fu-chih) combined the sense of order and morality prescribed by Confucian thinkers with a strongly Taoist "oneness" with nature: "Heaven is my father and Earth is my mother, and even such a small creature as I find an intimate place in their midst. Therefore that which fills the universe I regard as my body and that which directs the universe I consider as my nature. All people are my brothers and sisters, and all things are my companions."[47] For the neo-Confucians, human beings were "organically connected with rocks, trees, and animals and formed one body with the universe."[48] As Robert Weller and Peter Bol articulate,

> Neo-Confucianism continued to base ideas of personal and political morality on an understanding of "Heaven-and-Earth" as an integrated, coherent organism, largely consistent with the lines initially established by cosmic resonance theory. At the same time . . . the natural world [was] treated in practice as a metaphor for the integration and coherence that humans should try to establish in

social life; it generally did not lead scholars to the investigation of the coherence of the natural order or to a biocentric view of the world.[49]

Although modern neo-Confucians have tried to demonstrate an environmentalist spirit in their intellectual heritage, their predecessors were not environmentalists as we understand the term today (i.e., people committed to protecting the environment from pollution or degradation).[50] Rather, they were interested in exploring the place of human beings within the natural world and in establishing that people, as the "most advanced creatures," were "biologically endowed with principles for structuring perception, thought, and action that would, if realized, result in an integrated social world."[51]

Legalism

Legalism introduced yet a third, distinctive approach to governing human relations, one that developed over time, beginning as early as the seventh century B.C.E. The "final legalist synthesis" was achieved in practice by Li Si (d. 208 B.C.E.), chief counselor under the First Emperor of the Qin.[52]

Legalist thought was in some ways centrally rooted in the state of China's natural environment at the time. The Legalists argued that as China's population grew larger and food and other goods became scarce, strict controls and rules were needed. They believed that only the law could ensure that both the ruler and the ruled would do what was in the interest of the state as a whole. Laws were to be promulgated clearly and in great detail, with a system of rewards and punishments to encourage appropriate behavior.[53] Influenced by the Legalists, the Qin dynasty instituted a system of merit-based appointments for government service.

When the Qin collapsed, however, the Legalists fell into disfavor, and their system of governance was adapted to reincorporate many Confucian ideals. For example, once-absolute laws became far more relativistic and conditional. The magistrate was expected to consider every aspect of a case, including the circumstances, motivations, and consequences of the crime; "Quibbles about the letter of the law were not important."[54] Thus, the punishment for a local dyeing factory for polluting the water of nearby peasants might take into account how many people the dyeing plant employed and the impact of a severe fine on their livelihood.

Buddhism

Buddhism entered China via India by the second century C.E. and informed the Chinese approach to nature in a very different way. It encouraged reverence of nature by introducing the notion of equity between humans and other creatures.[55] In reincarnation, humans could return to the earth as an animal or insect; Buddhists, therefore, did not kill animals, and Buddhist monks were vegetarians. Buddhist monks also protected the environment in the mountains in which they typically lived. According to one Chinese scholar, the fact that "one-third of the most beautiful and famous scenic areas in China [today] are Buddhist temples surrounded by ancient trees" reflects the harmony between man and nature espoused by Buddhism.[56]

A Ravaged Land

Confucianism, Taoism, Legalism, and Buddhism share a healthy respect for the importance and power of nature to shape man's conditions and prospects for a fruitful and prosperous life. Yet it is the Confucian belief in man's ability to shape nature to fulfill his needs that is most evident throughout Chinese history. The efforts of early environmental thinkers and officials were overwhelmed by the imperatives of war, economic development, and population growth. Thus, the continual cycles of social transformations, including war, population growth, economic development, and eco-environmental change[57] resulted in astonishing levels of deforestation, desertification, soil erosion, and flooding.

Indeed, environmental historian Mark Elvin questions whether China ever achieved a balance between humans and the environment: "The restraint preached by the environmental archaic wisdom found in certain Chinese classical texts is both familiar and in all likelihood commonly misunderstood: it was probably not a symptom of any ancient harmony but, rather, of a rational reaction to an incipient but already visible ecological crisis."[58] As early as the Xia,[59] Shang, and Zhou dynasties, overexploitation of the land was evident: "As people completely relied on the natural productivity of the land, farmland was intensively cultivated to obtain maximum production."[60] The problem of "migratory farming" was especially severe as early Chinese peoples continuously relocated to find better land.[61]

Elvin describes a China in which the quest for power by both the state and the individual transformed the natural environment for the purpose of warfare. This transformation involved, for example, rampant deforestation for fuel for burning coal and intensive exploitation of the mountains and grasslands for ores to produce spears, cannons, and armor.[62] As he pointedly states,

> The Chinese search for power—both by the state and individual—was based, until very recent times, primarily upon an almost unending transformation of the lowland landscape to adapt it to an intensive agriculture, making use of hydraulic technology in the form of flood control, drainage, irrigation and seawalls to stabilize production in the face of irregularities in the weather, both seasonal and between years. . . . It has been the pay-off in power accruing to the "exploitation" of the environment at a rate overstressing its natural resilience and exceeding its capacity for self-renewal within a humanly relevant time-frame that has . . . made the process hard to restrain by conscious action, even when there has been a fairly widespread appreciation of its damaging effects.[63]

This was particularly evident during the 248 years of the Warring States period in which there were 590 recorded wars.[64] And, the Spring and Autumn Annals offer numerous references to war resulting from opposing armies raiding each other's crops and cutting off food supplies in time of famine.[65] The Annals also reveal that Qi State prime minister Guan Zhong convinced the leaders of other principalities never to "execute water works detrimental to the interests of the other states and never to impose a grain embargo in time of famine." But while Mencius, some 350 years later, cited the resulting Guiqiu Convention as a model for rulers of his time, he noted that such wise counsel was typically ignored.[66]

The ever-expanding search for fertile land also drew states into increasing competition and conflict. As Huang recounts, "On one occasion, perhaps in 320 B.C.E., the King of Wei, whose territory embraced both banks of the Yellow River, told the Second Sage [Mencius] that in times of serious crop failure he had to relocate the populace across the river in large numbers. By this time, the state of Lu had expanded its territory from its original authorization by five times, and neighboring Qi, by ten times."[67]

Even the consolidation of power after war often proved devastating to the environment. The first emperor of the Qin united six states and formed the first centralized state in Chinese history, an accomplishment that historians of China laud to this day. The emperor and his officials also constructed major irrigation works and canals to promote economic development and assist in the centralization of the state.[68] Yet the reality of state building placed an enormous burden on both the natural environment and the peoples of the time. Geping Qu and Jinchang Li detail:

> Unification by military force killed more than a million people and lay waste to 13 cities. Deaths related to hunger and displacement outnumbered those related to battle. After unification, large-scale construction detracted from other productive activities, leaving people with little respite. About 400,000 people helped build the Great Wall. Another 500,000 guarded mountains and suppressed riots. And 700,000 built the E'Fang Palace and Qin Shihuang's tomb at Lishan Mountain (site of the Terracotta Warriors). Diggers became sacrificial objects themselves. As a result, there were an insufficient number of men for farming and women for weaving. Although unification of the Qin was a great contribution to history, its rulers extorted taxes and forced military service on the people. The population of the Qin fell to below 20 million. Construction efforts during this period caused large-scale environmental degradation to forests and other natural resources. The poet Du Mu of the Tang dynasty approved of unification and the glory of E'fang,

but lamented deforestation: "Six states conquered, the world was united . . . with Shushan Mountain bare, E'fang Palace rose to glory."[69]

Thus, if war was one source of environmental degradation, the aftermath of war and the process of economic development was another.

The Han dynasty (202 B.C.E.–220 C.E.) illustrates how prosperity in China contributed to environmental degradation.[70] Population growth increased the demand for food. As arable land became insufficient, officials pushed the populace further afield to cultivate wasteland; more than 20 million acres of land were reclaimed for farming.[71] Local gazetteers during this time recorded the gradual deterioration and exploitation of the environment in individual regions. During the Han, for example, the people of Jiaxing, in the lower Chang (Yangtze River) delta, progressed from a situation of environmental affluence, where "food, including fruits and shellfish, was so abundant that the poor are said to have lived from day to day without keeping reserves," to a point in later imperial times where "economic, environmental and social stress is evident everywhere."[72]

As China's economy flourished during the Tang (618–906 C.E.), Song (960–1279 C.E.), and Yuan (1276–1367 C.E.) dynasties, settlers pushed southward, causing deforestation and soil erosion.[73] Still the needs of the people failed to be met. Qu and Li detail the unrelenting pressures of war followed by rapid development during these periods:

> Civilization was subsequently wrecked by natural and anthropogenic calamities, frequent wars, and general turmoil. The prosperous Yellow River Valley became desolate; water-saving facilities and farmland lay to waste; masses emigrated south or starved. . . . [74] [Even] in the heyday of the Tang dynasty, food production fell short of the needs of 53 million people. To meet the shortfall, 6.2 million ha [15.3 million acres] of land were reclaimed for agriculture, severely damaging many fragile ecosystems. . . . Soil erosion, river expansion, and flooding were other unintended costs. The Yellow River overflowed its banks more than 50 times in 100 years of Song dynasty rule.[75]

During the Ming and Qing dynasties, deforestation, flooding, soil erosion, and desertification all increased as the economy continued to develop:

> New approaches to agricultural production wreaked havoc on the environment; . . . entire forests were harvested for cultivation; reclamation additionally occurred on the frontier, prairies, mountains, and islands—all unique areas that buffered densely populated regions. . . . Employing various harvesting methods, the peasant farmers would leave nutrient-rich soils infertile after several years and deforest new areas. Centuries old [sic] forests north of the Qingling Mountains were left treeless. . . . An additional sign of environmental degradation includes unprecedented soil erosion. Sand content in the sedimentary layers of the Yellow River reflects soil erosion and frequent overflows. During the Ming dynasty, the river overflowed 127 times, approximately once every 2 years. Later, during the Qing dynasty, the river continued to flow over its banks, flooding more than 180 times in a 200 year period. . . . Cultivated areas and cities of the Han and Tang dynasties in the North and Northwest were literally submerged by sands during the Ming and Qing reigns. . . . The Badan Jilin, the Ulanbuhe, and the Maowusu deserts continuously expanded and destroyed vegetation. Desertified areas of Kergin in Northeast China were more or less created by land reclamation during the Qing.[76]

Beginning in the mid-seventeenth century at the onset of the Qing dynasty, grounds and parks were set aside for sightseeing and recreation, a practice that helped to protect animal and plant species that otherwise would have been endangered.[77] Yet the net effect of economic development during the Qing was an environmental disaster. There was a dramatic population increase, excessive cultivation of land, overherding, overfishing, and overcutting, all of which caused serious damage to forestry, agriculture, and fishery resources.

By the late 1800s, as Elvin details, China was a country wracked by "the exhaustion of resources, especially wood and mineral ores, shortages of water, erosion and lands ruined by salinization resulting from inappropriate development."[78] There was a "desperate anxiety about the supply of wood, and its quantity and quality . . . [as] the rate of depletion, driven by perceived economic need, exceeded the rate at which stocks renew[ed] themselves either solely naturally or with the help of an affordable silviculture."[79]

Natural disasters compounded these challenges. In 1876, thirteen million people died after a three-year drought. Ten years later, two million more people died when the Yellow River overflowed its banks.[80]

The Burgeoning Populace

The desire of successive emperors to increase the size of the population was a third contributing factor to the pressures exerted by man on the natural environment. Nearly all Chinese leaders regarded a large population as a necessity for a strong state, contributing both to greater tax revenues and a larger army. Shang Yang, the statesman that guided the development of the Qin state, argued that a large population and a strong army were the greatest assets of a ruler. Liu Yan of the Tang dynasty argued that if there were more people, there would be more tax payments. Similarly, Ye Shi of the Southern Song dynasty opined that "the most essential thing for a state is to have more people, because more people would till more land and pay more taxes and the army would have more recruits." And Qiu Jun of the Ming dynasty stated that "a peaceful life meant proliferation of people and if the population increased, the fundamental power of the state would be consolidated and the national strength would grow, thus bringing about great order and safety and stability to the throne."[81]

Not surprisingly, China has repeatedly confronted population issues. Elvin dates the problem to the Tang (618–906 C.E.) and Song (960–1279 C.E.) dynasties,[82] and Helen Dunstan as far back as at least the Sui dynasty (589–618 C.E.).[83] As Dunstan notes, "Confucian humanism was all in favor of the flourishing and propagation of the human species. For a region to be 'prosperous and teeming' was a positive phenomenon."[84] Mencius, for example, believed that "having no children" was one of the "three most impious acts."[85]

A few statesmen and scholars challenged the conventional wisdom concerning the value of a large population. Guan Zhong, for example, argued that population increases had to be regulated by two key ratios: land and the composition of the population. In the first instance, too many or too few people per unit of land would cause inefficiencies and potential food shortages. "A good ruler," he argued, "knows well how many people he reigns over; only sufficient arable land will make his people content."[86] In addition, balance between urban and rural populations and military and civilian populations was crucial. If there were too large an urban population, "there would not be enough farmland to support the population." Similarly, if there were too large a military, it would "leave base land uncultivated and also bring the nation to the brink of poverty."[87]

The Ming dynasty epitomized the impact of rapid population growth on the environment. During this period, the population expanded from an estimated 66 million in 1403 to approximately 100 million by the final years of the Ming in the mid-1600s. There were reports of widespread deforestation, massive land reclamation projects, soil erosion, and flooding as peasants left "nutrient-rich soils infertile" and moved to deforest other areas.[88] As a result, "floating" manual laborers and entrepreneurs migrated to the urban coastal areas in search of work.[89]

By the mid-1700s, Chinese officials formally acknowledged the difficulties of adequately providing for a large population by explicitly recognizing the link, for example, between the growing population and the increasing price of grain.[90] Yet it was not until a century later that Qing scholar Wang Shiduo proposed a set of measures to reverse the population trend. He advanced such draconian measures as the death penalty for men who married under the age of twenty-five and women who married under the age of twenty, a tax incentive for the infanticide of second daughters, and compulsory abortion.[91]

The Search for a Response

Throughout these centuries, China's system of governance was clearly inadequate to the demands of environmental protection.

Most responsibility for the environment lay with the provincial administrators, who made it an exceedingly low priority. To a Qing administrator, for instance, the two most important roles were the administration of justice and collection of taxes. He was also responsible for overseeing population registration, security, postal stations, public works (such as reservoirs and dams for local farm irrigation and roads), granaries, famine relief, poorhouses, and ceremonial observances, including sacrifices to the gods of earth and grain, wind, clouds, thunder, rain, mountains, streams, and agriculture. Finally, local magistrates were also charged with encouraging the people to farm and cultivate mulberry trees, dredge rivers, and build dams.[92] Yet few officials took the latter set of responsibilities seriously. One imperial edict complained that "it was difficult to find officials who would concern themselves with such things as farming and irrigation, which in ancient times had been encouraged by good officials."[93] As Dunstan comments, "Discussions of how to collect the land tax both successfully and with maximum sensitivity to peasant interests can be detailed, logical, perceptive and exhaustive. Environmental thinking was commonly attenuated by contrast."[94]

Nonetheless, some provincial officials took a serious interest in environmental protection. In Henan Province during the late 1600s, for example, Yu Sen, the province's assistant surveillance commissioner with special responsibility for watercourses proposed a massive reforestation program to address some of the devastation wreaked by the late Ming rebellions. While some aspects of the plan were not necessarily practical, his writings demonstrated a clear understanding of how willow trees could contribute to control soil erosion: "The soil of He'nan is not firm . . . and river banks are liable to become eroded. If one plants rows of willow trees, the roots will intertwine [so that] the protective dike is solid. At what point will it be possible for [it] to be washed away?"[95]

Yu also evidenced a broader philosophical approach to man's relationship to nature:

> The functioning of the five phases [wood, fire, soil, metal, and water] is such that failure to conquer means failure to generate. If now trees are scarce, wood will not conquer soil, and the nature of soil

will be light and easily blown away, while the human character will become crude and fierce. If trees are plentiful, the soil will not fly up, and men will revert to refinement and good order.[96]

Some officials also comprehended the correlation between development and environmental degradation and even developed overall plans for managing the ecosystem of a region. Chen Hongmu, Yunnan provincial administration commissioner in 1737, concerned himself with the full range of issues: reforestation, crop diversification, land ownership, and how to "brew" animal manure for fertilizer.[97] Chen's reports on reforestation indicate his clear understanding of how man had changed the landscape:

In mountainous Yunnan there were (originally) endless bamboo forests covering the serried hills, while trees and grasses grew luxuriantly and ample firewood was there for the taking. However, because the salt-works require wood, and mines and mints require charcoal, there has been daily cutting, resulting in denuded hills almost as far as the eye can see. Firewood and charcoal have gradually become dear and hard to come by; even the roots of grass and bark of trees are almost rarities. . . . Yunnan, being mountainous in all directions, has land on which grain crops cannot be grown, but it has absolutely no place in which trees cannot be planted. Besides, (since the province) was originally wooded with tall forests and dense bamboo thickets which have only now been felled almost to the last tree, reforestation should indeed be altogether feasible.[98]

At the same time, Shaanxi provincial governor Bi Yuan set forth measures to balance the burgeoning population with the increasingly scarce natural resources. He laid out a master plan for "managed settlement," which included resettling people, expanding irrigation works, and organizing a stock-rearing industry throughout the province, including camels, horses, oxen, and sheep.[99] During 1778–1779, he resettled over a hundred thousand people in the southern highlands.

The local people, too, were not oblivious to the harmful effects of poorly planned economic development on their livelihood and well-being. The damage to crops from local industry was a common concern during the Qing, and there are accounts of rural residents actively protesting environmental pollution. Dunstan recounts one case in 1737, in which 108 local residents submitted a petition to the local officials protesting that the dyeing workshops in the Huqiu hill district near Suzhou were polluting the local water supply, harming crops, spoiling drinking water, and damaging the scenic, religious spot. The authorities responded by prohibiting dyeing in the area.[100] In Yunnan, one citizen wrote a letter detailing the ways in which mining was harming the local crops by polluting the water and air and denuding the hills.[101]

Despite these scattered efforts, by the second half of the nineteenth century, the Chinese political system confronted a series of very serious challenges linked to the management of natural resources:

> Systems of water transport and control began to break down, partly through neglect but also ironically through over-expansion. Excessive dike building in central Hunan during the eighteenth century to create more farmland for the growing population restricted waterways and blocked drainage channels, leading to a protracted flooding in this rich agricultural area. Along the Yangtze, conflicting interests of officials and local elites inhibited dike repair. Water control elsewhere suffered from similar conflicts of interest and decay of old facilities. [Despite success in the earlier Qing period in raising] agricultural productivity [by introducing] improved seed strains and better farming methods, [during the later Qing and early republican period], agricultural production per unit of land began to stagnate and fall behind population growth.[102]

These problems were compounded by the large population in some regions, a failure to invest in public works projects, corruption, riots, protests against taxes, rebellions by minority people on the borders, and pressure from the West.[103]

The 1911 Revolution, which overthrew the Qing dynasty and the Confucian-based order, did little to relieve the deteriorating social, economic, and environmental circumstances of most Chinese. Approximately 80 percent were employed in agriculture, and most lived in terrible poverty. There were famines, mass migrations between provinces, widespread rural unemployment and poverty, and forced sale of land. Farmers fled the countryside to beg on city streets, and parents were forced to sell their children.[104] Customs officials of the time provided some insight into the rapid disintegration of the state, noting "the breakdown of law and order, the disruption of transportation and marketing, and widespread, uncontrolled flooding and drought throughout the country."[105]

The Nationalists did not entirely neglect the traditional imperial duty of economic development, and many urban centers realized economic growth rates of 7–8 percent under their leadership. The Nationalist leaders undertook flood control and irrigation projects as well as agricultural research to alleviate some of the environmental and agricultural problems faced by the peasants. Yet most failed to prosper thanks to "bureaucratic boondoggling" that resulted in "little positive achievement."[106] The peasants were further overwhelmed by demands from the tax collectors and other government officials for labor, supplies, and land.

Moreover, throughout the republican period (1911–1949 C.E.), the demands of continuous warfare either for the consolidation of power domestically or against an external foe, Japan, further contributed to the sustained agricultural crisis, environmental degradation, and social dislocation. By 1930, China's death rate was the highest in the world.[107]

Devastation under Mao

In 1949, the ascension to power of the rural-based Chinese Communist Party appeared to bring some initial relief to the economy and the environment. During the first five to seven years of Communist rule, the Chinese leadership repeated the practices of imperial leaders and began rebuilding the economy after a devastating war. Both agriculture and industry developed rapidly and, at the same time, some water and soil conservation guidelines were implemented. The Communists also launched major public works projects in water conservancy, afforestation, combating natural disasters, and other fields. Not all of these programs were effective. Liang Xi, the first minister of forestry, for example, stated in 1956, "As everyone knows, our afforestation statistics are not really based on actual measurements, but are fixed on the basis of mere eyeballing or guesswork. Consequently, there are mistakes, overestimates, and even totally unfounded reports."[108] Factories, especially power plants, were often built along rivers and without treatment facilities for waste water, waste gas, and industrial residue. Instead, the factories merely used the rivers for drainage.

Mao's vision for China as a great power[109] soon generated a renewed cycle of population growth, accelerated indiscriminate mobilization of resources in preparation for war, and grand schemes for economic development, which, in turn, contributed to severe environmental degradation and social turmoil. Moreover, while Mao praised the Legalist tradition of the Qin, articulating a strong belief in the importance of laws and regulations as "instruments for procuring happiness,"[110] his early writings suggested that people might often need to be "persuaded" of the utility of such laws. In his earliest recorded essay, "Essay on How Shang Yang Established Confidence by the Moving of the Pole," written when he was nineteen, Mao noted that the popular resistance to the brutal enforcement of Shang Yang's laws could be explained by "the stupidity of the people of our country," and their reluctance to undertake anything new: "At the beginning of anything out of the ordinary, the mass of the people always dislike it."[111] Rather than translating into an enduring legal system, Mao's understanding of Shang Yang's experience set the stage for a continuous cycle of campaigns and mass mobilization efforts, several of which had devastating consequences for the environment. Ultimately, few strides were made in advancing environmental protection regulations during the decades of Mao's rule.

Mao soon forswore even the pretense of respect for nature and for man's position in the cosmic hierarchy that had at least in theory guided the rulers who preceded him. His views suggested an exaggeration of Xunzi's approach; namely, that by understanding the laws of nature man could overcome nature. As historian Judith Shapiro notes,

The Mao-era effort to conquer nature can thus be understood as an extreme form of a philosophical and behavioral tendency that has its roots in traditional Confucian culture. . . . State-sponsored re-settlements and waterworks projects, extensive and excessive construction of dikes for land reclamation, political campaigns to change agricultural practices, and environmentally destructive land conversions in response to population shifts can be found in imperial times.[112]

As early as 1940, at a speech at the inaugural meeting of the Natural Science Research Society of the Border Region, Mao stated, "For the purpose of attaining freedom in the world of nature, man must use natural science to understand, conquer and change nature and thus attain freedom from nature."[113] Mao's later writings and speeches focused overwhelmingly on the need to conquer or harness nature for man's needs. As Murphey has described Mao's conception of nature, "Nature is explicitly seen as an enemy, against which man must fight an unending war, with more conviction and fervour and with a brighter vision of the ultimate results than even the Darwinian-Spencerian West held."[114]

Headlines in newspapers and magazines of the period offered evocative imagery in support of Mao's approach; for example, "The Desert Surrenders" and "Chairman Mao's Thoughts Are Our Guide to Scoring Victories in the Struggle Against Nature."[115] Mao himself penned an article in 1945 entitled, "How the Foolish Old Man Removed the Mountains," which retold the story of the legendary Yu Gong, who, in the face of scorn and mockery by his neighbors, was able to level two big mountains using only axes and the help of his two sons. In the retelling, however, Mao eliminated the conclusion, which acknowledged Yu Gong's supernatural aid from heaven, in order to avoid a contradiction with his message concerning the "boundless power of the people liberated and mobilized" to be able to move mountains.[116]

Mao's approach to the natural environment emphasized liberating and mobilizing the people to confront imminent threats from both environmental and human sources. He called on the people to prepare against war and natural disasters,[117] by digging tunnels deep, storing grain everywhere, and not attempting to dominate other nations.[118] Murphey bluntly states that this "assault on nature" was "a convenient rallying cry for an economically and technically underdeveloped society striking out, sometimes . . . blindly . . . ; the war against nature can be dramatized much more readily than the more prosaic processes of saving, accumulation, and investment."[119]

Mao's vision for China's future greatness had as its centerpiece a large population. In an August 5, 1949, white paper *The Relations of the United States and China* prepared for U.S. president Harry Truman, Dean Acheson argued, "The population of China during the 18th and 19th centuries doubled, thereby creating an unbearable pressure upon the land. The first problem which every Chinese government has had to face is of feeding this population. So far none has succeeded."[120] Mao's response to Acheson in his article "The Bankruptcy of the Idealist Concept of History" was to reiterate the utility of China's large population:

> It is a very good thing that China has a big population. Even if China's population multiplies many times, she is fully capable of finding a solution; the solution is production. The absurd argument of Western bourgeois economists like [Thomas] Malthus that increases in food cannot keep pace with increases in population was not only thoroughly refuted in theory by Marxists long ago, but has also been completely exploded by the realities in the Soviet Union and the Liberated Areas of China after their revolutions.[121]

At times Mao seemed to vacillate on whether there could be difficulty in meeting the needs of too large a population. At a 1958 meeting in Chengdu, for example, Mao said, "It would not do to have too large a population and to have too [little] land."[122] One of the hallmarks of Mao's rule, however, was the dramatic increase in population from 540 million in 1950 to 930 million in 1976, an increase for which China is still paying the price, having now attained a population of 1.306 billion.[123]

Mao also mirrored his Qing predecessors in failing to heed the wise counsel of an adviser on limiting the size of the population, in this case Ma Yinchu, a distinguished economist and former president of

Beijing University. In contrast to Mao's contention that "with many people, strength is great,"[124] Ma believed that if China's population continued to increase unchecked, it would become a major obstacle to the development of productivity. With population control, however, he argued "it would be not very difficult to make the lofty aspirations of building socialism a reality."[125] Ma proposed several measures, including family planning in the country's economic plans, late marriage, contraception, and a regular population census.[126]

Despite initial support from others within the scholarly community and the Chinese leadership, Ma, like thousands of other intellectuals, fell victim to the anti-rightist campaign during the late 1950s, losing his position and his livelihood. It wasn't until 1979, at age ninety-eight, that Ma was eventually rehabilitated by Deng Xiaoping: He was made an honorary president of Beijing University, and all charges against him were dropped—an acknowledgment of the wrongs perpetrated against him during Mao's tenure.[127] Such redemption, however, came twenty years too late to prevent the years of devastating consequences of Mao's population policy.

While Mao was to reverse himself many times on the issue of whether too large a population was problematic for China, it was not until 1974—when he perceived a reduction in the external threat to China from the United States and Japan and felt increasing pressure to feed and employ his people—that Mao called publicly for family planning population control.[128]

Campaigns of Destruction

Great Leap Forward, 1958–1961

In 1958, Mao's belief in the ability of man to conquer nature and his desire to achieve great-power status for China came together in the launching of the Great Leap Forward, a mass-mobilization campaign designed to catapult China into Communism and surpass the industrial achievements of Great Britain and the United States. The modest efforts at environmental protection of the early Communist years were quickly undermined as the country engaged in huge land reclamation projects for the purpose of planting grain, thereby laying waste to forests, wetlands, lakes, and rivers.

Qu Geping, who became the first director of China's National Environmental Protection Agency some two decades later, describes this period as one in which

> conceit began to emerge in guiding principles, and human will and capacity were exaggerated. . . . A 'leftist' tendency characterized by unrealistic targets, arbitrary guidance, exaggeration, and egalitarianism was rampant throughout the country causing great losses to the national economy and people's livelihood, as well as problems and damages to the environment and ecosystem. . . . During the Great Leap Forward, factories were built haphazardly without any consideration for environmental protection. . . . Biological resources, forests in particular, were seriously damaged, causing several losses to the ecosystem. . . . There was extensive destruction of the natural environment of our country.[129]

In hopes of raising grain yields to previously unattained heights, a wide range of misguided directives were issued. The Chinese people were exhorted to eliminate the four pests (rats, sparrows, flies, and mosquitoes); to afforest everywhere—"around every house and every village, by roadsides and watersides as well as on waste land and barren hills";[130] and to introduce new methods of raising grain yields, including close planting of seeds, deep plowing, extensive use of inappropriate fertilizers, tractors, and farm implements, and planting less (but producing more). As chronicler of the period Jasper Becker describes, many of the agricultural innovations were based on the specious science of the Soviet expert Trofim Lysenko. Some of the mistakes were mind-boggling. In Qinghai, for example, prison inmates tried to make iron-hard soil suitable for planting by "digging little holes and filling them with straw and grass which were set on fire." In Guizhou, peasants dug trenches for sowing seeds so deep (up to thirteen feet) that they had to tie ropes around their waists to prevent themselves from drowning. Finally, local leaders produced their own Potemkin villages to demonstrate success where there was none. Newspapers published pictures of children able to sit on wheat because it was so dense. Investigations later determined that the pictures were faked by putting a bench beneath the children.[131]

Mao also dramatically increased the pace and scope of infrastructure development for agriculture, including a massive effort to build reservoirs, dams, and irrigation projects: "Every county in China was ordered to construct a water reservoir by building a dam and water channels. . . . Most of the county dams had collapsed within two or three years and the dam on the Yellow River [Sanmenxia] quickly filled up with silt, rendering it next to useless."[132] Such waterworks projects necessitated huge forced relocations. In Zhejiang Province, 300,000 people were relocated from one county alone to make room for the Xinanjiang reservoir.[133]

Yet another environmentally devastating innovation of the Great Leap Forward was the campaign to produce iron and steel in backyard steel furnaces in an effort to surpass the industrial achievements of the West. Mao threw down the gauntlet: "In another two years, by 1962, it is possible [for us to produce] eighty to a hundred million tons [of steel], approaching the level of the United States. . . . [At the end of] the second-five year plan, we will approach or even surpass America."[134] As Becker notes, "The entire country, from peasants in remote villages on the Tibetan plateau to top Party officials in Zhongnanhai in Beijing, set up smelters in 1958 and 1959 to create 'steel' in backyard furnaces. Everyone had to meet a quota by handing over their metal possessions . . . bicycles, railings, iron bedsteads, doorknobs, their pots and pans and cooling grates. And to fire the furnaces, huge numbers of trees were cut down."[135]

The result was a massive amount of useless metal and skyrocketing pollution levels. Beijing was transformed from a city that "did not produce even pencils" to one that boasted "700 factories and 2,000 blast furnaces belching soot in the air."[136] All told, the Great Leap Forward yielded "600,000 shabby iron and steel making furnaces, 59,000 coal mines, 4,000 power stations, 9,000 cement factories and 80,000 farm repair shops. The number of factories increased from 170,000 in 1957 to 310,000 in 1959."[137]

Statistics bear out this period's devastating impact on the environment. One estimate held that to implement Mao's policy of backyard steel furnaces, for example, as much as 10 percent of China's forests were cut down.[138] Qu notes,

> The environmental situation quickly deteriorated. A lot of places were polluted by either smog, sewage waters or rubbish. Under a zealous drive, mineral resources were also exploited, resulting in startling losses and destruction to both topography and landscape. Biological resources, forests in particular, were seriously damaged, causing several losses to the ecosystem. There was extensive destruction of the natural environment of our country.[139]

Perhaps nothing could exceed the horror, however, of the massive famine wrought by the excesses of the Great Leap Forward. The death toll reached an estimated 35–50 million people during 1959–1961;[140] within one year alone (1959–1960), China's population shrank by 10 million.[141] In 1960, infant mortality reached 330 per 1,000.[142]

Cultural Revolution (1966–1976) and Its Aftermath

In the wake of the devastation wrought by the Great Leap Forward, Chinese leaders again began the slow process of rebuilding the social and economic infrastructure of the country. In 1966, only five years after the policies of the Great Leap Forward had been modified or repudiated, Mao initiated a second "revolution," with equally devastating consequences for the country and the environment.

The Cultural Revolution wrought even greater devastation on the economy and the social fabric of the country than the Great Leap Forward, with long-term negative implications for the environment. Qu comments, "The few environmental regulations in industry, agriculture and urban constructions were repudiated and negated as bourgeois and revisionist restrictions. Cases of environmental and ecological damages rapidly increased to a terrifying degree."[143]

Several policies associated with the Cultural Revolution contributed to the rapid destruction of the natural environment. Industrial production stressed quantity and high output with little concern for using appropriate technologies. Thus there was significant waste in raw materials and energy. Labor and environmental regulations were discarded, contributing to substantial increases in air and water pollution along with significant loss of biodiversity.[144]

The Cultural Revolution brought a renewed emphasis on grain production to the exclusion of forestry, animal husbandry, and fisheries. Forests and pastures were destroyed, lakes were filled, and man-made plains were cultivated to grow grains. One such campaign to expand the amount of cultivated land in northern Manchuria and Xinjiang was bound to fail since little could be done to "lengthen the north Manchurian growing season or ameliorate its soils, except at prohibitive cost."[145]

Vaclav Smil details the degradation that occurred to the land during the Cultural Revolution:

> Illegal felling of forest trees, always a problem in wood-short China, became truly rampant, and the worsening rural energy supply intensified the damage. . . . In most places the inevitable vicious circle set in soon after slopes were deforested to make way for grainfields: after a few years, as the accumulated organic matter was sharply reduced and the thin soil rapidly eroded, yields on the newly reclaimed land plummeted and more land was deforested just to maintain the harvests. The abandoned, barren land then succumbed to erosion, often with the irreparable result of all soil being removed to the bedrock.[146]

Mao's "third front" policy, which called for moving production away from the coastal regions to protect against an attack from a foreign power, led to the siting of factories "near the mountains, scattered and into the caves." As a result, officials constructed factories spewing toxic discharge in the mountains, polluting the atmosphere and water.[147]

Yet, as with the Great Leap Forward, the most destructive consequences of the Cultural Revolution were exerted on the whole of Chinese society. China's educated elite—and by extension the country's research and intellectual advancement in all fields, including environmental protection—were devastated. Tens of thousands of intellectual leaders and their families were sent to labor in the fields or factories. Others were imprisoned or killed. In the fifteen or so years spanning both the Great Leap Forward and the Cultural Revolution, Mao had easily equaled the worst excesses of Imperial China, tearing apart the social fabric of the country, devastating the economy, and ravaging the environment.

The Legacy

China's history suggests a long, deeply entrenched tradition of exploiting the environment for man's needs, with relatively little sense of the limits of nature's or man's capacity to replenish the earth's resources. Attitudes, institutions, and policies were rooted in and supported by traditional concepts and philosophies such as Confucianism that promoted man's need to overcome nature in order to utilize it for his own benefit, while the relatively eco-friendly philosophies of Taoism and Buddhism made limited inroads in the consciousness of the Chinese people and leaders.

In practice, the relentless drive to amass power, develop the economy, and meet the basic needs of a burgeoning population led to the plundering of forests and mineral resources, poorly conceived river diversion and water management projects, and intensive farming that degraded the land. The continual cycles of social transformations (including war, population growth, and economic development) and eco-environmental change resulted in large-scale deforestation, desertification, soil erosion, and flooding that only increased in scope and scale over time.

China's institutional capacity to protect the environment was strictly personal, with responsibility for maintaining harmony between man and nature resting primarily in the hands of the emperor or leader of the country and secondarily in the offices of regional administrators. Simply put, the emperor's "mandate from heaven" coupled with a Confucian-supported reliance on officials to behave morally and responsibly in executing their duties served as the mainstay of environmental protection for much of China's history. Thus, how effectively land and water resources were protected and conserved depended overwhelmingly on the proclivities of individual officials. While some enlightened statesmen and provincial officials, such as Guan Zhong and Yu Sen, advanced environmentally sound policies, most sought to develop the economy or military as rapidly as possible, giving little thought to the limits of the environment's resources.

At the same time, the general populace played virtually no role as advocate for environmental protection. Exceptions occurred in instances where their immediate environment and resources were threatened. Polluted water or damaged crops, for example, might incite serious local conflict. But for the average person in China, environmental protection was the purview of central and regional officials; only when immediate interests were threatened did a citizen take action.

The weakness of this personalistic system of environmental protection was compounded by a poor tradition of codification and enforcement of environmental laws. The blend of Confucian values and Legalist ideals reinforced the power of the local magistrate in determining on a case-by-case basis how best to balance competing interests rather than relying primarily on a set of codified laws. This greatly enhanced the ability of the emperor or local officials to act in an arbitrary manner with overwhelmingly negative ramifications for the environment. By extension, institutions devoted to the enforcement of codified law also were weak or nonexistent. Finally, the lack of a strong legal infrastructure enabled corruption to flourish within Chinese society, further confounding environmental protection efforts and contributing to social dislocation and turmoil.

Moreover, China's history suggests a remarkable consistency in the methods that the country's leaders adopted to manage their natural resources. From emperors to Mao, China's leaders favored campaign-style mass mobilizations for resolving environmental problems such as flood control or deforestation. But these campaigns often failed. In emphasizing the pace and scope of the effort, little consideration was given to the actual environmental and scientific factors necessary to achieve success, and without the freedom to question scientific beliefs and practices and to propose alternatives, the Chinese expert community was stifled in its ability to provide informed and useful analysis to the political elites.

The legacy of China's traditional environmental attitudes, institutions, and policy approaches therefore provided little foundation for building a sound environmental protection apparatus. The first decades of China's post-Mao leadership created new and frightening threats to the natural environment.

CHAPTER THREE

THE ECONOMIC EXPLOSION AND ITS ENVIRONMENTAL COST

The death of Mao Zedong in 1976 and the end of the Cultural Revolution opened the door to a fundamental shift in China's political position both domestically and internationally. Beginning in 1978, the Chinese leadership embarked on a reform program that continues today and has taken the country into uncharted territory. Increasingly, the market rather than the state drives the Chinese economy. There is far greater freedom to travel, speak openly, and engage in private social activities, and China has become integrated into the international community through trade and participation in an array of international organizations and agreements.

This reform process has also created a new set of environmental problems. Deng Xiaoping's early 1980s call to arms, "To Get Rich Is Glorious," set the stage, if inadvertently, for yet another state-sponsored campaign to exploit the natural environment for the purpose of economic development. Today, three decades of economic development, scarcely restrained by environmental protection institutions, have reinforced China's tradition of promoting rapid economic growth at the expense of the environment.

At the same time, the Chinese leadership has taken a number of important steps toward balancing the needs of a burgeoning population with the country's natural resources. In an effort to reduce the population growth rate, it has established an overarching family planning bureaucracy and adopted a range of restrictive population regulations. While successful by many measures (as discussed below), China's population policy has been undermined by the very economic reforms it has sought to enhance.

The state must also contend with secondary social and economic challenges engendered by the interplay of economic reform and the environment. What are these challenges? At the top of Beijing's agenda are the growing instability in rural and urban areas; increasing public health problems; and the significant costs to China's economy of environmental pollution and degradation in terms of lost work days, factory shutdowns, and remediation projects, such as cleaning up China's already highly polluted lakes and rivers. As environmental challenges continue to multiply, moreover, the policy measures necessary to respond effectively increase in scope and complexity, further increasing the economic and political burden on China's local and central leaders.

Economic Miracle

The reform of China's economy is one of the great success stories of the last three decades. From the late 1970s on, pressures from below and initiatives from above have transformed an economy crippled by decades of state control and poorly conceived state-sponsored development campaigns into a global economic powerhouse.

One key factor was the central government's decision in the early 1980s to devolve authority for economic development to the provinces, while conferring provincial status on a number of cities. Provincial leaders gained substantial fiscal authority, the ability to approve capital construction projects and foreign joint ventures, and greater leeway to appoint officials.[1] The results were striking: "Local government and CCP [Chinese Communist Party] leaders responded to the new incentives with a burst of entrepreneurial energy. They founded new local industries and pitched the merits of their provinces to foreign investors. Stimulated by local initiatives, local and national growth rates skyrocketed."[2] Gross domestic product (GDP) per capita increased almost forty times from approximately $84 (692 yuan) in 1984 to $3,259 (22,250 yuan) in 2008.[3]

In the countryside, pockets of such economic dynamism were evident even before Deng's reforms. With the complicity of local officials, farmers in some provinces had been experimenting with private plots and sideline enterprises. In 1983, Deng and his supporters explicitly acknowledged the farmers' achievements, and under the rubric "household responsibility system," sanctioned countrywide implementation of the reforms. Grain production in many cases doubled.

The farmers' economic success and growing financial autonomy spurred other far-reaching reforms of the Chinese rural and urban economies.[4] The farmers established a de facto labor and grain market, thereby undermining the system of grain rationing (*hukou*) that the state had established to keep farmers tied to the countryside. By the early 1990s, it was possible to buy grain openly in farmers' markets or through the black market. This led huge numbers of rural migrants to seek work in China's dynamic coastal cities, providing much needed low-end services but also stretching the resources of many of these cities.

The central leaders also began to plan, as early as 1987, to diminish the role of the state-owned enterprises (SOEs) in the Chinese economy. Beginning in the early 1960s, in many cities, these massive SOEs—sometimes employing upward of one hundred thousand people—were the bread and butter of the local economy. They dominated the key infrastructure sectors of the economy: power generation, ferrous metals, railroads, chemicals, machinery, and even textiles. Typically, they employed tens of thousands of people and provided for all the social welfare needs—education, health, and retirement—of their workers. Like their Soviet counterparts, however, they were by and large notoriously inefficient money sinks for state capital. A decade later, in 1997, Premier Zhu Rongji began to push aggressively to dismantle the system, an economically and politically challenging effort that has produced substantial unrest in many urban areas.

Since then, in place of SOEs as the foundation of the urban economy, the Chinese leadership has banked on collective, private, and joint venture enterprises. In the countryside, township and village enterprises (TVEs) have been widely touted as a key engine of economic growth capable of absorbing much of the excess labor in the countryside and encouraging farmers to remain on the land rather than migrate to the cities.

Foreign investment and joint ventures with Chinese enterprises have played an equally significant role in the new economy. In the early 1980s, the Chinese leadership designated some cities and provinces, primarily along the coast, as Special Economic Zones. As a result, total realized foreign direct investment skyrocketed from $430 million in 1982 to $92.4 billion in 2008.[5] The standard of living in the coastal areas similarly benefited; per capita GDP in Shanghai, for example, jumped from approximately $300 in 1978[6] to $10,529 in 2008.[7] International governmental organizations such as the World Bank and the Asian Development Bank began to play a substantial role in developing infrastructure such as highways, railroads, ports, and energy projects as early as the mid-1980s.

Throughout the first decade of the twenty-first century, China itself, with its newfound economic prowess and need for natural resources, has "gone out" (*zou chu qu*), becoming an important source of international development and investment throughout the developing world. In the process, it has rejuvenated many economies, but, as we will see in chapter 6, it has also exerted a profound negative impact on the local environments of many other countries.

As China's leaders survey the results of thirty years of reform, they have cause for great pride. Economic reform has brought revolutionary change to the lives of many Chinese citizens. Increasing standards of living, better access to goods and services, and greater freedom of movement and job choice all have reshaped the opportunities and life prospects of hundreds of millions of Chinese.

Environmental Havoc

The same dynamic that produced such success in the economic sphere, however, has also wreaked havoc on China's natural environment. The burgeoning economy has dramatically increased the demand for resources such as water, land, and energy. Forest resources especially have been depleted, triggering a range of devastating secondary impacts such as desertification, flooding, and species loss.

Environmental protection efforts have lagged. In the mid-1970s, the central government began to develop a small-scale environmental protection effort that gradually increased in scope and power. Local environmental protection bureaus, however, are wholly dependent on local officials for their economic welfare, and the central Ministry of Environmental Protection (MEP) has long struggled to make itself heard within the overwhelmingly development-oriented top leadership.

Without a strong, independent environmental protection apparatus, the devolution of authority to provincial and local officials has given them free rein to concentrate their energies on economic growth, pushing aside environmental considerations with few consequences from the center. Thus, in many regions, land, water, and forest resources have been squandered, without considering the necessity of conservation or replenishment of these natural resources.

The small-scale TVEs that have fueled much of China's growth have proved difficult to monitor and regulate. As they have increased in importance to the Chinese economy, they have rapidly proved themselves an equal, if not greater, threat to the environment than the SOEs. By 2000, these TVEs were estimated to be responsible for 50 percent of all pollutants nationally.[8] Even the most committed environmentalists, like Xie Zhenhua, the former head of China's environmental agency, tacitly recognize the primacy of economic imperatives in Chinese policy. When calling for heightening control on pollution by township enterprises, Xie simultaneously promised that environmental regulation would not hamper rural industrial development.[9]

Integration with the global economy, while providing some environmental benefits, has also contributed to China's new status as a destination of choice for the world's most environmentally damaging industries—petrochemical plants, semiconductor factories, and strip mining among others—and provided an insatiable global market for China's resource-intensive goods such as paper and furniture.

The results of decades of this interplay between the economy and the environment have been devastating. In many ways, the reform process is leaving as large a footprint on the natural environment as did centuries of imperial, republican, and early Communist rule.

Felling China's Forests

Within the first several years of economic reform (1978–1986), as local officials raced to take advantage of the new economic incentives and the relative lack of regulation, logging increased by 25 percent.[10] By the mid-1990s, local officials reported that of the country's 140 forest bureaus, 25 had exhausted their reserves and 61 had indicated that trees were being felled at unsustainable rates.[11] Highly skilled and productive lumberjacks became local heroes, felling trees as swiftly as possible to meet the growing domestic and international demand for China's timber products. Throughout the 1980s and 1990s, China's timber production skyrocketed as demand for chopsticks, furniture, and paper[12] drove an increasingly profitable legal and illegal logging business. China's integration into the international economy also led to an influx of Japanese and Taiwanese multinationals into China's logging industry. China, in turn, was able to tap into a lucrative international market for its wood products. Today, China is the world's largest exporter of wood products, the second largest importer of wood products, and is the largest importer of illegally logged timber.[13]

In a country where centuries of demands for fuelwood, cropland, and war had already reduced per capita forest reserves to one of the lowest levels in the world, the forests were ill-equipped to survive this new onslaught.[14] Today, China reports forest coverage of 18.2 percent,[15] well below the U.S. coverage of 33.1 percent and the world average of 30.3 percent.[16]

Reports from individual provinces highlight the dramatic decline in forest coverage over the past few decades. In Sichuan Province, for example, one of the most heavily forested provinces in the country and home to the country's famed pandas, the ratio of trees felled to trees planted through the 1980s and mid-1990s was as high as ten to one. The local inhabitants were said to be "replacing the forest of trees with a forest of arms and axes,"[17] and forest coverage in the province dropped from 28 percent in the 1970s to 14 percent in the 1980s. By the late 1990s, the province was left with just 8 percent of its original trees.[18] In 1998, the State Forestry Administration began a massive afforestation campaign known as the Natural Forest Conservation Project. The project, slated for completion by 2010, is aimed at collecting data to create an inventory of existing forests, designating areas prohibiting or limiting logging activities, converting 6 million hectares of farmland to forests, and restoring 39 million hectares of forest.[19] To an extent, the campaign has proved successful. From 1997 to 2000, timber harvests in China dropped by over half from 32 to 14 million cubic meters, and overall timber harvests declined steadily until 2002. In 2003, however, timber harvests began to rise again. In addition, while the proportion of China's land area covered by forest has increased by over 25 percent between 1990 and 2005,[20] these newly forested areas are mainly comprised of only one or two different tree species, closer to plantations rather than natural habitats.[21]

While China's forest resources have suffered substantial loss, so too have the country's grasslands. Grasslands now account for about 41.7 percent of China's territory,[22] primarily in the western areas of Tibet, Xinjiang, Qinghai, and Inner Mongolia. Overall, degradation has reduced China's grasslands by 30–50 percent since 1950; of the 400 million or so hectares of natural grasslands remaining, more than 90 percent are degraded and overgrazed, and more than 50 percent suffer moderate to severe degradation, contributing to decreased biodiversity and diminished capacity to serve as watershed protection. Annual reports from MEP indicate no improvement in the situation since 1996.[23]

Beginning in the 1950s and continuing until today, in an effort to boost China's domestic grain production, millions of hectares of grasslands have been converted to irrigated crop production, leading to severe degradation of the land. The reform period has further introduced new challenges to efforts to protect China's grasslands:

privatization of herds and grazing land, intensive grazing management strategies, and new farming techniques for growing forage and fodder have all undermined grassland protection.[24] Because grass output today is one-third to two-thirds lower than in the early 1960s, herds must graze over a larger geographic area to meet their needs.[25]

The loss of China's forests and degradation of its grasslands have both local and global consequences.[26] Domestically, China suffers from wood shortages, altered ecosystems, soil erosion, riverbed deposits, flooding, and changing local climates. Globally, deforestation contributes to climate change through the release of carbon dioxide when trees are felled, and from the loss of a carbon sink. Deforestation, along with the degradation of the grasslands and overcultivation of cropland, has also contributed to the growing desertification and increasing number of devastating sandstorms that are transforming China's north.

More than one-quarter of China's land is now affected by desertification or is degraded due to overgrazing by livestock, over cultivation, excessive water use, or changes in climate. In the northwest, the pace of desertification more than doubled from 1,560 square kilometers (sq km, approximately 600 square miles) annually in the 1970s[27] to 3,436 sq km (approximately 1,300 square miles) annually in the latter half of the 1990s.[28] Each year, an area equal to the size of New Jersey is degraded due to desertification, soil erosion, and salinization.[29] Four hundred million people in China, or more than 30 percent of the population, live in an area affected by desertification,[30] producing a continuous stream of migrating farmers and herders. As the Chinese say, "The desert marches on while human beings retreat."[31] In May 2000, then premier Zhu Rongji worried that the rapidly advancing desert would necessitate moving the capital from Beijing, although assessments by China's scientific community suggest that such a dire outcome is unlikely to result.

By the late 1990s, an annual average of thirty-five sandstorms was also wreaking havoc in northern China, compared with fewer than twenty sandstorms three decades ago.[32] Beijing has been repeatedly blanketed in dust from desert sandstorms, "obscuring the sun, reducing visibility, slowing traffic, and closing airports,"[33] and in which "thousands of kilometers of highways and railroads are blocked by sedimentation."[34] In April 2006, Beijing was hit with its largest sandstorm since 2001. The storm, which dumped four hundred thousand tons of sand and dust onto the city streets over the course of one night, created such low visibility that it halted construction projects and resulted in a massive clean-up. In 2007, clouds of dust from a storm originating in the Taklimakan Desert in northwestern Xinjiang Province took thirteen days to circle the globe, depositing mounds of dust into the Pacific Ocean.[35] According to MEP, in 2007 the total land area affected by sandstorms in China equalled one-and-a-half times the size of Alaska.[36]

In addition, logging, loss of grasslands, wetlands reclamation, and pollution directly threaten China's vast biodiversity: Of the 640 species listed by the Convention on International Trade in Endangered Species, 25 percent are found in China. Almost 40 percent of mammals and 70–86 percent of plant species in China are endangered.[37] China's endangered species recovery programs have had notable successes, as captive breeding programs have pulled the panda, Tibetan antelope, and Chinese alligator populations from the brink of extinction. Still, there have been a number of high-profile losses, such as the Yangtze River dolphin (*baiji*), which was declared extinct in 2006.[38] China's efforts to develop nature reserves to stanch this loss are impressive. As of 2007, China boasted more than 2,500 nature reserves throughout the country, up from about 1,000 in 1997.[39] Still, only two-thirds of the reserves actually have staff and budgets, and many suffer serious funding shortages—less than 200 million yuan ($29 million) was allocated to nature reserves in 2006.[40] Many have been forced to resort to commercial ventures within the reserves to raise money.[41]

Occurring over decades, if not centuries, the magnitude of China's deforestation and desertification has been difficult for the leadership to recognize and address. In 1998, however, nature sent the Chinese leadership a wake-up call. The great Yangtze River, stretching from the Tibetan plateau to the East China Sea, flooded, killing more than 3,000 people, inundating 52 million acres of land, and causing $20 billion in economic damages. Rampant logging, along with destruction of wetlands, which eliminated the natural capacity of the land to absorb floodwaters, was deemed the primary culprit. Then premier Zhu Rongji immediately banned logging for huge swaths of western Sichuan Province. The ban has been extended to seventeen provinces, autonomous regions, and municipalities. At the same time, the government announced a campaign in 2000 with an estimated cost of $725 million to prevent and control desertification by adding new grassland and forest and increasing the vegetated area throughout the northwest. Zeng Peiyan, then chairman of the country's top economic planning agency, stated that the government would provide peasants with grain from "overflowing warehouses" to encourage them to abandon farming and take on planting trees. Yet by the campaign's second year, details of future assistance to peasants remained absent, and regional officials began to complain that Beijing had not yet provided funding for the reforestation efforts.[42] Provinces in the northwest began turning inward to local businessmen for financial assistance. Beijing has since announced a number of other anti-desertification campaigns in the region, but they focus on planting new trees rather than rehabilitating grasses and shrubs native to the locale, which are typically more effective in halting desertification.[43] Some estimate that nearly forty cities have been abandoned in northwestern China as a result of desertification.[44] The government is also directing some resettled farmers and herders to change their sources of livelihood from agriculture to tree planting. Yet, the success of the campaigns is in doubt, as we'll explore in chapter 4.

The Search for Water

In the spring of 2008, with the Beijing Olympics around the corner, farmers in neighboring Hebei Province faced a dire situation. To ensure enough water for the Olympic Games, the provincial government had decreased the amount of water usually released for irrigation to divert the water to Beijing. By April, the amount of water allocated to irrigation had already been used up. An Zhenggang, who is responsible for managing Hebei's water supply, said at the time: "The farmers are crying out for more water. . . . Everything is up to the sky, so everybody is looking forward to a little more rain this summer hopefully."[45] Farmers in Hebei, who previously had dug wells in times of drought, found that even groundwater supplies were quickly depleting. In June, one farmer noted, "If you dig a well now, you hit rock before there's any water. It was never like that before. . . . We've had good fortune with the rain this year. But what happens when we have another drought? I don't think they'll be rushing to help us."[46] In March 2009, Hebei's Department of Water Resources reported that over-exploitation of groundwater had caused more than forty thousand square kilometers of land to sink, an area roughly the size of the State of Kentucky.[47]

For many regions in China, diminishing water supplies pose today's greatest social, economic, and political challenge. At 2,156 cubic meters (m^3) per capita (only a quarter of the world average of 8,549 m^3),[48] China's national supply of freshwater is well above 2,000 m^3, the World Bank's definition of a water-scarce country.[49] However, this figure does not account for the substantial regional disparities in water access. Water distribution is highly uneven, with availability greatest in the south and west, and much less in the north. Northern China has 42 percent of the country's total population and 45 percent of China's agricultural land, but only 11.3 percent of its water resources.[50] Average rainfall is approximately nine times more in the southeast (1,800 millimeters [mm]) than in the northwest (200 mm). Over 45 percent of China receives less than 400 mm precipitation annually. The distribution of groundwater resources is similarly skewed: average groundwater deposits in the south are over four times greater than in the north. Use of groundwater, a common alternative to using polluted surface water, has lowered China's groundwater tables in some areas by fifty meters since 1960.[51] The concerns do not end there. Groundwater depletion can create salinity intrusion, where brackish water intrudes from outside the water table; land subsidence, as underground geological formations containing groundwater compact due to water withdrawal and cause the land surface to sink; and increased power and monetary costs to pump water farther to the surface as the water table falls.[52]

It is no surprise, therefore, that officials in Shanghai, Guangzhou, and Taiyuan have all cited water scarcity as their number one environmental concern, and the Ministry of Water Resources predicts a "serious water crisis" in 2030, when the population reaches 1.6

billion and China's per capita water resources are estimated to decline to the World Bank's scarcity level.[53] According to the World Bank, 400 of China's 660 cities are already short of water[54] and 260 million people find it difficult to get enough water for their daily needs.[55] Moreover, 300 million people in rural areas lack access to piped water.[56] In the absence of adequate piped water, people must rely on surface water, which is often highly contaminated due to run-off from surrounding farm land and factories. As a result, 700 million people in China drink water contaminated with human and animal waste.[57]

Rapid economic growth has significantly increased demand for water in the agricultural, residential, and industrial sectors of China. Most of China's water is directed toward agriculture; 45 percent of China's total agricultural land is irrigated, accounting for 64 percent of China's total water use.[58] (In contrast, only about 11 percent of U.S. arable land is irrigated.[59] Although in California, where demand for water often exceeds supply and is beginning to constrain the development of new housing projects, the agricultural sector uses 48 percent of the state's water.)[60] Between 2003 and 2007, water use by Chinese industry increased at an average rate of about 3.8 percent per year,[61] while the total volume of urban water supplies increased by about 1.1 percent annually over the same period.[62] In some of the most dynamic regions of the country, demand is even greater: In Jiangsu Province, for example, water use rose by 44 percent during the same period. Such trends show no sign of abating. A 2007 study of Guangdong's drinking water concluded that by 2020 half of the province's water demand will not be met due to pollution and inefficient use.[63]

Years of drought have also depleted China's water resources. Baiyangding Lake, previously considered the "pearl of North China," is now dry, and hundreds of thousands of fishermen weave mats for their livelihood instead.[64] Over the past twenty years, main stream water flows have declined by 41 percent in the Hai River Basin, 15 percent in the Yellow River and Huai River basins, and 9 percent in the Liao River basin.[65] Since 2004, Beijing has resorted to drawing water from fragile groundwater supplies as deep as one kilometer below the surface.[66] Even still, the city's per capita water availability has plummeted from 1,000 m³ in 1949 to less than 230 m³ in 2007.[67] In 2008, a severe drought in the Yangtze caused the lowest water levels in 140 years, restricting the water supply to 5.9 million people.[68] China's plundering of its groundwater reserves, which has created massive underground tunnels, is causing a corollary problem. Some of China's wealthiest cities are sinking—in the case of Shanghai and Tianjin, by more than six feet during the past fifteen years. In Beijing, land subsidence has destroyed factories, buildings, and underground pipelines, and is threatening the city's main international airport.

As demand for water has skyrocketed, so, too, have levels of water pollution. According to MEP's 2008 annual report, over 70 percent of the water in three of the seven major river systems—the Huai, Songhua, and Hai—was grade IV or worse (not suitable for human contact). Nearly 57 percent of the water in the monitored sections of the Liao was also grade IV or worse. Only the Yangtze and Pearl river systems provided more reassuring statistics, with more than 80 percent of the water tested in both rivers reaching grade III or better (suitable for human contact). Moreover, despite a large-scale cleanup campaign for three of these rivers and three of China's largest lakes (*san he san hu*), water quality since the mid-1990s has either remained the same or deteriorated further.[69] In the three lakes—the Tai, the Chao, and the Dianchi—the 2007 statistics provided by MEP indicate that more than 75 percent of the monitoring stations for Tai Lake report water quality of grade V (suitable only for irrigation) or worse, while 50 percent of the monitoring stations for the Chao and 62.5 percent of stations for the Dianchi lake report water quality of grade V or worse.[70]

Perhaps most striking, an investigation conducted by the Ministry of Water Resources found that drinking water in 115 out of 118 cities surveyed was polluted, largely by arsenic (which can cause severe nausea, cancer of the internal organs, or, in the worst cases, death) and fluoride (which can lead to skeletal fluorosis, a bone disease that causes severe pain in the joints).[71] MEP's 2006 annual report analyzed drinking water sources in 107 Chinese cities and concluded that about 28 percent of drinking water failed to meet state water quality standards due to contamination by human sewage and nitrogen.[72] The challenge of providing clean drinking water is exacerbated by the steadily increasing amount of industrial and municipal wastewater discharge. MEP's 2007 annual report indicated an increase of 3.7 percent in the amount of industrial and municipal wastewater production relative to 2006.[73]

Outside China's major cities, the rise of TVEs has dramatically increased local water pollution. Factories and municipalities dump their untreated waste directly into streams, rivers, and coastal waters.[74] The proliferation of tanneries, chemical and fertilizer factories, makers of brick, tile, pottery and porcelain, small coal-fired power plants, and pulp and paper factories have all contributed to a dramatic increase in pollution outside China's major cities. It has been conservatively estimated that TVEs alone discharge over 10 billion metric tons of wastewater per year, accounting for about half of China's total discharge of industrial wastewater.[75]

Regulating these firms is difficult. Although there are occasional crackdowns on TVEs, Chinese scientists have stated that they have no means of controlling the pollution from these small-scale enterprises.[76] In some cases, too, local residents have accepted the pollution generated by the TVEs because they depend on the factories for jobs.[77] Complicating the problem is that more than 85 percent of China's population lacks access to operational wastewater treatment plants,[78] possessing no sanitation system other than "pipes that lead wastewater to the nearest ditch."[79]

Less visible but equally insidious has been the pollution generated from excessive use of chemical fertilizers. Indeed, China's use of chemical fertilizers has increased more than sixfold during the reform period, from 8,840,000 tons in 1978 to 57,470,000 tons in 2007.[80] According to the World Bank, the poor quality of fertilizers and their inefficient application is contributing to significant nutrient runoff, which in turn is contributing to eutrophication in many of China's most important lakes, in which the growth of dense algae depletes the shallow water of oxygen.[81] As a result, roughly 23 of China's 40 main freshwater lakes—including the Tai, Chao and Dianchi—have become eutrophic.[82] The impacts are far-reaching. For example, in late May 2007, Tai Lake became the site of a large-scale toxic cyanobacteria bloom, leaving the 2.3 million people living on the lake's shore without drinking water. The lake is prone to these large-scale events because of the nitrogen and phosphorus released by local factories—the northern section of the lake alone has 2,800 chemical plants—and agricultural run-off from nearby rice paddies. Despite government efforts to clean up the lake, these blooms continue to occur regularly.[83]

Water scarcity and pollution harm the Chinese economy by desiccating or polluting cropland, forcing investment of valuable domestic resources into large river diversion projects and cleanup efforts, and contributing to growing social tensions in both rural and urban areas. And there is little relief in sight. Chinese scientists have predicted that by 2020, water shortage may exceed 50 billion m^3, more than 10 percent of the country's total current annual consumption. By 2030, the Chinese government expects the country will have exploited its entire available water resources.[84]

Fueling China's Economy

The most visible sign of environmental pollution in China is the thick haze that periodically settles over cities around the country. In December 1999, then premier Zhu Rongji commented to Beijing city officials, "If I work in your Beijing, I would shorten my life at least five years. . . . Every year, after we start heating in the winter, Beijing's atmospheric environment deteriorates. Foul air from burning coal and car exhausts cannot disperse easily and forms a thick 'pan cover' over Beijing. Sometimes when passengers coming to Beijing ask air hostesses, 'Where is Beijing?' they simply answer: 'Under the cover of the pan.'"[85] Or, as one reporter has noted, "On the worst days, smog is still so thick in the capital that it can render a 50 story building invisible from 100 yards."[86] Although levels of air pollutants such as sulfur dioxide (SO_2) and particulates have decreased since the 1980s, China's cities remain among the most polluted in the world.[87]

Beijing is one of twenty Chinese cities among the thirty world cities with the most polluted air.[88] A 2005 survey determined that half of China's cities did not meet the government's own air quality standards.[89] Moreover, according to the World Bank, in 2007 only 1 percent of China's urban population breathed air considered safe by European Union standards.[90] In addition to total suspended particulates, which are the primary culprit in respiratory and pulmonary diseases, China's SO_2 emissions, which cause acid rain, are now the highest in the world, affecting one-third of China's territory.[91] Acid rain poisons the country's fisheries, ruins cropland, and erodes buildings. In 2003 alone, acid rain caused 30 billion yuan ($4.39 billion) in crop damages and 7 billion yuan ($1.02 billion) in damage to buildings.[92] Japan and South Korea also blame China for much of their problems with acid rain, a situation that has contributed to ongoing tensions in the region.

The rampant air pollution stems, in significant measure, from China's continuing reliance on coal to supply approximately 70 percent of its energy needs.[93] (By contrast, in Japan, the United States, and India, coal accounts for almost 20 percent, 22 percent, and 53 percent, respectively.)[94] Oil represents an estimated 21.2 percent of China's total energy consumption. Cleaner energy such as natural gas and hydropower, in contrast, accounts for only 2.7 percent and 5.8 percent, respectively, of China's total energy consumption.[95] One positive environmental trend is the steady expansion of coal gas and natural gas for district heating in urban areas: since 1985, their use has increased more than five times.[96] China's leaders have also set ambitious targets to increase the role of renewables in their energy mix to 15 percent by 2020.

Burning coal is responsible for 70 percent of the soot, 75 percent of the sulfur dioxide, 85 percent of the nitrogen dioxide, 60 percent of the carbon monoxide, and 80 percent of the carbon dioxide produced in China.[97] The economic reforms have only worsened the problem. Over the course of the reform period, China's coal use has more than quadrupled from just over 600 million metric tons in the late 1970s to more than 2.75 billion metric tons in 2008, making it the world's largest consumer of coal.[98]

The sources of this coal burning are diffuse and often difficult to control. Most troublesome are the inefficient industrial boilers used in outdated factories and power plants, as well as small household stoves used by many Chinese in rural areas.[99] More than 75 percent of China's households and almost all rural households use coal or wood for domestic fuel.[100]

China's leaders are trying to improve the efficiency level of the country's coal-fired power plants. In a move to achieve a target set by the eleventh five-year plan to improve the efficiency of coal-fired power plants, between 2006 and early 2009 the government closed over 54 gigawatts worth of small, low-efficiency coal-fired power plants—more than the total installed capacity of Australia. A further 31 gigawatts worth of small, inefficient coal-fired power plants are slated to be closed by 2012.[101] But while these plants may be closed, they are not being demolished; a frequent problem is that these small plants are brought back online when energy demand increases or local jobs are needed.

To help reduce air pollution levels, the Chinese government passed regulations in 2003 requiring that coal-fired power plants built after January 1, 2004, must install and operate SO_2 scrubber systems. By the end of 2007, over 270 gigawatts of generating capacity had been installed with some form of SO_2-scrubbing equipment. A 2008 Massachusetts Institute of Technology survey of eighty-five of these coal-fired power plants, however, found that while many plants have state-of-the-art SO_2 scrubbers installed, in a bid to cut costs they typically do not operate the equipment.[102]

China's integration into the world economy has been a dual-edged sword with regard to the country's air quality, especially in southern China. While many multinationals have significantly elevated the level of environmental technology employed in Chinese enterprises (as explored in chapter 6), others, with the complicity of local officials, have taken advantage of China's weaker laws and enforcement capacity to relocate their most polluting enterprises to the mainland. For example, in the late 1990s, the State Environmental Protection Administration (SEPA) accused Taiwanese and South Korean multinationals of establishing their factories in China in order to avoid stricter domestic environmental regulations.[103]

Hong Kong businesses, especially, have taken advantage of weaker environmental laws and enforcement on the mainland to site their highly polluting industries in nearby Guangdong Province. In the early 1990s, many Hong Kong businesses relocated there to take advantage of lower wages and to avoid a ban on sulfur-heavy fuel for industrial use.[104] Yet Hong Kong itself has begun to pay the price for shipping these factories across the Pearl River. Guangdong Province produces about 1.17 million tons of sulfur dioxide annually[105] (compared to Hong Kong's 73,900 tons)[106], and in October through April the wind blows sulfur and nitrogen dioxides from these factories into Hong Kong, producing noxious and poisonous "cloudbanks" over the island. In the words of one mainland engineer, "Hong Kong companies use us to make money, but in the end what they do goes back to haunt them."[107]

Other countries have begun to dump their toxic waste from the high-tech sector in China. Hong Kong and Taiwanese brokers, for example, buy hazardous electronic scrap from the United States and other countries to recycle in China. Whatever is of value is sold; the rest is typically burned and dumped, fouling the air and polluting China's lakes and rivers. In one case, in Guiyu, Guangdong Province, at a site where circuit boards had been processed and burned, levels of lead in the water were 2,400 times higher than WHO drinking guidelines,[108] and heaps of black ash dotted the area.

Hong Kong officials are greatly concerned about the impact of the mainland's environmental practices on the island's water and air quality and have established a number of joint working groups and collaborative efforts with various arms of the mainland government, notably the Guangdong provincial government, with which Hong Kong has established a regional air quality management plan for the Pearl River Delta. In August 2009, the two governments agreed to set up a Joint Working Group on Sustainable Development and Environmental Protection, to explore options for post-2010 air pollutant emissions reduction in the Pearl River Delta. In addition, they agreed to work together on recycling and public transportation. Yet success has been elusive. As one Hong Kong official stated, "We might have more stringent standards than Shenzhen, but we cannot enforce them across the boundary or ask them to do more to meet our standards."[109]

The greatest future challenge to China's air quality—both on the mainland and in Hong Kong—will likely arise from a new source: the country's rapidly growing transportation sector. The number of officially registered vehicles has risen from 1,358,400 in 1978 to 3,496,100 in 1985 to 168,030,000 in 2008.[110] China's passenger car sales, 12.7 million in 2009, surpassed the U.S. sales of 10.4 million cars.[111] By 2020–2025, China is expected to have more cars on its roads than the United States.[112]

Already, major cities such as Beijing, Guangzhou, and Shanghai suffer from severe traffic gridlock. Approximately 1,000 new cars hit Beijing's roads each day; in 2000 the city boasted 1.5 million vehicles, a number that jumped to 3.4 million in 2008, with an additional 2 million cars expected by 2012.[113] A trip from one part of downtown Beijing to another that took ten minutes twenty years ago may now take over an hour. By 2050, if China were to match the United States, with one of every two Chinese owning a car, the country would boast 600 to 800 million cars, a number equal to today's world total.[114]

China's leaders are taking action to help mitigate the negative air quality impact of such dramatic growth in personal car use. China's fuel economy standards, at 36 miles per gallon (mpg), are just higher than those in the United States, which has set a target of 35.5 mpg in 2016, up from the current 27.5 mpg.[115] Stringent new fuel standards launched nationwide in 2005 cut China's SO_2 emissions from automobiles by almost 2,500 tons in less than three years.[116] More recently, Beijing and Shanghai adopted vehicle emissions standards equivalent to those of the EURO IV standards used in Europe before the 2008 Olympic Games. These standards, known as the China IV standards, are intended to apply nationwide by 2010. However, lobbying by the state's major oil companies, which would be forced to invest billions to upgrade infrastructure, will potentially delay the national implementation of the higher emissions standards.[117]

The global economic crisis that began in 2008 and resulted in hundreds of thousands of factory closures throughout China has further complicated environmental protection efforts. The government launched a 4 trillion yuan ($586 billion) economic stimulus package to prop up the sagging economy—with 350 billion yuan ($50 billion) allocated to biological conservation and environmental protection. In March 2009, however, as the global recession deepened, the funds devoted to environmental protection slowly dwindled. During the National People's Congress in early March 2009, National

Development and Reform Commission (NDRC) director Zhang Ping announced changes in the planned stimulus spending that dropped the portion devoted to environmental protection by 140 billion yuan (about $20.5 billion, or 27.6 percent).[118] MEP enacted a "green passage" policy in late 2008 to speed up the environmental review process for new construction projects[119]—a move that also eliminated many obstacles that could have blocked these projects over environmental concerns. Over one hundred fifty large-scale infrastructure projects were approved under the "green passage" policy. Provincial governments also relaxed their environmental standards, reducing the review period for environmental impact assessments from sixty to as few as five days; in Hebei Province, local officials approved the construction of four cement plants in just one day.[120]

Economic Reforms and Population

In the waning years of Mao's tenure, China's leaders began to move away from the centuries-old notion that the country's future greatness was premised on a large population base. The first sign of this policy shift appeared in the early 1970s, when Premier Zhou Enlai proposed that population planning be incorporated into the state plans for the development of the national economy. During 1970–1973, a government slogan said, "One child will do, two are good enough and three are one too many." From 1974 to 1977, this was revised to "late marriage, fewer births and wider spacing," encouraging one birth and two at most. Encouraged by Beijing, the provinces implemented population control programs, cutting the birth rate in half.[121]

The ascension of Deng Xiaoping and a reform-oriented leadership in 1978 broadened the scope and accelerated the pace of this policy shift. In 1979, convinced of the necessity of further slowing the population growth rate to achieve economic progress, the National People's Congress approved the one-child policy.[122] This cemented the leadership's commitment to maintaining a low population growth rate. It also revived some of the more draconian policy prescriptions that previous population planning enthusiasts, such as the Qing scholar Wang Shiduo, had advocated. Compulsory abortion, for example, became prevalent in areas with aggressive family planning officials.

By all accounts, China's leaders have succeeded in slowing the rate of population growth from the prereform period. However, family planning efforts achieved their most dramatic impact early on, with less consistent results as the reforms progressed. Thus, despite official claims of success, China's leaders acknowledge that the biggest problem they confront is China's population size: in an interview with the *Washington Post* in 2003, Premier Wen Jiabao stated, "Any small problem multiplied by 1.3 billion will end up being a very big problem."[123] The National Population and Family Planning Commission (the government agency responsible for enforcing the one-child policy) credits the one-child policy with preventing some 400 million births since its inception and reducing the population growth rate from 1.2 percent in 1978 to 0.58 percent in 2007. According to the sixth national census, which was released in late 2005, China's population continued to grow, reaching 1.306 billion, up by 40.5 million since the previous census.[124] The population currently stands at nearly 1.34 billion,[125] and authorities aim to keep the population below 1.36 billion by the end of 2010.[126] The National Population and Family Planning Commission, meanwhile, projects that China's population will reach 1.5 billion in 2033.[127]

Repealing the one-child policy has been a frequent topic of debate during recent years. In 2008, Zhang Weiqing, the head of the National Population and Family Planning Commission, dismissed this speculation: "Given such a large population base, there would be major fluctuations in population growth if we abandoned the one-child rule now. . . . It would cause serious problems and add extra pressure on social and economic development."[128]

But the demographic effects of China's family planning policies may have equally destabilizing consequences, both socially and economically. China has thirty-two million more males under the age of twenty than females—meaning that for the next two decades, China will have increasingly more men than women of reproductive age. (This disparity is largely believed to be due to illegal sex-selective abortions, which became widely available after 1986.) According to the national census in 2005, 120 boys are born for every 100 girls, a gender imbalance that is the highest in the world and most pronounced in children ages one to four.[129] Within and outside China, there is concern about an increase in the illegal trafficking of women and violence, as a result of this disproportionate gender balance. As the Bucknell University professor Zhuqun Zhu has stated, "So many energetic, restless young men may create a lot of problems, such as violence, crime, and radical political extremism."[130]

Some of this may change as more Chinese are able to have two children. Ethnic minorities have long been granted the right to have more than one child, as are couples in which both spouses are only children. Virtually all children born since 1979 are only children, particularly in urban areas where family planning has been strictly enforced. With these children now of child-bearing age, China might well experience significant population growth in the coming years.

China's large and growing population size will remain one of the great challenges for the country's leaders as they attempt to improve their environment, straining natural resources, consuming ever larger amounts of energy, and burdening the country's land. As Hu Angang, an economist at Qinghua University in Beijing, notes, "We will have the social burden of a rich country and the income of a poor country. . . . No country has faced the same circumstances before."[131]

The Quest for Security

Mao's initial opening to the West toward the end of his tenure and the significant outward economic orientation of the reform leaders for more than twenty years have dramatically changed the calculus of external threat within China. During the Imperial era, and most of the Mao years, the quest for state security was a central contributing factor in the rampant degradation of the environment. War preparedness has not, however, been a significant factor contributing to environmental degradation during the reform period. Yet, some in the leadership continue to fear that tighter integration with the international community will breed dependency and contribute to a loss of sovereignty that could be dangerous should the outside world turn hostile. The mid-1990s quest for grain self-sufficiency reflects this latent security concern and illustrates how security concerns may continue to harm the environment.

In 1994, American environmentalist Lester Brown published a controversial article "Who Will Feed China?" in which he predicted that a declining capacity for grain production coupled with a surging demand for food in China would produce not only soaring levels of grain imports in China but also dramatic increases in the price of food worldwide. During the mid-1990s, Chinese grain imports did soar.[132] The piece elicited an unexpected political firestorm in China, arousing dormant but deeply ingrained beliefs about the centrality of grain in ensuring China's self-sufficiency and security. In early 1995, Xie Zhenhua, director of the National Environmental Protection Agency (precursor to today's MEP) flatly stated, "Who will feed China? The Chinese people will feed themselves."[133] Speech after speech by Chinese leaders decried the country's growing reliance on international grain markets. President Jiang Zemin criticized the coastal areas for their large purchases of grain from the world market[134] and their "drastic drop in the amount of acreage under cultivation and decreasing yields."[135] An editorial in China's most prominent Party newspaper, the *People's Daily* (*Renmin Ribao*), also attacked local officials for evading their responsibilities in grain production: "Some comrades believe that seizing the opportunity to accelerate development at present means undertaking a business which yields quick profit. There are also some comrades who unrealistically place their hope on other regions and rely on the state to solve the grain problem. They think that grain can always be bought with money."[136]

The response was a series of government-sponsored policies designed to increase Chinese grain production. Indeed, Chinese grain production during the successive four years swelled in response to these initiatives as well as favorable weather. China's reported grain yields rose dramatically from 394 million tons in 1994 to 508 million tons in 1999,[137] making it consistently the largest producer of grain in the world. In 2000, however, grain production declined by 9 percent as a result of the worst drought in fifty years.[138] And in

2001, drought continued, destroying millions of hectares of farm-land and killing hundreds of thousands of livestock,[139] resulting in a further drop in grain yields of 2.1 percent and a total output of just over 452 million tons. In 2003, grain output dropped to a ten-year low of 435 million tons.[140]

But the central government's policies only exacerbated already troublesome trends in agriculture and land-use practices. First, the government's urgings did little to persuade the fertile but already economically dynamic coastal provinces to shift from industrial to agricultural development. They perceived little economic incentive to pursue agriculture. According to Jiangxi Province's Director of Agriculture Liu Chuxin,

> It is now the universal view in all localities that they see slow re-turns from agricultural investment or no returns within a short time. They argue that no one will starve to death if less invest-ment is made in agriculture. Therefore, given the repeated calls for increasing investment in agriculture and the great pressure from the authorities, some departments will play tricks with figures, creating a false image. They have increased investment in figures. But in fact, they have done nothing at all.[141]

Given the opportunities that rural industry presented for far more rapid growth, it is not surprising that some officials also perceived a focus on agriculture as a sign of a less developed region. In the vil-lage of Xishan in Shandong Province, once a productive farming community, the head of the village stated, "Not even a single vil-lager grows grain now. We're not country bumpkins here."[142]

Recognizing the difficulties in reversing the trend toward indus-trialization in the wealthier provinces, in 1994, Beijing attempted to offset the loss by expanding the amount of cropland in other provinces by requiring that "all cropland used for construction be offset by land reclaimed elsewhere."[143] The unfortunate result was to encour-age coastal provinces such as Guangdong and Jiangsu, which were losing extensive amounts of cropland to development, to pay other provinces such as Inner Mongolia, Gansu, Qinghai, Ningxia, and Xinjiang to plow land to offset their losses.[144] These provinces then reclaimed vast tracts of grasslands and continued to plow more land, which exacerbated soil erosion, water shortages, and desertification.

A U.S. Intelligence study by MEDEA, a group of renowned social, physical, and natural scientists, summed up the environmental situation:

> China's land productivity potential is subject to environmental limitations. There is little potential for increasing production by bringing additional lands under cultivation. Loss of land due to industrialization and urbanization, and loss of fertility due to erosion, salinization, effects of air pollution, and fluctuations in weather patterns are limiting factors. . . . A water balance model of the five "breadbasket" river basins in North China showed that two of them are currently operating at a deficit.[145]

Thus, the campaign not only failed to achieve the desired results but also produced a system of perverse incentives that encouraged Chinese officials and farmers to worsen the situation. Moreover, the campaign in no way advanced the use of technologies or practices that would actually increase grain yields. As a result of China's focus on high grain yields over sound farming techniques, 4.5 billion tons of topsoil is lost annually due to soil erosion, while over 10 million hectares of cultivated land (one-tenth of the country's total) suffer from contamination from pesticides and fertilizers.[146] Overall, the quality of cultivated land in China is low; about 40 percent suffers from soil erosion, and only 45 percent of agricultural land is irrigated.[147]

In Heilongjiang Province, the country's largest grain production base, accounting for 6 percent of the country's GDP, the situation is dire. The black soil, the most fertile soil on earth, is eroding; it is now only 20–40 centimeters (cm) thick compared with 40–100 cm fifty-five years ago, and "15 percent has been washed away entirely, leaving the barren yellow soil in sight."[148] To counter these trends, Ma Zhong, a leading environmental economist in China, encourages the expansion of "traditional" eco-farming, in which farmers rely on organic fertilizers, crop rotation, and cultivation of the natural enemies of insect pests and weeds.[149] Such practices currently are followed on only 2 percent of China's cropland.

Degradation of agricultural land has also raised costs and lowered profits for Chinese farmers, who have increasingly turned away from grain in favor of growing highly profitable cash crops.[150] These cash crops can be grown in greenhouses, sidestepping land that may be contaminated, parched, or simply in short supply.[151] This boom in cash crops has also reduced grain production and threatens the country's desire for self-sufficiency. To compensate for this discrepancy, in recent years, China has joined other countries in the region in moving beyond its borders to purchase agricultural land in foreign countries. Private firms find agricultural land an attractive investment, especially in the context of rising food prices, and have bought up significant tracts of land in Africa, South America, and Southeast Asia in which to grow crops for export back to China.[152]

The government also seeks to maintain China's grain self-sufficiency by exporting only token quantities of food grains (in 2007, China's 1.34 million tons of rice exports comprised merely 1 percent of its total output of 130 million tons)[153] to assure sufficient domestic supply. To this end, the government has calculated that 120 million hectares (an area about the size of South Africa) of arable land are required to feed the population. Given that the amount of land available for farming is just about half of that number[154]—and that the supply of arable land grows smaller each year due to the pollution and degradation of land and water resources in addition to urban expansion[155]—it is likely that China's goal of maintaining grain self-sufficiency will become increasingly difficult to achieve.

While national security concerns no longer play a leading role as a source of environmental degradation in China, they remain latent in the consciousness of many within China's leadership and may emerge at times of international or domestic tension. The economic development campaign to "Open the West," which is explored in chapter 7, for example, has made explicit China's border concerns with Tibet and Xinjiang and raises difficult policy choices with regard to balancing rapid economic development and protecting the region's natural resources.

The Broader Costs

As China's leaders continue to press forward with economic reform, they must contend with a number of secondary, complex social and economic challenges engendered by the interplay of reform and the environment. Migration from rural to urban areas and the ensuing social tensions; growing instability in rural and urban areas; increasing public health problems; and significant economic costs from environmental pollution and degradation in terms of lost days of work, factory shutdowns, and costly pollution remediation programs all threaten to derail or slow China's economic growth as well as the nation's social stability.

Migration and Urbanization

The migration of farmers and rural laborers in search of greater economic opportunity has been an integral part of China's socioeconomic landscape for centuries. While Mao maintained strict residence requirements for all Chinese, the reform period granted rural workers far greater freedom to move in search of a better life. As economic reform geared up, migrants became an essential element of the service workforce of many large cities, working in areas such as garbage collection and construction. Throughout the country, the migrant worker population in early 2009 was estimated at 150 million, 35 million more than in 2006; in major cities, this "floating population" is estimated to constitute 10–33 percent of the population.[156] In Beijing, for example, it is estimated that one out of every three people is a migrant.[157] In Jiangxi Province alone, the outflow of farmers increased from 200,000 in 1990 to more than 3,000,000 in 1993, and by 2008, 6.8 million farmers from Jiangxi worked outside the province along with 8.2 million from Anhui and 7 million from Hubei.[158] Chinese officials in such poorer inland provinces explicitly encourage migration to the wealthier coastal regions because these workers remit substantial sums of money back to their families. On average, the migrant population earns ten to twenty times as much in urban employment as they did in farming.

While thus far migrant workers have integrated with relative ease into the burgeoning economies of cities, the future is much less certain. Increasingly, agricultural workers are moving not because of the economic opportunity in the cities but because of environmental degradation in the countryside. In the Ningxia autonomous region, for example, since 1983, 370,000 farmers have been relocated from their desertified villages to cities and newly irrigated areas along the Yellow River. By 2013, they will be joined by an additional 206,000 people from within Ningxia, and by 2027 another 150,000 people are expected to join from neighboring Gansu Province.[159] Today, a similar, though far smaller, relocation of people outside Beijing due to desertification is occurring. These are only small samples of a much larger problem. Chinese and Western analyses both suggest that during the 1990s, 20–30 million farmers were displaced by environmental degradation and that at least 30–40 million more may be relocated by 2025.[160] Desertification has already affected the lives and work productivity of some 400 million people,[161] and in southwest China alone, almost 100 million people will lose their land within 35 years if soil erosion continues at its current rate.[162] While much of this relocation may be accomplished peacefully, farmers, if not adequately consulted and properly compensated, will resist being moved, as they have during the resettlement process for the Three Gorges Dam, straining the resources and popular support of the government.

China's leaders are also addressing the problems of low rural living standards, land degradation, and migration through a monumental planned urbanization of the country. Between 2000 and 2030, the leadership wants to urbanize four hundred million people, more than the entire population of the United States. By 2030, an estimated one billion people will live in China's cities. The environmental impacts will be profound.

Urbanization will remove people from degraded lands and deforested regions, provide them with running water and sanitation systems, and offer them opportunities for increased standards of living. As hundreds of new cities are built to accommodate hundreds of millions of new urban dwellers, there is the potential to create urban environments that utilize the most advanced energy and water conservation technologies, urban planning methodologies, and public transport systems. China could become an environmental model for much of the rest of the world.

Conversely, there is the potential for things to go dramatically wrong if careful planning falls by the wayside. Already in China, urban residents use 350 percent more energy than their rural counterparts. Chinese buildings use 2.5 times more energy than those in Germany, and in 2008, half of all new buildings in the world were constructed in China. Arable land may well be squandered in the race to grow new urban centers. By 2020, urban China will demand about 20 percent of total global energy consumption and will account for one-quarter of growth in worldwide oil demand.[163] With growing private automobile use, moreover, air pollution levels are likely to rise. In many respects, how China's leadership manages this process of urbanization will determine the environmental future of the country.

Public Health

For Chinese citizens, perhaps the most frightening consequence of environmental pollution has been the range of public health crises popping up throughout the country. Although a system of country-wide environment-related health statistics has not yet developed in China, reports of specific, localized disease related to pollution are increasingly available, and are evident throughout the country:

- In January 2009, the National Population and Family Planning Commission vice-minister Jiang Fan announced that every thirty seconds, a baby with birth defects is born due to pollution or dietary habits in China and that the number of birth defects is constantly increasing in both rural and urban areas. According to a five-year study carried out by a group of doctors in Jiangsu, atmospheric pollution accounts for 10 percent of all birth defects in China, with the highest rate occurring in Shanxi Province, the heart of China's coal industry.[164]

- In Yunnan Province in 2008, villagers in Duqibao were poisoned by an iron-rich effluent dumped by a mining company into a local stream. The amount of iron in the stream was over eleven times greater than the acceptable level, and eighty villagers who drank the contaminated water experienced diarrhea, vomiting, and dizziness. The mining company refused to pay their medical costs.[165]

- Liukuaizhuang village, 120 km (75 miles) south of Beijing, was dubbed a "cancer village" by local media in 2008 after one in fifty residents was diagnosed with cancer over the past decade, well over ten times the national rate. The village is surrounded by rubber, chemical, and paint plants that all dump waste containing mercury and lead into the air and water. Wealthier villagers moved away to avoid developing cancer from breathing tainted air and drinking poisoned water.[166]

- In October 2008 government officials closed thirteen vanadium smelters in Jianli County, Hubei Province, after local farmers began suffering skin rashes due to emissions from the smelters and local waterways and farmland were polluted with toxic smelting waste.[167]

- Four hundred and fifty people from across two villages in Guangxi Province became sick in October 2008 after drinking water that was contaminated with arsenic. Local officials reported that torrential rains caused arsenic-containing wastewater from a local metallurgical company to pollute local waterways that provided drinking water to local residents.[168]

Pesticides, too, have become a significant health risk. An estimated three hundred to five hundred farmers die each year due to improper use of pesticides. Additionally, many farmers suffer liver, kidney, eye, and blood problems, along with headaches and skin and respiratory irritations due to pesticide poisoning. Farmers often lack the knowledge or money to invest in the proper equipment and clothing necessary for safe pesticide usage.[169]

China's poor air quality, too, has serious implications for public health.[170] A joint study by the World Bank and SEPA in 2007 estimated that 650,000 to 700,000 people in China die prematurely from air pollution annually.[171] In the country's most polluted cities, when children breathe, it is the equivalent of smoking two packs of cigarettes per day.[172]

China's long-time reliance on leaded fuel[173] has also contributed to lead poisoning among children in several major urban areas. (Lead poisoning can lead to lower IQ levels and other behavioral problems.) A 2005 government survey found that the national average rate of lead poisoning for children under age six was 10.4 percent,[174] while a 2007 survey of childhood lead poisoning in fifteen cities conducted by the Beijing Pediatric Research Institute found that 7 percent of children under age six in Beijing had blood lead levels that exceeded the national standard. Despite the prohibition of leaded gasoline in Beijing in the late 1990s, the study attributed the high lead levels to car emissions, since children near high-traffic roads or in lower-level apartments had higher blood lead levels.[175] In addition, lead persists in both the soil of polluted areas and the human body for many years after the initial exposure. This could account for elevated lead levels in food grown in ground polluted by lead from car emissions.

For the government, the import of this public health challenge is magnified by the role that the problem plays in engendering social unrest and in the cost to the Chinese economy.

Environmental Unrest

Social unrest over environmental issues is rising. In the spring of 2006, SEPA head Zhou Shengxian announced that there had been 51,000 pollution-related protests in 2005, amounting to almost 1,000 protests each week,[176] a 29 percent increase over 2004.[177] People from all across China take to the streets because few citizen complaints about the environment are resolved satisfactorily.

Damage to public health is one of the chief sources of environmental protests in China. For several months in 2006, the residents of six neighboring villages in Gansu Province held repeated protests against zinc and iron smelters that they believed were poisoning them. Fully half of the four thousand to five thousand villagers exhibited lead-related illnesses, ranging from vitamin D deficiency to neurological problems.[178] In late 2008, tensions between residents of Qingshan village near Chongqing and officials from a mine whose activities had polluted the local water supply and caused land subsidence that damaged many villagers' homes led to violence between villagers and men hired to protect the mine. When police arrived on the scene, the angry villagers reportedly smashed and burned several police cars. During the previous year, the mine had agreed to pay 4.5 million yuan ($660,000) in compensation to the local government to help clean the water supply and repair houses damaged due to subsidence. But when villagers learned that the local government had misappropriated the money, they blockaded the mine to prevent it from doing further damage to their health and the local environment. The blockade lasted for one month before the altercation sent twenty people to the hospital.[179]

In another case in August 2009, up to one thousand villagers stormed the Dongling Lead and Zinc Smelting plant in Shaanxi Province, tearing apart parts of the plant, pelting trucks with rocks, and smashing the fence. Tests indicated that 615 out of 731 children living near the smelter had excessive levels of lead in their blood. Of these, 154 were so sick that they were admitted to the hospital; many more children remain to be tested. Thousands of police were required to restore order.[180] The villagers had been complaining for three years about the plant, and although the local government has promised to relocate the affected families, villagers in the relocation sites pointed out that their children are similarly afflicted with lead poisoning.[181]

Damage to crops or reduced crop output due to pollution is also a common protest trigger. In Zhejiang Province, villagers were concerned that pollution was responsible for spoiled crops, poisoned air, and a heightened number of spontaneous miscarriages. After petitioning local, provincial, and even central government officials for two years to redress the problems, in the spring of 2005, thirty to forty thousand villagers swarmed thirteen chemical plants, broke windows and overturned buses, attacked government officials, and torched police cars. The government sent in ten thousand members of the People's Armed Police in response. The plants were ordered to close down, and several environmental activists who attempted to monitor the plants' compliance with these orders were later arrested.[182]

While most environmental protest is centered in rural areas, urban-based protests have also been on the rise. In January 2008, hundreds of Shanghai residents marched in protest against plans to extend the city's high-speed magnetic levitation ("maglev") train to Hangzhou, concerned that the train's proximity would expose them to radiation. Even after the city government announced in March that the train project would not be one of its top priorities in 2008, some fifty suburban homeowners gathered in a second protest against the plan's potential negative impact on their health and property values.[183] Despite local resistance, officials moved ahead with the project, settling for an alternate, less expensive rail line to be completed in time for the 2010 World Expo in Shanghai. After construction began, in July 2009, more than eight hundred families in Xihuan, a suburb west of Shanghai, staged a month-long sit-in protest at the rail line's construction site. One protester said at the time, "They started work without saying anything to us."[184]

Beijing officials are clearly aware of the growing threat of rural instability and the role of environmental degradation as a source of such instability. The Central Committee's organization department released a 308–page report that detailed the alarming increase in confrontational protests across the board, noting, "Protesters frequently seal off bridges and block roads, storm party and government offices, coercing party committees and government and there are even criminal acts such as attacking, trashing, looting and arson."[185] The head of MEP, Zhou Shengxian, stated that, "with the increase of environmental mass incidents, pollution has become the 'primer' for social instability."[186]

Economic Costs of Environmental Degradation

As local officials confront the social costs of environmentally degrading behavior, they must also negotiate the skyrocketing economic costs. There is widespread agreement among environmental economists that the total cost to the Chinese economy of environmental degradation and resource scarcity is between 8 percent and 12 percent of GDP annually.[187] Recent studies analyzing the economic effects of environmental pollution have broadened this range further. The Chinese government's own accounting of such costs in 2006, known as Green GDP, estimated that environmental pollution led to a loss of $64 billion in 2004, or about 3 percent of GDP that year.[188] Critics charged that the Green GDP report underestimated the true economic cost of environmental degradation, due in particular to the highly constrained set of factors consulted in the green accounting. A report published by the Information Office of the State Council in 2006 estimated the cost at approximately 10 percent of GDP each year. In 2007 the World Bank and SEPA report concluded that pollution alone costs China about 5.78 percent of GDP annually.[189] (A further discussion on Green GDP can be found in chapter 4.)

Health and productivity losses associated with urban air pollution top the list of economic costs. A survey of 111 Chinese cities found that in 2004 particulate air pollution accounted for approximately 281,000 deaths, 169,000 hospital admissions for respiratory and cardiovascular problems, 3.72 million outpatient visits, 2.78 million cases of bronchitis, and 2.65 million asthma cases, in total racking up a cost of $40.74 billion.[190] In 2007, a World Bank report estimated the cost of air and water pollution at about $100 billion.[191] Acid rain caused at least $13.3 billion in crop damage and damages to buildings.[192]

Local officials feel the economic impact most directly. Officials in the city of Chongqing, which sits on the banks of the Yangtze River, for example, estimate that dealing with the effects of water pollution on local agriculture and public health costs as much as 4.3 percent of the city's annual gross product.[193] Even if a specific dollar amount is not associated with an economic loss, the costs of pollution and degradation are evident. China's largest freshwater lake, Poyang, fell to a record-low surface area from overuse and drought in 2007 that left more than 760,000 people in Jiangxi Province to face water shortages and damaged 400,000 hectares of crops, including a loss of 37.4 million metric tons of grain.[194]

Even more striking, however, are the growing costs incurred from expensive river diversion plans to meet growing water shortages in the north and west. Even as cities grapple with the social implications of rising water prices and the necessity of improving water efficiency and pollution prevention, they increasingly look to river diversions as a costly but less politically volatile alternative. Currently moving forward, for example, is the $62 billion South-North Water

Transfer Project that will bring water from the Yangtze River to Beijing and Tianjin from provinces further south such as Hubei.[195] Such projects bring with them not only substantial expenses but also the threat of intrastate conflict and protests by displaced citizens.

Looming Crisis

The task of protecting the environment in the reform era presents a number of complex political and economic challenges. For example, deforestation contributes to biodiversity loss, soil erosion, and flooding. Yet, with pressures high to maintain employment in both rural and urban areas, protecting forested land puts millions of loggers out of work. Efforts to maintain high grain yields lead to overplowing of already degraded lands and a growing threat of desertification, while valuable fertile land is sold off at below market prices to industry, claimed for infrastructure, or incorporated into urbanization priorities. As economic opportunities in the countryside diminish, migration becomes an increasingly attractive option for millions of farmers; yet economic and environmental stresses in urban areas sharply constrain the willingness of officials and urban residents to accommodate the influx of migrant farmers.

Unless significant steps are taken, environmental trends suggest that resource degradation and scarcity will only continue to grow, as will the cost to the Chinese economy. One estimate predicts a 25 percent loss in arable land, a 40 percent increase in water needs, a 230–290 percent increase in wastewater, a 40 percent increase in particulate emissions, and a 150 percent increase in SO_2 emissions by 2020.[196] Although little systematic work has estimated the future economic costs of these growing environmental threats, the World Bank has predicted that unless aggressive action is taken, the health costs of exposure to particulates alone will triple to $98 billion by the year 2020, with the costs of other environmental threats similarly rising. Moreover, the impact of environmental degradation and pollution extends far beyond the costs to public health and the economy to impinge on core leadership concerns over stability in the countryside and urban areas.

To date, China's environmental protection efforts have been dwarfed by the magnitude and complexity of the environmental challenge in the country. Throughout most of the country, an effective response is further hampered by China's bureaucratically weak environmental protection apparatus, as we will explore in the next chapter.

THE CHALLENGE OF GREENING CHINA

O ver the past three decades, the rate of environmental pollution and degradation in China has far outpaced the capacity of the state to protect the environment. But this does not mean that China's leaders have done nothing. To the contrary, they have moved aggressively during the reform period to establish formal institutions, draft laws, and undertake large-scale programs in the name of environmental protection.

In many respects, their environmental strategy resembles their economic strategy. China's leaders provide administrative and legal guidance but devolve far greater authority to provincial and local officials; they utilize campaigns to implement large-scale initiatives of nationwide importance; they embrace the market as a force for change; and, as we'll explore in chapters 5 and 6, they rely increasingly on private citizen initiative and the international community to provide critical financial and intellectual capital.

Yet this mix of reforms, while wildly successful in spurring economic development, has proved insufficient to meet the challenge of protecting the environment. Without a strong central apparatus to serve as advocate, monitor, and enforcer of environmental protection, other interests often prevail. Local officials, confronted with a choice between upholding environmental protection laws and supporting a polluting factory employing thousands of local residents, for example, usually choose the latter, considering environmental protection a costly drag on their local economy. Moreover, both local environmental protection officials and local judicial authorities are beholden to the local governments for their funding. Unsurprisingly, conflicts of interest frequently are resolved in favor of local officials' priority on economic development.

Economic reform campaigns typically, although not always, relax central control over the economy, providing significant incentive to many actors to fulfill the campaign's goals. In the environmental arena, however, there are few incentives, economic or otherwise, for local officials to carry out the initiatives of the central government. When market-based approaches to environmental protection, popular in Europe and the United States, are implemented in China, they often lack the necessary administrative, market, and enforcement mechanisms. China's weak legal tradition, too, enables corruption to flourish, although there are increasing opportunities through judicial reform, broadcast media, and the Internet for Chinese citizens to seek redress for environmental wrongdoing through the judicial system.

Despite all these obstacles, China's leaders over the past thirty years have achieved some success in establishing institutions and norms to protect the environment and—perhaps more important— have laid the foundation for a transformation in how environmental protection will be integrated into future economic development. Whether this potential is achieved, however, will depend on the willingness of China's next generation of leaders, beginning with those selected in 2012 to build aggressively on the initial steps taken under Deng Xiaoping, Jiang Zemin, and Hu Jintao to strengthen significantly the central institutions responsible for environmental protection, to enhance the necessary adjunct institutions such as the judiciary and banks, and to reform the system of political and economic incentives underpinning environmental protection in China.

First Steps Toward Environmental Governance

Even before the ascension of Deng Xiaoping in 1978, the winds of environmental protection in China had begun to shift. In 1972, three events sparked a new environmental consciousness in Beijing.

The first two were ecological disasters. In the northeastern coastal city of Dalian, the beach turned black, millions of pounds of fish were lost, the port became clogged from polluted shells, and dikes eroded. Other coastal cities recorded similar incidents. That same year, tainted fish from the Guanting Reservoir outside Beijing appeared in the city's market. These events prompted then premier Zhou Enlai to establish a small leading group composed of officials from some of the country's provinces and largest cities to address the issue of treating and protecting the water resources of reservoirs.[1]

Perhaps most significant, however, the year 1972 witnessed the United Nations' (UN) first international environmental conference, the United Nations Conference on the Human Environment (UNCHE). This conference planted the seeds of environmental change in China and signaled a turning point in China's approach to environmental governance. In keeping with China's decision to reestablish political and economic relations with the rest of the world and the country's assumption of the Chinese seat in the UN in 1972, Premier Zhou Enlai sent a delegation to the UNCHE in Stockholm, Sweden,[2] opening the door to a new understanding of China's environmental problems and potential solutions.

While at the UNCHE, the delegation shied away from an open discussion of the country's environmental practices and experiences and sought to portray the issue of environmental degradation and protection in the context of conflict between the developing world and the superpowers. The official statements of the Chinese delegation largely reflected cold war rhetoric:

> The Chinese delegation is opposed to certain major powers practicing control and plunder under the name of the human environment, and the shifting by these Powers of the cost of environment protection onto the shoulders of the developing countries under the guise of international trade. . . . The urgent task before the developing

countries is to shake off the plunder undertaken by imperialism, colonialism, and neo-colonialism of various descriptions, and to develop their national economies independently.[3]

The delegation also proposed a set of ten principles to be incorporated into the final declaration of the conference, which included demands to:

- assure the right of developing countries to develop first and address their environmental challenges one by one;
- reject the "groundless" nature of others' "pessimistic view" in respect to the relationship between population growth and environmental protection;
- ban biochemical weapons and prohibit and destroy all nuclear weapons;
- assign responsibility to the superpowers for the destruction of the human environment through their "imperialist" policies of plunder, aggression, and war;
- sanction countries that plundered and destroyed the environment of developing countries;
- fight collectively against pollution;
- compensate any country polluted by another;
- support the free transfer of scientific and technical knowledge;
- develop an international fund by the industrial countries to support environmental protection elsewhere;
- ensure a country's sovereignty over its natural resources.[4]

In the end, some of these principles were incorporated into the UNCHE declaration, including the need to fight collectively against pollution and the importance of the free transfer of scientific and technical knowledge. Others were directly refuted, including China's assertion that no relationship existed between population growth and the environment. Most were simply not adopted.[5]

Upon the delegation's return to Beijing, its report prompted Zhou Enlai to take several steps toward establishing a national environmental protection apparatus. In June 1973, Premier Zhou organized the country's first National Conference on Environmental Protection. One year later, in May 1974, the State Council established a top-level interministerial Environmental Protection Leading Group of the State Council to study environmental protection issues, although it only met twice during the following nine years.[6] In addition, all provinces, municipalities, and autonomous regions were required to establish organizations for environmental control, research, and monitoring. Local governments also formed "three wastes offices," which had little bureaucratic authority, but nonetheless represented the first foray into institutionalized environmental protection at the local level. Through the mid-1970s, other small steps were taken to improve the environmental situation, including some environmental investigations by local officials. During this period, however, the political turmoil and large-scale development campaigns of the Cultural Revolution prevented real progress on environmental protection.[7]

As they did in the realm of the economy, Deng Xiaoping and his supporters greatly accelerated the development of a nationwide environmental protection effort. China's leaders recognized that China's path of economic development was having a ruinous effect on the environment, as noted in a report published by the Environmental Protection Leading Group:

> Environmental pollution is spreading in our country to such a serious degree in some areas that people's work, study and life have been affected. It also jeopardizes people's health and industrial and agricultural development. . . . It is an important component of our socialist construction and modernization to eliminate pollution and protect the environment. . . . We should not follow a zigzag path of construction first, control second. Environmental problems should be dealt with during construction.[8]

In 1978, the Chinese constitution was amended to acknowledge concern for the environment, with the proviso that the state had to protect the environment and natural resources as well as prevent pollution and other public hazards. And in 1979 the National People's Congress (NPC) approved the draft Law of the People's Republic of

China on Environmental Protection, which established basic principles to safeguard the environment and promoted the development of a legal network for environmental protection.[9]

In the 1970s and early 1980s, the Chinese government held a series of important meetings and passed regulations to control industrial and marine pollution. In addition, it enacted several structural reorganizations designed to strengthen the environmental protection bureaucracy—although some in fact had the opposite effect. In 1982, for example, the government created a Ministry of Urban and Rural Construction and Environmental Protection that incorporated the Leading Group on Environmental Protection. Many local governments followed suit, merging their environmental protection bureaus (EPBs) into new departments of urban and rural construction, in the process eliminating jobs and diminishing the bureaus' already weak authority.

Two years later, in the wake of the second National Conference on Environmental Protection in January 1984, the State Council in effect acknowledged its mistake in abandoning the Leading Group and established an Environmental Protection Commission. This commission, composed of participants from more than thirty government ministries and bureaus, reviewed environmental policies, initiated new plans, and organized environmental activities, such as inspections, into local implementation of environmental laws.[10] Later that year, the State Council also raised the profile of the Environmental Protection Bureau, elevating its status to the National Environmental Protection Bureau within the Ministry of Rural Construction and Environmental Protection, doubling its staff to 120 people, and enabling the agency to "issue orders directly to provincial EPBs, decide upon and conduct its own meetings, and receive Ministry of Finance funds directly earmarked for environmental protection, rather than waiting for these funds to be channeled through the Ministry of Construction."[11]

The following year, the Chinese leadership appointed Qu Geping the first chief administrator of the National Environmental Protection Bureau. Qu was an inspired choice to lead China's still-nascent environmental protection effort. With a background in chemistry, Qu had spent his early career at the Ministry of Chemical Industry and the State Planning Commission. A protégé of Zhou Enlai, he had participated in the 1972 UNCHE and served as China's representative to the UN Environment Programme during 1976–1977. While scholarly and possessed of a gentle sense of humor, Qu was also a skilled politician, respected by Chinese and foreigners alike for his willingness to speak frankly concerning China's environmental challenges.

Qu worked relentlessly to create an independent environmental agency; four years later, in March 1988, his efforts bore fruit when the National Environmental Protection Bureau, also referred to as the National Environmental Protection Agency (NEPA), finally achieved independent status from the Ministry of Urban and Rural Construction and was able to report directly to the State Council (although its bureaucratic standing remained one notch below that of a ministry).[12] In 1989, the standing committee of the NPC formally promulgated the Environmental Protection Law, which embraced four central principles: (1) coordination of environmental protection, (2) pollution prevention, (3) polluter responsibility, and (4) enhancement of environmental management.[13]

As China entered the 1990s, guarded optimism about the future of environmental protection prevailed. Although officials at the Third National Conference on Environmental Protection in May 1989 acknowledged some serious failings in the implementation of environmental regulations, they remained hopeful. Qu commented that the government now realized that environmental problems could exert a significant impact on development, on the strength of the country, and on the stability of the society.[14]

Much of the next decade, however, would suggest that China's leaders were not yet ready to bridge the gap between recognizing the importance of protecting the environment and acting to respond to the challenges. The reality of environmental protection remained much the same as it had at the end of the 1980s. As in many countries, China's environmental protection agency had little clout in interministerial negotiations. Few local officials paid attention to environmental protection laws, secure in the knowledge that environmental protection was not a central priority, and focused instead on raising the economic standards of their local citizens. Moreover, the imbalance between the rate of environmental degradation and pollution and the country's capacity to respond was both understood (however imperfectly) and accepted by many. "First development, then environment" remained a frequently articulated principle both within the Chinese leadership and more broadly in the country's media from the early 1980s to the mid-1990s.

Opening the Door: Rio and Its Aftermath

The two decades from the 1972 UNCHE to the 1992 UN Conference on Environment and Development (UNCED) in Rio de Janeiro, Brazil, were a period of profound economic, political, and social change in China. Yet in the months leading up to the UNCED there was little in the Chinese approach to the conference that evidenced such change. Prior to the UNCED, Chinese negotiators articulated five principles of environmental protection that were essentially an abridged version of those its delegation had delivered twenty years earlier at the UNCHE:

- environmental protection can only be effective when development has been attained;
- the developed countries are responsible for global environmental degradation;
- China should not talk about its responsibility for global environmental pollution and degradation;
- the developed countries should compensate developing countries for the efforts they undertake to meet international environmental agreements and should provide environmental technology and intellectual property at below-market prices; and
- the sovereignty of natural resource rights must be respected.[15]

To many international observers at the Rio conference, China was an inflexible obstructionist, intent on allying the developing countries against the advanced industrialized nations to prevent an international agreement on climate change, one of the key topics of the gathering.[16]

As was the case twenty years earlier, however, China's recalcitrance on the international stage was followed by a major shift in the consciousness and politics of the environment on the domestic front. The Chinese who prepared for and participated in the UNCED developed a new vocabulary for environmental protection. Chinese officials began to incorporate the ideal of sustainable development[17] into their planning process; in some cases, this was merely rhetorical, but in others the language represented real policy change, as discussed below.[18]

The UNCED also triggered a profound change in the Chinese leadership's conception of environmental governance by highlighting Western ideals of popular participation and reintroducing the notion of the nongovernmental organization (NGO) into Chinese society. While the centerpiece of the conference was the formal negotiations by the member countries, a parallel meeting of NGOs from the participating countries received even greater international attention. China's participation in the NGO forum, however, was limited by its inability to deliver any genuine NGOs; instead, China was represented by a set of government-organized nongovernmental organizations (GONGOs). This was a source of embarrassment to some senior leaders. Thus, one year later, in June 1993, the government for the first time cited public participation as a goal in environmental protection.[19] Around the same time, when a well-known Chinese historian, Liang Congjie—urged on by university students and friends, including a NEPA vice director—proposed the establishment of China's first environmental NGO, his proposal was welcomed by some government officials. Although governmental provisions for NGOs existed in China prior to this time, no formal application had been made to establish one. So Liang's effort represented a breakthrough for China.

The UNCED also spurred NEPA to issue an annual "Communique on the State of China's Environment" which reported on the state of the environment, progress made, and goals outstanding.[20] For Chinese officials not formally involved in environmental protection, the UNCED enhanced their awareness of the value of international contacts and assistance beyond bilateral and international governmental organization linkages.[21]

The Rio conference also reinforced notions already being advanced by the World Bank and other international actors about using the market as a basis for environmental policy reform, through measures such as raising the price of natural resources to properly reflect their economic value. Market-based pricing for coal was one of the first such reforms; in the mid-1990s, the government increased and deregulated coal prices. In many regions, this meant that new, higher coal prices finally covered the costs of production and delivery.[22] However, the full environmental costs of mining and burning coal were never incorporated into energy pricing, making it far cheaper to continue to use coal than, for example, to exploit the country's as yet largely untapped natural gas reserves.

China moved even further to improve its energy use policies in the wake of its ratification of the United Nations Framework Convention on Climate Change (UNFCCC) Kyoto Protocol in 2002. It set a number of domestic goals to increase its energy efficiency and the proportion of renewable sources in its energy mix. China's leaders pledged to reduce the country's energy intensity (energy consumption per unit of GDP) by 20 percent between 2006 and 2010, and to increase the role of renewable energy within the primary energy mix to 10 percent by 2010 and 15 percent by 2020. China has also become an active participant in UNFCCC conferences to negotiate a successor to the Kyoto Protocol, demonstrating how its engagement with global environmental issues has matured in the three and a half decades since the UNCHE. However, China's stance on climate change—detailed in a 2007 National Development and Reform Commission (NDRC) report—largely echoes its position at both UNCHE and UNCED. In a white paper published by the State Council in the lead-up to the UNFCCC conference in Poznan, Poland, in 2008, the Chinese government outlined its commitment to the principle of "common but differentiated responsibilities":

> Both developed and developing countries are obligated to adopt
> measures to decelerate and adapt to climate change. But the level
> of their historical responsibilities, level and stage of development,
> and capabilities and ways of contribution vary. Developed coun-
> tries should be responsible for their accumulative emissions and

current high per-capita emissions, and take the lead in reducing emissions, in addition to providing financial support and transferring technologies to developing countries. The developing countries, while developing their economies and fighting poverty, should actively adopt adaptation measures, reduce their emissions to the lowest degree and fulfill their duties in addressing climate change.[23]

In October 2008, China also proposed that the advanced industrial countries contribute 1 percent of their GDP to a fund that would support technology transfer to the developing world.[24] China has made genuine advances in environmental protection in the wake of both the UNCHE and the UNCED, and as a result of its participation in climate negotiations. According to MEP, China has signed on to 38 out of 48 international conventions relating to environmental protection.[25]

Despite such progress, Chinese environmental protection leaders remain deeply concerned about the future. At a forum on mainland water pollution organized by the All-China Environment Federation in 2007, SEPA head Zhou Shengxian painted a dark picture of the current state of the environment in his country, stating that "pollution problems have threatened public health and social stability and have become a bottleneck for sound socio-economic development."[26]

Challenges of China's Bureaucracy

Underlying Zhou's unhappy future scenario is the continued weakness of the state's environmental protection efforts. The core agencies behind China's environmental protection efforts—the NPC, which is the top lawmaking body in the country;[27] MEP;[28] and the judiciary, headed by the Supreme People's Court, along with China's fledgling environmental protection courts—together claim responsibility for the full scope of central governmental activities, including drafting of laws, monitoring implementation of environmental regulations, and enforcement. Yet each element of this bureaucratic apparatus exhibits fundamental structural weaknesses that undermine the best of intentions.

The Legal System

China's legal system has been widely criticized for its lack of transparency, ill-defined laws, weak enforcement capacity, and poorly trained advocates and judiciary.[29] In 1993, however, China's leaders addressed at least some of the weakness in the lawmaking process, establishing specialized committees within the NPC[30] on issues such as agriculture and rural affairs, and internal and judicial affairs. For the environment, the Chinese leadership tapped Qu Geping, head of NEPA, to head the new Environmental Protection Committee, now known as the Environmental Protection and Resources Conservation Committee (EPRCC)[31] within the NPC. Under Qu's leadership, and that of his successors, the committee spearheaded an impressive environmental lawmaking effort. Of the 28 environmental protection laws passed by China since 1979, 11 were passed between 2000 and 2007,[32] and two more were passed in 2008. (These laws are complemented by the more than 20 technical environmental regulations issued by the State Council, such as the "Implementing Regulations for the Water Pollution Prevention and Control Law," and the 100 environmental rules and methods and 400 standards formulated by MEP and other State Council ministries and agencies.)

Until he retired in 2003, Qu was relentless in his effort to improve the quality of China's laws—a duty since assumed by the former vice minister of construction Mao Rubai. According to many environmental protection officials and experts in both China and the West, most Chinese environmental protection laws are too broad, providing local officials with little guidance on implementation. This is because in China, administrative agencies—not the judiciary—are responsible for the implementation of environmental laws, while the legislature, NGOs, and private citizens share responsibility for supervising that implementation. But the still nascent opportunities for public participation in the Chinese legal system means that proper supervision and implementation of environmental laws is either undeveloped (on the part of citizens and NGOs) or improperly or unequally enforced (on the part of government administrative agencies).[33]

To compound the problem, many environmental laws passed by the legislature lack a feasible or appropriate method of execution.[34] They may provide an opportunity for pollution victims to seek compensation for environmental wrongdoing, but they do not clearly state the proper procedure for doing so. The end result is that many Chinese citizens, particularly victims of pollution, do not know how to state their case or claim damages—resulting in limited participation in the legal system.[35] Many legal experts have remarked that China's environmental laws are like policy statements rather than laws in the Western sense—which may also account for their inconsistent enforcement. For example, Xin Qiu and Honglin Li's analysis of the Solid Waste Pollution Prevention and Control Law (effective 2005) explains:

> For a long time, Chinese legislators believed that "something is better than nothing" and "general is better than specific." Thus, legislation under this concept tended to be vague, granted too much flexibility, lacked feasibility, and potentially resulted in overlapping authority. For example . . . Article 10 [of the Solid Waste Pollution Prevention and Control Law] states: "[T]he competent environmental department under the State Council [referring to the MEP] is responsible for the united supervision and management of the nation's solid waste pollution prevention and control in general; other related departments under the State Council are responsible for the supervision and management of the nation's solid waste pollution prevention and control within their specialized areas." However, this provision is too vague to actually identify responsible agents and define responsibilities. Who are the other related departments? What are the responsibilities of each department? What is united supervision and management, and what kind of authority does it have? How should the government enforce such a mandate if responsible departments ignore their duties? Without clear answers to these questions, any department can interpret the law in ways favorable to themselves, and thus cause controversies in implementation.[36]

It is therefore difficult for the Chinese to know what is prohibited and what can be called to account through legal redress. In one case, in Changzhou, Jiangsu Province, when a local environmental protection bureau attempted to sue a local chemical company for failing to pay its discharge fees over a two-year period, the bureau at first could not decide whether the basis for the suit rested on the enterprise's failure to pay four small amounts for its discharge fees or its failure to pay overstandard fees. Moreover, the Changzhou court, scheduled to hear the case, pointed out that inconsistencies between national regulations and Changzhou's rules might make a suit difficult.[37] Similarly, although regulations passed by SEPA in 2007 mandate that all facilities should monitor their own pollution emissions, there are no stipulations as to how often they must do so.[38]

Ambiguity in the laws also permits conscious exploitation by enterprises or other actors. As Xiaoying Ma and Leonard Ortolano point out in their study of environmental regulation, "The Chinese even have a common saying, 'National policies, local countermeasures' [*shang you zhengce xia you duice*], to describe the practice of exploiting the ambiguity of national laws and regulations to figure out ways around them."[39]

Furthermore, as in other countries, lawmakers must balance environmental protection needs against other social considerations. In China, the chief concern is the potential link between stiffer environmental protection laws and economic disruption. Over the past decade, the Chinese government has fueled this debate by proposing to implement an environmental protection tax, which would tax polluting enterprises as a market mechanism[40] to finance pollution control and enforcement efforts at the national level.[41] This tax would replace the system where local environmental protection bureaus collect fees from polluters.

Whether the new tax proposal would be based on the profits earned or the quantity of pollution discharged by an enterprise remains an open question. Nonetheless, the proposal highlights the central tension inherent in China's environmental protection efforts: how to balance the development of the economy with environmental protection, while maintaining the government's belief that less central government involvement is better.

An equally challenging factor in China's laws is the exhaustive consultative process. Law drafting involves a wide range of ministry representatives, local officials, and technical experts, all of whom may lobby for significant changes until, frequently, the law is watered down to the point that it serves no real use.[42] The negotiations over the energy efficiency law, for example, lasted more than four years, and today the law is still not well implemented, a function of both the complexity of the law and the weak enforcement apparatus.[43]

Yet China's environmental lawmakers have demonstrated increasing sophistication in their understanding of how to negotiate and draft a technically sound and politically viable law. The Water Pollution Control Law, for example, was first passed in 1984, just five years after the landmark Environmental Protection Law, and was amended twice since, in 1996 and 2008.[44]

The amendments clarified how to control water pollution and better enforce the law at the local level, including how to penalize violators. The revisions of the law in 2008 came on the heels of a string of high-profile water pollution incidents, most notably the 2005 Songhua River benzene spill near Harbin, in northeastern Heilongjiang Province. This accident was noteworthy because not only did officials cut off water supplies to Harbin's 3.4 million residents[45] but they also attempted to cover up the incident.

Lawmakers responded by proposing amendments to the Water Pollution Control Law that sought to prevent a repeat of the Songhua incident. The resulting broad-sweeping changes included mandating the local governments to incorporate water protection into their economic planning rather than choosing between GDP growth and environmental protection; increasing opportunities for public participation by requiring MEP to disclose publicly information about nationwide water quality; and instituting stiffer fines for polluters by removing the 1 million yuan ($142,855) cap set in 1996 and ordering that owners of seriously polluting enterprises could be fined up to 50 percent of the enterprise's income for the previous year. What was particularly noteworthy was that the draft law was made available for public comment in late 2007—the first time a draft piece of Chinese environmental legislation was subject to public comment. After just one month, the Legal Affairs Committee of the Standing Committee of the NPC received over 1,400 public comments, many of which were incorporated into the final draft of the law.[46]

The latest amendments to the Water Pollution Control Law, effective since June 2008, include tougher fines and fine-tuned enforcement measures. The amendments include, for example, a mandate that requires a heavily polluting enterprise be fined 20 to 50 percent of the previous year's income, to be paid directly by the owner of the responsible factory or business. The amendments also authorize local EPBs to dismantle any illegal power outlet or underground pipe and fine the violator for the cost.[47]

It is too early to tell whether the amendments passed in 2008 will provide the Water Pollution Control Law with the authority it needs to diminish incidences of water pollution and strengthen enforcement of regulations at the local level. However, this process of amending this law into a workable, enforceable, and effective piece of legislation that is responsive to public concerns (and even takes public opinion into account) demonstrates the initiative required to achieve this same level of success when enforcing other environmental laws on the national scale.

MEP and Its Environmental Protection Bureaus

Management of environmental protection in China is shared by many agencies and other actors, depending on the issue. Rather than cooperating, different government bodies usually compete for limited resources and influence where environmental protection is concerned.[48] Resolution of large-scale water pollution problems, for example, might involve the Ministry of Water Resources, which is in charge of water allocation; the Ministry of Construction, which handles water and sewage treatment; the State Forestry Administration, which takes care of water within reservoirs in nature reserves; the State Oceanic Administration, which is responsible for coastal waters; the Bureau of Fisheries under the Ministry of Agriculture, which is responsible for monitoring water pollution in fisheries; and MEP, which monitors water pollution in areas not overseen by other ministries. In addition, economic agencies such as the Ministry of Finance play a key role in determining the level of fines assessed against factories for water pollution, and the Environmental Protection and Resources Conservation Committee (EPRCC) of the NPC is responsible for coordinating and drafting laws regarding water pollution. However, involvement in the full range of environmental protection activities, including law drafting, monitoring, enforcement, environmental impact assessments, and research rests with the Ministry of Environmental Protection (MEP) and its local bureaus.

In many respects, MEP's rise within the bureaucratic hierarchy of China's state apparatus mirrors the rise in the importance of environmental protection within the Chinese government. In 1998, as part of sweeping administrative reforms that reconstituted many institutions within the Chinese bureaucracy, then premier Zhu Rongji elevated the agency from its long-time subcabinet status to ministerial rank, changing the name from the National Environmental Protection Agency (*Guojia Huanjing Baohu Ju*) to the State Environmental Protection Administration (*Guojia Huanjing Baohu Zongju*). During the National People's Congress in March 2008, SEPA was promoted to cabinet level and renamed the Ministry of Environmental Protection (*Zhonghua Renmin Gongheguo Huanjing Baohu Bu*). As a cabinet-level body, MEP can now cast a vote in the State Council, granting environmental protection a stronger influence on national policymaking. Moreover, MEP's position in the government bureaucracy means that, unlike NEPA and SEPA, its rank is superior to that of many of the state-owned enterprises (SOEs) it regulates, strengthening MEP's ability to enforce environmental laws. Still, MEP cannot force other ministries to adhere to its recommendations. A number of contributing factors have limited the broader influence of MEP and other environmentally inclined actors. As noted, former premier Zhu Rongji—a reform-oriented leader in charge of China's economic development and considered a strong supporter of environmental protection within the Chinese leadership—elevated NEPA's status in 1998 as part of an overall reorganization of the state's bureaucracy. Yet shortly thereafter, during a lunch in New York with the newly named SEPA director, Xie Zhenhua, I asked Xie to describe the most important change for

SEPA as a result of its new ministerial rank. He replied, with no small degree of irony, "They cut my staff in half." In fact, SEPA's already meager staff further decreased from six hundred to three hundred people.[49] The current size of MEP's staff is far from adequate—and helps explain why enforcing environmental laws has proven to be so difficult in China. Consider that in the United States (population 300 million), the Environmental Protection Agency (EPA) has more than 17,000 employees spread out over the agency's headquarters, 10 regional offices, and 18 satellite locations and laboratories. In China (population 1.3 billion), however, MEP has 300 employees in its Beijing headquarters, about 30 employees in each of its 5 regional offices, along with a total of about 60,000 employees at the local provincial and township levels, and 2,600 employees including affiliate agencies and institutes.[50] In other words, MEP's workforce is less than one-sixth the size of the EPA but is responsible for administering environmental laws over a population five times that of the United States. It is no wonder that, according to prominent Chinese environmental lawyer Wang Canfa, barely 10 percent of China's environmental laws and regulations are actually enforced.[51] In 1998, Zhu also eliminated the overarching State Environmental Protection Commission, which was the only standing forum for top-level coordination on environmental protection. This diminished the environmental agency's ability to coordinate high-level environmental policy and stretched its capacity very thin.[52]

MEP's bureaucratic challenge is compounded by the low level of funding accorded to environmental protection. While Chinese investment in environmental protection had hovered around 0.8 percent of GDP during the ninth five-year plan (1996–2000) and increased significantly to 1.3 percent of GDP in the tenth five-year plan (2001–2005) (about 700 billion yuan or $85 billion),[53] investment in environmental protection during the eleventh five-year plan (2006–2010) was 1.35 percent of GDP.[54] This remains far below the 2 to 3 percent of GDP that some Chinese environmental experts believe is necessary simply to keep the environment from deteriorating further.[55] Moreover, funds invested in environmental protection are often spent on unrelated projects. In 2007, the Chinese Academy for Environmental Planning (which reports to MEP) disclosed that only half of the 1.3 percent of GDP that China had devoted to environmental protection during the tenth five-year plan was used for legitimate projects. Moreover, 60 percent of environmental protection funds spent in urban areas during that period were used to construct parks, gas stations, and sewage treatment plants rather than waste- or wastewater-treatment facilities that would have substantially improved urban environmental protection efforts.[56]

In addition, despite MEP's cabinet-level status, it still lacks jurisdiction over local EPBs, which are controlled by local governments typically focused on growing local economies at the expense of local environments.[57] Enforcement rests with some 3,000 EPBs and their 50,000 inspectors spread throughout the country. Although the number of inspectors rose by 116 percent between 1997 and 2003, this figure is still insufficient to administer and enforce environmental laws at the local level.[58] While nominally responsible to both MEP and their local governments, EPBs rely on the latter for virtually all their support, including their budgets, career advancement, number of personnel, and resources such as cars, office buildings, and employee housing.[59] Not surprisingly, EPBs are typically quite responsive to the needs and concerns of the local government— because despite recent regulations to the contrary, local government leaders are evaluated on GDP rather than their environmental performance.[60] MEP maintains only a supervisory role with regard to the EPBs. Many EPBs are ill-equipped to manage the task of environmental protection at the grassroots level. It has been reported that in some cases, EPB workers have resorted to anonymously reporting local environmental violations to MEP out of fear that the local government would perceive an EPB's enforcement of environmental regulations as favoring the environment over the economy, costing those workers their jobs.[61]

Recent reforms have attempted to bolster MEP's authority by strengthening the accountability of EPBs as part of a government-wide effort to increase transparency. In May 2008 the Open Government Information Regulations were issued, obliging government agencies at all levels of the bureaucracy to disclose information that "involves the vital interests of citizens," giving "citizens, legal persons, and other organizations" the right to request information from the government.[62] At the same time, MEP announced that the Measures for the Disclosure of Environmental Information would also go into effect. These measures established a procedure for citizens to request specific information from EPBs regarding environmental pollution and/or protection,[63] obligating EPBs to compile and publicly disclose a "blacklist" of enterprises in their jurisdiction whose pollution discharges exceed both their permitted amount and national standards.[64]

These new regulations may well represent a significant step forward for transparency at all levels of government, although implementation remains a question. In Heilongjiang Province in April 2009, for example, the provincial EPB held a news conference to outline the bureau's planned environmental enforcement activities for 2009. According to the measures, Heilongjiang EPB officials were required to release the polluter "blacklist" to the press during this meeting. But when reporters inquired about the list, they were told it was confidential information to which the EPB would not grant them access.[65]

The administrative rank of an EPB is also sometimes lower than that of the enterprises it is supposed to oversee. This is because EPBs are both institutionally and financially subordinate to provincial and local governments and are generally low-ranking in the overall government hierarchy.[66] Limited resources and local politics have further reduced the efficacy of environmental protection efforts at the local level. Environmental protection bureaus are responsible for monitoring waste and pollution from enterprises and, if necessary, levying and collecting fees[67] and fines. While fees and fines nominally punish polluters whose pollution exceeds permitted limits or local standards, it remains far less expensive for polluters to simply pay a fine for their pollution rather than investing in pollution prevention and/or treatment at their facilities. For example, in 2006, the investment required to build a wastewater treatment facility at a paper mill near Nantong in Jiangsu Province was 100 million yuan (about $14.5 million)—while the maximum fine on wastewater discharge was a mere 100,000 yuan (about $14,500).[68]

Repeated violations do not necessarily result in additional fines, further boosting the incentive to pay a fine rather than eliminate pollution at the source. This stands in direct contrast to U.S. standards, which require companies in violation of environmental regulations such as the Clean Water Act to incur daily penalties of up to $32,500[69] in addition to criminal charges. Although fee collection in China has increased over time,[70] barriers to effective monitoring and enforcement efforts remain.

First, monitoring and inspection teams are typically inadequate to the task. Although EPBs reportedly conduct more than two million inspections throughout China each year,[71] they are chronically understaffed and underequipped. One local EPB enforcement official interviewed in Yunnan Province in 2009 stated that although he was required to inspect every factory in his district once per quarter, he lacked regular access to a car and thus could not get himself to the factories to perform inspections.[72] This lack of human and material resources prevents many environmental violations from being investigated.[73]

Local officials often look the other way when it comes to inspecting polluting enterprises under their jurisdiction. In some cases, an EPB official may have a personal relationship with the head of an enterprise and will levy a smaller fee. Even development may trump environmental protection. In Zhejiang Province in late 2006, it was discovered that county-level government officials had promised factories with an annual industrial output of at least 10 million yuan ($1.2 million) that they would not be subject to government inspections without prior approval from the factories.[74]

When central government teams from MEP, NDRC, the State Forestry Administration, the Ministry of Supervision, or even provincial teams undertake inspection sweeps throughout a province, they often detect gross violations. Sometimes these mass inspection campaigns follow major industrial accidents, in a bid by government agencies to prove to the public that they will not let a similar mistake happen again. For example, SEPA investigated more than one hundred sites just four months after the 2005 Songhua River benzene spill, ordering the cleanup of twenty chemical and petrochemical enterprises.[75] A nationwide inspection campaign of 720,000 enterprises in 2006 reportedly closed 3,176 of these enterprises due to excessive pollution discharges and/or unsafe working locations.[76]

The low administrative standing of EPBs also hinders their efficacy. Alternatives to fines, such as shutting down a polluting enterprise, usually cannot be ordered directly from the EPB due to its low standing, and instead must be referred to the local government or mayor—whose higher standing allows them to ignore the EPB's order. So EPBs may be caught in a situation in which they observe an issue and bring it to the attention of both the polluter and higher officials in the local government but lack any authority to enforce fines or other punitive measures against the polluting enterprise.[77] According to a study by the World Bank, social, political, and economic considerations often dictate which firms are more likely to be required to pay the full fee. Private firms and those whose pollution has a higher social impact (in particular if citizens complain) have less bargaining power with the local EPBs. State-owned enterprises and those firms with a precarious financial situation, however, have relatively greater bargaining power.[78] In some cases, even when firms pay the fee and receive 80 percent of it back to retrofit their factory, they use the money to pay for other needs of the enterprises' environmental protection departments rather than pollution prevention measures.[79]

Pollution violation fees issued in 2004 totaled 460 million yuan (about $250 million), encompassing 80,000 individual violations.[80] But, according to the OECD, the overall collection rate of pollution fines was less than 50 percent nationwide—standing at 80 percent in coastal areas but a mere 10 percent in the western provinces.[81] Furthermore, polluters often negotiate the fines paid to EPBs and may pay a sum that is significantly lower than the cost of environmental damage inflicted by the pollution: generally, the pollution violation fees collected by EPBs cover less than 5 percent of the costs required to properly clean up that pollution.[82]

Most startling, perhaps, is that the fee collection process has also produced a perverse incentive for EPBs to encourage the persistence of pollution problems. In Wuhan, for example, municipal EPB officials developed what they considered to be an effective mechanism to encourage local EPBs to enforce fee collection by appealing to local EPB officials' desire to increase their personal wealth.

To address the institutional weaknesses of local EPBs, strengthen regional coordination, and combat local government interference, in 2006 MEP began to establish regional environmental supervision bureaus. These centers answer directly to MEP. Upon opening the sixth bureau in Northern China on December 19, 2008, MEP vice minister Zhang Lijun outlined the goals of regional environmental supervision bureaus as such:

> Failure to properly address the issue of environmental protection is a result of two factors. One is that some local governments have eased pollution controls in order to favour GDP growth. The other is that as an administrative authority, the Ministry of Environmental Protection lacked effective supervisory capacity over the relevant local departments. . . . In the past, it has been difficult to resolve some long-standing transboundary pollution disputes because local governments alone could only deal with problems within their own administrative areas. . . . Now the regional supervision centers have been granted wider powers to deal with such disputes.[83]

Despite the bureaucratic reforms, the regional bureaus lack the authority to coordinate provincial offices and remain understaffed. One report suggests there are only about thirty people staffing each of the regional environmental supervision bureaus.[84]

The Judiciary

The third prong of China's environmental protection effort rests in its nascent system of advocacy. China historically has operated under the rule of men rather than the rule of law. During much of Mao Zedong's tenure, the law was perceived as a means of oppression, and qualified judges were dismissed in favor of party officials with strong ideological credentials. In 1978, however, Deng Xiaoping began to work to change this conception of the law and to develop a legal system modeled at least in part on western systems.[85] Unlike in the United States, however, past cases do not serve as binding precedents, although they are sometimes referred to for guidance.[86] The top judicial authority, the Supreme People's Court, is the only body permitted to issue official interpretations of the law.[87] As with the economic and environmental bureaucracies, the judiciary is also highly decentralized. The Supreme People's Court possesses a supervisory role but has no real power over the personnel or budgets of the lower courts. Such control rests with the local government.

Not surprisingly, this system raises problems for the independence of the courts. A study of the Chinese court system found that judges often reach decisions by "relying on CCP (Chinese Communist Party) policy, the views of the local government, and a court's individual sense of justice and fairness in contractual dealings."[88] Since courts are dependent on the local government for their funding, local officials wield a "potent weapon against judges who would be more willing to enforce the law despite adverse economic consequences."[89] As one environmental lawyer pointed out, "In all the suits that we have lost, the courts have not followed the law. Instead, they ignored the legal or technical merits of our case in order to support the local enterprises."[90] Even when a court order is issued, there is no guarantee that an EPB will be able to enforce its mandates.[91] Thus, when powerful local interests block enforcement of environmental protection laws, Party intervention is often necessitated. Such intervention, however, as law professor John Copeland Nagle notes, "robs the law of its independent force."[92] Chinese lawyers also complain that judges cannot render an informed ruling because they do not understand the basic facts of the case.[93] In many cases, judges are civil servants or demobilized soldiers with only a high school education and no training or practice in the law.[94] When one law professor questioned the logic of having military men with no legal training serve as judges, the People's Liberation Army responded by pointing to the military's historical contribution to the country.[95] Nor is every lawyer or judge well trained. In the first eight months of 1998, Chinese officials estimated that nearly 10,000 cases were "incorrectly prosecuted or wrongly decided."[96]

Nonetheless, in some respects, the court system has emerged as the strongest leverage that MEP and its local bureaus possess to ensure that environmental laws are effectively enforced, and there have been significant success stories. In early 2008, a court in Foshan, Guangdong Province, sentenced three men to prison and ordered them to pay monetary damages after they illegally dumped toxic hydroxybenzene-containing waste in several locations throughout the city. The dumping attracted the attention of local authorities after students and staff at a primary school located near one of the dumping sites experienced adverse health effects from inhaling hydroxybenzene fumes in their classrooms.[97] In 2009, a court in Yunnan Province jailed three executives from a fertilizer plant that had released large quantities of arsenic into Yangzonghai Lake over a period of several years, contaminating the primary drinking water source for 26,000 people. The executives were also fined 16 million yuan ($2.3 million) for not taking appropriate preventative measures to protect the lake from pollution. Twelve local government officials, including the city's vice-mayor, were also fired as a result.[98]

Perhaps the most important innovation in China's legal system is the establishment of a network of courts that exclusively hear cases regarding environmental protection and the enforcement of environmental regulations. In 2007, the Supreme People's Court established three courts to address judges' insufficient capacity to solve environmental disputes, eliminate the challenges faced by plaintiffs in bringing environmental lawsuits, and strengthen the enforcement of judgments against defendants who are influential in local economic matters.[99] These courts were established in areas where there was a particular concern about water quality issues: the court in Guizhou Province was in the vicinity of four lakes and reservoirs that provide drinking water, the court in Jiangsu Province hears cases concerning Tai Lake, and the court in Yunnan Province hears cases concerning the Dianchi Lake.[100]

Unlike most Chinese courts, the environmental protection courts hear criminal, civil, and administrative cases.[101] The courts also have the authority to enforce the judgments they issue, nominally granting them more authority and independence than any other division in the Chinese court system.[102] And the courts have already heard (and issued rulings) on a number of cases: the Kunming court in Yunnan Province heard 12 environmental law violation cases during the first half of 2009,[103] while the Guiyang court in Guizhou Province accepted 45 environmental cases (and ruled on 37 of them) in its first 6 months of operation.[104] More environmental protection courts are expected to open throughout China as the success of established courts becomes determined. However, several challenges could hamper the long-term effectiveness of these courts: They currently lack procedural rules; the problem of determining which parties which have standing to bring public interest cases remains unresolved; and an insufficient number of environmental cases fill their dockets. Only 5 percent of cases heard in the first year involved water, the topic that they were ostensibly established to address.

An important force behind the establishment of these courts is Wang Canfa, a charismatic and hard-driving professor of law at the China University of Politics and Law. In 1998, Wang established the Center for Legal Assistance to Pollution Victims (CLAPV). The center trains lawyers to engage in enforcing environmental laws, educates judges on environmental issues, provides free legal advice to pollution victims through a telephone hotline, and litigates cases involving environmental law. Between 2001 and 2007, the center trained 262 lawyers, 189 judges, and 21 environmental enforcement officials in environmental law. Additionally, by 2008 the pollution victims telephone hotline set up by the center in 1999 had aided 9,500 callers.[105] The center's resources, however, are stretched thin: It must raise its own funds through private sources, undertake the investigation of the cases, and prosecute them.[106]

Over the years, I have had many opportunities to chat with Wang about his work. In spring 2009, I met with him in New York. While he was quick to point out the challenges he faces—funding shortages, corruption within the system, and too few counterparts throughout the country—he was optimistic about the new court system and his work in training judges. For the first time, too, he had received funding from a private Chinese company, suggesting a new awareness on the part of Chinese companies of the importance of his work.

CLAPV has had a number of successes over the years; it wins about 50 percent of its cases. In a 2005 case, a court in Fujian Province ruled that a potassium chlorate plant should pay 684,000 yuan (about

$100,127) in damages to 1,721 villagers whose crop yields dropped dramatically after the plant's operations polluted their farmland with hexavalent chromium. The court also ordered the plant to conduct on-site cleanup and treatment of the pollution—but the amount of damages it awarded was far short of the 13 million yuan ($1.9 million) CLAPV and the villagers had originally sought.[107] In 2006, CLAPV won concessions from a factory that had dumped waste containing cyanide and sulfur on surrounding farmland and caused a farmer's orchard to stop producing. CLAPV had taken the farmer's case to court for restitution after the farmer unsuccessfully appealed to the local EPB for assistance. The court ruled that the factory should pay the farmer 150,000 yuan (about $21,958) and dig him a new well after the pollution had rendered his old well unsuitable.[108]

One promising, albeit underutilized, avenue for enhancing enforcement is the occasional alliance between the courts and the banking system. China's state-owned banks have become engaged in environmental protection through both fund-raising for environmental projects[109] and denying credit to firms that do not maintain pollution standards. In the mid-1990s, the People's Bank of China adopted a policy of refusing to extend credit to firms that did not correctly dispose of their industrial waste or that failed to meet state standards for environmental protection,[110] but it was not enforced.

Other environment-related alliances with banking institutions have met a similar fate. In mid-2007 MEP launched the Green Credit policy, providing state-owned banks with a list of over thirty thousand companies for whom loans should be limited or denied due to their status as a serious polluter.[111] During the first year this policy was in effect, banks successfully blocked loan applications from twelve companies due to their history of excessive pollution.[112] But in early 2008, MEP officials charged that local officials were sabotaging the Green Credit initiative: MEP vice minister Pan Yue stated, "Some provinces and financial institutions have not implemented the policy at all." Provinces had found it difficult to cut credit to highly profitable, high-polluting and/or energy-intensive companies that were usually protected by local governments.[113] MEP also launched the Green Securities policy in January 2008, which required that heavily polluting industries applying for an initial public offering (IPO) must make environmental disclosures and undergo an environmental assessment. In 2008, MEP inspected 38 companies, and the 20 that failed their environmental inspection were not able to undertake an IPO.[114]

The institutional weakness of MEP, the problems of the legislative and judicial organs, the power of the financial and planning agencies, and the relatively low level of central investment in environmental protection all have far-reaching negative implications for the center's ability to implement its policy mandates. Moreover, the decision to devolve authority for environmental protection to the local level as well as the nature of decision making at the local level have produced a situation in which environmental protection is spotty throughout the country. Only a small number of the wealthiest locales with the most proactive leaders and strong ties to the international community have made real progress toward redressing the environmental degradation of the past and are working to respond to the challenges of the future: about 10 percent of China's almost seven hundred cities have received MEP's designation as a National Model Environmental City, reflecting their success in meriting a number of environmental goals. Still, these areas offer hope that as China continues to integrate into the international economy, as wealth increases, and as officials become more educated about the benefits of environmental protection for the continued prosperity of their region, more environmental leadership will emerge from local officials.

Devolution of Authority

In 1989, the Environmental Protection Law established the "environmental responsibility system" (*huanjing baohu mubiao zerenzhi*). In theory, this placed the responsibility for environmental protection in the hands of local officials, who together with local EPBs would work together to improve environmental protection.[115] Investment decisions, experiments with new policy tools, engaging the public, and establishing linkages with international actors all fell within the portfolio of these leaders.

In some cases, this has allowed for exciting experimentation. In the eastern province of Jiangsu, for example, the World Bank and the Natural Resources Defense Council have launched the Greenwatch program, which grades twelve thousand factories according to their compliance with standards for industrial wastewater treatment and discloses publicly both the ratings and reasons for them. Without a strong central apparatus, however, this highly decentralized system of environmental protection has continued China's prerevolutionary reliance on the environmental proclivities of individual local officials. When the mayor is environmentally proactive, income levels are high, and the city is tightly integrated into the international community, environmental protection has evidenced substantial progress over the past two decades. When these conditions are not present—and especially when the mayor or governor is not committed to environmental protection—the EPBs are unlikely to be effective actors.

A province or city's wealth largely determines the resources it can devote to environmental protection, especially the funds allocated to treating environmental protection. Thus, Shanghai, with a gross product per capita of $10,529, and Nanjing, with $7,788, devoted approximately 3 percent ($5.34 billion and $1.44 billion, respectively) of their local revenues to treating environmental pollution in 2007. By contrast, the city of Lhasa, with a per capita gross product of $2,877 in 2007, devoted less than 0.01 percent of its revenues to environmental protection that year.[116]

High income levels also generally translate into higher levels of environmental education and a greater number of citizen complaints about environmental issues. In wealthier provinces, the number of complaints is five to seven times higher than in less-developed regions.[117] Complaints are important because they often inform EPBs of situations of which they were unaware. In Dalian, for example, 40 percent of the almost two thousand cases investigated by the EPB stemmed from citizen complaints.[118] Major cities throughout China have set up hotlines so that local people can report environmental concerns; in the wealthy coastal region of Zhejiang, the provincial-level EPB received more than 830 phone calls during the first half of June 2001.[119] Over 80 percent of environmental agencies at the county level operate 24-hour telephone hotlines for citizens to lodge complaints.[120] SEPA established the first national environmental hotline in 2001,[121] and MEP head Zhou Shengxian reported in late 2008 that 1.6 million cases of water pollution alone had been reported on the hotline between 2003 and 2008.[122]

Wealth is not the only or even the most important determinant of how well a city manages its environmental protection efforts. Much of the difference stems from the commitment level of mayors. Zhongshan, Shanghai, and Dalian—all cities recognized for their environmental protection efforts—have had mayors who have made the environment a top priority. These cities boast not only physically beautiful environs but also a positive trend line in their pollution statistics and cleanup efforts. Their EPBs also possess enough clout (thanks to mayoral support) to persuade other local bureaus to engage in cooperative activities. For example, in Dalian, the EPB has worked well with the local public security bureau to enforce the monitoring of auto emissions. Confident of mayoral support, some EPBs become more proactive in developing policy initiatives.

Even when officials recognize the benefits of a more environmentally proactive course of action, concerns for social stability often prevent them from adopting such measures. Despite the fact that agriculture in China rarely employs the most efficient irrigation technologies, for example, water prices are often artificially depressed to encourage farmers to remain on the land. By 2009, Beijing water prices (which are different for residential, industrial, and agricultural uses) had risen to 5 yuan per cubic meter (m³). Yet the rate for residential use was only 3.7 yuan per m³ [123] and overall water prices were only one-fifth the cost paid by residents in other major cities around the world. According to Wang Dangxian of the China Institute of Water Resources and Hydropower Research, such price increases are inevitable because "the current prices are not sustainable for a water-scarce city like Beijing."[124] In May 2009, Beijing's water resources bureau announced that it would raise water prices further to conserve supplies, since completion of the South-North water transfer project (which will divert one billion m³ of water to Beijing annually) was delayed from 2010 to 2014.[125]

Judgments issued by Chinese courts against polluting enterprises are another instance where concerns for social and economic stability may trump an environmentally proactive course of action. Although courts do rule in favor of pollution victims and order polluters to pay compensation and/or environmental cleanup costs, rulings are often subject to heavy pressure from local governments because these polluting enterprises are usually a major source of tax revenue and local jobs. In the CLAPV case involving a potassium chlorate plant in Fujian Province described earlier in this chapter, for example, legal experts have noted that the monetary damages awarded by the court were only about one-twentieth of the amount originally sought by the plaintiffs because the factory provided one-third of the county's tax revenue. So to maintain the county's economic security it was in the best interest of the local government to keep the factory in operation. The lead plaintiff who brought the suit was also subject to pressure in his village to drop the case; both he and his wife were assaulted and the county government closed his place of business.[126]

China's top environmental cities also have extensive ties with the international community, including long-term, comprehensive cooperation efforts with the World Bank, Asian Development Bank, and countries such as Japan, Germany, and Singapore. For example, Japan has an exchange program with Dalian's EPB, and the Japanese Overseas Cooperation Agency assists in urban planning, establishing environmental priorities, and pollution monitoring. Japanese companies, a major source of foreign investment in Dalian, are also considered environmentally friendly.[127]

Still, these wealthiest, most environmentally proactive cities present their own set of challenges. They often pursue environmental cleanup by exporting their polluting industries to points just outside the city limits. While this can be an effective strategy if the outlying regions are sparsely populated, population pressures in the major cities often drive the development of satellite communities in these outlying areas. In the past twelve years, Shanghai has moved more than seven hundred factories outside the city limits. Guangzhou, too, relocated its cement factories due to their heavy pollution; local media reported in 2007 that the city spent 1 billion yuan ($125 million) to do so.[128] In the run-up to the 2008 Olympics, Beijing officials ordered approximately two hundred industrial facilities to refit, shut down, or relocate outside Beijing to decrease the amount of air pollution produced by those facilities.[129] Zhongshan, another model environmental city located a few hours from Guangzhou, is surrounded by strip mining enterprises, petrochemical plants, semiconductor factories, and other polluting industries. Many of them are joint ventures with Taiwan.[130] During a drive with the vice mayor of Zhongshan in which he proudly recited the economic and environmental statistics of his beautiful city, I gently pointed out that the environmental achievements of the city might be even more impressive had they not been achieved on the back of outlying towns. While the irony of my comment seemed lost on the vice mayor, the local EPB director laughed heartily at my remark.

The Campaign Mentality

While China's leaders have devolved both authority and responsibility to local officials for environmental protection, they continue to intervene in environmental management through broad campaigns to address problems of nationwide importance and scope. They use campaigns to pressure local officials on the full range of macro-environmental threats: land degradation, water pollution, and water scarcity. Campaigns, however, suffer from three major shortcomings: (1) they tend to be highly politically charged with significant investment up front but little follow-through past the stated target of completion; (2) they rarely consult local officials and businesses to engage them in the campaign; and (3) they often do not employ the best set of technologies or incentives to change behavior. Overall, these campaigns place extensive burdens on localities with little follow-through from the center and thus, often, fail to achieve the desired results.

One major MEP campaign, more political in nature, targeted the country's overall emphasis on economic development at the expense of environmental protection. In 2005, SEPA and the National Bureau of Statistics (NBS) launched the Green GDP campaign. Designed to calculate the costs of environmental degradation and pollution to China's economy in terms of GDP, this project—a dramatic political statement—was viewed as evidence that the Chinese leadership would finally take action after years of rhetoric concerning the need to improve the environment. Local officials would be evaluated not only on how well they grew their economy but also on how well they protected their environment.

A chief proponent and architect of the Green GDP campaign was Pan Yue, vice minister of MEP. Pan has spearheaded an array of national environmental initiatives since his first appointment in 2003 as SEPA's deputy director, including the Green Credit policy and the Measures on Open Environmental Information. Still, he is perhaps better known for being one of the most outspoken environmental advocates within the Communist Party; he often criticizes unabashedly the Chinese leadership's shortcomings in environmental protection.

Despite the efforts of Pan and others behind the Green GDP campaign, however, the report issued by SEPA and NBS in September 2006 fell dramatically short of expectations. According to the government's calculations, environmental pollution had cost China $64 billion in economic losses in 2004, accounting for 3.05 percent of its GDP that year. Considering that China's 2004 GDP growth was about 10 percent, the pollution-adjusted GDP growth rate fell to 7 percent. While a figure of 3.05 percent is not insignificant, it was a far cry from what international and domestic observers had anticipated: indeed, for more than a decade, scientists, economists, and the World Bank (among others) had calculated that environmental degradation and pollution cost the Chinese economy the equivalent of 8–12 percent of GDP annually (see chapter 3).

The unexpectedly low figure provided by the Green GDP report was largely due to stonewalling at the provincial level and the central government's inability to formulate an economic accounting based on disparate environmental information. SEPA had originally envisioned that the report would provide detailed regional Green GDP statistics, as a first step in evaluating local officials based on their environmental performance and the economic growth of their region. But many local leaders felt threatened by the results and balked at providing environmental information. They feared that the Green GDP figures would essentially erase their hard-won economic gains. Furthermore, SEPA and NBS announced that they were able to account for only half of the items they had originally intended to include in the report: data concerning the economic impacts of major environmental problems such as groundwater and soil contamination were not even included in the final Green GDP calculations. Further muddying the waters, SEPA vice minister Zhu Guangya issued a separate environmental report almost concurrently, claiming that damage to China's environment cost the government roughly 10 percent of GDP annually—far closer to the figure that had been expected in the Green GDP study.[131]

Soon after the report was published, MEP officials quietly let it be known that the accuracy and fullness of the study had been sharply constrained by political opposition by both local officials who refused to participate and by officials from within the NBS. Some NBS officials opposed the Green GDP accounting effort on the grounds that they did not have the statistical tools to accomplish it well. Some also argued that Green GDP should not be used to evaluate local officials. After the report's release, the comments of the deputy director of the Beijing Bureau of Statistics, Yu Xiuqin, reflected such sentiments publicly: "Green GDP is not that important by itself. . . . The importance of the concept is not about the figures we are going to see. . . . Green GDP figures can only serve as guidance for public opinion; they will not have an actual impact on environmental protection." Moreover, she noted that it would not be a good idea to link the Green GDP to officials' performance evaluations because it would promote the production of false statistics.[132]

After publication of the Green GDP report in 2006, SEPA and NBS intended to release updated figures sometime in 2007. Whether due to pressure from local and provincial government officials or to genuine concerns that the government could not accurately monetize the cost of environmental degradation to economic growth, however, in 2007 the government put the publication of further Green GDP reports on hold. Vice minister Pan Yue disagreed with the decision. In February 2008, he said, "Although it will be a long process to establish the system because of difficulty obtaining data and the approach, we have to kickstart it. China cannot wait till all the preconditions are ready. Otherwise it will be too late to save the country's environment."[133]

In a bid to address severe water pollution, in 1997 the government initiated the Three Rivers and Three Lakes campaign to clean up the Liao, Huai, and Hai rivers and Tai, Chao, and Dianchi lakes. Government reports in 1999 touted the measures taken by the Kunming government to clean up China's sixth largest freshwater lake, the Dianchi:

> The Kunming city government banned the sales and use of detergent which contains phosphorus which was then discharged into the Dianchi Lake valley. It also closed down more than 20 enterprises found to be responsible for pollution. A project to dredge the bottom of the lake is also going on smoothly and should be completed by April this year.[134]

EPB officials in Kunming, however, report a very different story. In part, as they note, the sheer magnitude of the problem is overwhelming:

> Over the years, lots of industrial wastewater has been emptied into the upper section of Dianchi. As a result, the lake's purification ability is very weak. No matter how much dredging we do, there will still be pollutants in the water. Because of years of abuse, the ecosystem is very fragile. Blue algae blooms are common.[135]

In fact, the sediment at the bottom of the lake contains a toxic mix of arsenic, lead, and chromium. Even after absorbing almost 6 billion yuan ($878 million) in central and local government funds over the decade since the campaign was launched, most of Dianchi's water

fails to achieve even grade V standard.[136] According to the deputy director of the Yunnan Provincial Institute of Environmental Science,
Xu Haiping, it would take twenty to thirty years for the water in the
lake to be as clear as it was in the 1950s[137]—but even that may prove
to be optimistic as officials decry their ability to prevent polluters
from continuing to pollute.

Perhaps the central government's most audacious bid to address
both water scarcity and water pollution in China's northern
provinces, however, is the South-North Water Transfer Project. This
project, which was initially proposed by Mao Zedong in the 1950s,
began construction in December 2002 and encompasses three canals,
diverting up to 44.8 billion cubic meters of water from the Yangtze
River to the Yellow, Huai, and Hai rivers (more than half of California's annual water consumption) at an estimated cost of almost $62
billion.[138] While construction of at least two of the canals (the eastern and central) is not in doubt, the third (the western) requires such
an enormous investment of technical and financial resources that
many believe it will never be completed.[139]

This massive project first had to overcome the serious resistance
of a number of provincial leaders. During the discussion phase of
the project, many officials in the southern provinces complained
with good cause that Beijing was wasting a tremendous amount of
water from easily addressed technical problems such as leaky toilets, and thus they resented Beijing's looking south to meet its water needs. Even former Chinese president Jiang Zemin complained,
"If a country can send satellites and missiles into space, it should
be able to dry up its toilets."[140] At the same time, Hubei and Henan
provinces will be adversely affected: The project will require the resettlement of upwards of 300,000 people from these provinces.[141] As
discussed in chapter 7, China's experience with resettlement during its Three Gorges Dam project does not augur well for this process.

An even greater challenge for Beijing will be to ensure the cooperation of all the affected provinces in cleaning up the pollution that
plagues much of the area along the proposed canals. Moreover, the
environmental impact of the canals themselves remains in ques-

tion. There are widely varying analyses, including some that predict a largely positive impact for the eastern route.[142] The World Bank, meanwhile, fears significant disruption of the local ecology, salinization of the soil that would cause the water quality in Shanghai to deteriorate, and damage to freshwater fisheries.[143] And a geologist at the Chinese Academy of Sciences claims that redirecting water on the central route will increase sedimentation and the risk of floods, making navigation of the rivers diverting water to the project much more difficult.[144]

Perhaps of greatest concern, between 2006 and 2007, an independent geologist named Yong Yang led expeditions along the western reaches of the Yangtze, tracing the route of the diversion project and recording water levels during different seasons. Yong found that the average water flow in that section of the river equals about seven billion m^3 per year. This indicates that during some seasons, the government's goals to divert between eight and nine billion m^3 of water northward each year will exceed the amount of water available.[145]

These environmental concerns came to the fore in late 2008 when the government announced that completion of the central route, originally slated for 2010, would be postponed to 2014.[146] The central route, which runs through Hubei Province, created concerns over the impacts it may have on surrounding waterways, such as pollution and sedimentary build-up. Many Chinese scientists and environmental advocates fear that the government's failure to address these issues will prevent the project from being successful in the long term.[147] Even as Beijing has mobilized provincial support for the construction of the South-North Water Transfer Project, it will require a commitment of substantial financial and political resources to ensure its success. Resettlement, pollution control, and limiting the ecological impact all will require continual oversight by Beijing. The campaign approach to environmental protection, while useful for garnering official attention and mobilizing public support for a particular environmental challenge, has little chance to succeed. It emphasizes above all a crisis mentality and grand, sweeping gestures. Instead, China's leaders will have to undertake the careful planning, long-term investment, and closely monitored implementation that typically eludes them as they seek to ensure that this grand-scale development project and cleanup campaign fulfills its goals.

The Failures of Reform

Deng's early steps toward institutionalizing a bureaucracy and legal framework for environmental protection during the 1970s and 1980s, as well as later initiatives under his successors Jiang Zemin during the 1990s and into the twenty-first century under Hu Jintao, have not been able to meet the rapidly multiplying set of environmental challenges that have emerged in the wake of the economic reforms. In virtually every respect, China's environment overall has deteriorated, contributing to additional social and economic problems. In particular, China's central environmental protection bureaucracy remains weak, forced to negotiate with more development-oriented ministries and commissions from a position of lower status within the central bureaucracy and unable to enforce its directives through a strong chain of command to local EPBs.

At the same time, China's formal environmental protection institutions have all taken important steps to enhance their efficacy. They have improved the process by which they develop new policies and draft new laws, experimented with new policy approaches, and developed a coterie of talented and highly qualified experts throughout the policy, legal, and judicial arenas.

While the devolution of authority to local officials has left many regions suffering from lack of leadership or lack of resources or both, it also has produced some striking examples of success. Local initiative in Dalian, Shanghai, and Zhongshan, for example, has earned all three cities recognition for their environmental achievements.

Moreover, as chapters 5 and 6 explore, greater change may be forthcoming from forces outside the government. China's reforms also have introduced nongovernmental actors, including international and domestic NGOs, the media, and multinationals as important sources of environmental change, providing access to new policy approaches, new technologies, and funding opportunities. Often at the margins, but sometimes in critical ways, these actors are helping to push China's environmental protection capacity beyond the limits of its formal institutions.

CHAPTER FIVE

THE NEW POLITICS OF THE ENVIRONMENT

Citizens should have the right to shout out that the emperor has no clothes on whether they are right or not. Without democracy there can be no way to approach truth. History without clear conclusions will only repeat its blind and restless past. . . . I found the chief guarantee of nature protection to be the practice of democracy. Without real democracy there can be no everlasting green hills and clear waters. I am convinced that nature conservation is a cause for a whole nation.

Tang Xiyang, *A Green World Tour*

China's leaders have come to understand that failure to protect the environment incurs significant social and economic costs, and they are eager to find a means to reconcile their desire to achieve both unimpeded economic growth and improved environmental protection. As we will see in chapter 7, the path they have elected to follow is the one taken by the East Europeans and Asians over a decade ago, establishing an environmental protection bureaucracy and legal system and supporting the existence of environmental nongovernmental organizations (NGOs). Beginning with the launch of the first environmental NGO, Friends of Nature, in 1994, China's leaders have opened the political space for popular participation in environmental protection, permitted the establishment of NGOs,[1] encouraged media investigations, and supported grassroots efforts.

At the same time, China's leaders have resisted widespread implementation of tough economic policies, such as raising prices for natural resources or closing polluting factories, that might engender social unrest. By promoting the growth of environmental NGOs and media coverage of environmental issues, the Chinese leadership hopes to fill the gap between its desire to improve the country's environment and its capacity to do so.

This trend in inviting greater political participation in environmental affairs represents a much more widespread phenomenon in state-societal relations: the emergence of nongovernmental associations and organizations to fill roles previously occupied by national or local governments and state-owned enterprises. The rapidly expanding market economy has diminished the capacity of the state to regulate the economic and social activities of the Chinese people.[2] At the same time, the state has intentionally abandoned its commitment to the "iron rice bowl," in which the state provided for all the basic needs of society. The Chinese leadership no longer desires sole responsibility for much of the burden of social welfare that it has borne for the past fifty years, including the provision of housing, medical care, education, pensions, and environmental protection. Instead, it is encouraging the private sector to respond to the social welfare needs of the public, opening the door to the emergence of civil society, permitting greater openness in the Chinese media, and encouraging the Chinese people to assume greater responsibility in managing their own economic and social affairs.

This is an enormous gamble. As the Soviet and Eastern Bloc experience shows, social forces, once unleashed, may be very difficult to contain. While the Chinese leaders seek the antidote to a dysfunctional political and economic system, they are also desperate to avoid the political turmoil that convulsed the Eastern Bloc countries and ultimately transformed those political systems. Chinese officials have expressed concern that social groups could contribute to "peaceful evolution" or call for the transition of China to a western-style democracy.

China's leaders therefore have been careful to circumscribe both the number of NGOs and the scope of their activities. Yet there is evidence—nascent still—that the Chinese leadership will prove no more adept than the East Europeans at managing reform while avoiding revolution. As was the case in some of the countries of Eastern

Europe and republics of the Soviet Union, as well as countries in Asia, environmental NGOs in China are at the vanguard of nongovernmental activity. Thus the question is not only whether nongovernmental actors can shape the future of environmental protection in China but also whether they may play a role in effecting broader political change in the context of the ongoing transformation of state-societal relations.

Tightrope Act: NGOs and the Response from Beijing

The Chinese government's decision to alter the social contract that has governed state-societal relations for the past several decades has been met with both enthusiasm and concern by the Chinese populace. While people welcome the opportunity to exercise greater freedom of movement, association, and so on, they are also wary of the new responsibilities entailed. Public opinion polls, for example, reflect a growing concern with social issues emerging from the reform process. In a 2008 Internet poll of thousands of Chinese citizens conducted by the Chinese Academy of Social Sciences, for example, the environment ranked fourth as a concern, behind other social concerns such as medical care, unemployment, and the income gap.[3]

In response to these growing social welfare concerns and demands, a variety of social organizations—NGOs as well as government-organized and supported efforts—has emerged, addressing issues as wide-ranging as domestic violence, job retraining, and environmental protection. According to the Ministry of Civil Affairs, which oversees such organizations, by 2006 there were 354,000 officially registered NGOs.[4] A broader definition of social organizations that includes all types of citizen-based organizations and economic associations yields a number over one million. And if one attempts to account for NGOs that are not registered with the government, the number by some accounts is as high as eight million.[5]

The Chinese leadership has generally welcomed the efforts of these organizations. They are somewhat reminiscent of organizations that appeared during the republican period, when religious groups, literary societies, and relief organizations emerged and prospered, at least until the demands of mounting a war against Japan in the 1930s led to a government crackdown on independent societal organizations.[6] During the 1980s, in the wake of Deng Xiaoping's initiation of economic reform, some of the same kinds of relief organizations emerged, as did a few groups calling themselves NGOs. Some of the latter even became active in policy research and advocacy.[7] Again, a crackdown followed, this time on the heels of widespread protests for democracy and political change.

China's leaders today remain worried about the potential for the current generation of NGOs to serve as a locus for intellectual, worker, peasant, or general societal discontent. They already have to contend with substantial organized urban and rural unrest, significant ethnic protest in Xinjiang and Tibet, a resurgence of triad (i.e., China's traditional criminal gangs) activity, and growing participation in religious organizations that are not sponsored by the state. The controversial Qigong movement Falun Dafa,[8] which embraces Chinese from all sectors of society and has demonstrated the capacity to mobilize thousands of people without being detected by the Chinese public security apparatus, epitomizes the type of challenge the government fears.

Such concerns have produced a duality in the government's approach to the NGO sector. On the one hand, NGOs fill societal needs and earn international praise. On March 5, 2004, during the tenth National Committee of the Chinese People's Consultative Conference (CPPCC), Premier Wen Jiabao announced the government's intentions to turn over certain government responsibilities in social services to NGOs and intermediary agencies. CPPCC National Committee member Wang Min echoed Wen's announcement, stating, "For such a country as China still in a transition from a planned economy to a market one, the help from NGOs will prove especially important." In particular, with regard to the environment, Yang Haikun, another committee member, stated that NGOs can play an important role in environmental protection.[9] Speaking before an annual conference of Chinese NGOs in Beijing in late October 2007, the deputy director of the State Environmental Protection Administration (SEPA), Zhou Jian, stated, "NGOs have become an important social force in promoting China's environmental protection and acted as advisers to the government."[10] On the other hand, during 1995–1997, the government placed a two-year moratorium on the registration of new NGOs, and in September 1998, the State Council issued a set of restrictive Regulations for Registration and Management of Social Organizations.[11] Previous NGO guidelines had been vague.[12] These new regulations, however, required all NGOs to reregister, stating that, in the future, all such organizations would have to receive approval from a government organization before applying for NGO status and that there would be no appeal process if an organization's application were rejected.[13] They also stated that a national-level NGO would have to "prove [that it had] a 'legitimate' source of funding, raise at least 100,000 yuan [$12,000] and comprise of [sic] more than 50 individual members."[14] Local NGOs would have to raise 30,000 yuan ($3,750).[15] Moreover, anyone who had ever been deprived of political rights, such as a former political prisoner, would be barred from participating in an NGO.[16] Many NGOs, to avoid the bureaucratic obstacles of gaining legal status and maintaining it, operate unregistered or register as business organizations, existing in a tenuous legal zone. This is true particularly for groups working on human rights and civil rights issues, because it is illegal for them to register as an NGO and domestic funding is sparse.

Why the mixed message? One Chinese scholar assessed the government's concern over the NGO sector this way: "The Party knows from its own experience that it is possible to start a mass movement capable of overthrowing a government from just a small group of about a dozen people. . . . As such, control is vital. They feel they cannot allow any non-official group to gain ground in society for fear it will grow into a potentially threatening movement."[17] The emergence of a particular NGO, the China Democratic Party (CDP), highlighted just such potential. Using the Internet to communicate among a small membership scattered throughout the country, the CDP tried to register as an NGO in one-third of China's provinces and autonomous regions. This was despite its openly stated mission of establishing itself as a political alternative to the Communist Party, which was clearly a subversive activity outside the boundaries of acceptable NGO behavior. Beijing launched a crackdown.

Within several months of its inception, the CDP was banned, and there was an aggressive manhunt to arrest those linked to the organization. The crackdown on CDP and leaders of other groups viewed as political threats intensified in the lead-up to the 2008 Beijing Summer Olympics. Media reports in July 2008 suggested authorities harassed several members of the CDP, the leader of the New People's Party, and detained the president of the Chinese House Church Alliance and his wife.[18]

Thus, while permitting the NGO sector to develop in China, the government has been vigilant about limiting the range of its activities. In addition to the formal regulations, it retains a number of mechanisms by which it can effectively shut down an NGO. A Public Security Bureau circular issued in 1997 sets out three avenues by which local officials can effectively neutralize a "troublesome" NGO: (1) the sponsoring organization can cease its support; (2) the NGO can be closed down for financial reasons; and (3) key leaders of the NGO can be transferred to other jobs that leave them little to no time for outside work with the NGO. Anthony Saich, former Ford Foundation representative in Beijing, has noted that all three tactics have been employed. The Women's Hotline in Beijing (which provides counseling and advice to women), various NGOs in Shanghai, and "Rural Women Knowing All" (a group of activists concerned with women's issues in rural areas) have all been subverted through these methods.[19] According to Saich, who worked extensively with Chinese NGOs, the government is determined to maintain a high degree of Communist Party and state control over NGO activities.[20] In 2005, moreover, the government launched a nationwide investigation of foreign and domestically-bred NGOs under suspicions that western political agendas were behind a series of color revolutions in Central Asia.[21]

Beijing's mixed messages toward NGOs have continued in recent years. In May 2007, Sun Weilin, director of the bureau for NGO administration under the Ministry of Civil Affairs, announced that China will revise its laws to encourage NGO development by simplifying the NGO procedure, improving communication between NGOs and the government, and setting up a foundation that will recognize and reward NGOs with good performance.[22] Several other developments have signaled Beijing's desire to ease NGO management and financing. China's 2009–2010 National Human Rights Action Plan states that "revisions will be made to the Regulations on the Registration and Management of Social Organizations, Interim Regulations on the Registration and Management of Private Non-enterprise Entities, and Regulations on the Management of Foundations to ensure social organizations conduct activities in accordance with the law and their respective charters." According to one analysis, there has also been discussion within the Ministry of Civil Affairs to eliminate the requirement for NGOs to have a government sponsor.[23]

To a degree, Beijing's desire to ease restrictions on the NGO community has translated into policy. The Social Organizations Registration and Administration Act, for example, now includes an amendment that says organizations that have been disqualified from registering may still acquire legal status under a separate filing system.[24] In 2007, amendments to the Enterprise Income Tax Law raised the limit on charitable tax-deductible contributions by corporations from 3 to 12 percent of total annual profits; the Ministry of Civil Affairs and tax officials have begun to promote NGOs as candidates for such contributions.

Still, concerns remain. The Ministry of Civil Affairs has also issued a directive requiring local authorities to establish an evaluation system for NGOs and assigning them to numerical ratings on a scale from one to five.[25] According to the directive, NGOs should be evaluated based on a number of criterion, including the extent of their compliance with regulations, the scope of their activities, and the strength of their ties with the Communist Party.[26] Organizations ranked highly would receive perks such as access to government services, while low-ranking organizations would lose their eligibility for tax-deductible contributions. What impact such revised regulations will have on China's NGO community remains to be seen.

The government has also continued to exert its power to shut down unfavorable NGO operations. In July 2007, officials closed down China Development Brief, a nonprofit online publication that tracked civil society news and connected NGOs in China. The founder of China Development Brief, Nick Young, has since been denied re-entry into the country.[27] On July 29, 2009, moreover, authorities detained Xu Zhiyong, the founder of a legal reform think tank called Open Constitution Initiative (*Gongmeng*). Xu, whose group is registered as a business and receives funding from overseas, was under suspicion of tax evasion. In one news report, a researcher commented, "It's what you do with the money that matters."[28]

The government has also pursued development of its own NGOs, referred to as government-organized nongovernmental organizations (GONGOs). The Ministry of Environmental Protection (MEP), for example, has six GONGOs under its auspices: the China Environment Science Association, the China Environment Protection Industry Association, the China Environmental Culture Promotion Association, the China Environment Fund, the All-China Environment Federation, and the Chinese Society for Environmental Sciences. In some cases, GONGOs serve as a resting place for former government officials and staff when their agency is downsized during a period of bureaucratic reform such as 1998 and 2003. They may also serve essentially as front organizations for government agencies. In fact, there is a state-directed effort to train government bureaucrats in the establishment of NGOs.[29] Some of these efforts are a legitimate means of establishing a cooperative venture with a foreign counterpart. For example, the Chinese government set up an NGO to work with the U.S. NGO, the National Committee on U.S.–China Relations, to work on land use planning for the Ussuri watershed on the border between China and Russia.[30]

Many other such GONGOs, however, are simply tools by which government agencies may take advantage of the desire of foreign governments and international NGOs to support the NGO movement and civil society in China. One example is the Chinese Society for Sustainable Development, which is linked to the Chinese government's Agenda 21 office and designed to attract money from western counterparts interested in working with NGOs to develop and implement projects directed toward sustainable development. Despite one official's claim that the NGO is a "genuine" NGO, the Society is headed by the director of the Agenda 21 office, staffed by Agenda 21 officials, and located on the fifth floor of the building in which the Agenda 21 office is housed.[31]

Over time, some GONGOs are likely to evolve into genuine NGOs, having already become significantly independent in their fund-raising or membership; there are also instances in which GONGOs and NGOs develop strong and mutually beneficial relationships, or in which GONGOs act as a bridge between government and genuine NGOs. As Wu Fengshi suggests in her excellent analysis of the community of environmental GONGOs, this evolution in the nature of GONGOs may have a profound impact in strengthening the development of green civil society in China, moving many of them well outside the boundaries initially established by the government.[32]

Notwithstanding the government's efforts to manage the activities of GONGOs as well as NGOs, the environmental NGO community in China has become adept at expanding the boundaries of the permissible while avoiding government censure. While NGOs do not explicitly violate government policy, they have achieved a level of national integration and potential for coordinated action against which the government has explicitly attempted to guard. For example, although NGOs are technically forbidden to establish branch offices, many province-based NGO leaders have been trained by or been members of Beijing-based environmental NGOs before setting off to establish their own organizations. There is now a growing network of provincial and local NGOs throughout China whose leaders have all received training or guidance from a dozen or so Beijing-based NGO activists. Moreover, the advent of the Internet has meant that environmental student groups as well as professional NGOs communicate with great ease, sharing both technical data and administrative knowledge on how to raise funds and increase membership. Also, some NGOs with national-level status have broad mandates such as conservation and protection of biodiversity and undertake activities throughout the country, although they are technically based in Beijing. They thereby have avoided the geographic stricture altogether and have members spread throughout the country.

Such circumventing of the spirit of official policy has not prompted a crackdown, primarily because these environmental NGOs have yet to challenge central government policy. Thus far, the government and environmental NGOs have operated under the tacit agreement that their mission and work are mutually reinforcing. Yet a closer examination of the environmental movement reveals that it has evolved into three distinct, albeit closely linked activist efforts.[33] Each of these strains within the movement has its own set of goals and means of operation, not all of which coincide with those of the government. Thus, the government–NGO alliance may be a tenuous one.

1. *Conservation.* The first and largest group of environmental activists devotes its time to nature conservation and species protection. These leaders, such as Liang Congjie from Friends of Nature, Yang Xin from Green River, Wang Yongchen from Green Earth Volunteers, Xi Zhinong from Wild China, and Yu Xiaogang from Green Watershed, form a loose network of committed environmentalists throughout the country who often work closely together.

While Beijing is supportive of the efforts of these NGOs, local officials often resist their involvement to protect entrenched local political and economic interests. As time has passed, some NGO leaders within this group are also beginning to raise questions concerning central directives. A public anti-dam campaign in southwestern Yunnan Province has met a degree of success in this area. In 2005, plans to build thirteen dams along the Nu River spurred dozens of mainland environmental groups and individuals to publish a letter calling on the government to release an environmental impact assessment (EIA) in accordance with Chinese law. Although an EIA was never published, the government scaled back the project to four dams, and in May 2009 Premier Wen Jiabao halted the construction of a hydropower station on the Nu River until the project underwent a more thorough environmental assessment.[34]

2. *Urban Renewal.* A second approach to environmental activism focuses on issues related to urban renewal. Geng Haiying, a doctor in Dalian, and groups such as Green Cross in Xiamen, Friends of Green Environment in Jiangsu Province, and others who are concerned with urban issues are disinclined to challenge the center and more likely to try to work in a consensual fashion with local governments. Indeed, the nature of their work—recycling programs, en-

ergy efficiency, and environmental education—often demands at least passive assistance from local officials.

3. *Pollution Prevention.* Finally, the third group of environmental activists has interests and goals that may push the boundaries of the current political system, taking advantage of new technologies and regulations to deal with the causes as well as the consequences of factory pollution for the Chinese people. Ma Jun, Wang Canfa (discussed in chapter 4), and Wu Lihong have been outspoken activists on this front.

Furthermore, underpinning all environmental activism in China are the Chinese media, which have been a critical partner to the NGOs in publicizing their accomplishments, working to expose corrupt local environmental practices, and informing and educating the Chinese public. Many of the brightest and most promising environmental activists of the next generation, such as Wen Bo, Hu Kanping, and Hu Jingcao, boast both environmental and journalistic credentials and may well revolutionize the manner in which Chinese NGOs pursue their goals in the years to come.

Three Pioneering Environmental Activists

The contemporary intellectual roots of environmental activism in China took hold during the mid-1980s and early 1990s with the writings of two prominent journalists, Tang Xiyang and Dai Qing, and one noted scholar, He Bochuan. While none of the three has established an NGO, each has had a profound impact on the evolution of the environmental movement.

Tang Xiyang

Revered by many in China as a spiritual and philosophical leader of the environmental movement, former *Beijing Daily* reporter Tang has had a tremendous impact on the ideas and thinking of environmental NGO leaders within China. Tang was born in 1930 in Hunan Province and graduated from the foreign language department of Beijing Normal University in 1952. Within five years, like thousands of other intellectuals who heeded Chairman Mao's call to let "a hundred flowers blossom and a hundred schools of thought contend," he came under political attack during the anti-rightist campaign, which condemned all those who had voiced their dissenting opinions openly. During the Cultural Revolution, Tang's wife was beaten to death by the radical, overzealous Red Guards, who were committed to rooting out all potential political opposition. Tang turned to nature as a refuge:

> Driven into a corner, I could think of only two ways to relieve my suffering: kill myself or kill somebody else. Nature saved me. . . . Instead of twisted faces, hypocrisy, ruptured relations, and unending, unavoidable nightmares, nature offered the most sublime words, the most beautiful music, the purest emotions, perfect philosophy. . . . We spoke no words, yet we understood each other. . . . The more I love her, the more I understand her and her suffering, which is more terrible and intense than mine. . . . Now I no longer appeal for myself, but for her.[35]

After Deng Xiaoping's accession to power, Tang was rehabilitated in 1980, and he joined the Beijing Museum of Natural History as the editor of the museum's magazine, *Nature*. The journal became a vehicle for his and others' musings on issues such as species protection.

In 1982, Tang met an American cultural education specialist, Marcia Bliss Marks, and the two began to travel together to national parks. They fell in love and were married. In 1996, Tang and Marks established the first Green Camp, which served both to train future environmental activists and to draw attention to the plight of some of China's most precious resources and endangered species. Tragically, Tang realized their dream alone. Early on the morning they were scheduled to travel to Yunnan for the first Green Camp, Marcia succumbed to a long battle with cancer. She had placed herself in a hospital, strictly in opposition to her religious beliefs as a Christian Scientist, so that Tang would not feel compelled to stay with her and care for her at home but rather would forge ahead with the Green Camp. With as many as thirty college students, Tang journeyed to northwest Yunnan to study and work to protect snub-nosed monkeys. In 1997, Tang's Green Camp traveled to southeast Tibet to protect the primitive forests, and in 1998 they visited the Sanjiang Plain in Heilongjiang Province to protect the wetlands. Many of the students who participated in these Green Camps have returned to their homes in other cities, such as Shanghai and Nanning, to establish their own green camps.[36]

In 2007, Tang, now in his late seventies, won international acclaim as a recipient of the Ramon Magsaysay Award, often dubbed "Asia's Nobel Prize." He continues to write and publish articles and to lecture regularly about China's environment. Tang's greatest influence on the thinking of Chinese youth, however, is probably through his 1993 book, *A Green World Tour*. The book—a personal account of Tang's eight-month-long travels through nature reserves and encounters with various people in countries in Europe, the former Soviet Union, Canada, and the United States, as well as in China—has inspired many Chinese to take steps to improve the environment, such as investing their own money to establish a nature preserve.[37] But Tang himself believes that much more must change for the environment to be protected in China. He comments,

> If my trips abroad can be compared to the journey to the West of the Tang Dynasty priest Sanzang, whose mission was to bring back Buddhist sutras, then what I am after is "the green sutra." I found the chief guarantee of nature protection to be the practice of democracy. Without real democracy there can be no everlasting green hills and clear waters. I am convinced that nature conservation is a cause for a whole nation. It won't do to depend on a wise emperor or president. Hundreds of millions of people must realize and show concern for this problem. When they all dare to speak and act, the emperor or president has to do something; otherwise he cannot continue in office. After visiting many countries and observing others' attitudes, I feel democracy is necessary to the protection of nature.[38]

The underlying message of the book, therefore, is a sharply political one. In response, the government censors have stepped in, deleting

from both the 1993 Chinese and the 1999 English language editions
Tang's ruminations on the Cultural Revolution, Tiananmen Square,
and the imperative of democracy for China. He has countered the
censors by amassing a large number of copies of the book at his
home and reinserting the censored portions by hand. Many of his
views run counter to the official line:

> The Tiananmen Square incident has left a very deep impression on
> me. All the [Chinese] newspapers, journals, radio and TV programs
> changed to uniform words and tone almost overnight, as if the hap-
> pening involving a million people that had taken place the night
> before was unreal. A downright lie became 100 percent truth. In an
> instant, intelligent men devoting themselves to the cause of democ-
> racy became criminals, while those engaged in repressing the masses
> were honored as "Defenders of the Republic" . . .
>
> Let's compare conditions in Eastern Europe. When the peoples of
> Poland, Hungary and Eastern Germany awakened to the necessity
> for reform, reform became an irresistible tide. However, when the
> Chinese people awakened and began to act, they induced bloody
> suppression. That reminds me of various farmers' rebellions in for-
> mer eras. Even if some of the rebellions were successful, the result
> was simply a shift in rulers, the fruits of success never passed into
> the hands of the common people. I'm also reminded of the burning
> of books and burying alive of scholars by the Emperor Qinshi-
> huang, the state examination system started in the Tang Dynasty,
> and the various political movements started by Mao Zedong aimed
> at punishing intellectuals, which I experienced myself. In such a
> cultural environment, prolonged, closed, dictatorial, lacking in
> democracy, domestically and in interflow internationally, it was
> very difficult to develop science and technology as well as a tradi-
> tion of loving nature.[39]

When asked directly, "What are China's biggest environmental
problems?" Tang answers, "Democracy. If you don't have democracy, you can't have real environmental protection."[40]

In 2004, Tang published a second book, *Wong! Wong! Wong!*, an
anthology of essays by 180 friends and environmentalists that in-

cludes his own thoughts. In 2005, Tang said, "They can disagree with me. What I wanted was a book that will leave future generations our ideas on nature." Within a year, the book sold 10,000 copies in China.[41]

He Bochuan

Tang's *A Green World Tour* remains in print in China, albeit in censored form. But distribution of one of the most controversial treatises, He Bochuan's *China on the Edge*, was halted a year after it was released.

Published in 1988, when the reform movement was in full swing and political openness in China had reached new heights, the book describes a grim environmental situation in China and predicts an even grimmer future unless radical political and economic reform are undertaken. The author, He Bochuan, was a lecturer in the department of philosophy at Sun Yat-sen University in Guangdong. In 1983, he contributed a section on education to the prestigious collection of essays *China in the Year 2000*. Using this piece as an intellectual launching pad, He wrote a number of articles on the related issues of population, ecology, energy, and economics that eventually became *China on the Edge*. By the time publication was halted in 1989, in the wake of Tiananmen, it had already sold more than 400,000 copies.[42] The book was, in fact, widely distributed among students during the Tiananmen Square protests.[43]

At the time, He's contribution was unique not only in its critique of environmental practices but also in its clarion call for political and economic reform. He linked issues such as inefficiencies in water supply to irrationalities in the economic system, noting, "These economic difficulties are a major factor in environmental problems because they create the inefficiency, waste, lack of innovation, and ineffective use of capital which compound environmental damage and obstruct solutions to it."[44] He later broadened his critique to include a more sweeping call for political reform: "Until reform of the political system achieves concrete results, and particularly in political democratization, liberalization, and legalization, and systems for enforcing them, it will be impossible to devise an overall plan for

China's current reforms."[45] Had the book continued to be sold, it might well have had the same impact as Rachel Carson's 1962 book *Silent Spring*, which is widely credited with catalyzing the environmental movement in the United States.

Though He has since concluded his tenure at Sun Yat-sen University, his writings remain extensively read and discussed in China. He continues to decry China's approach to development and environment, noting that "China is following an approach to development that measures progress only through economic growth, while ignoring the disastrous effects on the environment. . . . Economic growth is supposed to solve the problem of poverty, but it causes so much environmental destruction that poverty continues and development is undermined. It is a vicious circle."[46]

Dai Qing

Around the same time, in the mid-1980s, Dai Qing began the long personal odyssey that would transform her from an inquisitive reporter into a political pariah at home and an acclaimed human rights and environmental activist abroad.

In 1986, while a reporter at *Guangming Daily*, Dai attended a conference in Beijing on the Three Gorges Dam. A small group of Chinese scientists had organized the meeting to report on their environmental concerns about the dam. While Dai did nothing with the information at the time, she maintained an interest in the issue. During a visit to Hong Kong one year later, she encountered a writer named Lin Feng, who provided her with information on the dam from Hong Kong newspapers over the next few years.[47]

In early 1989, when the National People's Congress (NPC) and the Chinese People's Political Consultative Conference were scheduled to discuss the proposed dam, Dai attempted to inform the debate by arranging for several prominent journalists to interview the scientists she had met in 1986. When it became clear that no newspapers or journals would publish the interviews, she arranged to have the collection published by the Guizhou People's Publishing House,[48] with the same editor, Xu Yinong, who had published He Bochuan's book. Guizhou People's Publishing House, an obscure press in one of China's poorest provinces, likely operated under the central government's radar screen. Generally, officials permit far greater latitude in political expression and economic reform away from the capital of Beijing.

Dai's book, *Yangtze! Yangtze!*, was quickly acclaimed in the West and banned within China (although 25,000 copies remained in circulation) for its articulate and scientifically based evidence opposing construction of the Three Gorges Dam. The book includes essays by journalists, scientists, and well-known political figures within the Chinese Communist Party's leading group responsible for evaluating the dam's feasibility who dissented from the government's final published report, as well as by others involved in assessing the dam's viability.[49] Implicit and occasionally explicit throughout the book is a critique of the lack of political openness in the environmental assessment process of the dam, the silencing of dissident opinions, and the blatant disregard for truth displayed by the leaders who favored the dam.

One of the most telling criticisms comes from the highly respected former personal secretary of Mao Zedong, Li Rui:

> [D]ue to the practice of relying on the leader's personal experience and will in decision making, we have yet to establish a complete scientific and democratic decision making process. . . . There are, however, some encouraging signs of improvement, such as when different views can be seen in the newspapers and many more scientists and specialists have the courage to voice their different opinions. But we are still in a transitional period between "rule of men" and "rule by law."[50]

Yangtze! Yangtze! may have represented the reform era's first public lobbying effort involving intellectuals and public figures in an attempt to influence a governmental decision-making process.[51] While the effort failed, its impact was also unprecedented in Chinese history: three years later, in 1992, when the NPC finally voted on the issue of construction of the dam, one-third of the delegates voted no.

Dai's opposition to the dam is as much political as environmental. As she once commented, "I got involved in this issue not for scientific reasons, but to promote the freedom of speech."[52] Her voice holds weight in China because of her family background. Dai's "second father" was Marshal Ye Jianying, one of Mao Zedong's chief lieutenants during the war, and then a long-standing member of the Politburo, who also served as a defense minister and then chairman of the standing committee of the NPC. Despite her family connections, Dai was forced to pay a steep price for her views: In 1989, she was sentenced to ten months in the maximum security Qincheng prison. The reason for her imprisonment was ostensibly her role in trying to broker a compromise between the students and the government during the Tiananmen crisis. However, she believes that the real reason for imprisonment was her vocal opposition to the dam.

Officially, Dai is not permitted to publish, to participate in any organizations, or to have a job. When she attempted to participate in a tree-planting project, the organizers were told that her name had to be removed from the list.[53] Still, she stays vocal throughout the world. In 1993 Dai received two international awards, the Goldman Environment Prize and the Condé Nast Traveler Environmental Award. In 2003 she completed a book about her experiences, *Tiananmen Follies: Prison Memoirs and Other Writings*, published in the United States in November 2004. In 2007, Dai served as a visiting fellow at the Australian National University, and she continues to publish articles in publications such as the *New York Review of Books* and the *New York Times*. All throughout, she has remained a controversial figure in the eyes of the Chinese government. In September 2009, during Dai Qing's address at an international symposium in Frankfurt, Chinese delegates walked out of the venue, returning only after the organizers apologized for allowing Dai to participate.[54] China had initially demanded that Dai's invitation be rescinded and threatened to otherwise boycott the Frankfurt Book Fair in October, where China was the guest of honor. The organizers initially conceded to the request to disinvite Dai but later reversed their decision.[55]

Tang, He, and Dai represent the contemporary intellectual and political roots of the environmental movement in China. They, themselves, have not established environmental NGOs. Yet their ideals resonate with many of those who have. The current leadership of the environmental NGOs is at once emboldened and cautioned by the experience of these three writers and thinkers. And Dai and Tang especially continue to involve themselves heavily in environmental efforts. The environmental NGO community is small enough that, as Tang Xiyang states, "All of the movement people know one another."[56]

The Conservationists

The largest, best funded, and best organized of the environmental NGOs in China are those that focus primarily on species and nature conservation and environmental education. Many of the founders of these NGOs are intellectuals—historians, journalists, and university professors—who combine a reverence for nature with a sense of civic duty and political activism. Species protection also has been a politically acceptable issue to tackle because, at first blush, it does not challenge the deeply entrenched political priorities placed on urban and coastal modernization. Rather, species protection involves illiterate peasants, loggers, or officials in poorer, more remote regions of the country, where species still exist but are on the verge of extinction.

The conservation-oriented NGOs often work with national authorities to counter local officials' failure to implement central policies. As a result, these environmental NGOs have clashed with powerful local interests, sometimes with life-threatening consequences. More recently, they have even begun to challenge, in modest ways, the decisions of central authorities, suggesting that success may be emboldening them.

Foremost among these conservation activists is Liang Congjie, who founded the first environmental NGO in China, Friends of Nature. Indeed, the birth of the contemporary environmental movement in China might be dated to the early 1990s, when a group of students and scholars searching for an activist outlet in the post-Tiananmen period approached Liang, an unassuming and highly articulate historian, with the idea of establishing an environmental NGO.

Liang's distinguished reform lineage made him a natural choice. His grandfather was the famous Qing dynasty reformer Liang Qichao, and his father, Liang Sicheng, was a renowned architect in Beijing, who attempted (unsuccessfully) to preserve much of the old city of Beijing during Mao's time. In addition, he holds a position in the Chinese People's Political Consultative Conference, a formal government body with a notable reform orientation, affording him a political platform as well as a degree of political protection that less well-positioned Chinese would not have.

While Liang doubted his ability to start such an organization, given his lack of expertise in environmental affairs and China's lack of tradition in nonstate organized activity, he consulted with some friends, such as Dai Qing, who encouraged him to give it a try. Liang was also inspired by the idea of a Chinese environmental NGO, having heard of an expatriate Chinese environmental group based in Boston, Green China. Perhaps most important, a vice director of the National Environmental Protection Agency (NEPA), precursor to the MEP, had suggested to Liang that he use his voice to accomplish something positive in environmental protection.

With the support and guidance of his friends, Liang drafted a mission statement and charter for an environmental NGO. Rather than emulate Greenpeace, with its confrontational and often contentious tactics, he decided to emphasize environmental education. Mission statement in hand, Liang approached NEPA to serve as his NGO's "mother-in-law" (*guakao*). However, NEPA had already established its own GONGO, the China Environmental Cultural Association. Officials within NEPA suggested that Liang instead invite the Chinese Academy of Culture (*Zhongguo Wenhua Shuyuan*), of which Liang was a key member, to oversee the organization. With the Academy's support, Liang registered the NGO as the Green Culture Sub-Academy on March 30, 1994.[57] By the end of 1994, Liang had received the government seal from the Ministry of Civil Affairs.

Even prior to receiving formal government approval for his organization, Liang held a first organizational meeting on June 5, 1993. About sixty people attended, primarily Liang's friends and friends of friends.[58] While Liang's friend Dai Qing herself was not permitted to participate because of her outspoken criticism of the government's plans to build the Three Gorges Dam, her friends attended the meeting.

The group focused its initial efforts on environmental education, publishing popular science–oriented books on environmental protection[59] and involving the public in conservation efforts such as tree planting. Soon, however, Liang expanded his group's activities well beyond the original mandate of environmental education to take on more controversial issues, including protection of species, such as the Tibetan antelope and Yunnan snub-nosed monkey, and preventing deforestation. The membership also grew rapidly, reaching 8,000 people by 2007.

While there are no branches of Friends of Nature in other cities—both because of the government's restrictions on such branches and because Liang was afraid of losing control of branch practices—several members of Friends of Nature have left Beijing and established their own environmental NGOs elsewhere. For example, renowned environmentalist and nature photographer Yang Xin, a former member of Friends of Nature, has established Green River Network in Chengdu, Sichuan Province.[60] Friends of Nature member Tian Dasheng also founded Green Volunteer League in Chongqing. Moreover, the NGO has spawned numerous offshoots that focus on specific aspects of environmental and wildlife protection, such as bird watching and animal rescue.[61]

Liang has become nationally and internationally renowned for his work, frequently traveling abroad and winning plaudits both domestically and internationally for his efforts. The Chinese government, for example, has awarded him the Giant Panda Award and sponsored him for a United Nations Environmental Programme Global Village Award. MEP, especially, has appreciated Liang's work in calling to account local officials who ignore center directives. For example, in 1998, at a meeting sponsored by the Hainan environmental protection bureau (EPB), Liang challenged a local EPB official's account of Hainan's success in combating deforestation. A SEPA representative who had also been present later thanked Liang, stating that in his official capacity he could not so directly contradict the word of a local official, especially in a public meeting.[62]

Despite such acclaim, Liang maintained a modest demeanor and continued to work out of cramped offices in downtown Beijing. His ambition to improve China's environmental situation, however, remained large. During a visit with Liang and his wife in Beijing in 2000, he described to me the ways in which he and other NGO leaders had begun to try to reform Beijing's policies. For example, in late 1999, when the government announced its campaign to "Open the West," one of the five major tenets was "ecological construction." Yet SEPA was not among the twenty-odd ministries involved in advancing this policy, casting serious doubt on the government's real commitment to environmental protection. Liang, in his capacity as a member of the Chinese People's Political Consultative Conference, wrote a letter to the State Council calling on it to include SEPA in the leading group.

Liang also told me that he was planning to tackle new issues such as water resources and energy development, moving far beyond his previous emphasis on nature conservation and into the much more politically and economically sensitive realm of pollution prevention and resource use in urban areas. Still, two years later, when I visited with his staff in summer 2002, they appeared focused almost entirely on expanding their environmental education efforts rather than on undertaking new issues. An innovative program was Friends of Nature's environmental education van, which transports volunteers to China's poorer, interior provinces, where they live for several weeks at a time and use pictures and games to educate schoolchildren on the particular environmental challenges of the region. Friends of Nature is also using its relatively senior status and strong endowment to provide small grants—perhaps one to two thousand dollars—to help nascent NGOs get started throughout the country. Liang stepped down as head of Friends of Nature in 2009. (The new director, Li Bo, is moving in new directions, for example working with Ma Jun to hold enterprises and cities accountable for meeting their pollution targets.)

Yet Liang's greatest contribution to environmentalism in China may well be in his service as an activist above reproach. With his distinguished reform lineage, as well as his nonconfrontational approach to change, he was able to work within the system to push the boundaries of what the government considers acceptable activities for NGOs. Moreover, with high official and unofficial standing in government circles, he was able to serve an important role in conveying other environmentalists' concerns to government leaders. For example, one NGO based in Yunnan, the Green Plateau Institute, sent a letter to the National Minority Affairs Bureau via Liang, so that he could use his influence to press the government to stop government-sponsored groups from climbing the holy Meili Snow Mountain in Yunnan's northwestern region. Thanks to Liang's intervention, the treks were halted. Nonetheless, even Liang's Friends of Nature is not exempt from the government's strictures. In 2003, the government threatened not to renew the organization's registration as an NGO unless the secretary and a cofounder of the organization, Wang Lixiong, were dismissed from the organization. Wang had publicly come to the defense of two Tibetans convicted of separatist terrorist activities earlier in the year. Although Wang fought his dismissal, Friends of Nature decided that he should leave rather than endanger the organization's future.[63]

The Monkey and the Antelope

Liang also played a central role in two campaigns that galvanized environmental activists throughout China: the campaign to protect the Yunnan snub-nosed monkey, which was threatened by illegal logging in Deqin County, Yunnan, and the effort to protect the Tibetan antelope from poachers in the western reaches of China. These campaigns not only energized the environmental activists but also helped catalyze a nationwide environmental movement and establish a foundation for future campaigns.

In 1995 nature photographer Xi Zhinong, while employed by the Yunnan Forestry Department, had spent months documenting the ways of the near-extinct Yunnan snub-nosed monkey, which makes its home at the edge of the Tibetan plateau in Deqin, Yunnan.[64] The monkeys' diet consists almost exclusively of lichens from the branches of the trees in the old-growth forests on mountains separating the upper Yangtze and Mekong rivers,[65] and logging—both legal and illegal—had devastated the monkeys' habitat. Soon after completing his filming, Xi learned that the county government had plans to sell extensive tracts of the forest to loggers. When Xi protested to the provincial forestry department's leaders, they explained that the forest lay outside protected areas. Even the media, many of which had become actively engaged in environmental investigative journalism, refused to become involved, concerned that the issue was "too sensitive" because the Tibetan minority was involved.[66]

A friend of Xi's then contacted Tang Xiyang, describing Xi's work and the plight of the monkeys. Tang followed up by calling Xi and persuading him to write a letter to Song Jian, then the head of the State Environmental Protection Commission, linking concern for the nearly extinct monkeys to the larger threat of deforestation along the upper Yangtze, noting that silt from the denuded slopes could clog the Three Gorges Dam.[67] At the same time, Tang passed the letter to Liang Congjie, who then passed copies of the letter to the media. The letter was first published by the Associated Press and quickly picked up by the Chinese media, generating significant domestic and international attention. Concurrently, budding journalists and student environmental activists, Wen Bo and Yan Jun, organized a group of more than two hundred students at the Beijing Forestry University to view Xi's film at the end of 1995.

These letters and the exhibition generated a tremendous amount of attention within various state agencies. As a result of this internal and external pressure, in April 1996, the government launched a formal investigation. China Central Television's (CCTV) *Evening News* (*Xinwen Lianbo*) followed up with a program on the logging, did a feature story on Xi, and invited him to work on the popular television program *Oriental Horizon*. Later, in summer 1996, Xi helped Tang manage the first Green Camp in Deqin, leading over thirty students to the forest and adding to the publicity. Finally, the State Council instructed the local government to stop the illegal logging and promised to compensate the loggers for a three-year period at a rate of eight million yuan ($970,000) annually.

In 1998, however, Xi was tipped off that the logging was continuing. CCTV's investigative program *Focus* went undercover and filmed the logging, following up with an interview with the Fuxi-anzhang County head. By chance, the program aired the evening before the devastating Yangtze River floods. Premier Zhu Rongji then stepped in to take control of the situation personally, phoning the director of Yunnan's forestry department to insist that action be taken. As a result, the Yunnan Forestry Department's vice director held a meeting at which the head of Deqin County had to "confess his mistakes," and the deputy-head of the county was fired.[68]

Although sixteen high-level officials signed onto the campaign, the local government has not effectively halted the logging, likely because the economic interests are too strong.[69] Some officials have threatened that they could "make Xi disappear,"[70] and he was fired from his job at the Yunnan Forestry Bureau. Liang Congjie believes that the government and NGOs will have to undertake greater grass-roots education in Yunnan to educate the public and the officials for the protection effort to succeed.[71]

While the campaign may have attained only limited success in preventing deforestation and protecting the monkeys, it transformed the landscape of environmental protection in China, galvanized the environmental protection movement, and gave the activists a sense that they could indeed accomplish something through their efforts. It was the first time China's environmentalists had coordinated their activities and affected policy at the most senior levels of the Chinese government.

Several of those involved were inspired to become even more involved in the NGO movement. For example, Xi and his wife, Shi Li-hong, returned to Deqin in 1999 to try to register their own NGO. Shi was already a veteran activist in the world of international environmental NGOs. Originally a reporter with *China Daily*, Shi had viewed a documentary on women environmental activists produced by Liao Xiaoyi and was inspired to take action. In 1996, she, along with Wen Bo and several other young activists, attended the Deqin Green Camp sponsored by Tang Xiyang. Shi then joined Friends of Nature and Global Village of Beijing as a volunteer, and began working part-time at the World Wildlife Fund (WWF) as an environmental education assistant in March 1997 and then as a full-time communications specialist in October 1999.

Yet, despite their excellent credentials, when Shi and Xi applied for NGO status, they were turned down by the local Party secretary, likely because of Xi's campaign to save the monkeys.[72] At the provincial level, however, top officials were favorably disposed to their work, and their application was approved. Finally in March 2000, they registered as the Institute of Ecological Conservation and Development (now called the Green Plateau Institute)[73] under the Xicheng District Bureau of Commerce and Industry in Beijing. They focused their work primarily on biodiversity and soil erosion, although much of the emphasis was on "community based natural resource conservation and development."[74] They undertook a variety of projects such as enabling local women in Deqin to sell their carpets, working to enlarge a small regional hydropower station, assisting environmental architects interested in improving the interior of Tibetan homes to use less wood, and training teachers. They also continued their investigative efforts. Reporting on the government's efforts to clean up Dianchi Lake, Shi Lihong stated that despite billions of dollars of investment, the water quality in the lake had actually declined.[75]

The energy and personal sacrifice required to serve as a leader of China's environmental movement, however, takes its toll on even the most committed. I met up with Shi while she was attending the 2002 World Economic Forum in New York as one of the "World's 100 Future Leaders." She told me that she and her husband had left Yunnan and returned to Beijing. Despite all their hard work in Yunnan, they were not native to the area, and decided to leave their work in the hands of a local environmental activist that they had trained. Back in Beijing, they had already established an independent documentary studio, Wild China, which concentrated on producing television movies on rare species in China.[76] Six months later, in June, I met with Shi in Beijing. Normally dynamic and articulate, Shi seemed exhausted and concerned about leading a life that placed her constantly under the spotlight. Liao Xiaoyi had earlier counseled Shi that life as one of China's top environmental activists necessitated a substantial loss of privacy and sacrifice of one's personal life. Perhaps bearing such advice in mind, Shi decided to accept a long-standing invitation from a well-known China scholar, Orville Schell, to take a year sabbatical in the United States at the University of California, Berkeley.

The cause of the Tibetan antelope provided a second rallying cry for China's nascent environmental movement. Over the past several decades, the Tibetan antelope has become increasingly endangered as a result of the international trade in shahtoosh, the wool from the neck of the antelope, which is coveted for its exceedingly fine quality. The link between the decline in the numbers of antelope and the shahtoosh trade was originally established by noted American environmentalist George Schaller, who has spent years in China documenting and working to preserve China's rare species. Although the Tibetan antelope has been under the protection of the Convention on International Trade in Endangered Species (CITES) since 1979, their numbers have declined from almost 1,000,000 at the turn of the nineteenth century to under 75,000 by the turn of twentieth century.[77] If poaching continues at the current rate, the species will likely be extinct by 2020.[78]

The antelope range throughout Kekexili, Qinghai, as well as Xinjiang and Tibet, a vast, largely barren region of western China. The shahtoosh trade is driven by three sets of actors: the poachers; the producers of shawls made from shahtoosh, primarily based in Kashmir; and, most important, the very wealthy consumers in the West, where a shahtoosh shawl may retail for more than $10,000. Crackdowns have taken place in the United States and England, among other western countries. India, however, has remained impervious to entreaties from environmentalists to shut down its mills. Dr. Farooq Abdullah, until 2002 the chief minister of Kashmir, stated that "as long as I am the chief minister, shahtoosh will be sold in Kashmir." He argued that there was "no evidence of Tibetan antelope being reduced in number or their being shot to acquire wool for shahtoosh."[79]

Within China, a battle between poachers and the Wild Yak Brigade, an unofficial group that patrols the area in search of poachers, has emerged.[80] The brigade was first formed in Zhiduo County, of which Kekexili is a part, and initially headed by Gisang Sonam Dorje, a local official. When he was killed by poachers in 1994, his brother-in-law, Zhawa Dorje, assumed his position. In 1998, Zhawa Dorje was found dead from a gunshot wound in his home in Golmud, Qinghai; it was ruled a suicide, but other explanations including murder and a family argument have also been advanced. At that same time, Liang Congjie, Xi Zhinong, and Yang Xin of Green River Network decided to become involved in the effort to protect the antelope.

In 1997, Xi traveled to Tibet with Yang Xin to profile Yang for *Oriental Horizon* and spent two weeks on patrol with the Wild Yak Brigade. Upon his return, Xi persuaded Shi Lihong to involve WWF. Shi's boss, Lu Zhi, then spoke to Liang Congjie and Grace Ge, the International Fund for Animal Welfare (IFAW) representative in Beijing, about what NGOs could do to help. Shi began collecting information on the challenge, eventually contacting the CITES office in Geneva, which agreed to participate in a meeting sponsored by WWF along with IFAW in Geneva.

In July 1998, Friends of Nature and a young journalist from the forestry bureau's newspaper *Green Times*, Hu Kanping, invited Zhawa Dorje to give a series of lectures in Beijing. The lectures inspired the public and mobilized support behind the Wild Yak Brigade; just one month later, however, Zhawa Dorje was killed.

Despite this tragedy, the Beijing-based NGOs continued to press forward. Yang Xin, who had been a close friend of Gisang Sonam Dorje, began to work to create a vast preserve in the region that would house facilities for climate change research, as well as five ranger stations to monitor the area and combat poachers. Simultaneously, Liang Congjie and Friends of Nature raised money to buy two Beijing Army jeeps for the brigade.[81] Liang also sent a report about the Tibetan antelope to NEPA and the Ministry of Forestry, calling for more funds, weapons, and manpower. Most important, Liang recognized that if the poachers were to be stopped, all three provinces and regions that were home to the antelope would have to crack down simultaneously.

The NGO effort also received assistance from the media. In spring 1999, after a year of effort, Xi Zhinong was able to persuade budding young television producer Hu Jingcao to produce a feature on the

Tibetan antelope. After officials were persuaded to cooperate in a crackdown in April 1999, more than twelve groups of poachers were arrested. But by June, the poachers were back in action.

In early August, the Qinghai government dealt a serious blow to the antipoaching efforts by stating that it wanted to replace the Wild Yak Brigade with an "official" nature reserve administration. Liang Congjie and other conservationists, along with the Wild Yak Brigade itself, strongly opposed this shift, in part because training and developing such an official presence would likely take upwards of a year but also, one might presume, because the opportunities for corruption would be great. Despite personal lobbying of the NGOs by Qinghai officials, the NGOs resisted the change.

Still, some NGO leaders had their own reservations about the activities of the Wild Yak Brigade. The group had been illegally charging local residents to harvest worms in the area. In addition, there were accusations within the group of misappropriation of funds. However, after so much time and effort had been invested, the NGO community in China was reluctant to let the Wild Yak Brigade disintegrate. As one NGO leader commented, "The Wild Yak Brigade has become a sort of flag for the Chinese environmental community. No one wants to let it fall, but now many people are afraid to be associated with the brigade because of their behavior."[82] By 2001, however, Qinghai officials had succeeded in disbanding the brigade and had organized an official effort. At least one NGO leader believes that this official effort is now succeeding.

The Tibetan antelope and Yunnan snub-nosed monkeys have served as causes célèbres for the Chinese NGO environmental movement, both solidifying a nationwide network and inspiring new activists to take part. They also exemplify the reach of the Beijing-based NGOs and their capacity to alert the national leadership to environmental problems and work in support of national environmental policy at the local level, when local actors are ineffectual. Yet if China's environmental movement is to thrive, it must broaden the range of activities it supports and incorporate more regionally based NGOs to sustain the work over the long run. This has proved a difficult task. Outside Beijing, the nongovernmental movement is less politically well-connected, possesses fewer ties to the international NGO community, and is more often subject to the vagaries of local politics.

Grassroots Environmentalism in the Hinterlands

Many regional NGOs have emerged in cities and towns rich in biodiversity, such as Kunming, Yunnan. In several cases, the government has been effective in constraining the development of NGOs through its registration requirements. However, even with limited human and financial capital, these NGOs have proved remarkably adept at sustaining their work; in fact, there are some striking examples of environmental activism that reach beyond what has been attempted by Beijing activists, which may well serve as models for future environmental activism in China.

Yang Xin's Green River is perhaps the most successful of the regional NGOs. Yang, an accountant in his early forties, focuses his work on environmental conservation in the headwater of the Yangtze River and has published four books, including *The Source of the Yangtze*, which had significant U.S. sales and has brought in additional revenue for the organization. He is also quite organizationally savvy, spending part of each year in Beijing and maintaining close links to Beijing-based NGOs such as Friends of Nature and Global Village of Beijing. In addition, Yang has developed a website for Green River.

In spring 2000, Yang organized scientists, reporters, and government officials to travel to the source of the Yangtze to install a stone monument with an inscription from Jiang Zemin. Yang's most significant work, however, as noted earlier, has been the establishment of the nature protection station in the headwater region of the Yangtze, developed in 1997 in part as a response to the poaching of the Tibetan antelope and in part to encourage ongoing research and environmental monitoring in the area. In September 2008, Green River announced its plans to construct a second nature protection station downstream from the first one, an area inhabited by endangered species such as the giant and red panda, the takin, and the golden monkey. Once open, the new center will focus on environ-

mental education for young Chinese and nature conservation training.[83]

Yang is successful because of both his personal abilities and his
good connections with local government officials. He had no difficulty registering as an NGO in 1998, although the Sichuan EPB
warned him to stay clear of politics. Since then, Yang has received
both domestic and international recognition for his work, among
them WWF's J. Paul Getty Award for Conservation Leadership in
2003. In 2006, after receiving nominations through Internet votes
and public opinion polls, Yang was named by MEP as one of China's
Green Warriors.[84]

Other NGOs, like the Green Volunteer League of Chongqing and
Action for Green in Kunming, have encountered serious difficulties
in sustaining their environmental work. Green Volunteer League
was founded by Tian Dasheng, a professor of German at Chongqing
University, who developed a love of nature through Russian author
Ivan Turgenev, Tang poetry, and the German Romantics and was inspired to take action by the leftist Green movements in Sweden and
Germany during the 1980s. In 1996, after Tian learned about Friends
of Nature from a television broadcast, he joined the organization
and participated in a tree-planting campaign in Inner Mongolia.
When he returned to Chongqing University, he helped establish a
student group called *Luse Jiayuan* (Green Homeland).

Wu Dengming, co-founder of Green Volunteer League, was for-
merly a People's Liberation Army (PLA) officer. He views his involvement in environmental protection as a means of repaying the debt he
feels for the wildlife he helped destroy as the leader of the hunting
team for his PLA unit during the Great Leap Forward in the 1950s. As
a steel worker, he also worried that China would end up as polluted
as western industrialized countries. He became an activist after he
met Tian, who inspired him with stories of environmental protection.

In establishing Green Volunteer League, Tian and Wu faced several obstacles. Tian originally planned to establish a branch of Friends
of Nature; however, he was instructed that branches were not permitted. Indeed, he was told by the local government that since there
was already an NGO in the region, he would not be permitted to

establish one at all. Together, Wu and Tian then approached the leaders of what had become a defunct organization, the Green Volunteer League of Chongqing, took it over, and adopted their registration. Wu and Tian have tried to improve their position by establishing ties to other NGOs. Both Wu and Tian are members of Friends of Nature, and they participated in Liao Xiaoyi's Earth Day activity in March 2000 in Beijing. As a result of that activity, they also began to work with Yang Xin.

With over 1,800 volunteers in their organization, Tian and Wu have pursued a bold approach to environmental protection. They went undercover to expose illegal logging activities, in one case posing as a businessman and geologist, gaining the confidence of the loggers. Their investigation and subsequent report led to the head of the village being sentenced to three years in jail, although in the end it turned out to be a relatively relaxed form of house arrest. With extensive media coverage of such exploits, Wu and Tian became celebrities of sorts.[85] In addition, Wu has faced periodic threats and been harassed by local authorities. The group's efforts in 2003 to expose polluting factories in the valley of Pulu, fifty miles west of Chongqing, led to the arrest of one of Wu's researchers for interviewing local villagers.[86]

Yu Xiaogang has met a greater level of success but paid an even greater personal price for his activism. A native of Yunnan Province, Yu grew up surrounded by a rich landscape of mountains, rivers, and lakes. In 2002, Yu completed his postgraduate research on the environmental impacts of the Manwan Dam on the Mekong (Lancang) River. The dam had ruined the local fishing economy and left villagers without a steady food supply. Yu, who began his career in one of Yunnan's government ministries, received Premier Wen Jiabao's endorsement for his work. That same year, Yu founded a Kunming-based NGO, Green Watershed, to educate local communities about the negative effects of dams and other development projects, particularly a series of thirteen dam projects that had been proposed for construction along the Nu River. Green Watershed argued that the dams would displace 50,000 people and negatively affect the UNESCO World Heritage site that the river runs through. Yu lobbied the government and in 2004 brought a group of villagers to a UN-sponsored hydropower conference in Beijing. The group also organized a series of public debates around the dam proposals.

Yu's efforts, along with those of the NGOs, led to a government order by Wen Jiabao to temporarily suspend the construction of the dams along the Nu River. In 2006, Yu was awarded the Goldman Environmental Prize for his contributions to protecting the Nu River. Within China, however, Yu has been forbidden to travel abroad in retaliation for his work on educating villagers about the potential downsides of the Nu River dams. Yu has nonetheless continued his environmental activism, expanding his campaign to other dam sites and providing training in natural disaster management. In 2008 alone, Green Watershed trained over 100 NGOs and over 60 communities. Yu's group currently focuses on the Lashi Lake near the city of Lijiang, where they developed an integrated watershed management program. In 2008, moreover, Yu launched the Green Banking project, a coalition of environmental NGOs that recognizes banks and financial institutions that include the environment in their corporate agenda with a "Green Banking Innovation Award."[87] Upon receiving the 2009 Ramon Magsaysay Award, Yu said that at China's current rate of environmental deterioration, "our pride in our GDP will change into GDD, Gross Domestic Disaster."[88]

Despite their difficulties, Tian, Wu, and Yu all remain committed environmental activists with a deep philosophical belief in the need for environmental protection and social change. Thus, in several ways, both environmental and political, the NGOs focused on conservation issues tend to reflect the ideals put forth by Tang Xiyang and Dai Qing, calling for greater official transparency and accountability, albeit in less directly oppositional terms. While many of the NGOs outside Beijing suffer from lack of funding, staff, office space, and other politically induced constraints, they continue to pursue their work. At the same time, they are beginning to establish linkages with NGOs more directly interested in urban renewal, such as Liao Xiaoyi's Global Village of Beijing, and thus broadening the range of their environmental activities.

Beyond Conservation: Cleaning Up the Cities

Like Liang Congjie, Liao Xiaoyi (or Sheri Liao as she is known abroad), has become internationally renowned for her work on environmental protection. In 1996, she established the Global Village of Beijing, with the purpose of improving the urban environment and advancing environmental education through television programming.

Originally a researcher at the Chinese Academy of Social Sciences, Liao traveled to the United States to serve as a policy fellow at North Carolina State's Center for International Environmental Politics. She began to study the role of environmental NGOs and produced a documentary, *Daughters of the Earth*, which featured the work of forty female environmental activists. Inspired, she returned to China and established the Global Village of Beijing, whose main purpose was to raise public awareness of the environment in China through television programs.

Liao's work differs from that of Liang and other conservation-oriented environmentalists in several respects. Unlike Liang, Liao has registered her organization as a business. When she initially attempted to register an NGO with the Civil Affairs Ministry in 1995, the two-year moratorium was in effect. In addition, she was told that she would have to solicit permission from her supervising agency prior to undertaking any new activities or holding meetings. By registering as a business, Liao avoided these difficulties and has maintained a greater level of independence, although, as a business, she has to pay taxes.[89]

Liao's organization also differs from most Chinese NGOs in focusing predominantly on urban issues such as community development. With government support, she established a pilot recycling project in Xuanwu district in Beijing that has now been expanded to other districts. She is also working with Xuanwu to make it a "green community." Eventually, Xuanwu will employ a wide range of efficiency technologies such as energy-saving lights, water-saving faucets, recycling bins, and so on. To accomplish this, Liao works closely with the local EPB as well as with other departments of the local government to ensure that they are vested in the process.

Liao has also supported the Dacheng Lane Neighborhood Committee in the Xicheng district of Beijing, a group of retired teachers who have banded together to clean up the local environment. Perhaps most impressive, Liao founded an environmental protection education and training center outside Beijing, where forty families practice a green lifestyle, which includes sorting garbage, reusing everyday articles, and not using chemical fertilizers.[90]

Liao's strategy, which has been an effective one, is to change government policy by example and through media attention. According to Liao, former SEPA administrator Xie Zhenhua was persuaded of the efficacy of green communities and indicated at the time that fostering green communities should be one of the main tasks of SEPA. As of 2002, with the financial support of Canadian International Development Agency (CIDA), Liao was hoping to develop green communities elsewhere in Beijing, as well as in Wuhan and Shanghai, where local officials have indicated interest.

Liao views Chinese environmentalism as a triangle, involving the government, private enterprise, and the nonprofit sector. In her view, the role of NGOs is to educate the public, help the government implement environmental protection policies, and encourage business to demonstrate more care for the environment.[91] She held a conference on sustainable consumption that involved senior Chinese officials, NGO leaders, officials from the United Nations Environment Programme and United Nations Development Program, and business leaders from companies such as BP and Royal Dutch Shell.

In contrast to other environmental activists, Liao is resolutely apolitical in her public comments. In one interview, for example, she stated, "I don't appreciate extremist methods. I'm engaged in environmental protection and don't want to use it for political aims. This is my way, and my principle too."[92] She is extremely reluctant to become engaged in thorny political issues like the Three Gorges Dam. While she will state that she does not "like" the project, she adds that she does not want to "make trouble." Believing that her focus must remain on the positive work that she can do to change people's behavior with regard to environmental protection, she maintains an aggressively forward-looking approach. In one private chat, she told me that in response to pleas from Dai Qing to become involved in protesting Three Gorges, she argued, "We have a lot of things to do in China besides Three Gorges. The most important thing for us is to avoid other mistakes like Three Gorges."

At the same time, Liao has reached out to NGO leaders throughout China, holding an annual Earth Day celebration that attracts regional NGO leaders to Beijing as well as environmental activists from abroad. In 2002, twelve NGOs participated. Liao also took the lead in organizing an exhibition for the World Summit on Sustainable Development in Johannesburg, South Africa, during late August–early September 2002. While several NGOs attended the summit, many more were introduced to the international community through a World Bank–funded video. The video exemplifies the transformation in Chinese society since the 1992 UN Conference on Environment and Development, when China was embarrassed by its lack of nongovernmental participation.

Liao is a strong believer in the power of the media, and she was a pioneer in the area of media and the environment. Her television program, *Time for the Environment*, was broadcast weekly on nationwide CCTV for five years from 1996 to 2001, airing a total of three hundred episodes. In 2002, with the support of the U.S. Department of Agriculture and CCTV, she completed a series of nine programs on model environmental medium-sized farms in the United States, and she continues to work as a producer for environmental programs on CCTV, including the shows *Green Talks* and *Daughters of the Earth*. Indeed, her work highlights the importance of the media as purveyors of information and as a foundation for future environmental NGO activism.

Not only Liao's work but also her administrative skills serve as a model for other NGOs. Liao has raised $500,000 for her operations, primarily from overseas sources, and maintains a full-time staff of seven in a small but bustling complex of offices in the Asian Games complex on the outskirts of Beijing. Liao has won a number of awards in recognition of her work, including CCTV's Annual Economic Figure Social Commonwealth Award, and she has twice been named by *Chinese Women* magazine as one of the Ten National Outstanding Women in China.

The Media and Environmental Advocacy

Spurred in part by Liao Xiaoyi's pathbreaking work, the media have become an essential element of environmental activism in China. In a 2007 public opinion poll, over 81 percent of Chinese indicated that they learned about environmental protection–related issues primarily from television and radio.[93] Government publicity was a distant fourth at 13.5 percent.[94]

In recent years, many media personalities and journalists have assumed leadership roles in environmental education. Wang Yongchen, the effusive director of Green Earth Volunteers, was perhaps the first radio host to explore environmental issues, using her talk show to raise issues such as the Tibetan antelope. In 2003, Wang helped lead a campaign—successful to date—to halt the construction of the Yangliuhu Dam on the Min River in Sichuan Province, arguing that the dam could damage Dujiangyan, possibly the world's oldest functioning irrigation system. China's mainstream media criticized the dam heavily, and the Chinese public voiced its strong opposition on Internet websites. Wang argues that this is the first time that the Chinese people have had input into such an important project.[95] In 2004 Wang won the Condé Nast Traveler Environmental Award for her efforts to stop damming projects along the Nu River. She now works as a senior environmental reporter for China National Radio and organizes monthly meetings for reporters to raise and discuss pressing issues affecting the media and environment.

Chinese television is also playing a critical role in environmental protection efforts by investigating and protesting environmental crimes. As one former CCTV anchorwoman stated, "Seeking justice for the public has evolved as an important function of the Chinese media. Such a function may be part of China's *guoqing*—unique national situation. It is unique because rule of law has not been fully established in the country."[96] One of the most popular such television programs is *Focus*. Modeled on the U.S. news program *60 Minutes*, *Focus* went on the air in 1994 as an outgrowth of another trial investigative program, *Oriental Horizon*. While only thirteen minutes long, Focus has become a phenomenon on Chinese television, drawing 200–250 million viewers and spawning a range of investigative efforts into environmental and other issues within the Chinese media.[97] In a 2007 CCTV survey, *Focus* was rated the second most watched program in the country, after the *Network News Broadcast*.[98]

In a fascinating paper on the role of the media in China, Li Xiaoping, an executive producer of *Focus*, recounts how people wait in line outside the *Focus* studio to ask the reporters to investigate various cases of environmental or other types of official wrongdoing. She also notes that bureaucrats have developed a saying, "Avoid fires, avoid theft, avoid *Focus*."[99] The local media are also getting into the act. In 2005, after local media reported on a rising number of cancer incidents in Shanba Village in Guangdong Province, the local government and a mining company secured funds to build a reservoir to provide the villagers with a source of clean drinking water.[100] The media also play a prominent role in enlightening top government officials about environmental problems. Former premier Zhu Rongji was especially likely to take action after learning of environmental problems via television programs; his campaigns against desertification and illegal logging in the late 1990s both stemmed initially from television reports.[101]

Grassroots environmentalism may also be spurred by television programming. For example, the media have played an important role in engendering a public groundswell of support for battery recycling in China.[102] In one case, Geng Haiying, a young doctor from Dalian, first became interested in the environment after viewing a television program on battery recycling. The program was produced by Hu Jingcao, a young woman who had become integrated into the environmental movement in Beijing through Liang Congjie and others, producing a number of environment-related programs on issues such as the Tibetan antelope, the Huai River, and deforestation.

Based on Hu's program, Geng suspected that local dumps in Dalian, which were filled with batteries, were leaking and poisoning the local water supply and produce. She investigated the issue further through Green Beijing, SEPA's website, and by reading about the solid waste problem. She then single-handedly began a program to recycle batteries in Dalian. The local EPB was supportive, but since there was no formal law on the books, it did not take an active interest in addressing the problem. However, when SEPA stated that battery recycling would be a priority, she extracted a promise from the Dalian EPB to collect batteries. She then approached department stores to see if they would be willing to serve as collection points for the batteries. While the department stores were initially suspicious of her motives, by April 2000, she had persuaded three of them to establish recycling bins. Her environmental activism was also supported by Wen Bo, a Dalian native, who helped her gain access to outlets such as radio programs for publicizing her work.

Geng's experience touches on one of the greatest difficulties that grassroots environmentalism faces: the failure of the state to address the environmental protection desires of the populace. In 2000, another crusader for battery recycling, Tian Guirong, had collected 30 tons of batteries from throughout Henan Province. However, she commented, "I collected them to help with environmental protection, but I didn't realize there would be nowhere to dispose of the batteries."[103] In Beijing, the EPB has established a hotline and "Useful Rubbish Recycling Center" to collect used batteries and other refuse, but its disposal site for batteries does not meet the state's own environmental standards, so the Center has had to hold on to the batteries. According to one official, the staff is so fearful of phone calls asking where batteries may be sent that it is suffering from "battery-phobia."[104]

Thus, even with media attention and strong public support, China's environmental protection bureaucracy falls short of meeting public needs. Indeed, the range of individuals in China undertaking private environmental activities, such as private nature reserves and garbage collection,[105] only points out further the weaknesses of the local EPBs.

Geng Haiying's experience, however, also suggests that the combination of an activist orientation and media attention can generate further action. In fact, many of the next generation of environmental activists have been trained as journalists in China, often with further study and fellowships at universities, think tanks, and NGOs abroad, and they bring to environmental protection not only strong technical expertise but also facility in communicating their ideas to audiences both at home and abroad. They will be a potent force for environmental protection, some in service of Beijing, but many more in service of the broader public's interests.

The Next Generation of Activists

The future of the environmental movement in China will depend largely on the outlook of the next generation of environmental activists. There is reason to be optimistic. Tang Xiyang, Liang Congjie, and other NGO leaders cultivated this group closely. This new generation has been heavily influenced not only by its interaction with senior NGO leaders but also by its international exchanges. The result is a highly skilled, articulate, and politically savvy set of environmentalists, among them Wen Bo, Ma Jun, the co-founder of Green Plateau Institute Shi Lihong, and Hu Kanping, editor of *China Green Times*.

Preeminent among these young environmental leaders is Wen Bo. At twenty-five years of age, Wen was already a renowned environmentalist with excellent journalistic and environmental credentials. In many ways, Wen exemplifies the new environmental activists in China. Early on, he interned at *China Daily*, working for Shi Lihong, and then continued to write for several years for *China Environment News*. At the same time, he organized student environmental groups at universities throughout China, helping to link them into the China Green Students Forum, which now has a membership of 250 student groups. He also participated in Tang Xiyang's Green Camp and has spent substantial time working with international environmental NGOs such as Environmental Defense Fund, International Snow Leopard Trust, and International Rivers Network, which is the most prominent lobbying organization opposed to the Three Gorges Dam. In 2001, Wen assisted Greenpeace in establishing its first office on the mainland.

By 2001, Wen had joined Pacific Environment, where he provides organizational and financial aid to local environmental NGOs across China. He has received international acclaim for his work and was named a Young Global Leader by the World Economic Forum in 2009.

Hu Kanping, unlike Wen, has remained primarily a journalist, focusing his reporting on issues related to forestry for the State Forestry Administration. A literature major in college, Hu came of age politically in 1986–1987 in Shanghai, joining in student demonstrations in support of the political reform leader Hu Yaobang. An idol for many Chinese youth during the late 1980s, Hu Yaobang was ultimately stripped of his position as general secretary of the Communist Party in January 1987, and his death in April 1989 triggered the Tiananmen demonstrations. Hu Kanping has spent his career within the forestry administration of the central government as a reporter for the agency's newspaper, *Chinese Forestry News*, which was renamed *Green Times* in 1997. Hu is the editor-in-chief of *Environmental Protection Journal* and is responsible for special projects at the Ministry of Environmental Protection. He has also written several books on how Chinese people can live more environmentally friendly lives.

Both Wen Bo and Hu Kanping recognize the limitations of the media. In discussing *Green Times*, for example, Hu stated that while his reporters are permitted to report on local corruption, they cannot report on violence or personnel issues. Moreover, while the forestry administration will give free rein to reporters to publish articles on issues like pollution that are outside the bureau's jurisdiction, it may limit reporters' publication of articles on some areas under its jurisdiction.[106] However, Hu has also pushed the boundaries of the acceptable, attempting to make environmental reporting accessible to the general public. He and Wen, for example, first became friends in October 1995, when Hu attended a newspaper bazaar to peddle his independent newspaper *Green Weekend*. While not a commercial success, it attracted significant positive attention from the forestry officials who appreciated the lack of official pronouncements and the lively, informative writing style. They encouraged him to enliven the official newspaper with such articles and writing. As Hu became well-known for his work, he was later invited to join the board of Friends of Nature.

Ma Jun also began his work in environmental protection as a journalist. Born in the coastal city of Qingdao, Ma grew up in Beijing. He began learning English at an early age, largely due to his father's encouragement. In 1993, Ma started working as an assistant at the *South China Morning Post*'s Beijing bureau, and became known there for his investigative pieces on the environment; later he was promoted to Beijing bureau chief.

In 1999 Ma published the book *China's Water Crisis*, a chronicle of the devastating impact of economic development on the country's rivers. The book, which boosted public awareness of China's water issues, is widely compared to Rachel Carson's *Silent Spring*. In 2005, Ma founded the NGO Institute of Public and Environmental Affairs (IPE). IPE collects data on air and water pollution levels from local Environmental Protection Bureau reports. Based on these data, Ma launched an online public database in 2006 that maps the sources of pollution. One year later he published a similar map for air pollution. The database, the first of its kind in China, now highlights some 30,000 violators of air and water quality regulations. Most of the firms on the list are domestic companies, but a small percentage can be traced to multinationals. Companies identified on the pollution map are added to a watch list and can be removed only after undergoing a third-party environmental audit.

Ma's work quickly catapulted him into the international spotlight. In 2006, *Time* magazine named Ma as one of the one hundred most influential people in the world. Ma's efforts to expose polluting companies have also meant regular collisions with businessmen and local officials. Despite the controversial nature of his work, Ma has been able to keep his operations running with the help of partnerships with the Ministry of Environmental Protection and with international groups like the WWF. His choice to target multinationals and use only government-approved data has also helped protect him.

In August 2008, IPE launched a program known as the Green Choice Alliance for Supply Chain Management, in which corporations pledge to review their list of suppliers and remove those who are on the IPE watchlist. Within four months, sixteen enterprises on the IPE polluters list had been audited, and ten of them were removed from the list. Ma has begun to expand his work by involving local NGOs in the auditing process.

In August 2009, Ma received the Raymon Magsaysay Award for "harnessing the technology and power of information to address China's water crisis, and mobilizing pragmatic, multisectoral and collaborative efforts to ensure sustainable benefits for China's environmental and society."

Environmental activist Wu Lihong has met a less fortunate fate. Wu, a former factory salesman in his forties, worked for sixteen years to address the rampant pollution in Tai Lake in Jiangsu Province, gathering evidence and writing letters to local officials, and eventually bringing about the closure of almost two hundred factories. In 2005, Beijing honored Wu as one of the country's top environmentalists, but in 2006 one of the local government's Wu had criticized arrested and jailed him on dubious charges of blackmail and fraud. Wu was tortured until forced to confess to the charges. In 2007 Wu was sentenced to three years in prison and lost when he appealed to overturn the sentence.[107]

The orientation of this younger group of environmentalists is open and aggressive. For example, one young journalist with whom I spoke said he would like to see NGOs increasingly challenge central government policy, produce high-quality reports that will help increase the government's efficiency and effectiveness, act as lobbyists and pressure groups, and use actions like those of Greenpeace to dramatize environmental issues. Still, he remains cautious about voicing his opinions openly, preferring to push the boundaries through his actions.

Others are even more explicit in their demands for change:

China's transition to a market economy has broadened the base for civil society. At the same time, the government is still very powerful. I think that environment groups can develop under the current situation, but that in the end, environmental work may lead to greater democracy in China. In fact, environmentalism and democracy are related. Many NGO leaders are hesitant to say that we are related, but I believe that the NGO movements are creating democracy.[108]

Overall, the tone is one of wariness but also cautious optimism. This generation of environmentalists seems to understand that the very existence of the nongovernmental sector is tenuous, but it believes that time is on its side.

> There is no real environmental movement because the government would be very unhappy if there were a movement. The Party has almost all the power and NGOs have no money, no power, and no social resources. The government wants NGOs to help but not to make trouble [*keyi bangmang bu neng tianluan*]. But I agree with Tang Xiyang. More and more media and NGO focus on environmental issues will lead to more democracy and greater freedom. The hope is that we will educate the young people about the problems we have and the need to do something about them. In twenty years, these young people will be the leaders of China. In this way, we will build-up a democratic country.[109]

The Future of the Environmental Movement in China

In a China characterized by constantly shifting political winds, environmental NGOs have moved rapidly into the political space opened to them during the early to mid-1990s. They have had a significant impact in raising environmental consciousness among the Chinese people through Earth Day information campaigns and a barrage of television programs devoted to environmental issues. They have exposed inadequate local implementation of national environmental protection laws, especially with regard to species protection and deforestation. And they have begun to work in urban areas to employ environmentally sound technologies and practices to improve both the environment and people's lives. In these ways, they have served the interests of the Chinese people, their own concerns, and the needs of the government in Beijing.

Understandably, the NGOs have avoided open conflict with the central leadership in Beijing. Now, however, some environmental activists have begun to prod Beijing directly, opening the door to the possibility of more direct criticism and lobbying by the next generation of environmental leaders. We can expect this next generation to be bolder. They possess the full complement of skills necessary to organize effectively: technical expertise on the environment, strong backgrounds in journalism and media, and extensive ties to environmental activists both throughout China and abroad.

Why does Beijing tolerate the increasingly activist environmental NGOs? For one thing, they provide an inexpensive mechanism for monitoring local pollution efforts and educating the public on environmental protection. While MEP has not established any extensive linkages or programs with environmental NGOs, their interests are frequently allied, and outgoing vice-minister of MEP Pan Yue, in particular, has been a vocal supporter of working with the country's NGOs. NGOs also offer a degree of political cover to an otherwise authoritarian government, signaling to the world that China does tolerate independent societal organization.

Veteran NGO leaders in China are sensitive to the possibility that the government will use them for propaganda purposes. For example, in its bid to host the 2008 Olympics, the government solicited the support of Friends of Nature, Global Village Beijing, and twenty other environmental groups for the "Action Plan for Green Olympics." As Liang Congjie and Sheri Liao both commented at the time, the NGOs agreed to lend their support in hopes of realizing long-term environmental benefits. Liao stated, "Whether Beijing finally wins the 2008 bid or not, the Action Plan for Green Olympics will be of great significance to Beijing's sustainable development."[110] After winning the bid, Beijing's organizing committee for the Olympic Games, known as BOCOG, invited a number of NGO leaders to offer recommendations on environmental policies for the games. In 2004, BOCOG asked both Liang and Liao to serve as environmental advisors in formulating regulations and work plans for the Games. Christine Loh, who heads the Hong Kong-based think tank Civic Exchange, also served on the board of the Olympic Air Quality Science panel.

Newspaper articles in the lead-up to the Olympics decision mentioned the possibility that Beijing's largest polluter, the Capital Iron and Steel Company, would have to be moved if the city won the bid, and in January 2003, Chinese officials announced a $341 million effort to relocate 75 percent of the company to a rural part of Qian'an city in Hebei Province.[111] Such a move had been proposed five years earlier, in July 1996, when Liang's Friends of Nature held a forum on the pollution generated by the enterprise and issued a report suggesting where the company might be relocated.[112] In the wake of China's Olympic bid victory, however, Liang evidenced more concern than elation, noting, "My greatest worry is that the committee will focus on making Beijing into a showcase city with water-wasting stretches of grass."[113]

As the city finalized its blueprints for the Olympic games in 2004, both Liang and Liao felt that their advice to the city had fallen on deaf ears. Much of the city's plans to host a Green Olympics consisted of aesthetically appealing projects rather than measures that would tackle air pollution or the city's critical water shortages. Plans to roll out vast green lawns, for example, led to concerns that they would exacerbate the city's already critically low water supply. In August 2004 Liang told *Time* magazine of the organizing committee, "They didn't listen to us." Liao shared the sentiment in her interview with *Time*: "I'm very disappointed. . . . It's a very sensitive issue. I can't really talk about it." [114] In February 2008, Loh told *BusinessWeek*, "They will do everything that is humanly possible, but there is no guarantee that would be enough."[115]

In the end, as Greenpeace China's environmental report card of the Beijing Olympics concluded, the city missed important opportunities to ensure the sustainability of Beijing's environmental efforts introduced in time for the games.[116] The government's support of NGOs remains qualified. The range of restrictions it has placed on NGOs regarding registration, funding, staffing, and location have constrained the number of NGOs as well as the range of their activities. If the government is committed to an active and engaged public effort to protect the environment, especially as a means of overcoming the state's decreasing capacity to meet the country's environmental protection needs, it will need to relax these restrictions and free NGOs to flourish.

But this is unlikely in the near future. The promised new regulations suggest a continued uncertainty in the leadership's outlook on the NGO sector: a desire for it to flourish but a fear that it will not be loyal to the Party. While environmental activists, with the exception of Dai Qing, have been wary of pushing too hard or too fast for political reform as a means of enhancing environmental protection, they have not shied away from articulating similar political ideals. The Communist Party leaders recognize that, in the context of the rapid socioeconomic changes occurring in China today, the potential for environmental NGOs and other social groups to press for greater political change, as in the cases of some Eastern European countries, former Soviet republics, and Asian neighbors, poses a real danger to their authority and leadership.

CHAPTER SIX

THE DEVIL AT THE DOORSTEP

The Chinese leadership has embraced the international community as an essential component of its long-term strategy to improve China's environment, welcoming cooperation not only with other countries and international governmental organizations, such as the United Nations (UN), the World Bank, and the Asian Development Bank (ADB), but also with multinationals and international nongovernmental organizations (NGOs).

At the same time, China's economic reforms and its integration into the global economy have opened the door to new policy approaches and technological possibilities in environmental protection. Attributes valued by the market such as efficiency, transparency, rule of law, and managerial expertise have begun to permeate environmental protection in China. Moreover, China's participation in trade-based regimes such as the Asia-Pacific Economic Cooperation (APEC) and the World Trade Organization (WTO) now offers opportunities to reinforce the integration of environmental protection objectives into the process of economic development. Over time, the transformation of China's economy has the potential to redefine radically China's approach to environmental protection.

But significant impediments to international environmental cooperation remain. Much of the infrastructure for effective policy or technology implementation is not in place. Inconsistent enforcement of environmental laws, lack of transparency, poor management, and weak incentives for environmental protection all curtail the viability of many of the most desired technologies and policy tools. China's continued emphasis on economic development means that the leadership may also ignore pleas from members of the international community for more proactive policies on regional and global environmental issues. Moreover, the international community at times ignores China's real needs, focusing instead on technologies that may not be appropriate for China's current level of commitment to environmental protection.

China Meets the World

As we've seen, the 1972 United Nations Conference on the Human Environment (UNCHE) marked China's first foray into the arena of international environmental politics. China's participation raised the profile of environmental issues on the agenda of China's leaders and contributed to the establishment of the country's first formal environmental protection apparatus.[1] The UNCHE also launched China into a new world of global environmental concerns. Through the UN, the international community soon engaged China in battling trade in endangered species, marine dumping, trade in tropical timber, and the degradation of sites of natural and cultural value.

As the international community impressed on China's leadership the importance of participating in the full range of environmental treaties and regimes, China responded by establishing a leadership group for each treaty, consisting of the relevant ministries and agencies under the auspices of the State Council, to study the issues and develop recommendations. This process created small communities of experts, including many who had been forced to give up scientific or intellectual pursuits during Mao Zedong's reign, and who formed the basis of an emerging scientific and environmental elite.

In some cases, for example marine dumping, the Chinese were not significant contributors to the problem. In acceding to the London Dumping Convention, therefore, Chinese leaders' motives were primarily political: to rejoin the international community, to prevent Taiwan from asserting itself as the representative of China in international bodies, and to develop a coterie of trained environmental and scientific experts who could transmit relevant knowledge to the Chinese leadership to help with domestic environmental problems.[2]

But in order to sign on to any treaty, China had to develop the capacity to implement it. This required the drafting of new laws, the training of experts to understand and meet the demands of the treaty as well as to implement it, and coordination among as many as ten or more bureaucracies, each of which controlled a different aspect of the treaty.

This preaccession process is often long and complex. In the case of the London Convention against Ocean Dumping, the Chinese signed on in 1985, over a decade after the convention had been established internationally, first ensuring that their domestic laws and capabilities were reasonably in keeping with the demands of the international agreement. Before signing on, for example, China passed its own Marine Environmental Protection Law modeled on the convention. The long lead time also permitted the relevant Chinese ministries to study the domestic ramifications of the issue, jockey among themselves for the lead position in the international negotiations, and balance their competing interests to arrive at the formal Chinese negotiation position.

During the course of the negotiations, the Chinese representatives maintained a low profile, studying the technical points of the proposed treaty and developing expertise by participating in training seminars and technical development efforts. The various UN secretariats that oversaw the international environmental agreements typically offered extensive educational programs and some technology for the expert communities in developing states. Once China became party to the London Dumping Convention, China's State Oceanographic Administration took advantage of training courses on monitoring ocean dumping and developing an adequate legal system offered by the UN Environment Programme (UNEP) and the International Marine Organization.

Others in the international community also helped the Chinese develop the capacity to fulfill their treaty commitments. For example, several years after China acceded to the World Heritage Convention in 1985, the World Bank and the Getty Museum in Los Angeles together assisted the Chinese in restoring and protecting the Yungang Grottoes and the Mogao Grottoes of Dunhuang—ancient Buddhist sites that contain spectacular rock carvings, paintings, and painted clay figures from as early as the fourth century. They coordinated efforts to reduce sandstorms in the area and to conduct environmental monitoring inside the caves, and the Getty supplied instruments and trained workers. In turn, China exported some of its newly trained experts to Cambodia to contribute to the international effort to protect Angkor, the site of Khmer empire ruins, including the famous temple of Angkor Wat.

China's 1981 accession to the Convention on International Trade in Endangered Species was similarly aided by the World Wildlife Fund (WWF), the International Union for the Conservation of Nature (IUCN), and the U.S. Department of Interior, which helped with the training of Chinese officials, database development, and wildlife studies. The WWF and IUCN even worked with Chinese officials in an undercover sting operation to catch those who trade in tiger bone for use in Chinese traditional medicine, a practice that has contributed to rapid decline of the South China and Siberian tiger populations.[3]

During the 1980s, many of China's domestic environment and resource issues captured the attention of international actors. For example, the World Bank initiated projects on fisheries, rural water supply, and the development of natural gas, while the WWF became deeply involved in species protection in China, including a multiyear effort to protect the rapidly declining number of China's famed pandas in Sichuan Province.[4]

Raising the Stakes: Ozone Depletion and Climate Change

As China gradually developed the scientific and technical expertise as well as the practices to support its full participation in international environmental affairs, growing world awareness of ozone depletion and climate change in the late 1980s and early 1990s placed Chinese environment and development policies under intense international scrutiny and raised issues of environmental protection to the highest level on the agenda of the Chinese leadership.

Ozone depletion and global climate change pose potentially devastating health, environmental, and economic challenges to the countries of the world, up to and including, in the case of climate change, the destruction of some small island states because of sea level rise. These global environmental phenomena also differ substantially from other environmental problems because the treaties designed to respond to them entail substantial financial and human resource commitments.

Before the 1980s, China's contribution to these problems was inconsequential. Both global climate change and ozone depletion result primarily from industrial processes related to development rather than from natural phenomena. China's relatively late industrial development meant that compared to Europe and the United States, the country bore little responsibility for the current global environmental state. However, owing to China's sheer size and the rapidity and scale of its industrial development throughout the 1980s, China quickly became one of the chief contributors to both problems. In 1986, China's consumption of ozone-depleting substances was roughly 3 percent of the world total; by 2001, it had become the chief contributor to ozone depletion and remained so in 2007. That year, China closed five of its last six plants producing the most potent ozone-depleting substances.[5] However, in 2008 China continued to be the largest producer, by volume, of less dangerous ozone-depleting substances because of their use in refrigerator and air conditioner manufacturing.[6] Similarly, during the late 1980s, China ranked third in total contribution to global climate change; in 2007, China overtook the United States as the world's largest emitter of the greenhouse gas carbon dioxide.

Participating in the treaty negotiations for the 1990 London Amendments to the Montreal Protocol on Substances That Deplete the Ozone Layer and the Framework Convention on Climate Change dramatically raised the stakes for China's commitment to global environmental problems. When negotiating the London Amendments, the government established a leading group under the auspices of the National Environmental Protection Agency (NEPA) to evaluate the costs and benefits of signing the protocol. This group concluded that there were three reasons China should sign the agreement. The most important was market-based—the treaty's potential sanctioning mechanism. China was interested in becoming a major exporter of light industrial products, such as refrigerators, that use ozone-depleting substances. The protocol, however, forbade signatories from purchasing such products and sanctioned those countries that traded in them. Second, some within the Chinese leadership believed that, as a member of the international community, China should contribute to the resolution of ozone depletion and that it would enhance China's image to sign. Finally, according to one member of the working group, strong scientific evidence and interactions with the international scientific community were also key reasons for supporting accession.[7]

Yet in the end what drove China's negotiating position were the financial implications of joining the Montreal Protocol. Along with India, China refused to sign the accord until significant financial support and transfers of technology from the international community were promised. Once the international community agreed to establish a special multilateral fund for this purpose, China ratified the treaty in 1991. China's emission of chlorofluorocarbons (CFCs), potent ozone-depleting substances, has decreased from 55,000 metric tons in 1998 to 550 metric tons a decade later.[8] China's successful reduction of CFCs has in part been fueled by continued financial incentives from the international community.

A similar pattern emerged with regard to global climate change. Because of the complexity of the science inherent in the problem of climate change, the formal negotiations were preceded by lengthy scientific discussions involving Chinese scientists, leading to unprecedented consultation between domestic and international expert communities. This convention also demanded research and data collection by the experts from each country. In China, this effort prompted the establishment of an extensive coordinating bureaucracy, whose job it was to collect the necessary data for the scientific discussions. By 1989, one year after scientific negotiations began, China had organized a climate change research program encompassing forty projects and involving about twenty ministries and five hundred experts.[9]

The international community was instrumental in funding this scientific research. The World Bank, the Asian Development Bank, the UNEP, the UN Development Programme (UNDP), Japan, and the United States all provided monitoring equipment for greenhouse gas emissions, shared computer modeling techniques, offered technological assistance in developing response measures, and trained Chinese environmental officials. For example, the State Planning Commission's (SPC) Energy Research Institute became a focal point for international work on energy and climate change (despite having no history of such research) when an expert from the U.S. Department of Energy Lab, Pacific Northwest National Laboratory (managed by the nonprofit corporation Battelle), identified a few talented economists from the Institute and trained them in the United States. China eventually used a variant of one of the lab's models for estimating emissions of carbon dioxide in preparation for the political negotiations,[10] and one of the SPC's U.S.–trained experts later served as a member of China's climate change negotiating team. Several Chinese members of the various international climate change working groups emerged from their participation with a new appreciation of the importance of China's contributing to the international climate change effort.[11]

Yet as the negotiations moved from the scientific to the political, the influence of the international community diminished. Within China, the lead agencies were no longer the more proactive scientific, technical, and environmental ministries but rather the Ministry of Foreign Affairs and the SPC. Concerns over economic development and sovereignty now dominated the domestic debate, overshadowing the potential benefits such as access to technology, environmental capacity building, and international goodwill.

The majority of the Chinese leadership believed that the advanced industrialized countries should restructure and reform their own wasteful practices and not simply look to the developing countries as a cheap alternative. As one science official commented, "The policy making on climate change depends on social issues, not science."[12] In addition, the potential economic costs of taking action on climate change were far greater than those involved in reducing ozone depletion. A meaningful Chinese response to global climate change would require a significant reorientation of the Chinese energy industry and substantial investment in new energy-efficient technologies.

Therefore, in the end, despite the wide-ranging impact of the international community on the development of domestic Chinese institutions, the establishment of a scientific community, and a flow of funds to China for scientific research, China's stance on climate change was regressive. China refused to consider any targets or timetables for reducing its greenhouse gas emissions. It was unwilling even to permit other countries to undertake joint implementation activities, such as reforestation, within China in order to fulfill their obligations within the treaty.[13]

Subsequently, the international community and proactive domestic actors continued to press the Chinese government to adopt a more flexible position in its response to the challenge of climate change. During the late 1990s and into 2000–2001, there were signs of some movement in China's position. Former premier Zhu Rongji, for example, reportedly indicated to foreign and domestic scientific and policy elites in 1998 that China should find some constructive role to play on the issue of climate change. In addition, he requested that an international group of environmental and economic experts explore potential strategies for China to reduce its carbon dioxide emissions. Meanwhile, the growing role of the State Economic and Trade Commission (SETC) in the wake of the 1998 administrative reforms (see chapter 4) reportedly gave greater voice to those in the government who were interested in pursuing a more proactive climate change policy in order to gain access to new technologies from abroad. According to one Chinese scientist, there was increasing dissatisfaction with the recalcitrance of the Ministry of Foreign Affairs and the State Development and Planning Commission (SDPC). The sentiment was that China was missing significant opportunities to advance its technological know-how because of a reluctance to cooperate on climate change.

In 2002, China took a significant step forward at the UN World Summit on Sustainable Development in Johannesburg when it announced that it had ratified the Kyoto Protocol to curb greenhouse gas emissions. As a developing country, China is eligible under the Clean Development Mechanism (CDM) to earn credits by undertaking emissions-reduction activities;[14] however, it is not required to meet any emissions targets or timetables. Nonetheless, China's taking this first step meant that it could later be pressured to agree to emissions reductions commitments.

Eight years later, when the world's leaders gathered in Copenhagen in December 2010 to try to frame a 2012 post-Kyoto climate agreement, China had become one of the most important voices at the table. In 2007, China surpassed the United States as the largest contributor of the greenhouse gas (GHG) carbon dioxide, a transition that drew significant international attention. Getting China on board with serious emissions reductions commitments became a focus of the international community. China's leaders themselves had become more convinced that climate change would negatively affect the country's future. Chinese government analysts and think tank experts predicted that if climate change were not abated the country would suffer a 37 percent decline in agricultural output of three out of the country's four major grains by 2050; rising sea levels that would threaten hundreds of millions along China's wealthy coastal region; and increasing desertification that already plagued over 20 percent of the country's land.

By the December 2010 climate summit, China's negotiators came prepared to do business. While still resisting binding targets and calling on the advanced industrialized countries to devote one percent of their GDP to a green technology fund for the developing world, China nonetheless wanted to contribute to a global accord. It proposed a reduction in carbon intensity of 45 percent from 2005 levels by 2020. This represented a cut in the amount of carbon used per unit of GDP but not an absolute cut in the reduction of greenhouse gas emissions. It also was well in keeping with the leaders' plans domestically to reduce energy intensity throughout the Chinese economy to make it more efficient. Some in the international community praised the initiative, while others called it far too little given the anticipated growth in the Chinese economy and thus emissions over the coming decades.

At the conclusion of the Copenhagen convention, China had succeeded in avoiding a binding accord, had not committed to absolute cuts in greenhouse gas emissions, and had staved off an intrusive regime of international verification. Yet with pressure mounting from the rest of the developing world, China was forced to renounce its claim on the funds from the international technology fund it had desired; many developing countries believed that China was not in need of such assistance and, moreover, would naturally attract the lion's share of such funding were it made available. In addition, China's reputation was eviscerated by many at the conference who blamed China for the failure to reach agreement on the target of a 50 percent reduction in global emissions and an 80 percent reduction in emissions by developed countries by 2050. Additional reports of Premier Wen Jiabao snubbing world leaders by sending lower level officials to meetings in his stead and a senior Chinese official insulting President Obama did little to improve China's reputation at the negotiations.

If China has remained steadfast in its commitment to resist binding targets and timetables that might limit Chinese economic growth, it has nonetheless moved quickly to establish itself as a potential world leader in green technologies. It has become the test bed for the rest of the world's GHG reduction efforts, technology development and transfer, and capacity building. As of September 2009, about 35 percent of the world's CDM projects under the auspices of the Kyoto framework were in China.[15] These projects have helped China expand its wind power capacity, develop coal bed methane capture projects, and provided a profit of several billion dollars for the Chinese government. (The windfall is reportedly slated for a green technology fund.) The international community is also actively pursuing eco-city or province partnerships. The European Union (EU), for example, has established partnerships with the cities of

Jilin and Chongqing, as well as Guangdong Province, Singapore has teamed up with Tianjin, and California with Jiangsu Province. While these partnerships are not yet well defined, they all will likely embrace both capacity building for the local governments as well as the development of industries that will serve a low-carbon economy, such wind turbine production. The private sector, including multinationals and international NGOs, is deeply engaged in climate-related activities in China. BP has established a clean energy research center at Qinghua University in Beijing; Wal-Mart has launched a campaign to reduce significantly the energy used by its stores and factories; the Natural Resources Defense Council is working to promote energy-efficient buildings and demand-side management; and the Environmental Defense Fund has a pilot project to help reduce GHG emissions from the agricultural sector.

As a result of its involvement in international climate discussions, and its desire to promote domestic energy security, China has set out a number of targets and policies to improve its energy use patterns. For example, it has pledged to reduce energy intensity (energy consumption per unit of GDP) by 20 percent between 2006 and 2010.[16] It also plans to increase the role of renewable energy within the primary energy mix to 15 percent by 2020.[17] It has levied a fuel consumption tax on gasoline of 1 yuan per liter;[18] replaced and added to the country's stock of coal-fired power plants with more efficient models; and a massive afforestation program has raised the level of forest coverage in the country from approximately 12 percent in 1998 to 18 percent in 2009.[19] Discussions of a voluntary target to reduce the growth of GHG emissions, a carbon tax, and a carbon emissions-trading regime also proliferated as China prepared for the post-Kyoto round of negotiations in Copenhagen in 2009.

China is also actively investing in new technologies that will help slow the rate of growth of the country's GHG contribution. It has announced a $1.5 billion research subsidy for automakers to improve their electric vehicle technology.[20] State-owned power developer China Huaneng Group has announced that it will pursue the development of technologies for carbon capture and sequestration (CCS) with the assistance of the ADB and the Chinese government.

Shenhua Group is also pursuing CCS technology in conjunction with its planned coal-to-liquid fuels plant in Inner Mongolia.

A few Chinese companies have already become environmental technology leaders, such as BYD, which focuses on battery development for electric cars. Others are manufacturing powerhouses, such as Suntech in solar panels. Moreover, power plant efficiency technology may begin to be transferred not only from the international community to China but also from China to the rest of the world. In April 2009, Xi'an Thermal Power Research Institute, a subsidiary of Huaneng, signed a preliminary agreement to supply Houston-based Future Fuels with a two-stage pulverized coal pressure gasification technology for an IGCC plant to be built in Schuylkill, Pennsylvania, in 2010.

China's climate policy to date has been driven by the belief, widely shared within the government elite, that a lower carbon economy will be good for economic modernization, that there is money to be made through the development and sale of climate-related technologies, and that domestic energy security depends in part on expanding the role of renewable energy resources at home. When useful, China's leaders also link climate change mitigation to domestic environmental concerns such as air quality and flood prevention. Still, China's efforts to combat climate change have stopped short of its imperative for economic growth.

The cases of global climate change and ozone depletion suggest both the importance and the limitations of the international community's influence. It is clear that the international scientific and policy-making communities had little influence in determining the outcomes of China's decision-making processes regarding these issues. In the case of global climate change, the science has remained incidental to political decision-making. In the case of ozone depletion, although the scientific community played a role in domestic deliberations, it was not until China's financial demands were met that the country assumed a more proactive orientation.

However, interaction between the international community and domestic actors and institutions on climate change continues and may yet produce more substantial changes in both process and outcome. Moreover, the relatively high degree of institutionalization of a new, broad-based environmental bureaucracy with direct and extensive international ties suggests the potential for additional policy change in the future.

Setting a New Agenda for International Environmental Cooperation

Global climate change and ozone depletion brought to the fore a new global discourse on issues related to the environment and development. These issues were given further impetus by the 1992 UN Conference on Environment and Development (UNCED), which focused attention on the broad issue of how best to integrate environmental objectives with economic development goals. Inspired and impelled by these three sets of global environmental discussions, Chinese environmental and scientific elites along with their international counterparts launched a domestic and international offensive to advance the cause of environmental protection in China.

In the run-up to the Rio conference, Chinese environmental and scientific officials held a series of meetings to educate and pressure their planning and industry colleagues about the importance of incorporating environmental objectives into China's plans for economic development. With significant encouragement from Martin Lees, a former UN official, and funding from the international community, the Chinese leadership sponsored a three-day high-profile international meeting in October 1990, hosted by environmental, scientific, and social science communities, represented most prominently by then NEPA head Qu Geping, State Science and Technology Commission (SSTC) chairman Song Jian, and president of the Development Research Center of the State Council Ma Hong. The International Conference on the Integration of Economic Development and Environment in China brought together Chinese leaders and international experts to discuss issues pertaining to the program's theme, "China and the World in the Nineties." This was the first of several international conferences hosted by Beijing to focus on environmental concerns, and participants from outside China included representatives from the World Bank and UNDP, business executives from Shell and Sumitomo, and the heads of NGOs like the Rockefeller Foundation and the WWF.

Qu Geping used his position as conference chairman to bring international pressure to bear on the somewhat less environmentally inclined ministry representatives from the Ministry of Energy, the State Planning Commission, and the Ministry of Foreign Affairs. The officials from these agencies stressed either the economic imperatives of advancing development in China or the primary responsibility of the developed countries—which had consumed, they argued, global resources and degraded the environment in their drive to industrialize—to address pollution issues.[21] By contrast, representatives from the Ministry of Agriculture, the Ministry of Water Conservancy, and the Development Research Center of the State Council claimed that China's pollution stemmed primarily from China's inappropriate pricing system for natural resources, the traditional view that resources are inexhaustible, and poor local management techniques.[22] In his summation, Qu Geping delineated the industrial and environmental arenas in which China should take stronger action to improve environmental protection measures.[23]

Soon after this meeting, then chairman of the State Environmental Protection Commission Song Jian publicly set out an alternative formula to the one typically articulated by Chinese leaders. Rather than simply pushing forward on economic development and then playing cleanup afterward, Song argued for balancing the two simultaneously, or even slowing down economic growth in order to protect the environment: "As we develop the economy, we must guarantee a balanced ecological environment and maintain in good order our natural resources so that future generations will have their rightful heritage. To this end, we should be ready to pay more or, if necessary, slow down the economic development."[24]

This 1990 meeting also launched the China Council for International Cooperation on Environment and Development (CCICED), which many Chinese environmental actors consider one of the most prestigious and effective forums for international environmental cooperation. The first formal meeting of the CCICED, which was coordinated by China's NEPA and the Canadian International

Development Agency, was held in April 1992. Chaired by Wen Ji-abao until he became premier in 2003, along with then vice-premier Zeng Peiyan (2003–2007) and vice-premier Li Keqiang (2007–2011), CCICED has served as a forum for international and Chinese experts to exchange views and develop recommendations for Chinese leaders.[25]

The advent of the UNCED in 1992 gave a dramatic boost to the establishment of a formal institution for international and Chinese cooperation on environmental protection. Although the Chinese delegation to the UNCED, led by Premier Li Peng, not surprisingly reflected China's traditional values and rhetoric,[26] the conference had a profound effect on environmental policies, institutions, and thinking in China.[27] Within one year of the UNCED, China became the first country to develop its own national Agenda 21 based on the global Agenda 21 action plan to promote sustainable development. Here, too, the international community was instrumental in shaping the domestic policy process. The UNDP proposed the idea, provided financial support, offered international expertise, reviewed the proposed priority projects, and arranged the international donor meetings.[28]

Chinese environmental actors called directly on the international community to assist in supporting Agenda 21. During the summer of 1994, SSTC vice president and daughter of Chinese leader Deng Xiaoping, Deng Nan, stated:

> The development of the economy and technology has made it possible for us to increase investment to deal with environmental problems, but economic development in China at present is basically resource oriented. It is possible that development will bring about destruction of the ecology and worsening of the environment. If environmental problems are ignored in the process of development, economic development will be severely hampered. We should extensively launch international cooperation.[29]

In July 1994, shortly after Deng Nan's statement, China held a second high-level meeting to garner international financial support for the national Agenda 21 projects. Representatives from twenty countries, international institutions, and businesses agreed to support approximately forty of the sixty-two high-priority projects that the Chinese had outlined, including projects focused on cleaner production, sustainable agriculture, pollution control, clean energy, and the development of communications. For Agenda 21 to succeed, the international community, according to Song Jian, would have to supply 30 to 40 percent of the estimated $4 billion cost.[30]

China's participation in the UNCED was also a catalyst for institutional change, contributing to the development of environmental NGOs and the formation of an Administrative Center for China's Agenda 21, directed initially by the SSTC and the SPC, but later directed primarily by the SDPC.

Perhaps most important, for the Chinese leadership, the UNCED also served to reinforce and, for the general public, introduce the concept of *sustainable development*. The term now provides an accepted framework within which Chinese officials press for the incorporation of environmentally sound practices into future economic development.[31] Throughout many regions of China, local governments have developed their own Agenda 21 bureaus to ensure that sustainable development principles are incorporated into urban planning.[32]

The international community has responded to the rise of Chinese environmentalists with both institutional and financial support. In many cases, different international actors send the same message. For example, CCICED advocated enhancing the State Environmental Protection Administration's (SEPA) authority. At the same time, the World Bank's 2001 report, *China: Air, Land, and Water*, explicitly called not only for raising SEPA's profile but also for reconstituting the State Environmental Protection Commission, the environmental oversight body that was dismantled in the 1998 administrative reforms.[33]

In another example, the UN's Clean Development Mechanism (CDM) in particular has proved a popular program through which foreign companies support Chinese GHG reduction efforts. Under the CDM, companies in China that reduce emissions generate certified emissions reduction (CER) credits that can be purchased by companies in countries party to the Kyoto Protocol to offset emissions in those countries. Chinese companies often undertake emissions reductions with guidance and investment from the Multinational Corporations (MNCs) that later purchase the CERs. Through the CDM, MNCs and carbon funds have provided companies in China with economic incentives to cut emissions, and companies in China have been quick to take advantage of this opportunity: as of January 2010, China had over seven hundred projects approved to receive CER credits, the largest number of any country. A GHG reduction project at the Jiangsu Meilan Chemical Company is expected to generate $740 million in revenue from the CDM over the next seven years. The UN's Multilateral Fund, also established under the Kyoto Protocol, has already invested $150 million in Chinese CFC and hydrofluorocarbon-23 (HFC-23) reduction projects. The UNEP estimates that the market value of CER credits will reach $18.3 billion in 2009.[34] China's success in attracting investment through CDM has raised some criticism. Some analysts argue that Chinese companies are playing the market by creating heavily polluting factories only to profit through the CDM from subsequent reductions.[35] Moreover, the Chinese government is reaping large profits from a sales tax on CER credits. Those credits generated by projects the government encourages, such as installing alternative energy technologies, are taxed at 2 percent; those credits generated by projects Western investors favor, such as HFC-23 reduction projects, are taxed at 65 percent.[36]

As the Chinese experience with the CDM suggests, China's efforts to attract international investment for environmental protection from international organizations have been extraordinarily successful. According to one estimate, fully 80 percent of China's environmental protection budget is derived from abroad.[37] Overall, China is the largest recipient of environmental aid from the Global Environment Facility, the third largest recipient of loans from the World Bank behind Brazil and India, and has received extensive assistance from the ADB and UNDP.

The World Bank during 2007–2008, for example, provided more than $700 million in loans for projects on such environmental problems as water conservation and waste management, climate change education, and improving energy efficiency in large- and medium-size industrial enterprises. As of April 2009, the World Bank's International Bank for Reconstruction and Development, along with the Global Environment Facility, had approved project funds totaling over $4.6 billion since July 2007. However, only about $1.4 billion, roughly 30 percent of the total, is allocated to environmental projects, compared to $3.2 billion for infrastructural development, such as railroad and highway repair and construction. The project receiving the most funding in this period was the Wenchuan Earthquake Recovery Project, aimed at restoring essential infrastructure, education, and health services.[38] On a smaller scale, during the past decade, the ADB has set aside several billion for environment-related projects in China; in 2007, it provided almost $400 million in loans and grants for urban environmental improvement and water supply projects. In the same year, however, the ADB also provided over $900 million for transportation infrastructure, including roads and airports.[39] As the EU has become China's largest trading partner, Germany and France joined Japan as the largest annual providers of bilateral technical and financial assistance to China.[40] In 2008, France provided China with over €235 million ($343 million) in grants and loans. Germany was the second largest provider of grants and loans. In both cases, the aid was directed at efforts to curb climate change and promote sustainable development. The European Commission is also a multilateral donor to China, having provided approximately €900 million ($1.3 billion) since aid began in 1975 to projects addressing a broad range of issues.

Japan has traditionally been the largest bilateral provider of assistance to China and has made environmental assistance a priority within its overseas development aid budget. Japan has a strong interest in shaping China's environmental practices; it is affected by both the acid rain and dust that emanates from China and by such issues as fishing rights. Japan also perceives a direct economic benefit from its assistance in terms of opportunities for environmental technology transfer. China is the largest recipient of Japanese technical cooperation.[41] In December 2007, then Japanese prime minister Yasuo Fukuda pledged to finance ten new centers in China dedicated to the promotion of environmental and energy technology transfer and cooperation, and to educate ten thousand Chinese students over three years about environmental protection technologies.[42] Prime Minister Yukio Hatoyama, elected in September 2009, will likely continue and even expand such assistance, having pledged to improve relations with China as well as enhance Japan's efforts to combat climate change. The United States provides extensive policy advice and technical training opportunities to China, primarily through NGOs. (Its formal bilateral assistance is sharply constrained by political and financial considerations, although environmental cooperation has increasingly been emphasized in the bilateral relationship.) The newfound influence of the Chinese and international environmental communities has also been evidenced by the inclusion of environmental issues—both global and domestic—on the agendas of the high-level summits between the United States and China since 2006. In December 2008, following the fifth round of the Strategic Economic Dialogue that was spearheaded by former U.S. treasury secretary Henry Paulson, the United States announced its desire for China to enter the International Energy Agency (IEA) as a non-OECD member, which could be another forum for U.S.–China cooperation on energy.[43] (China has remained resistant to this proposal, in large part due to its reluctance to comply with the IEA's transparency requirements and to relinquish control over its energy policy and infrastructure.)[44] Unlike with Japan, however, extensive U.S. environmental diplomacy with China has not been matched by an equally impressive set of collaborative projects (though U.S.–China cooperation on environmental projects is on the rise). The U.S. Department of Energy has had difficulty exploiting the potentially vast China market for U.S. cleaner coal technologies. The lack of assistance, and especially of financing mechanisms for U.S. corporations, has meant that U.S. firms find it difficult to compete with their European and Japanese counterparts. However, U.S.–China cooperation is improving. A pilot program in Guangdong Province, run under the auspices of the U.S. consulate in Hong Kong, provides energy efficiency auditing. Factories that apply for energy audits can take out loans from participating banks to pay for efficiency upgrades, with the expectation that they will pay the loans back over time out of the savings they will realize from using fewer materials or conserving energy.[45] Since the June 2008 signing of the

Ten Year Framework on Energy and Environment Cooperation under the auspices of the Strategic Economic Dialogue, the U.S. and Chinese governments are also supporting new "EcoPartnerships" between American and Chinese companies, such as the venture between Ford Motor Company and Chang'an Motors and the cities of Denver and Chongqing to develop electric cars. As of April 2009 there were six other EcoPartnerships between universities, businesses, and municipalities. In July 2009, the United States and China announced plans to develop a U.S.–China Clean Energy Research Center. The new center, with an initial cost of $15 million, will serve as a clearinghouse for research on boosting energy efficiency, clean coal technologies, and clean energy vehicles.[46]

The international community may also play a role in spurring China's leaders to take action on environmental issues because of concern over outsiders' perceptions. Certainly, international concerns over Beijing's air quality in advance of the Beijing Olympics provided significant motivation for many of China's environmental initiatives (discussed in chapter 3).

Tensions between China and the international community, for example, have increased, particularly around the question of who should be held responsible for China's GHG emissions. Finally, growing cross-border trade and investment has contributed to muddying the waters of responsibility for pollution or emissions. China blames much of its high levels of GHG emissions on MNCs from developed countries operating factories in China. Under the Kyoto Protocol, emissions are registered in the country in which they are produced, but developing nations such as China reject this as an inequitable structure. Under the Kyoto Protocol structure, the United Kingdom can claim that it has reduced emissions by 18 percent since 1990, but the Stockholm Environment Institute estimates that, if factories outsourced from the United Kingdom and international transport are included, the United Kingdom's emissions have risen 20 percent.[47] China would prefer an emissions control regime that acknowledged the negative impact of outsourcing from the developed world. The counterargument is that since China benefits from the increased economic activity of MNC outsourcing, it should bear responsibility for the emissions.

While the West may contribute to China's pollution challenge, China is also guilty of environmental exploitation beyond its own borders. For example, in Papua New Guinea the China Metallurgical Group operates the Ramu nickel and cobalt mine, which dumps mine tailings into pristine waters, a disposal method illegal in Canada and the United States. The company has run into serious opposition over its environmental practices. On the one hand, the Ramu mine is the largest business venture in the country and supports the economy of the nation's highlands. It employs four thousand people and adds 10 percent to the national economy. On the other hand, many of the laborers at the mine are Chinese who have immigrated to the country, squeezing out the domestic workforce and failing to pass the benefits of development onto the local population. "They were supposed to help us develop," says Reuben Andonga, a teacher, "but we are still living in a primitive way. We still live in houses of grass and coconut leaves. We still get our light from hurricane lamps. They haven't given us any electricity or permanent houses."[48] Furthermore, the mine presents an ecological threat to which the citizens of Papua New Guinea are sensitive. "The Chinese don't understand the value of the land to the people," says Ben Kedoga, a local radio journalist.[49] Chinese mining and petroleum interests have also been active in Gabon. In 2006, Sinopec was accused of illegally surveying for oil in one of Gabon's natural wildlife reserves. Despite efforts from local conservationists and the Wildlife Conservation Society, Sinopec engineers did not desist until the Gabonese government intervened. More recently, the China National Machinery and Equipment Import and Export Corporation (CMEC) signed a $600 million contract with the Gabonese government to dam the Kongou River in the Ivindo National Park to create an iron mine. The dam threatens not only the rare wildlife in the national park but also Gabon's longstanding ambitions to create a vibrant ecotourism industry. Construction of the dam has been delayed due to the fall in the price of iron and negotiations between CMEC and the Gabonese government.[50]

Economic Reform: Challenges and Opportunities for Environmental Cooperation

China's current stage of industrialization, transition to a market economy, and integration into the international economy has contributed to the pollution and degradation of the environment over the past three decades. Yet it also has provided a substantial opportunity for rethinking and reorienting the country's approach to environmental protection.

The same attributes needed for a successful market economy and integration into the global economy, including transparency, rule of law, managerial expertise, and a premium on efficient production, are the keys to realizing China's environmental goals, such as those outlined in China's Agenda 21 and in the country's eleventh five year plan, ending in 2010. As China's leaders press forward with economic reform and integrating China into the global economy, the international community has taken the opportunity to advance environmental cooperation in four areas: policy design, capacity building, technology transfer, and enforcement and incentives.

Policy Design

The international community and China have developed an extensive range of cooperative activities focused on policy reform. Many of these efforts target China's energy sector, including plans to develop new strategies and laws at the national level, as well as local initiatives, such as developing energy efficiency building codes in Chongqing.

Foreign governments, international governmental organizations, international nongovernmental organizations, and multinationals have all established partnerships with Chinese ministries and other institutions focused on these issues. The World Bank and the National Development and Reform Commission (NDRC) are collaborating on a cleaner coal and renewable energy strategy; the U.S. government committed in the Strategic Economic Dialogue to implement fifteen coal mine methane capture projects in China to recycle the methane released from mines; the U.S. Department of Energy agreed in December 2006 to the sale of four state-of-the-art nuclear reactors by Westinghouse as part of China's efforts to double its nuclear power capacity by 2020; in 2008 General Electric (GE) built China's first "trigeneration" power plant, which not only emits less carbon dioxide in producing power but also provides cooling and heating to the Taiyanggong neighborhood in Beijing; and BP is funding multiple Chinese Academy of Sciences research projects at a cost of tens of millions of dollars, including a new Clean Energy Commercialization Center.[51] Already, a gradual increase in the use of natural gas in Beijing has contributed to an improvement in air quality. The Natural Resources Defense Council has begun several long-term projects to develop building codes for the Yangtze River Basin region, a painstaking effort that involves the preparation of detailed manuals; training for a range of stakeholders, including enforcement officials, designers, builders, and component manufacturers; the development of financial incentives; and improvement of China's domestic capability to manufacture energy-efficient building materials.[52]

Chinese environmental protection officials have also stated that they will increasingly rely on financial incentives and the market rather than simply on fines[53] and the court system to improve the environmental situation. In the water-scarce northern city of Zhangjiakou, Hebei Province, for example, officials, acting on the advice of the ADB, raised the price of water 40 percent but varied the price according to the type of consumer. In one year, water consumption in the city fell by nearly 14 percent, primarily due to reductions by factories that had finally instituted water recycling.[54]

Some international actors, including the U.S. EPA and NGOs such as Resources for the Future and the Environmental Defense Fund (EDF) have developed pilot projects employing market-based tools. To assist China in meeting its target of reducing sulfur dioxide emissions by 20 percent, for example, EDF managed a pilot program from 1999 to 2005 with the Huaneng Group—China's largest state-owned power generation company—to institute a system of tradable permits for sulfur dioxide in the provinces of Shandong, Shanxi, Jiangsu, and Henan, as well as in the Shanghai and Tianjin municipalities. This system, which EDF introduced in the United States in

1990, establishes an overall level of permissible emissions for a given region, assigns targets for individual companies, and then permits the enterprises to buy and sell the rights to pollute. Firms whose emissions fall below the permitted level can store the reduction credits below their quota for future use or sell the credits to others who cannot meet their emissions levels. Not surprisingly, the Chinese have encountered some hurdles in their efforts to utilize a market-based tool in a transitional economy. As William Alford notes, the hybrid nature of the Chinese economy often stymies policies that otherwise might be important mechanisms for environmental protection:

> Adherence to the "polluter pays" principle and the establishment of a workable system of tradable discharge permits presumes more in the way of market mechanisms overseen by independent regulatory authorities than is now available in China or likely to be in the foreseeable future. . . . The "polluter pays" principle, for example, depends on such variables as readily identifiable corporate entities that operate under meaningful budget constraints, the free flow of information needed to make a market, and a clear dividing line between those who are regulated and those doing the regulating.[55]

Researchers involved in the experiments for tradable permits for sulfur dioxide also noted that Chinese officials and enterprise directors have only a weak understanding of the concept of property rights. There is no established mechanism for property rights transfer in China and thus no logical transaction agent (i.e., a person to hold the money in escrow during the transaction). In December 2007, under the auspices of the U.S.–China Strategic Economic Dialogue, the United States agreed to assist China in implementing a ten-year program to introduce a country-wide system of sulfur dioxide tradable permits. The long implementation phase suggests a recognition of the substantial evolution in the policy environment that will need to occur for the system to operate effectively. EDF has also been piloting a market-based program for the reduction of agricultural GHGs since 2005. Working with provincial- and county-level Environmental Protection Bureaus in Xinjiang and Sichuan,

EDF has provided the technology for precise fertilizer application, no-till agriculture, drip irrigation, household biogas/methane digesters, and water management to farmers. The Chinese Academy of Agricultural Sciences then certifies the emissions reductions generated by these technologies. The emissions reductions can be bundled as Voluntary Emissions Credits, which can be sold to investors. The EDF project generated 310,000 tons of carbon dioxide reductions by April 2008, which were purchased by an American-based MNC. The revenue was then recycled back to the farmers.

A broader carbon exchange may take some time to implement. Beijing, Shanghai, and Tianjin each founded emissions exchanges in late 2008 and intend to begin trading credits in 2010, but the new exchanges will be effective only once the central government corrects several problems in the country's emissions regulatory regime. As of September 2009, there were too few member companies in each exchange to sustain trading. A systemic obstacle to the exchanges is the method by which China assigns emissions credits: the central government allocates credits to provincial governments, which in turn often simply apportion credits to favored companies. Jeff Huang, assistant chairman of the Tianjin Climate Exchange and vice-president of the Chicago Climate Exchange, advocates that Beijing should instead allocate credits to companies directly.[56] The exchanges also will most likely not handle carbon trading, which is a critical shortcoming. They will facilitate transactions of energy conservation and environmental protection technologies; energy conservation quotas; and pollution rights, including sulfur dioxide and chemical oxygen demand; but Gao Guangsheng, the director of the Office of National Coordination Committee on Climate Change at the NDRC, announced in October 2008 that "conditions were not mature" enough to facilitate carbon trading.[57] Only after China puts a price on carbon emissions will trading be possible.

Capacity Building

The case of tradable permits for sulfur dioxide underscores the importance of capacity building within China if environmental cooperation is to be effective. Without the proper education and training for Chinese partners, and the appropriate coordination among them, many policy initiatives will never be fully implemented.[58] According to an assessment of ADB projects in China, "more than half of the pollution discharges can be reduced at many enterprises through strengthening management rather than upgrading equipment."[59] Capacity building, therefore, has become a central element of most international cooperative ventures.[60]

The Dow Chemical Company, for example, has partnered with the UNEP and the Ministry of Environmental Protection (MEP) to provide training in chemical safety, emergency preparedness and response, and local awareness in China's chemical industry. The program, started in 2008, will last until 2010 and is the latest of a series of capacity-building programs Dow has undertaken with MEP to strengthen both national and local actors in China's chemical industry. According to Neil Hawkins, Dow's vice president for sustainability: "[China is] an important center of global transformational growth. Collaborating with partners like MEP and UNEP will make a positive and lasting impact on a wide range of people, and Chinese society as a whole."[61] Other companies, such as General Electric and General Motors, also hold wide-ranging training programs for their Chinese plant managers, covering legal issues, environment, health and safety questions, audit skills, and work plans for specific issue areas such as maintaining air and water quality, pollution prevention, and industrial hygiene.

Given the long-term investment in capacity building and training necessary for many partnerships, multinationals and other international actors often stress the importance of selecting the right partner for a cooperative venture.[62] General Motors, for example, searched five years before selecting Shanghai Automotive as its Chinese partner.

Still, officials from one U.K.–based multinational believe that when a Chinese company or ministry is looking for cost reduction in a planned venture, the first thing to be eliminated from the budget is training. Moreover, they have found that although there has been a "sea change in attitudes" within Chinese enterprises over the past decade, these new understandings are "not always reflected in implementation." While the company's Chinese partners, for example, have been well-briefed in the International Standards Organization (ISO) 14001 standard, by which an organization can be certified as having attained a certain international standard for its environmental management system, they do not always implement the guidelines fully.[63]

Bridging the gap between policy design and implementation in China also requires extensive bureaucratic coordination, a challenge often not met adequately. Both Chinese and international participants of CCICED, for example, believe their environmental recommendations are often not adequately implemented because there is little to no participation by the ministries responsible. As one Chinese CCICED participant has noted, "When it comes to the relevant ministry, due to lack of institutional relationship between the Council and this Ministry, it's likely that neither the minister nor its key departments or divisions know anything whatsoever about the CCICED." Similarly, the ADB has found that weaknesses in interagency coordination "frequently lead to turf wars among agencies."[64] For example, as discussed in chapter 4, the Green GDP effort collapsed in 2007 amid disagreement between SEPA, the National Bureau of Statistics (NBS), and provincial governments.

Technology Transfer

China's economic development and reform also raise the potential for significant environmental advances through the introduction of new technologies. A 2001 World Bank/SEPA assessment of the state of environmental affairs in China notes, "The switch to a more competitive, demand-driven industrial sector is resulting in increased earnings retention and re-investment. This is increasing technological innovation and resource use efficiency, allowing more industrial growth to be achieved at less environmental cost."[65] Chinese officials often express the belief that technology is the answer to their environmental problems. Premier Wen Jiabao said in January 2009, "Cooperation in technological transfer shall be strengthened so as to help the developing countries get the advanced greenhouse gas control technology," urging the European Union to abrogate export restrictions on high-tech products in the process.[66]

To facilitate this effort, China instituted a cleaner production program in 1993 and ISO 14000 environmental management system certification procedures in 1997;[67] in 2007, China was awarded more ISO 14001:2004 environmental management certificates than any other country, suggesting at least that Chinese manufacturers are eager to pursue internationally recognized environmental ratings for their perceived economic benefit.[68] (The 2007 awards represent standards that the ISO published in 2004.) Both international governmental organizations and multinationals have developed a number of impressive cooperative ventures employing cleaner production. Successful ventures, not surprisingly, combine policy change, technological innovation, and capacity building. For example, Wal-Mart, itself China's eighth largest trading partner, has joined the Environmental Defense Fund to support clean production in Wal-Mart's supply chain, which comprises some 100,000 Chinese factories. Starting in 2009, Chinese factories that supply Wal-Mart were expected to demonstrate compliance with environmental laws, improve their energy efficiency, and operate with greater transparency. In an attempt to ensure the widespread distribution of cleaner production, as suppliers adopt new technologies and best practices, Wal-Mart requires that these advances be shared with competitors.[69] Alcoa is also working in China to provide new, cleaner technologies in the aluminum industry. In 2007, Alcoa partnered with the Zhengzhou Yutong Bus Company to develop lightweight, more efficient municipal buses for use during the Beijing Olympics.[70] Two years later, Alcoa entered into a strategic agreement with mineral-rich Henan Province to provide new low-energy and cleaner technologies, aluminum recycling capacity, and cleaner waste disposal mechanisms.[71] Alcoa's activities in Henan promise cleaner aluminum production, leading in turn to greater use of aluminum in sustainable technologies, such as fuel-efficient vehicles.

Establishing new institutions to facilitate technology transfer and environmental education is also an important means of enhancing China's environmental protection efforts. The World Bank, for example, has supported the development of energy service companies (ESCOs)—independent companies that advise Chinese companies on buying, installing, and maintaining energy-efficient technologies. ESCOs are then paid with the financial savings that the technologies brought to the companies. According to China's national ESCO association, the Energy Management Company Association, there were fewer than fifty ESCOs in China in 2002 but over two hundred by the end of 2006, a rate of expansion that suggests ESCOs may eventually become a significant component of national environmental management.[72]

Many multinationals, however, have been stymied in their efforts to transfer and/or employ environmental technologies successfully. Even when coupled with capacity building and policy reform, the effectiveness of new technological advances is impaired by China's weak enforcement capacity and incentive system. Case after case demonstrates that "technology is not a substitute for enforcement."[73] Many firms possess the technological capacity to address their pollution problems, whether it is wastewater treatment or electrostatic precipitators to control sulfur dioxide emissions, yet they avoid using this equipment because they believe it is too costly.[74]

Enforcement and Incentives

China's weak capacity to enforce its environmental laws and regulations is well known both within and outside the country. A 2003 World Bank report notes, "[The] ability to implement comprehensive national environment policies has been limited by the high degree of administrative decentralization, local prioritization of investment and employment, vertical and horizontal fiscal imbalance, and absence of clear accountability for environmental conditions. The legal system for compliance and enforcement is used sparingly, although it is slowly increasing."[75]

A press release from the MEP in 2009 illustrates both the increase in enforcement activity and its persistent shortcomings: "Last year, environmental departments sent out more than 1.6 million officers to inspect about 70,000 enterprises. To date they have punished 15,000 enterprises for breaking environmental laws." However, "about 15.5 percent of [construction] projects started construction without approval, and about 9.6 percent of enterprises closed for environmental reasons resumed production without permission.

Treatment facilities at about 25 percent of the main sources of pollution were not running properly."[76] Moreover, the global recession has likely hindered the adoption of cleaner industrial practices. As MEP minister Zhou Shengxian remarked, "The economic slowdown w[ill] put more pressure on environmental protection as some enterprises may be reluctant to turn on their pollution treatment facilities."[77]

For the international community, enforcement challenges take several forms. For example, following the 2007 publication of the list of heavy polluters by the NGO the Institute of Public and Environmental Affairs, Chinese public and official censure fell disproportionately on the MNCs listed. Many ventures have stalled or dissolved over the failure of China to protect intellectual property.[78] And other firms have found that their Chinese partners elect not to utilize some end-of-the-pipe technologies because of their perceived additional cost. Many factories operate pollution abatement facilities only during inspections, if at all. Even if multinationals provide the necessary pollution control equipment, Chinese firms may not fit it at industrial sites because the cost is much higher than the small financial penalties they will have to pay for exceeding pollution limits.[79]

Not surprisingly, weak enforcement may affect the willingness of firms to transfer their best technology. Multinationals are understandably reluctant to employ their advanced technology, which typically adds more to the start-up costs of the venture, if they do not believe that inferior technology will be penalized.[80] The challenge of enforcement is matched by the need for development of a stronger incentive system for enterprises to invest in technical measures to improve plant efficiency.[81] For cleaner production to be adopted, enterprises need incentives such as resource shortages, higher prices, and increased regulatory pressure. To date, cleaner production has been centered in regions with strong incentives, such as the water-scarce areas of northern China,[82] joint ventures in which the technology was provided by the international partner, or companies that are able to sell emissions credits through the CDM.

Even if a Chinese enterprise employs the most advanced environmental technologies, the local infrastructure as well as the capacity of the enterprise management may be insufficient to support their use. As one analysis reports, "The latest environmental technologies are often inapplicable in China, where existing systems are often many years out of date. Grafting new technologies onto China's old systems may lead not only to sub-optimal output but even to outright failure."[83] Dupont and Dow officials, for example, found that "unstable power supply often disrupted their ultrasensitive high-tech chemical manufacturing process. Computerized production components failed, and onsite technicians were often ill-prepared to handle the consequences."[84] In one case, the company was compelled to bring in experts from abroad, which increased the cost of the venture far beyond initial expectations. Company officials were especially unhappy because the Chinese government had insisted that only the most advanced technology be used, and the venture had been predicated on the government's assurances of appropriate infrastructure support.[85]

China's continued evolution to a full market economy, well integrated into the global economic system, provides a number of opportunities and challenges for environmental cooperation. However, given the range of potential institutional, policy, and technological impediments to effective collaboration, an integrated approach, which supports a variety of assistance needs, is needed to achieve the best results.[86] This means that all four potential areas of cooperation—policy design, capacity building, technology transfer, and enforcement/incentives—must be targeted for international involvement. As China's economy becomes further integrated into the global economy, there is also the potential for environmental objectives to be advanced by environmental activities or requirements embodied in the various trade regimes to which China accedes.

Reinforcement by Trade Regimes

The tensions inherent in integrating environmental protection with international trade are evident even in the most environmentally oriented international declarations. For example, Principle 12 of the Rio Declaration states:

Trade policy measures for environmental purposes should not constitute a means of arbitrary or unjustifiable discrimination or disguised restriction on international trade. Unilateral actions to deal with environmental challenges outside the jurisdiction of the importing country should be avoided. Environmental measures addressing transboundary or global environmental problems should, as far as possible, be based on international consensus.[87]

Some sectors in China have already been affected by green requirements in international trade, including textiles, agricultural products, and wood crates for packing that have been banned by the United States and Canada.[88]

Regional and global trade regimes such as WTO and APEC have the potential to reinforce positive trends in China's development and environment trajectory. China's implementation of Restrictions of the Use of Certain Hazardous Substances (ROHS) in order to sustain electronics exports to the EU is an example of positive reinforcement of environmental standards through trade. In 2005, electronics exports to the EU accounted for 35 percent of China's exports and were valued at $380 billion. When the EU passed a directive on ROHS, banning certain toxic compounds commonly found in electronics, effective January 1, 2007, it cost the Chinese an estimated $37 billion in lost foreign trade.[89] In response, China issued its own version of the ROHS, the "Administration of the Control of Pollution by Electronic Information Products," which brought Chinese electronic manufacturing in line with the EU's ROHS and improved disclosure requirements. China's new restrictions apply also to products not for export to the EU.[90]

China's accession to the World Trade Organization in December 2001 also raised hopes that the country's integration into trade networks and market liberalization would increase awareness in China of environmental and safety concerns and give the international community greater leverage over China's manufacturing and exports. Other potential positive changes resulting from WTO accession included publication of environmental laws and regulations affecting trade, international insistence on greater legal transparency and effective enforcement mechanisms in China, and the continued closure of inefficient state-owned industries. Indeed, since acceding to the WTO, China's general tariff has decreased from 15.3 percent in 2001 to 9.8 percent in 2009.[91] However, especially in the areas of product safety and international property right protection, China's integration into trade regimes has not met expectations. Rather, China's progress on these fronts has been made haltingly through protracted negotiations and disputes with its trading partners.

WTO accession has not significantly altered China's environmentally deleterious industrial practices. During 2002 to 2007, overall energy intensity in China increased.[92] As of early 2009, China was responsible for 38 percent of global steel production, only 12 percent of which was for export.[93] International trade regimes have only limited leverage over energy intensive, highly pollutant production for domestic consumption. For reasons primarily of energy security, China has taken steps to lower its energy intensity and met some success. There have been efforts to meet the eleventh five year plan goal of reducing China's energy intensity by 20 percent by 2010. During the first three years of the program (2006–2008), China achieved a reduction by a cumulative 10.04 percent.[94] The Top-1000 Energy-Consuming Enterprises Program, launched by the NDRC and the University of California, Berkeley's Lawrence Berkeley National Laboratory (LBNL) in 2006, provided incentives for energy efficiency for one thousand enterprises in nine industries, including iron and steel production, coal mining, construction materials, and power generation. In return for voluntary energy intensity reductions, the LBNL provides technologies and capacity building, and the enterprises enjoy positive press. By September 2008, the program was on track to reduce CO_2 emissions by 450 million tons by 2010, equal to the total annual emissions of South Korea.[95]

Unfortunately, the global financial crisis threatens to reverse many of China's gains and overwhelm the environmental goals of the eleventh five-year plan. China's $586 billion stimulus plan announced in 2008 has lavished investment on energy-intensive industries. In a nod to domestic and international concerns about the negative impact of capital and resource intensive development projects, in 2003 then-SEPA instituted the Environmental Impact Assessment Law requiring an environmental impact report for all new major construction. In a concession to economic pressure, on January 10, 2009, a spokesperson for the MEP announced the availability of a "green passage," an expedited and less rigorous impact assessment process, for large infrastructure and capital-intensive projects deemed to be beneficial to China's slowing economy.[96] In Tianjin, the sixty-day statutory time limit for environmental impact assessments was reduced to just seven days.[97]

In the area of product safety, a series of international incidents in 2007 involving contaminated Chinese exports drew international scrutiny and revealed China's insufficient monitoring of standards. In September 2008, for example, Chinese dairy products contaminated with the chemical melamine led more than twenty countries to ban imports of Chinese milk-based products. The melamine incident was responsible for the deaths of at least six Chinese infants and harmed the health of more than 300,000 Chinese children. Previously, in March 2007, pet food adulterated with melamine caused kidney failure in pets, precipitating the recall of Chinese-made pet food in North America, South Africa, and Europe; in April 2007, the U.S. Food and Drug Administration impounded all imports of vegetable proteins from China; in May 2007, a toxic substance was discovered in toothpaste shipped from China to Panama, the United States, Canada, India, and Nigeria; and in June 2007, farmed fish were discovered to be contaminated with antibiotics; also during the summer of 2007, several toy brands, but most notably Mattel, recalled millions of toys when they were found to be contaminated by lead paint. Following precedents established since 2007, India instituted a six-month ban on Chinese toys in January 2009 in response to a similar health scare. The United States has had a ban against imported Chinese poultry since fears rose about avian influenza in 2004. While WTO membership has not pressured China to improve its product safety record, it has given China a forum in which to dispute such bans: in the spring of 2009, China leveled accusations of protectionism against India and the United States in the WTO's highest courts.

China's integration into global trade regimes has, however, raised awareness within China about the country's shortcomings. Chinese judges, motivated at least in part by the political desire to assuage the fears of trading partners, meted out harsh punishments to those responsible for tainted export and food products: one manufacturing executive was sentenced to life in prison, two were sentenced to death, and one committed suicide. In June 2007, the head of China's food and drug administration was executed on corruption charges. Actions like these may bring attention to the need for reforms, but the problems are systemic and difficult to uproot.

With regard to intellectual property rights (IPR) protection, China's efforts have been slow to meet international standards. The United States filed suit against China in April 2007, arguing that China's legal regime for IPR protection was insufficient to meet the requirements of the WTO under the Agreement on Trade-Related Aspects of Intellectual Property Rights (TRIPS Agreement). The United States held that China was in violation of the TRIPS Agreement because the Chinese copyright law did not protect works that did not meet China's "domestic content requirement"; China's disposal process for seized counterfeit goods damaged the reputation of the legitimate product; and China had a legal threshold for criminal prosecution of counterfeiting and piracy that exempted most commercial infringements of IPR. In a decision circulated on January 26, 2009, the WTO ruled in favor of the United States on the first two counts and cited the need for further evidence before reaching a judgment on the third.[98] Such IPR infringements make MNCs wary of product and technology transfer to China. To remedy this situation, some MNCs, such as GE, have taken it on themselves to support China's IPR legal regime. GE offers legal expertise and training to the Chinese government and law enforcement agencies.[99]

Furthermore, China's accession to the WTO has strengthened the export potential for those exports deemed safe for consumption but threatening to the environment; textile exports, for example, increased by almost 8.2 percent year-on-year between 2007 and 2008.[100] Especially worrisome is the Chinese government's resurging encouragement of the expansion of environmentally harmful and energy-intensive industries such as tin mining and production, particularly since the global economic downturn began in late 2008.[101] Similarly, car ownership in China is projected to increase sevenfold before 2030.[102]

While APEC, unlike the WTO, does not impose requirements or binding commitments on its participants, it does provide a stock-taking exercise in which each member economy reports on steps it has taken to promote sustainable development in several key areas, including cleaner production, protection of the marine environment, food, and energy.[103] In addition, the APEC energy ministers devote substantial attention to the clean use of energy, renewables, energy efficiency, and so on, even encouraging member economies' participation in activities to reduce greenhouse gases.[104] The 2007 *APEC Leaders' Declaration on Climate Change, Energy Security and Clean Development* set an aspirational goal of decreasing energy intensity 25 percent compared to 2005 by 2030. The 2009 APEC meetings in Singapore included a three-day symposium on climate change. Recent projects facilitated by APEC include a campaign sponsored by the United States to decrease trade barriers between APEC economies for renewable energy technologies and an assessment, carried out over 2008 and 2009, of the potential for carbon sequestration projects to reduce emissions from natural gas production in Southeast Asia.[105]

Still, the environmental component of APEC appears decidedly less important than economic and other concerns. While APEC's Energy Working Group sponsors many projects, the Sustainable Development initiative has none. The environment ministers met last in 1997, despite pledging to meet annually. Although APEC sponsored a "High-Level Meeting on Sustainable Development" in 2006, the meeting concluded only that APEC economies should share information on sustainable development with each other, with international organizations, and civil society groups and did not set ambitious targets.[106] Instead, regional environmental issues are usually addressed through small commissions or organizations involving only those countries directly affected. South Korea and Japan, for example, work directly with China to monitor acid rain. The same three countries also continuously negotiate marine fisheries agreements.

More difficult for regional cooperation are issues that involve sensitive sovereignty issues, such as control over resources in the South China Sea or utilization of the water resources of the Mekong River. In June 2008, China's third hydroelectric power dam on the Mekong

River began power production; twelve more are either planned or already under construction. China's actions have caused great consternation among the affected countries downriver, including Burma, Laos, Thailand, Cambodia, and Vietnam; Vietnam has accused China's dam construction of cutting the flow of water, resulting in saltwater intrusion into the Mekong Delta, which is home to about half of Vietnam's agricultural output.[107] While China did begin to participate in the Greater Mekong Subregion Commission that is focused on development issues, despite significant international pressure, China has refused to join the Mekong River Commission that coordinates environmental issues among these states. In 2003, in a notable concession to its downstream neighbors, China began providing information on the river flow and water levels of the Mekong.

Thus, China's growing participation in international trade regimes, its development of domestic environment and development institutions to further cooperation with the international environmental community, and its transition to a market economy all contribute to an increasingly dense network of linkages on issues related to environmental protection. There are few if any potential risks to China in such cooperation. As China seeks to invite foreign participation in the full range of its environment and development activities, however, its continued penchant for large-scale development campaigns has opened the country to mounting criticism from both within and outside China.

The Great Campaigns: Reconciling Environment and Development

Three Gorges Dam

The construction of the Three Gorges Dam has received perhaps the lion's share of international (as well as domestic) criticism. Sun Yat-sen initially proposed the project back in 1919, but the process of realizing his vision began in earnest only in the 1980s and early 1990s.[108] The dam is a massive undertaking that will eventually provide China with 22,000 megawatts of energy annually, more than 10 percent of China's total electricity needs. The physical structure was largely completed in 2006, standing 200 meters tall, with a reservoir more than 600 kilometers long and 175 meters deep. In a two-stage process, the dam first provided electricity to a region in the immediate vicinity of the dam; some time after 2010, when the dam reaches its full capacity, the government plans to transmit power as far north as Beijing and as far south as Hong Kong. Whether the demand for energy will be there at that time has yet to be fully addressed.

The Chinese scientific community has been divided on the merits of the dam. Although the U.S. government provided technical assistance for the Three Gorges Dam during 1984–1993, many international experts have since condemned the project and serious debate occurred within the National People's Congress during the early 1990s. At the time, those opposed to the dam, both within and outside China, argued that the project was unsound on several grounds: (1) it would force the relocation of over one million Chinese citizens; (2) it would flood precious arable land and destroy ancient cultural relics and historic cities such as Fengdu, also known as the "ghost" city; and (3) the reservoir created by the dam would become filled with sediment and prevent the passage of some ships. Nonetheless, the Chinese government elected to proceed with the dam and began construction in 1994.

At first, international financial support for the dam was scanty. The World Bank refused to help,[109] and Chinese plans to issue bonds on the international financial market were dashed by the lack of interest. However, the Three Gorges Project Development Corporation began to raise money through the China International Capital Corporation, which is 35 percent owned by Morgan Stanley. Moreover, U.S. investment firms, including Morgan Stanley, Merrill Lynch, and Chase Manhattan Bank helped underwrite over $1 trillion in China Development Bank bonds, whose top loan commitment was the Three Gorges Dam.

Meanwhile, international forces began to fight the dam. International Rivers Network, the international nongovernmental organization, undertook a broad-based campaign to force Morgan Stanley to withdraw from providing any assistance in fund-raising for the dam, including boycotting the company's Discover Card. In addition, Trillium Asset Management, a Boston-based firm that promotes "socially responsible" investing, has been active since 1995 in exerting pressure on several other financial institutions, including Citigroup and Chase Manhattan Bank, not to contribute assistance in any form to the dam, and has met with some limited success, as when Bank of America agreed not to commit any direct lending and to "carefully weigh any transactions that might indirectly benefit the dam."[110] In addition, in part as a result of Trillium's efforts, Citigroup began to incorporate environmental, human rights, and public relations risk criteria into its lending and underwriting deals.

Contributions to the capital construction of the dam also ran into some roadblocks. While many governments helped their domestic firms win bids on various aspects of the project by providing financial assistance and insurance through their export credit agencies, the United States, led by the U.S. Department of State, withheld support through its Export-Import Bank.

Progress on the Three Gorges Dam's construction was mired with problems, giving rise to even greater international and domestic concern. The project has been plagued by corruption. According to a 2008 report, local officials involved in managing the construction and resettlement process have embezzled as much as $700 million, or 12 percent of the $5.86 billion resettlement budget, and 350 people have been tried and found guilty on corruption charges.[111] Shoddy construction that caused a bridge to collapse, killing several people, led former premier Zhu Rongji to term the construction "tofu engineering."[112] He then invited foreign experts and engineers to oversee the construction process to ensure that top-quality practices were enforced.

Social unrest continues to surround the resettlement process. Since the late 1990s, there have been many demonstrations involving hundreds of farmers who believed they were being inadequately compensated during the resettlement process. Probe International and Human Rights Watch have joined International Rivers Network in monitoring the resettlement process and the local political situation around the dam and have issued several scathing reports regarding the corruption that has plagued the resettlement efforts. In July

2002, when fifty-six migrants from Gaoyang, located 225 kilometers from the dam site, attempted to travel to Beijing to lodge complaints concerning the lack of compensation for their resettlement, they were accused of being Falun Gong supporters and arrested at the direction of the local county leadership. They were released after their plight was brought to the attention of officials from the Three Gorges Project Construction Committee.[113] Many older Chinese, too, were reluctant to leave their homes, many of which had been in their families for centuries. Indeed, all along the Yangtze, beautiful stone houses that seem to be embedded in the rocky landscape stand shuttered as new, often spanking white, multistory apartment buildings sprout at higher elevations in newly developed cities. The deserted towns have also spawned another industry: private "grave robbers" search in the villages for ancient stone tablets that might provide historical records. Already, 1.2 million people have been relocated, which is in line with original estimates. The vice mayor of Chongqing, Yu Yuanmu, announced in October 2007, however, that a further four million people would be resettled by 2020 because of the dam's impact on the surrounding area, raising the total number of relocated persons to almost six million.[114] Many of those resettled have lost their homes and livelihoods, and the compensation provided by the state has been insufficient for many to begin anew. "These relocated people sacrificed a lot for the Three Gorges Dam and their living standard dropped," said Xu Yuming, a researcher involved in planning the project. "Now we are facing a new challenge of how to improve their living standards. . . . There are now more people than the land can sustain."[115]

Social problems have been compounded by the unexpected geological effects of the Three Gorges Dam, particularly seismic activity and devastating landslides. Following the 2008 Wenchuan earthquake in Sichuan Province, there has been increased awareness of reservoir-induced seismicity, especially in China's southwestern provinces. Scientists recorded 822 tremors around the reservoir in the seven months following the September 2006 rise in the water level.[116] The increase in seismic activity created by the new reservoir has in turn increased the number of landslides on the steep banks of the gorges. In 2007, a total of thirty-six kilometers of shoreline collapsed into the reservoir, destroying the homes and liveli-hoods of relocated people.[117] The government has invested a further $1.75 billion to mitigate the damage caused by geologic activity.[118] Yet another concern is the pollution generated by the towns and cities surrounding the reservoir. Aware of the potential environ-mental damage, the government announced a planned investment of $5.5 billion for 150 new sewage treatment plants and 170 new waste disposal centers; however, as of 2007, fewer than half of the facilities were under construction.[119] Less than one-third of the industrial and one-tenth of the urban domestic wastewater is treated before being dumped into the reservoir.[120] The city of Chongqing alone generates one billion tons of untreated wastewater per year.[121] The official government English-language newspaper, *China Daily*, reported that six million tons of rubbish and ten million tons of solid industrial waste are dumped into the Three Gorges area and the upper reaches of the Yangtze every year; more than twenty mil-lion tons of garbage are dumped in the areas just around the reser-voir. Sailing down the Yangtze during summer 2002, I was not sur-prised to see mounds of garbage floating all along the river from Chongqing to Wuhan. Of even greater concern to many in China, however, is that the government will not have enough time to clean up all the factories and coal mines along the river banks before the reservoir is formed and that there is already massive underwater pollution.

The Chinese government is well aware of these challenges, al-though it has tried desperately to downplay their significance. Only in September 2007 did Chinese government officials attending a conference in Wuhan admit that "the Three Gorges Dam project has caused an array of ecological ills, including more frequent landslides and pollution, and if preventive measures are not taken, there could be an environmental 'catastrophe.'" A month prior, the secretary general of the Yangtze River Forum told the *Wall Street Journal*, "We thought of all the possible issues. But the problems are all more seri-ous than we expected."[122] The dam has so far cost almost $45 billion, but as early as 2000, a senior scientist working on the dam, Zhang Guangduo, predicted that managing the impending environmental crisis would necessitate a further investment of $37 billion.[123] The true extent of environmental and social costs associated with the Three Gorges Dam has yet to be fully understood. While the international NGOs have generated a significant amount of negative publicity for the dam and have had an impact on the thinking of the World Bank, the United States, and some investment firms, they do not appear to have exerted much influence, even indirectly, on Chinese practices.

Opening the West: Development or Exploitation?

China's "Great Opening of the West" (*Xibu Da Kaifa*), or "Go West" campaign—one of the country's most important domestic initiatives at the outset of the twenty-first century—raised a red flag throughout the country and the international community, highlighting the extent to which the Chinese government has opened itself to domestic and international pressures.

Launched in 1999, the Go West campaign was designed to "reduce regional disparities and to eventually materialize common prosperity" by developing six provinces (Shaanxi, Gansu, Qinghai, Sichuan, Yunnan, and Guizhou), five autonomous regions (Ningxia, Tibet, Inner Mongolia, Guangxi, and Xinjiang), and one municipality (Chongqing) in western China. The area encompasses approximately 5.4 million square kilometers and a population of 363 million people, 56 percent of the land, and 27.5 percent of the country's population.[124] The region is rich in natural resources, including gold, oil, natural gas, and coal, but much of it is difficult to access. Moreover, unlike the coastal provinces, the region remains poorly connected to the outside world, and the region comprises China's poorest provinces. Guizhou, one of the poorest provinces in China, boasts an average per capita income of just over 9 percent that of Shanghai.[125]

The west-east oil and gas pipelines from Xinjiang to the east coast exemplify the development projects imagined by the campaign. The pipelines, developed and constructed primarily by China National Petroleum Corporation (CNPC) and its subsidiary, PetroChina, have been publicized as beneficial for the economies of the western provinces. The pipelines should attract investment to the region's oil and gas resources. The first pipeline, which connects the Tarim

Basin in Xinjiang to Shanghai began commercial operation on January 1, 2005. Construction of a second west-east pipeline began in February 2008 and will run to Guangdong. It is scheduled for completion in 2010; at that time, it will be the longest natural gas pipeline in the world.[126] In March 2009, GE won a $300 million contract to supply the turbines to pressurize the gas as it travels across the country. (GE has won over $600 million in bids for projects in China since 2005, including the first west-east pipeline and a pipeline from Sichuan to East China to be completed in 2010.)[127] The third and fourth west-east pipelines are being planned.

The Go West campaign confronts the Chinese leadership with a critical test of its commitment to environmental protection. Leaders insist that environmental protection is a top priority in the campaign, but their claims are not supported by the evidence. Construction of the first pipeline would have necessitated the destruction of part of the Great Wall had the route not been changed following the social and environmental impact assessment carried out by Royal Dutch Shell, which originally partnered with PetroChina in the project.

Other aspects of the campaign have exacerbated severe regional ecological degradation arising from rampant deforestation, mining, overgrazing, and intensive plowing of cropland. According to at least one report, much of Tibet's environmental degradation appears to have come at the hands of Han settlers following investment in the Tibetan Plateau. The Han settlers are believed to be responsible for the destruction of up to 40 percent of Tibet's old-growth tropical and subtropical mountain forests. Rare plant and animal species are becoming extinct as Chinese officials exploit them for foreign markets, and the grasslands are suffering as Chinese demand for meat has led to overstocking of yak, goat, and sheep and the loss of Tibetan traditional herding and grazing practices.

Jiang Gaoming, a professor at the Chinese Academy of Sciences' Institute of Botany, notes that the government has spent 60 billion yuan ($8.7 billion) on reforestation and planting efforts to reduce soil erosion, but that the frequency of sandstorms in eastern China demonstrates that these funds and efforts have been in vain. He suggests that the replanting efforts have been conducted halfheartedly without rigorous examination of the methods. For example, officials have planted trees instead of grass, even though grass holds loose soil better and does not deplete precious groundwater. Officials have also limited their efforts to areas in sight of roads and towns, ignoring the larger, unseen problems because "who would notice?"[128] Mining has also been particularly destructive to Tibetan ways of life. Toxic tailings from mines have killed many livestock and Tibetan farmers are unlikely to receive appropriate compensation.[129]

The environmentally ruinous impact of the Go West campaign is magnified by the explicit linkage between the campaign and national security. China's leaders view the Go West campaign as essential to their solidification of control over border regions such as Tibet and Xinjiang. These regions have the highest proportion of non-Han minorities in the country, including twenty million Muslims as well as Tibetans and other ethnic groups. (Throughout China, the Han are the dominant ethnic group in the country equaling almost 92 percent of the population. In Xinjiang and Tibet, however, despite a massive influx of Han Chinese since 1949, Uighurs and Tibetans outnumber Han in both regions.)

Ethnic clashes in both Tibet and Xinjiang have been on the rise in recent years. In March 2008, massive riots broke out in the Tibetan capital of Lhasa, reportedly due to a conflict between Tibetan and Han Chinese traders. Beijing immediately deployed armed forces to shut down access to the city and tighten surveillance throughout the Tibetan territory, but clashes continued for weeks, spreading to the neighboring provinces of Gansu, Qinghai, and Sichuan. Xinjiang, too, is the site of frequent bombings, protests, and riots by separatists and independence advocates, and has consequently become the frontline of China's counterterrorist efforts. In July 2009, thousands of Uighurs took to the streets of Urumqi to protest ethnic discrimination, following news a few weeks earlier of two Uighur factory workers who were killed by a mob after rumors spread that they had sexually harassed Han women. Authorities reportedly arrived at the scene of a peaceful demonstration, but it soon spiraled into a bloody clash between Han Chinese and Uighurs that lasted for days, defying hundreds of military police in the process.[130]

As one report noted, the Go West campaign is the "fundamental guarantee for us to foster national unity, to maintain social stability, and to consolidate the borders."[131] Such plans to "colonize" the region further have already become problematic for Beijing. International observers and ethnic minority groups in Western China oppose the west-east pipelines as tools by which the Eastern power centers consolidate economic and political control of the western provinces. A range of NGOs, such as Tibet Vigil, Tibet Society, and Free Tibet Campaign joined the Tibetan government-in-exile in urging Western MNCs to withdraw from the original pipeline project because it represented a "significant escalation of China's exploitation of oil and gas on the Tibetan plateau and will accelerate China's policy of transferring Chinese settlers into Tibetan areas."[132] At least one multinational company that competed for the development rights to the first pipeline became concerned not only about pressure from international NGOs but also about possible attacks on the pipeline by local ethnic minorities.

As multinationals examine their business prospects in China's west, they are cognizant of the political, social, and environmental landmines that await them. For some, the potential cost far outweighs the potential gain. BP withdrew bids for the west-east pipeline project in 2001 and sold its 2 percent share in PetroChina in 2004 following pressure from environmental groups.[133] Other MNCs, however, have attempted to work with their Chinese counterparts—in some cases dragging them along—to mitigate these costs by addressing them up front. Royal Dutch Shell took such a tack by insisting on conducting its own environmental impact and social impact assessments during the west-east pipeline projects.

International attention has waned since the completion of the first west-east pipeline. The World Bank, which withdrew support for the large-scale construction aspects of the campaign early on, and Global Environment Facility have now provided at least $165 million in funds to rehabilitate the environment in China's western provinces. Projects include a forest management initiative in Guangxi and the development of sustainable cultural tourism in Gansu.[134] The Go West campaign illustrates that international organizations, western MNCs, and activism groups can have a limited positive impact China's major infrastructural projects though lobbying and leading by example. However, international pressure is unlikely to derail such major campaigns, in which national security and politics become intertwined with perceived economic necessities.

China's Eco-cities: Challenges to Cooperation in Sustainable Urbanization

As China moves forward with its plans to urbanize four hundred million people by 2030, the government and the international community have focused on the environmental opportunities and challenges of the hundreds of new cities that will be constructed in the process. Eco-cities have become a popular model for meeting this challenge and have received a great deal of government and media attention both within China and abroad. The most dramatic of the proposed eco-cities have also garnered vast investment from foreign firms and governments. Unfortunately, these large-scale development partnerships have so far not yielded the desired results. Differences in expectations between the international and Chinese partners have undermined these groundbreaking development campaigns.

Dongtan was intended to be the world's first fully-formed eco-city. In 2004, the Shanghai Industrial Investment Corporation (SIIC) hired the consulting firm McKinsey & Company to find an international firm to develop a city on the eastern tip of Chongming Island, an island three-quarters the size of Manhattan in the Yangtze River delta north of Shanghai.[135] The eastern tip of the island is also a wetlands critical to the migratory route of thirty-four endangered bird species and is a breeding ground for Chinese sturgeon.[136] Chongming is also the last undeveloped space near the city of twenty million residents and is referred to as Shanghai's "green lung."

The U.K.–based engineering firm Arup won the bid to develop Dongtan in 2005, which was treated as a milestone in U.K.–Sino relations. Arup was already contracted to engineer several of the showcase buildings for the 2008 Olympic Games, including the National Stadium (popularly known as the Bird's Nest) and wielded significant political capital in Beijing. The deal between Arup and SIIC to develop Dongtan was signed at 10 Downing Street, where both President Hu Jintao and then-prime minister Tony Blair witnessed the event.[137]

The initial plans for Dongtan were commensurate to the political spectacle. The city was to be constructed in phases, the first of which would cost an estimated $2 billion and house fifty thousand people in time for the 2010 Shanghai World Expo.[138] By 2040, the population would reach half a million. Clusters of low-rise buildings housing integrated business and residential space would be interlaced with paths, parks, and waterways. Only zero-noise, zero-emission cars would be permitted, but more importantly, cars would be unnecessary. Although the compact residential areas would be surrounded by farmland, Arup also dreamed up rooftop plots and subterranean "plant-factories," in which crops would be grown on stacked trays under LED-lights to increase output per acreage. SIIC requested that even in its initial phase, concluding in 2010, over 60 percent of Dongtan's power be generated by renewable resources. Solar panels, wind turbines, and innovative biomass converters fed with rice husks, developed by the University of East Anglia, would power the new city. All waste would be recycled and put to productive use as biomass or fertilizer. Arup also invested in new technologies to ensure that fuel conversion would be 80 percent efficient, many times more efficient than today's standard technologies.[139]

International environmental organizations were consulted about the potential effect on the neighboring wetlands, critical to migrating birds. The government-sponsored Sino-Italian Cooperation Program for Environmental Protection began impact assessments in 2004. In keeping with the Ramsar Convention on Wetlands, a three-decade-old international treaty governing the development of wetlands, the Chinese government imposed a 3.5 kilometer buffer zone between Dongtan and the wetlands. Arup's plans accommodated the protected wetland area.[140]

Despite Dongtan's auspicious start, the project was short-lived. First, it became apparent that both Arup and SIIC expected the other party to fund the construction, both hoping to cash in on the positive publicity generated by the project without having to pay for it.[141] Next, the primary backer, Shanghai Communist Party chief Chen Liangyu, was jailed in April 2008 for eighteen years on fraud and corruption charges.[142] Without Arup's knowledge, Chen constructed a hotel and visitors' center on the Dongtan site, neither of which appear in Arup's plans. This suggests Chen had different ideas about what Dongtan would represent. Following Chen's imprisonment, the Dongtan eco-city appears to have become politically unviable and Chen's successors have not adopted the project.

Four years after the initial agreement, Arup has not realized any aspects of its plan for Dongtan. While Arup denies that the project has ended, the firm has backed away from some of the revolutionary design commitments. At a conference in February 2008, Arup's Urban Strategies Leader, Gary Lawrence, said, "While cars are not excluded, they are the least attractive transportation option"—a significant shift from earlier declarations regarding cars in Dongtan.[143] Meanwhile, a bridge connecting Dongtan to Shanghai has been built. Instead of the eco-city, Chongming Island residents now look forward to luxury hotels and weekend homes for wealthy Shanghai residents.[144] Some observers also believe that rather than allow Dongtan to languish as evidence of failed plans, it should be the site of several national pavilions during the 2010 World Expo, certainly opening the door to further unsustainable development after the pavilions are removed.[145]

Although conceptually less grand, the eco-village of Huangbaiyu met with considerably more success before it, too, eventually fell prey to divergent expectations. Huangbaiyu is a small, rural town of approximately four hundred families in Benxi County, Liaoning Province. In 2002, the China–U.S. Center for Sustainable Development, co-chaired by Deng Nan, daughter of former premier Deng Xiaoping, and Bill McDonough, renowned pioneer of environmentally sustainable architecture and founding partner of the design firm William McDonough & Partners, set out to redesign Huangbaiyu as China's first eco-village. The Center used McDonough's firm for the project.[146] Huangbaiyu was to serve as a model for Chinese towns throughout the country. In a lecture given in 2005, McDonough described his goal as "developing the protocols to house 400 million people in twelve years."[147]

In 2005, William McDonough & Partners submitted a design plan to the Benxi Municipality. The plan for Huangbaiyu called for southward-facing tract homes, commercial space, government buildings, and a school packed tightly into the valley and surrounded by agricultural land, obviating the need for automobiles to access either social facilities or their farms.[148] The homes would be constructed of pressed-earth bricks and straw mortar to avoid the pollution and waste generated in the production of traditional bricks. The walls would be thick for insulation and the homes powered by solar panels. Each home would be constructed for approximately $3,500. Hewlett-Packard, BP, and Intel each invested in the project. The Vermeer Manufacturing Company of Iowa donated the press for the earthen bricks.[149]

The project stalled in 2006 after the developer, a local businessman named Dai Xiaolong, constructed the first phase of the project and failed to meet a number of the eco-design standards set out in the initial plan. Only two of the forty-two homes built have been occupied, and, as of 2007, the few residents had no heat and no gas.[150] The intended residents of Huangbaiyu complain that there is insufficient room in each home's plot to raise crops or livestock; the development is too far removed from their original homes; the construction is substandard; the homes are equipped with garages, although there are fewer than ten cars in the village; and that there are no factory jobs, which they claim had been promised to them. There are also no solar panels on the roofs. In the aftermath of the project, it is evident that each of the parties had different expectations for Huangbaiyu and that these expectations were not clearly communicated to the other parties.

The concerns of the American and Chinese partners motivating each to undertake the Huangbaiyu eco-village project were very different. The China–U.S. Center for Sustainable Development set out to create a demonstration village that might have revolutionized Chinese rural village design and positively affected the world's environment. The local partners, however, were more interested in the economic opportunities presented by the eco-village. Without agreement on the goals of the project, disagreements about the specifics were unavoidable.

The Chinese government and a conglomerate of Singaporean companies broke ground on the Sino-Singapore Tianjin Eco-city 150 kilometers (93 miles) east of Beijing on September 28, 2008. The $10 billion project espouses twenty-six "key performance indicators," including that the eco-city not occupy agricultural land, 90 percent of transportation within the city be in the form of "green trips" (on foot, bicycle, or public transportation), and CO_2 emissions per unit of GDP be restricted to 150 tons per $1 billion. However, in some respects, the Tianjin Eco-city is less ecologically ambitious than Dongtan. For instance, construction of the 30-square-kilometer (11.6-square-mile) site will involve desalinating currently uninhabited salt flats and filling in part of Tianjin's harbor with landfill.[151]

Despite concessions to traditional urban development practices, the Tianjin Eco-city may represent progress in China's eco-city campaign. Most importantly, it is a for-profit joint venture funded by the Singaporean conglomerate, lead by the Keppel Group, the Chinese Tianjin TEDA Investment Holding Company, and international investors, including the Qatar Investment Authority. The developers hope to generate investment returns through environmental research and development, service-sector businesses, and tourism. The for-profit nature of the project provides additional motivation to see the project through to success, perhaps creating a new model for China's future eco-cities.[152] Gu Xiaosong and Li Mingjiang, two Chinese academics, published an opinion article in Singapore's *Straits Times* encouraging an analogous collaboration between Singaporean and Chinese companies in the Beibu Bay region in southern China.[153]

The failure of the most ambitious eco-city projects has also led to a preference for smaller collaborative projects between international and Chinese partners on environmentally sustainable urban infrastructure. In these projects, the partners' expectations are easier to define and success is therefore more assured. In 2008, the Swedish International Development Cooperation Agency, the Stockholm Environment Institute, and the Erdos Municipal Government, in Inner Mongolia, completed the construction of 825 apartments in four-

and five-floor multistory buildings each equipped with no-flush, urine diversion toilets and urinals.[154] In 2006, the Urban Sustainability Initiative at the University of California, Berkeley entered into a partnership with the city of Chengdu and Southwest Jiaotong University to redesign Chengdu's public transportation system. By integrating the city's rapid transit, subway, and bus systems, the team hopes to increase use of public transportation in the city to 30 percent of total vehicular transport.[155]

A true eco-city of any size has yet to be realized in China. Dongtan will not be the world's first eco-city; Masdar, in the United Arab Emirates, will likely have that honor. The international community has been excited about the prospect of eco-cities in China, both because China is in urgent need of such developments, and because China's growing economy and authoritarian system appear to make it possible to undertake risky urban development projects. The eco-city projects have centered mostly on environmental engineering technology and knowledge transfer. The failure, to date, of the large-scale projects to produce a model environmentally sustainable urban space illustrates the challenges to international technology transfer to China. The international partners have been interested in how the Chinese political and economic environment seemingly allows for large-scale experimental development projects. The Chinese partners have been motivated by the political and economic bottom line. These aspirational differences have undermined several of the projects and are guiding future eco-city experimentation towards either for-profit ventures or smaller projects.

A Transforming China

In the three decades since the 1972 United Nations Conference on the Human Environment, the world has witnessed a sea change in Chinese environmental protection attitudes and practices. The country has been transformed from one with no environmental protection apparatus, no environmental legal system, and only the smallest environmentally-educated elite, to one in which numerous bureaucracies are engaged in protecting the environment, the legal infrastructure embraces virtually every aspect of the environment, and there is a vast, ongoing environmental education effort throughout the society.

The international community has played an essential role in this transformation. China's participation in international environmental regimes has contributed to the development of a domestic environmental community, environmental laws, and new bureaucratic arrangements to manage environmental protection. These new actors and arrangements, in turn, have provided new opportunities for international environmental cooperation. Over the years, this synergy has produced an enormous range of cooperative ventures involving every sector of Chinese society and level of Chinese government, as well as the full range of international actors.

Moreover, the modernization of China's economy now invites an entirely new level of cooperation, involving innovative policy approaches, advanced technologies, and greater technical expertise. And the country's increasing involvement in international trade regimes holds promise for reinforcing the integration of environmental objectives in China's future economic development.

But the need for a strong enforcement capacity as well as an incentive system for environmental protection remains a significant obstacle to the implementation of many new market-based environmental policies and advanced technologies. While some cooperative ventures have succeeded despite these impediments, many have failed to achieve their full potential. Moving international environmental cooperation forward will depend heavily on the ability of the Chinese leadership to make progress in these two areas of enforcement and incentives. In addition, the continued penchant of China's leaders for large-scale, environmentally degrading development campaigns not only draws into question their commitment to environmental protection but also opens the door to substantial international, and increasingly domestic, criticism of both China and the country's international partners.

Future cooperation on environmental protection between China and the international community holds as many challenges as opportunities. The interest of the international community and proactive actors within China in advancing such collaboration and significantly enhancing China's environmental protection capacity is clear. What remains is for China's leaders to invest the necessary political and financial capital to develop an effective incentive system in which environmental best practices will thrive.

China is not alone in the particular blend of policy measures it has adopted to respond to its environmental challenges. The former states of Eastern Europe, republics of the Soviet Union, and several Asian countries shared many of the economic, political, and institutional challenges to effective environmental protection that China currently faces. Moreover, the boldest policy choices of these countries to protect the environment—to open the door to NGOs and greater public participation, as well as deeper integration into the international community—are the same ones China is now pursuing. In so doing, these countries became vulnerable to far greater challenges to their systems of governance and seismic shifts in the nature of their polities. In chapter 7, we'll consider the implications for China of these lessons from other countries.

CHAPTER SEVEN

LESSONS FROM ABROAD

M any countries face challenges similar to those of China in balancing environmental and economic demands while maintaining social stability. The scale of China's environmental degradation and pollution, however, dwarfs that of most countries. China's economic and political transition further complicates efforts to compare China with other countries and draw useful lessons from their experiences. Nonetheless, there are broad similarities between China's current set of challenges and that confronted by other Asian countries, as well as several countries of the former Eastern Europe and republics of the former Soviet Union. Taken together, these countries reflect the range of China's environmental problems, as well as the political and economic dynamics of China's transition from a totalitarian to an authoritarian regime and a command to a market economy. The recent history and contemporary situation of these countries thus help provide a forecast of potential changes and trends in China's environmental protection efforts.

More than a decade ago, the Eastern Bloc countries and republics of the former Soviet Union confronted the challenge of rapid industrialization and massive environmental degradation within the framework of socialism, much as China has for the past several decades.

Their economies were dominated by highly polluting state-owned enterprises (SOEs); they treated natural resources as free goods; and they paid little attention to energy consumption or pollution control.[1] The leaders pursued large-scale development projects, including dams, river diversions, and agricultural experiments, with devastating environmental consequences. Environmental protection was of little real concern.

Yet in critical ways, China today presents a very different picture from Eastern Europe and the former Soviet Union in the late 1980s and early 1990s. China has moved much further along the path to a market economy and integration into the global economy. The Chinese leadership continues to shed parts of its communist system, privatizing the economy, breaking free of SOEs, developing land tenure laws, pushing toward a free labor and genuine housing market, and in the process, permitting large-scale economic inequalities to emerge. While continuing to cloak its behavior in claims of social justice, the Chinese Communist Party (CCP) has become largely devoid of ideological content, serving primarily as a patronage machine committed to rapid economic development.

In this way, China has begun to resemble more closely the countries of Central and Eastern Europe today, as well as its neighbors to the south and east—the economically free-wheeling but politically constrained authoritarian states of Asia. At various points in their recent history, Korea, Thailand, Malaysia, Indonesia, and the Philippines have shared with China several of the daunting challenges inherent in balancing environmental protection with rapid economic development. In addition, these authoritarian states lacked, and in some cases still lack, the transparency, accountability, and political institutions necessary for effective environmental protection.

In confronting their environmental challenges, these other countries' initial decisions favored redressing environmental degradation through a combination of political and institutional reform rather than by increasing investment in environmental protection or restructuring the economy to encourage economic actors to integrate environmental protection into their development plans. Thus, they began by developing an environmental bureaucracy and legal system. Like China, they later opened the door to greater public participation in environmental protection as a means of both addressing the populace's growing environmental concerns and releasing the broader pent-up pressures for political change. The international community also played an important role in shaping the environmental situation in many of these countries. In the end, this approach affected not only the evolution of the countries' environmental situations but also their broader political economies.

Eastern Europe and the Soviet Union

Rapid industrialization after the Second World War brought a host of environmental problems to Eastern Europe and the former Soviet Union, many of which resemble the challenges facing contemporary China. Into the 1980s, much of the region relied exclusively on coal for its energy; in the German Democratic Republic (GDR) and Czechoslovakia, for example, more than 80 percent of the countries' energy needs were met by coal. As a result, Czechoslovakia produced more sulfur dioxide than any other country in central Europe,[2] with harmful consequences for agricultural productivity, plant life, and human health. Bohemia registered shocking levels of respiratory disease, digestive ailments, heart problems, and birth defects from its coal-based air pollution.[3] East German scientists also acknowledged that the incidence of heart and respiratory diseases as well as cancer were 10 percent to 15 percent higher in highly polluted regions of the country. In addition, mining and coal use contributed to the loss of agricultural land, falling groundwater levels, and increasing rates of water pollution from sulfates, phenols, sulfuric acid, and particulate matter.[4] Importing clean coal technology, such as desulfurization equipment from the West, was viewed as too expensive.[5]

Poland and Hungary also posted frightening statistics with regard to water quality. By the late 1980s, Polish officials believed that only 1 percent of their surface water was safe to drink, and as much as 49 percent was unfit even for industrial use. Moreover, almost half of all major Polish towns had no sewage treatment plants and dumped their wastewater untreated into rivers and lakes.[6] In

Hungary, two-thirds of the sewage water remained biologically un-purified.[7]

The negative impact of development on the environment was compounded by the nature of the political system. Environmental laws were not enforced, managers were not rewarded for environ-mentally sound production but solely the quantity of goods pro-duced, access to information was limited, and the right to organize politically was restricted.[8] In Poland, for example, in 1983, the Council of Ministers cited twenty-seven environmentally endan-gered areas and put into place regulations to prevent the creation of new industries harmful to the environment.[9] Yet there was virtually no enforcement of these regulations. This system of political con-straints and perverse economic incentives produced shocking levels of pollution and related social costs.

First Steps: Enhancing Government Awareness

As in China, the governments of Eastern Europe began to acknowl-edge the challenge of environmental protection during the 1970s and 1980s, particularly in the aftermath of the 1972 United Nations Con-ference on the Human Environment (UNCHE). During this time, many of these countries established environmental protection agen-cies,[10] and officials began to acknowledge publicly the interdepend-ence between economic growth and environmental protection. In East Germany, the mantra became "an efficient economy assures adequate investment funds for environmental protection."[11] Numerous envi-ronmental laws were enacted.[12] By the late 1980s, for example, Poland had passed thirty environmental laws and resolutions; Czechoslovak-ia had adopted fifty-three laws and regulations; and Yugoslavia had is-sued more than three hundred. East Germany, Romania, and Hungary all passed comprehensive state environmental protection laws during the 1970s, and Bulgaria enacted a set of revised environmental man-agement guidelines.[13]

Yet the impact of these efforts was limited. As two analysts have commented, "It was one of the greater paradoxes of the communist period that governments were prolix in legislation aimed at limiting environmental damage, yet this legislation did very little to halt the degradation."[14] Corruption impeded implementation: "Past experience suggests that money voted for environmental protection is often diverted to other purposes by local people's committees and that exemptions to the water pollution laws are often granted on a wholesale basis."[15] The primacy of economic development was also a constraining factor: "Managers were rewarded for fulfilling their plans and severely penalised for not doing so. . . . The result was considerable waste, notably of energy resources, and with it pollution on a massive scale."[16] As in China, too, outdated factory equipment, low fines for polluters, and environmental inspectors who were overruled on economic grounds all contributed to poor implementation.[17]

At the same time, the governments also engaged in efforts—which presaged those of China during the mid-1990s—to raise the profile of environmental protection in their countries. Many countries doubled their investment in environmental protection in their 1986–1990 plans, and environmental impact assessments were enacted. There was recognition in Poland, for example, that environmental degradation was a barrier to further socioeconomic development, and environmental protection was rated as highly as housing, food, and energy in public opinion polls. In Yugoslavia, banks were required to account for environmental demands when granting loans for new projects.[18]

Finally, the governments sponsored official environmental protection organizations devoted to scientific assessment of environmental degradation and public campaigns to clean up the environment. Most often, they were also focused on issues of conservation. For example, in Czechoslovakia during the 1980s, the Slovak Association of Guardians of Nature and the Homeland used youth volunteers to clear up polluted regions and to plant trees.[19] Together with its Czech counterpart, it boasted almost 30,000 individual members in the early 1980s. In Bulgaria, in the early 1980s, the journalists' union and the National Committee for the Protection of Nature jointly agreed to cooperate on environmental protection measures.[20] In the former GDR, by 1986, nearly 60,000 people had joined the officially sponsored Society for Nature and the Environment.[21]

These state-sponsored groups did not, however, develop a broader or more systemic critique of environmental protection. Constraints included poor access to reliable data, severe limits on the activities they could undertake, and limited interactions with foreigners.[22]

East European scientists also began to focus on environmental issues. In Hungary, scientists were among the leaders to initiate environmental protection. They focused their attention on the environment at the 1971 Annual Assembly of the Hungarian Academy of Sciences, and in 1972 held a special conference on the topic.[23] In the mid-1980s, the Polish Academy of Sciences recommended that state investment in environmental protection for the 1986–1990 five-year plan ought to be increased by 6 percent.[24] These scientific and environmental experts were the "most visible and authoritative spokespersons for the environment," forming a community that crossed professional boundaries and included legal experts, scientists, and social scientists who knew each other from their universities or by virtue of their involvement in one of the nascent environmental organizations.[25]

The Next Stage: Environmental Activism

Yet these state-sponsored efforts failed to address the underlying problems—both environmental and political—that plagued the region. What emerged to fill the vacuum were environmental clubs with broad societal representation that responded aggressively to the overwhelming pollution problems.

Non–state-organized environmental activism in Eastern Europe dates as far back as the establishment of the Polish Ecology Club in September 1980.[26] The development of the club was spurred by concern throughout the country about threats to health within heavily polluted areas such as Silesia, and there was broad public support for reviving the long-held Polish tradition of maintaining national parks and nature reserves.[27] Polish scientists, cultural elites, trade union members, and environmentalists banded together to call on the local Kraków government either to close or to modernize several of the major factories in the city's vicinity. With the support of the Kraków mayor, they achieved some success, and by July 1981, the Polish Ecology Club had fourteen branches and twenty thousand members.[28]

In Hungary, as early as the early 1970s, citizens' groups petitioned Budapest concerning air pollution and unbearable noise. In one case, in 1977, citizen pressure resulted in the closure of a polluting factory after children became ill from lead poisoning.[29]

In the GDR, the Protestant Church led the fight for environmental protection. In the 1970s, the church promoted environmental discussion groups and activism among parishioners. According to one estimate, at least several hundred people were involved in such unofficial groups, which held "environmental worship services" in heavily polluted areas.[30] While much of their work was devoted to activities such as tree planting or riding bicycles, they also protested a chemical works plant and sponsored discussions on nuclear power.[31] The Lutheran Church even published a clandestine environmental journal, *Umweltblatter* (Environmental Pages).[32]

The Catalyst: Chernobyl and Its Aftermath

In April 1986, the nuclear disaster at the Chernobyl Nuclear Power Station in the republic of Ukraine provoked a radical change in Soviet politics, with effects that rippled not only through the republics of the Soviet Union but also through the satellite nations of Eastern Europe. The now infamous explosions at Chernobyl on April 26 emitted more radioactive material into the atmosphere than the atomic bombs that leveled Hiroshima and Nagasaki.[33] The radioactive gas and particles dispersed as far as Greece, Yugoslavia, Poland, Sweden, and Germany. The Soviet leadership, however, did not report the accident to the public until two full days after the accident, and even then attempted to minimize the disaster by claiming that "the radiation situation in the power station and the surrounding area is stabilized."[34]

The domestic and international outrage at the way the disaster was managed proved a spur to openness in the Soviet Union and emboldened the populace to challenge the government's policies on other environmental issues. Throughout the Soviet Union, intellectuals, students, and scientists led the drive to establish ecology clubs that pressed officials to address local pollution problems. In the face of massive protests in 1986 against the Siberian River diversion project, which was to provide water to the parched cotton and rice fields of Central Asia, for example, the government canceled the project, which had been decades in the making.[35]

By the late 1980s, environmentalists in the Soviet Union were having a noticeable impact on the path of economic development. Almost two-thirds of the thirty-six projects planned by the Ministry of the Medical and Microbiological Industry—reputed to be a serious polluter—had to be canceled when local groups refused to grant the necessary land.[36] In 1989, more than one thousand factories were shut down or had their operations scaled back as a result of environmental violations.[37] Thus, as Murray Feshbach and Alfred Friendly conclude, the "passage from pollution to politics was an easy one."[38]

Simultaneously, pressures were building in Eastern Europe for both enhanced environmental protection efforts and greater public input into governmental policy making. In Poland, many environmental groups attributed both Chernobyl and problems in the Polish environment to the lack of a public voice in the decision-making process.[39] The media played a crucial role in opening up the political space for public debate and discussion. As East European analyst Christine Zvosec argued at the time, "This is due not to any liberalization in reporting policy, but to the inability of ignoring pollution problems."[40] Environmental problems provoked media criticism of unusual frankness. In Poland and Czechoslovakia, the media referred to the respective environmental situations in each country as an ecological catastrophe or disaster.[41] In Yugoslavia, for example, the press extensively publicized the efforts of environmental experts to prevent the construction of the Tara River Dam, and a Belgrade radio program not only provided information on pollution but also exposed environmental polluters.[42]

The Third Stage: Beyond the Environment

For the governments of the Soviet Union and Eastern Europe, environmental protest appeared, at least initially, as a "relatively safe outlet for expressions of more general discontent."[43] As one Russian environmentalist stated, "Green activities were tolerated because officials did not at first identify them as threats to Communist rule."[44] From the perspective of government officials, properly managed, popular participation in environmental protection could be constructive:

> Criticism should not be superficial or one-sided, but rather sympathetic to the dilemmas facing decision makers. Environmentalists should be willing to seek realistic solutions and to propose alternatives. Apart from criticizing existing government policy and warning about potential hazards, social organizations can also play an important role in increasing the public's awareness of environmental questions. Active cooperation between governmental and nongovernmental organizations is a precondition for effective environmental protection.[45]

But the ecology groups quickly disabused these officials of their belief in the relatively nonthreatening nature of their activities. Activists who began by fighting pollution became leaders in the broader battle for "cultural, economic and political independence."[46] In Latvia, for example, the first "environmental" protests were in fact cultural in nature: In 1984, the activists were devoted to restoring churches and monuments.[47] The Latvian Environmental Protection Club (*Vides Aizsardzibas Klubs*; VAK) organized activities devoted to reinstating the Latvian language, commemorating the Latvian flag, and honoring the Latvians deported by Stalin in 1940.[48] As one Bulgarian activist noted, "Ecological activity was the only permitted form of action. If you acted around human rights or religious freedom you just went to prison. Environmentalism was the only way to express civil disobedience without being arrested."[49] Consequently, VAK served as a point of coalescence for activists of all stripes. In an interview with Jeffrey Glueck, Valdis Abols, a VAK vice president, stated, "Many, maybe even the majority of people who joined us in 1987, were very far from green thinking. They just saw that this was a political force. They could use this for their political ambitions."[50] Similarly, a Slovak activist stated that environmental protection organizations were "the only game in town." This meant that activists interested in other issues, for example assisting the rights of the disabled, joined environmental protection organizations because they were the only nongovernmental organizations (NGOs) legally sanctioned.[51]

Other social organizations incorporated environmental issues into their platforms. In Czechoslovakia, for example, in 1983, Charter 77, an association of human rights activists founded in 1977, published information from a report by the Czechoslovak Academy of Science that had been denied publication by the Czech authorities.[52] Charter 77 often discussed environmental issues in its publications, and in 1985, two environmentalists were sentenced to jail for drawing attention to the deterioration of the forests in Bohemia and publicly criticizing the Czech government's environmental protection efforts.[53] This did not deter the organization; in April 1987, Charter 77 published a full-length treatise on the environment that called for restructuring the economy and elevating the environment to a first priority issue for the government.[54]

In Poland, the labor organization Solidarity also made the environment part of its political platform. In May 1981, for example, Solidarity's Interfactory Workers Committee advanced a resolution calling for work to stop at an extraction area until environmental damage could be addressed.[55] By 1988, there was a Green party in Poland.

The linkage between the environment and broader political issues such as nationalism and anticommunism was often made explicit through opposition to large projects such as nuclear power stations, dams, and river diversions.[56] Severe problems of transboundary pollution and other environmentally related disputes also fostered environmentalism in Eastern Europe. For example, in 1987, Polish students demonstrated against the accidental discharge of heating oil into a tributary of the Oder River by a Czech factory. When the Czech government did not report the incident for several days, the Polish government complained about the lack of information and demanded compensation.[57] Similar conflicts arose between Austria and Hungary. As Miklós Persányi explains,

> A very heated nationwide debate developed over the importation of waste from Austria. An enterprise supported by the local council in Mosonmagyaróvár in western Hungary contracted to dump garbage sent from Graz. The Austrian partner paid with hard currency and promised to provide high technology waste management equipment. Chemists from a local environmental group analyzed the waste and determined that it contained heavy metals and that its pollutants were reaching groundwater. The group informed the public and the authorities, leading the National Authority for Environmental Protection and Nature Conservation to stop the importation. Subsequently, a regulation prohibiting the importation of hazardous wastes was adopted.[58]

Two of the most compelling cases were the conflict over the treaty between Czechoslovakia and Hungary to build the Gabcikovo-Nagymaros Dam on the Danube with construction by Austrian firms and the transboundary air pollution dispute between Romania and Bulgaria.

In the former case, the debate began when leading Hungarian environmentalist Janos Vargha argued in a 1981 article that the dam would "change the hydraulic, physical, chemical, and biological conditions of a nearly 200 kilometer section of the river itself and also that of the surrounding ground water. These changes would be harmful to the drinking water supply, the quality of the river and ground water, agriculture, forests, and fish, as well as the picturesque landscape."[59] By 1984, a grassroots environmental organization, the Danube Committee, had been established to oppose the dam. This organization later grew to encompass other environmental concerns as well as anticommunism, becoming known as the Danube Circle, which was registered as an official organization in 1988 and soon began to work with groups in Austria and other international NGOs. At the same time, Hungarian environmentalists began to protest Hungary's agreement to dispose of toxic waste from Austria.[60] In 1988, forty thousand people demonstrated in Budapest against the construction of the dam on the Danube.[61] One year later, the government of Hungary decided to halt construction of the dam, while the Czechs continued its development. However, both domestic NGOs and international NGOs became active in pressing the government to cease construction. The International Coalition Against Large Dams and the International Rivers Network (both of which have agitated against China's Three Gorges Dam) also pressed international investors and the government to stop the development of the dam.[62]

Even in Bulgaria, one of the most repressive of Eastern European societies, the issue of transboundary pollution awakened an environmental spirit within the populace. In 1987, the Bulgarian town of Ruse recorded dangerously high levels of chlorine pollution, sparking a series of demonstrations that fall. The Bulgarian government was forced to raise the issue with Romanian officials.[63] This became the first real challenge to the Communist Party. The Committee for the Defence of Ruse, which was established to address the issue of the chlorine pollution, later gave rise to the broader Ecoglasnost, which then became a core component of the Union of Democratic Forces.[64] Although the official bilateral negotiations successfully resulted in Romania shutting down more than 80 percent of the factories, environmental activism was unable to emerge under President Nicolae Ceausescu, despite terrible circumstances.[65]

Environmental issues also served as a catalyst for political change in several of the Soviet republics. As D.J. Peterson points out, "To many citizens, the destruction of nature in their homelands epitomized everything that was wrong with Soviet development, the Soviet economy, and the Soviet state itself, and these great injustices against nature were obvious and easy focuses for action. Nature became a medium for social change."[66] In 1989, the Lithuanian greens argued that "besides a lack of pollution control equipment, the republic suffers 'a lack of control over its production and resources' . . . [and] accuse[d] Soviet occupiers of turning the republic into 'a colonial industrial dump site producing goods and services far beyond the needs of its own inhabitants.' "[67] In Georgia, in 1988, popular protest against the Transcaucasus Main Railway laid the foundation for the creation of the Ecology Association under the auspices of the All-

Georgia Rustaveli Society. This became the forerunner of the movement that asserted Georgian independence.[68]

Finally, "there were those for whom environmental groups were merely a vehicle for pursuing the main goal of overthrow of the Communist regime. . . . This was to be especially so in countries where environmental interests were not deeply rooted in the value system of the people, such as Romania."[69] In such cases, these "environmentalists" might do little to enhance environmental protection, electing instead to focus their energies on more politically salient issues.

Romania, for example, had one of the most polluted cities in Eastern Europe, Copsa Mica, where the people were routinely covered in black carbon powder emitted from a local tire factory. Within the town, more than half the almost three thousand people tested showed symptoms of lead poisoning. During 1983–1993, about two thousand people were hospitalized for severe lung and stomach pains or anemia due to the lead poisoning. Ninety-six percent of the children between ages two and fourteen had chronic bronchitis and respiratory problems.[70] Yet, the local people were so dependent on the factory for their livelihood, they perceived the pollution as "part of reality"[71] and were reluctant to agitate. Moreover, despite promises from the United Nations that it would provide financial support for improving the situation, Romanian environmental NGOs, such as the Ecological Movement of Romania, made no push for change. They were more concerned with blocking Ceausescu in his efforts to turn the Danube delta into agricultural land plots because this issue was directly linked to the dictator's legacy.[72]

Postscript: Two Decades Down the Road

The political and economic transition of Eastern Europe and the former Soviet Union has produced some environmental success stories. In some of the wealthier countries, such as the Czech Republic, Poland, and Hungary for example, a combination of economic reform, public pressure, and environmental activism has produced significant declines in air, water, and soil pollution.[73] These countries have greater resources to invest in cleaner, more efficient technologies, and have moved away from the pollution-intensive industrial practices of their communist past toward more efficient production methods.[74]

Significantly, the desire of many of these countries to join the European Union (EU), which imposes stringent environmental standards for prospective members, is forcing the governments to ratchet up significantly their environmental protection efforts. Poland, for example, has achieved some notable progress in its environmental record driven in part by EU mandates, taking tough steps to ban the import of waste from other countries, to increase the fees for environmental pollution, and to experiment with market-oriented measures such as tradable permits. In Hungary, some believe that the government's desire to accede to the EU, rather than the actions of Hungary's flourishing environmental movement, is the key to understanding the country's efforts to improve its environmental record.[75]

Yet in other countries in the region, the promise of a greener future heralded by the rise of environmental activists and NGOs and the downfall of communism has yet to produce significant improvement in the environment. There are several reasons for this. Primary among them is the continued economic straits in which many countries find themselves. The case of Bulgaria, for example, suggests that the government's perceived ability to invest in environmental protection has varied according to its overall economic situation; thus during the mid-1990s, as the economy continued to deteriorate, Bulgaria's investment in environmental protection dropped from 1.3 percent of gross domestic product (GDP) in 1993 to 0.9 percent in 1995. Slovenia similarly witnessed an overall economic decline and corresponding decrease in investment in environmental protection.[76]

Even as the countries of east and central Europe continue to negotiate the legacy of their communist years such as aging nuclear facilities and highly polluting heavy industrial factories, rapid economic growth has provided an unsettling array of new environmental problems similar to those of China: growing air pollution from the increasing number of cars on the roads; increasing contamination of the water supply from new pollutants, such as detergents; and substantial increase in problems of waste management from plastic packaging.[77] In many of these countries, environmental NGOs have had difficulty transitioning from broader social activism to the nuts and bolts of shaping environmental policy to resolve such new challenges.

Political considerations, too, often constrain the opportunities for these NGOs. Senior Russian officials, for example, have attempted to prevent environmentalists from reporting on ecological damage by Russia's military by framing the issue of nuclear waste as a security issue and accusing the activists of treason. Former Russian president Vladimir Putin, with support from other Russian officials, also successfully blocked a national referendum that garnered more than two million signatures opposing the import of nuclear waste, a program that would earn Russia more than $20 billion over ten years.[78] Indeed, the Russian government's evident reluctance to respect the role of popular involvement in environmental affairs has led some environmental activists to link environmental protection with democracy once again: "[The referendum] is not just a fight against nuclear waste import, but a fight for establishing democracy and strong civil society in Russia."[79]

With few exceptions, too, the environmental protection agencies throughout the central and east European states remain weak, particularly in the face of continued demands to raise the population's standard of living. In the case of Russia, President Putin dissolved Russia's State Committee on the Environment in 2000, further hampering the work of Russia's environmentalists, particularly since environmental oversight was then passed to the Natural Resources Ministry, the primary agency in charge of mining, oil exploration, and timber extraction.

Finally, many environmental NGOs remain elite-oriented organizations with stronger ties to international funding institutions than to their domestic constituents. Grassroots organizations, in contrast, may be more effective in reaching their constituents but often lack the funds or organizational skills to sustain them over the long term.

Asia Pacific: From Economic Miracle
to Environmental Catastrophe

At first glance, the Asia Pacific countries appear to have little in common with those of Eastern Europe and the former Soviet Union. From the 1980s until the onset of the Asian financial crisis in the late 1990s, the Asia Pacific region enjoyed unparalleled economic growth. Economies grew at unheard of rates, producing unprecedented levels of affluence throughout the region.

Yet this rapid development also produced an environmental disaster that was largely ignored in the planning calculus of the region's leaders. Like the countries of Eastern Europe and the former Soviet republics, the Asia Pacific region as a whole suffered from disregard for environmental protection, weak environmental protection institutions, and little opportunity for public participation. Moreover, like China, the Asia Pacific region also suffers the environmental burdens of growing automobile use, urbanization, and migration, among other concerns.

Rapid economic growth in the Asia Pacific has exerted a number of negative environmental impacts. Water pollution is the chief problem. Factories dump their untreated domestic waste directly into streams, rivers, and coastal waters. Throughout Southeast Asia, denuded uplands have contributed to devastating cycles of flooding and drought. Agricultural runoff, untreated domestic sewage, and industrial waste also degrade ground, surface, and coastal waters. Some estimates indicate that in the Philippines, Indonesia, Vietnam, and Thailand, CO_2 emissions are growing two to ten times faster than the underlying economies. In metro Manila, more than half of city residents have no direct access to water supplies due to underdeveloped infrastructure, while less than 4 percent of the metro population has access to the sewer network.[80] Poor water quality and water scarcity have threatened both the health of the region's populace and its continued economic development. In the Java Sea, increasing levels of waste, including toxic waste from industrial and processing activities, are causing declining fish stocks and increased morbidity among the human population from the spread of infectious diseases. One study of thirty-four different fish species in the

Java Sea found elevated mercury concentrations in the majority of the samples taken from the coasts of Cambodia, Indonesia, Malaysia, and Thailand.[81] In July 2008, a cholera outbreak that spread through contaminated drinking water killed 172 people in Indonesia's Papua Province.[82]

Even in such wealthy nations as Korea and Taiwan, industrialization threatens water quality. In Taiwan, high levels of cadmium and copper have contaminated several major waterways used for drinking, aquaculture, and agriculture.[83] In Korea, untreated industrial waste has polluted several primary sources of drinking water.[84] While Japan has successfully reduced levels of mercury and arsenic in its coastal waters, the development of coastal resorts and golf courses has devastated fish stocks. Between 1988 and 2003, Japan's capture of marine fish declined from 12.5 million tons to 6 million tons.[85] Overall, degraded water resources hamper continued economic growth throughout the region through increased morbidity and mortality rates, increased costs to industry, constrained supplies to agriculture, and decreased value of freshwater and coastal fisheries.

However, as in China, the most visible sign of environmental pollution in Asia may be the poor air quality. The pollution generated by automobiles, coal and oil use, and inefficiencies in the supply and distribution of energy have led to significant health and economic problems for the region. Air pollution has been growing two to three times faster than the economy, and the death toll from air pollution in Asia is alarmingly high. Fine particulates in Bangkok's air exceed World Health Organization limits by 250 percent. One study conducted in 2006 found that in highly polluted areas of Bangkok, symptoms of respiratory disease and decreased lung functions are prevalent among children between the ages of ten and fifteen.[86] In Manila, air pollution is responsible for an estimated five thousand deaths annually.[87]

These problems are compounded by increasing population, migration, and urbanization in many of these countries. By 2015, it is estimated that almost two billion people, or more than half of the entire population of Asia, will live in cities.[88] By this time, it is projected that 15 of the world's 23 megacities will be in Asia.[89] The infrastructure necessary to meet basic environmental, population, energy, and sanitation needs such as sewage systems, housing, plumbing, power, and transportation is lagging far behind this growth.

The rapid and devastating manner in which the Asian Pacific countries have degraded their forest resources has also contributed to cycles of drought and flooding, soil erosion, and climate change. Many countries have derived a significant portion of their wealth from logging. Domestic needs for agricultural land and firewood for fuel are partly responsible for this deforestation. But as in China, the substantial income derived from wood-related products is the driving force behind much of the region's loss of forest cover. The process of economic development has also contributed to the loss of valuable arable and forested land. In Thailand, for example, Thai developers have turned fertile land over to developers of golf courses, resorts, and industry. Forested land has decreased from 53 percent of the total land area in 1961 to a mere 28.4 percent in 2005.[90] In the Philippines, forested land similarly declined by almost 50 percent during 1969 to 1993, transforming the Philippines from a major world exporter of wood in the 1980s to an importer by the 1990s.[91] Today, the country remains a net importer of timber, while forest coverage has continued to decline from 35.5 percent in 1990 to 24 percent in 2005.[92]

In addition to its large wood exporters, the Asia Pacific region is home to some of the most significant consumers of timber and wood products. While Japan maintains an approximate 70 percent forest coverage and strictly regulates domestic timber-cutting, it is the third largest importer of softwood and hardwood in the world, after China and Finland.[93] Korea and Taiwan are also significant importers; South Korea's imports more than tripled between 1994 and 2003, while Taiwan now imports over 95 percent of raw materials used for its wood-based products.

The Politics of Resource Exploitation

Despite growing economic affluence and the simultaneous decline in environmental health, political leaders in the Asia Pacific have been slow to rise to the challenge of environmental protection.

Chief among the impediments to more effective environmental protection is the close financial, friendship, and often familial connection among elites responsible for environmental protection and those in the business communities. The importance of these ties is enhanced by weak legal infrastructures, especially in the economically less advanced Asian states.

In Malaysia, for example, leaders traditionally have held the right to allocate logging concessions to their political supporters. Despite measures to improve the situation, international NGOs, such as Friends of the Earth and Greenpeace, have stated that corruption is undermining these initiatives, noting that the political structure is closely intertwined with vested interests.[94] In Indonesia in 2003, experts blamed illegal logging for floods that caused the death of more than 100 people. The minister of environment stated at the time, "It is difficult to combat illegal logging because we must face financial backers and their shameless protectors both from the Indonesian armed forces and police and other government agencies."[95] This same pattern emerged in the Philippines, where loggers often bribed forest inspectors in order to log the timber illegally; in the Philippines, the illegal timber trade is valued at four times that of the legal trade.[96]

Weak environmental agencies also are a central problem for implementing successful environmental policies in virtually every Asia Pacific country. In part, this is because states typically established their environmental protection agencies later in the overall development of their bureaucracies or as spin-offs from other ministries whose primary commitment was not to environmental protection. Malaysia still does not have an independent environment agency; rather it is lumped together with scientific issues in a Science, Technology, and Environment Ministry. Typically, these environmental agencies are plagued with low levels of funding, poorly trained staff, inadequate equipment and technology, and mandates that overlap or conflict with those of other, more powerful agencies. In Thailand, for example, there are "about twenty government agencies with responsibilities related to the problems of water pollution, . . . many [of these] have made no commitment to enforce environmental regulations."[97]

Moreover, while environmental protection agencies may have regulatory power, most have no mandate to influence sectorwide development paths that are responsible for environmental degradation, such as energy or transportation. In Japan, the Environment Agency is generally considered among the most ineffective of all the government organizations. In 1993, for instance, when that agency attempted to advance a new Environmental Basic Law, the law was substantially diminished in scope by the resistance of various business and government officials, who were concerned that the law would elevate the status of the Environment Agency and hinder Japanese economic development.[98] In Korea, too, the Ministry of Environment did not assume control over monitoring tap water quality from the Ministry of Health and Social Affairs and the Construction Ministry until 1994, after the country experienced a high level of contamination at several key sources of drinking water. However, as the ministry had only two or three employees who possessed the qualifications to be classified as professional technicians, it turned over much of the management responsibility to the private sector.[99]

Even when national elites have supported stronger environmental protection efforts, regional authorities have often undermined them. In Malaysia, for example, regional authorities who received revenues from timber royalties have hampered the efforts of the national government to curtail illegal logging. Moreover, each state has autonomy over its forests and is responsible for issuing its own forestry ordinances, for zoning forest areas, and for instituting the mechanisms to enforce the laws. Yet in one heavily logged area—Sarawak—during the mid-1990s, there was only one forestry department official.

The reluctance of Asia Pacific leaders to take strong action by increasing investment in environmental protection, raising fees for polluters, or strengthening enforcement has left gaping holes in environmental protection efforts throughout the region. What has emerged to fill this gap in each country—with or without the active encouragement of the government—has been a hybrid of environmental protection efforts led by NGOs, the media, individual localities, and business leaders. This amalgam of approaches parallels that of China.

In a few cases, as in China, individual regions have led the national governments in environmental protection efforts due to citizen interest or especially motivated local elites. In Japan, for instance, Kawasaki City approved a "basic environmental plan" that was more stringent than the national government's plan to improve air, water, and soil quality and to enhance energy efficiency in its urban heating. In Minimata, where mercury poisoning in the 1960s affected people in areas around Minamata Bay and resulted in the birth of environmental activism in Japan, the municipal government has now transformed the region into a model environmental area. It established an extensive recycling program in which residents separate their household garbage into twenty-three categories, which is further refined into eighty-four types. In 1999, about five thousand people representing corporations and local governments visited Minimata to learn from the city's experience.[100]

In some of the wealthier, more industrially advanced countries of Asia, businesses are playing an active role in advancing environmental protection. In Japan, for example, Sony established a Green Partner program in 2001, which requires its suppliers to commit to a specific set of environmental standards in procuring materials for the company's global operations. Since 2003, Sony has mandated that all new suppliers join the program, while existing Green Partners must be recertified every two years.[101] Sony's Green Partner program complies with the international environmental standards outlined in ISO 14001.

Pushing the Boundaries: The NGO Sector

Throughout the region, however, one of the most potent forces for environmental protection has been NGOs. Along with the media and international NGOs, domestic NGOs have played a crucial role in raising the profile of environmental issues both among government elites and within the general populace. They transmit information, educate, monitor the implementation of laws, and challenge official findings. Often they provide important technical expertise, contributing to both the identification and the solution of a problem.

Once unleashed, governments have found NGOs a difficult force to contain. Frequently they go beyond the mandate of the central

government, challenging not only local actors but also central officials. In some cases, they have become enmeshed in broader political movements, providing cover for democracy and human rights
activists.

Indonesia, Malaysia, and Vietnam are evidence of the complex relationship between government and NGO activity. To a degree, governments in these countries have recognized the importance of NGOs in
environmental protection and call on them to increase public awareness of environmental issues. Indonesia's Environmental Management Law, for example, stipulates that environmental protection
"constitutes a community interest, . . . which can be channelled
by people individually, environmental organisations, such as non-
goverment organizations, traditional community groups, and others
for maintaining and increasing environmental supportive and carry-
ing capacity, which becomes a mainstay of sustainable development."[102] In 2003 the Vietnamese deputy prime minister Vu Khoan
praised environmental NGOs, stating, "Vietnam will continue to create favourable conditions, including improving the legal environment
for NGOs' operation in Vietnam."[103] Malaysia's first Minister of the
Environment Tan Sri Ong Kee Hui, moreover, credited Malaysian
NGOs with influencing the country's environmental movement.[104]

At the same time, watchdog organizations including both the
press and NGOs are carefully monitored and intimidated by authorities, with force when deemed necessary. In mid-September 2009, fifteen leaders of four indigenous communities in the Malaysian state
of Sarawak were detained after sending the chief minister of the state
a memorandum protesting two dams being built in the region. The
memo stated that the dams were being built without the consent of
the local communities. The fifteen leaders were released on bail for
3,000 Malaysian ringgits (about $866) and summoned to appear in
court.[105] One local newspaper reported that the operation of one of
the dams would result in the relocation of one thousand Penan people and twenty Kenyah families, while destroying their lands, crops
and burial sites.[106]

In May 2009, in Indonesia's North Sulawesi province, authorities
reportedly forced the shutdown of a meeting of a coalition of farmers and environmental activists in the capital city of Manado. Police

not only arrested fishermen and activists during the time of the meeting but also intervened in the planning of the meeting by pressuring the owners of the meeting venues to cancel reservations made with the Manado Alliance.[107]

In Vietnam, in May 2008, the government shut down the biweekly publication *Du Lich* (Tourism) for three months and fired the paper's editor for running two articles that voiced criticism of China's increasing influence in Vietnam. The two stories at the center of the controversy were about the Nam Quan Border Gate and three archipelagos in the South China Sea, where China pushed to expand its territorial claims. The paper had also written about the development of bauxite mines in Vietnam's Central Highlands, which attracted investment from Chinese companies such as the Aluminum Corporation of China Limited (Chalco).[108] Despite the potential threat of government intervention, these NGOs have remained vocal through their partnerships with other domestic NGOs. In both the Sarawak and Manado cases, other NGOs stepped in to protest the government interventions. In Sarawak, the Bruno Manser Fund circulated a letter of petition asking authorities to drop all charges against the indigenous leaders and to apologize for the arrests. In North Sulawesi, the group Sarekat Hijau Indonesia published a letter it submitted to the Indonesian chief of police, condemning the "police outrageous action in Manado," and voicing "concerns and protest against any undemocratic actions."[109]

In the Philippines, Thailand, and Korea, NGOs have extended themselves well beyond the boundaries of environmental issues and have been frequent and vocal opponents of state policy. During periods of military or authoritarian rule in each of these countries, environmental issues were closely entwined with broader political protest movements.

In Thailand during 1974–1975, a student opposition movement protested the government's decision to grant valuable, illegal mining concessions to the Thailand Exploration and Mining Corporation (TEMCO). It was the first time that the authority of the military government had been so challenged. Eventually, the students won, the government rescinded the concessions, and environmental groups blossomed throughout the country.[110] Over time, NGOs have become an accepted part of the Thai decision-making process, aided by several factors. As the Thai middle class grew during the 1980s, their concern over environmental degradation increased, the military government opened the space for popular participation on environmental issues, and the international community stepped in with substantial financial and organizational assistance.[111] Thai NGOs, for example, worked with the Electric Authority to reconfigure the Pak Mun hydropower project to minimize the number of people who would need to be relocated due to flooding. This process was facilitated because the government fully expected that its plans would undergo public review before the project was initiated.[112]

In the Philippines and South Korea, environmentalism became even more closely linked to calls for democracy. Under the rule of authoritarian dictator Ferdinand Marcos during the early 1970s, environmental protests in the Philippines were closely integrated into the broader struggle for democracy. The democratic movement shaped the agenda of the environmental movement by highlighting the link between environmental degradation and authoritarianism and pointing out the abuses that occurred from the "exclusion of public participation in development planning, the concentration of resources in a few hands, and the intolerance to alternative development strategies fostered under undemocratic political and economic structures."[113]

By the time Corazon Aquino assumed power in 1986, NGOs had become a strong, independent force, in large part because international donors were channeling aid through the NGOs rather than through a government that was perceived as corrupt and inefficient.[114] In 1997, the government halted construction of a coal-fired power plant outside Manila, largely due to political pressure by the environmental NGO Crusade for Sustainable Development. The group proved that the power company and local officials had colluded to conceal public opposition to the project and that there had been numerous environmental violations.[115]

In South Korea, democracy activists often used environmental movements for political cover; throughout the 1970s, environmental protection was one of the few issues over which the military regime permitted public protests.[116] At the same time, the environmental movement learned from the democracy movement, adopting its strategies of protest and confrontation.[117]

As in the Philippines, as South Korea began the transition to a democracy in 1987–1988, the environmental movement shifted its tactics from active confrontation to peaceful action, putting a priority on "creating a mass base, acquiring expertise . . . and [seeking] mass media attention and public sympathy."[118] In 2000, Green Korea United, one of the largest environmental organizations in Korea, filed a lawsuit against the government via one hundred children throughout the country, alleging that the government had permitted the quality of life to deteriorate with its "reckless and unruly urban development."[119] Green Korea United also launched a successful campaign to prevent Taiwan from shipping its nuclear waste to North Korea.[120]

Thus, NGOs have sometimes been a powerful force in setting the environmental agenda in Asian countries. Yet many governments remain wary of NGOs and limit their activities through various restrictions and requirements. Some of this wariness stems from the link that has emerged between environmental activism and broader issues of social change. According to one editorial in a Malaysian newspaper, this link has two negative consequences. First, it suggests that environmental NGOs are remiss in not focusing on their core issues such as the "illegal infrastructure encroachment in national parks and invasion of watershed areas."[121] Second, and undoubtedly of greater concern, is the belief that environmental NGOs may use their base of public support to agitate for human rights. As the editorial noted,

> It is not an exaggeration to say that pure environmental movements today have become intertwined. In fact they could even be described as being a prisoner of the 1990s global spread of concern for human rights. This variation was born out of Europe and has become very effective, particularly in promoting democracy in developing countries. . . . It may, therefore, be time to reconsider the perception of NGO groups so that the entire community is not discredited by human rights groups that disguise themselves as environmental NGOs. In this way the legal and technical matters are

not confused by sentiment or ideology that are western-based rather than relevant and home grown.[122]

In wealthier Asian nations, such as Japan and Taiwan, environmental activism has progressed along two distinct paths, much like in the United States. First, are the NGOs concerned primarily with local or "not in my backyard" issues, such as polluting enterprises, incinerators, or nuclear power plants. Such groups might utilize traditional rituals, religion, and folk festivals to agitate for change. Taiwanese activists, for example, organized a parade in opposition to China Petrochemical Plant, including martial arts performing groups with real weapons; their performances were threatening enough to cause one thousand riot police to back down.[123]

A second, sizable element of the environmental movement in Taiwan is devoted to global environmental issues. Because the movement has been advanced largely by intellectuals trained in the United States, its focus has mirrored that of the West, emphasizing global issues such as deforestation, nuclear power, the ozone layer, and climate change.[124]

In Japan, the vast majority of Japanese NGOs are locally based; only 10 percent consider themselves national organizations.[125] Their primary focus is nature protection, and secondarily global environmental protection and pollution. They direct the majority of their energy toward recycling, antipollution campaigns, and organic food and other cooperatives.[126]

The political structure in Japan is not conducive to a flourishing NGO community. For example, gaining tax-exempt status requires either capital assets of about $2.5 million or a vast membership. (The number of members needed is determined by the ministry with which the NGO is affiliated.)[127] In addition, NGOs rely heavily on government funds, especially from the Environment Agency, which during the mid-1990s, was criticized for disbursing money to "industry affiliates and quasi-governmental organizations" rather than genuine environmental NGOs.[128] Finally, NGOs have few entry points into the Japanese political structure; there are no provisions, for example, for public participation in environmental policy making or implementation. Environmental litigation is also rare because the scope of activities that may be challenged by environmental activists is narrow, and the highest court tends to support the government.[129]

Despite the decades-long history of environmental NGO activity throughout the region, many NGOs face overwhelming difficulties. In Japan, the Philippines, and Thailand, NGOs rely heavily on external funding: in Thailand, many NGOs receive as much as 80 percent to 90 percent of their financing from overseas supporters.[130] And in several Asian countries, the media is still controlled to a large extent by the government, which limits access to information.

Government and business have also co-opted many Asian NGOs. In Thailand, for example, while grassroots NGOs still protest dam construction, mining, and urbanization, big business has fostered a "cooperative" approach toward environmental protection pursuing green technology and beautification campaigns.[131] They thereby escape public censure and, to a large extent, neutralize potential criticism from environmental activists.

Nonetheless, environmental NGOs have pushed the envelope of environmental protection throughout the Asia Pacific region, challenging central government plans and, in some cases, mobilizing the populace for local environmental protection concerns. While restricted in activity—whether for economic or political reasons—they nonetheless provide one model for China's future environmental protection efforts.

Lessons for China

Throughout the Asia Pacific region, Eastern Europe, and the Soviet Union, during the 1980s, the tale of environmental protection is a relatively straightforward one. Senior government officials placed a premium on economic development, believing that it held the key to social stability. The environmental consequences of this relentless drive to develop, however, inevitably began to damage public health, the standard of living, and society's overall well-being.

The leaders' initial response to their environmental challenges is a political one: to develop an environmental protection apparatus with a central agency (often with regional or local bureaus); to promulgate an array of laws; and to open a degree of political space for citizen involvement. Two decades later, in countries that have prospered economically such as Japan, Korea, Poland, Hungary, and the Czech Republic, government leaders are enabling these environmental bureaucracies, grassroots efforts, and legal infrastructures to fulfill their missions by devoting greater resources to environmental protection and supporting the legitimacy of environmental actors. In the central European states, international pressure from the EU also has been a critical factor in energizing the governments' commitment to environmental protection.

Still, the majority of governments in Asia, central Europe, and Russia remain focused overwhelmingly on economic development to the near exclusion of environmental protection. They avoid the more difficult choices—to invest substantially in environmental protection, to assess heavy fines for polluting enterprises and other environmental malpractice, and to raise the prices for natural resources—fearing that such policies will jeopardize economic growth. Their integration into the international economy is a mixed blessing, bringing both international environmental assistance and access to better environmental technologies from trade and foreign investment but also the potential for more rapid exploitation of their natural resources and import of others' polluting industries and waste. NGOs flourish in some countries, but their efforts often are hampered by legal and illegal means. Even in wealthy democratic nations like Taiwan and Japan, the role of environmental NGOs has been effectively circumscribed by political considerations.

Compared to their counterparts in the United States and Europe, Asian NGOs and media have been less well institutionalized. They often depend on financing from governments and multilateral development banks, considerably weakening their autonomy.[132] In addition, in East Asia, there has not been a "strong participatory culture" or a "well-developed charitable ethic"[133] to support a more proactive environmental movement. In the countries of Eastern Europe and the former republics of the Soviet Union, especially Russia, too, NGOs have encountered significant political roadblocks in attempting to continue their environmental activism. And when governments feel threatened by environmental activism, such as in Russia or Malaysia, for example, they may resort to accusing environmental NGOs and activists of acting against the best interests of the state.

The experience of these countries reinforces much of China's story to date and is suggestive of both future challenges and opportunities in China's environmental protection effort. As we have already seen, economic development has provided the wherewithal for a few regions within China to begin to respond more aggressively to their environmental challenges: investing greater resources, empowering local environmental officials, and attracting environmentally sound foreign investment. The demands for accession to international regimes such as the European Union accelerate a commitment to environmental protection, suggesting that China's accession to the World Trade Organization may, in a more limited fashion, produce similar results.

Still as the majority of countries continue to struggle economically, their environmental institutions remain weak, their willingness to enforce laws and insist on environmentally sound foreign investment remains poor, and their tolerance for wide-ranging, fully independent environmental activity remains limited. Much of China seems to be on this environmental trajectory.

Broader Political Change and the Environmental Factor

Beyond the consequences for the environment, however, the path elected by these countries to respond to environmental degradation and pollution has had enormous consequences for the broader political economies of the countries. In Eastern Europe, especially in Bulgaria, Poland, Hungary, and Czechoslovakia, environmental groups and activists were key players in the downfall of communist regimes.

Green movements throughout Eastern Europe shared several features. They were rooted in the intelligentsia (writers, academics, scientists, and other professionals) and the younger generation, especially college students.[134] They also boasted prominent intellectual leaders who were interested both in political change and environmental reform. For example, Alexander Dubcek—who had led Czechoslovakia during the 1968 Prague Spring, which brought six months of political openness in the country before Soviet troops invaded—was a forester. In Armenia, one of the first environmental protests was led by 350 intellectuals, such as the writer Zori Balayan, who petitioned general secretary Mikhail Gorbachev to address the devastating air pollution problem in Yerevan, the capital.[135] Yury Shcherbak, a famous cardiologist-writer, also served as the head of Zelyonny Svit (Green World), a NGO organization in Ukraine.[136] He later became Ukraine's environmental affairs minister.

Environmental movements also served as a "school of independence for an infant civil society." Glueck has termed this a "shelter function"—these movements or organizations provided cover for grievance sharing and civil association.[137] As Glueck eloquently states,

> The environmental appeal drew on deep chords of feeling: a sense of assaulted nationhood, moral pollution, and social helplessness. Environmental degradation occurred under the direction of bureaucracies unaccountable to local communities; it occurred amidst a deepening sense of social despair; and it occurred without freedom of information, without public review, and without the secure right of remonstration. These frustrations, along with the infant associations of civil society, blossomed within the politics of ecology.[138]

He goes on to note,

> Green campaigns and organizations were meeting grounds for liberally-minded individuals, breeding grounds for activist citizens and alternative elites, and training grounds in organization and tactics. They were an education in self-initiative for people long reconciled to waiting for state directives and in cooperation for people used to distrusting their neighbors. Utilizing the resource of their being "apolitical," they undertook activities that challenged the State's control over communication and human mobilization.[139]

Glueck also points out the "values function" performed by environmental movements; that is, especially among youth and the intelligentsia, environmentalism provided a new world view that was devoted to a more "harmonious, post-materialist, and caring politics—one directly opposite the consumerist and self-directed values promoted by neo-totalitarian life."[140] Glueck cites the Hungarian campaign against the Danube dam as emblematic of this function. The dam brought together a wide range of value-oriented concerns: environmentalism (the dam would destroy an irreplaceable ecosystem, and Hungary's largest underground water source would lose its self-cleansing capacity and eventually dry up); nationalism (the dam would mean the destruction of a historic national site); and democratization (the dam represented an opportunity to mobilize the public in criticism of the Communist Party).[141]

In some cases, then, transboundary pollution issues or large, unpopular government projects served to raise the flags of both environmentalism and nationalism, thereby forging broad societal consensus against both the project and the ruling government. In otherwise totalitarian states, environmental issues provided a state-approved outlet for public discontent. Environmental degradation and other political considerations fueled awareness and political activism, environmental NGOs became the lightning rods through which popular social and political discontent was channeled. The result was not necessarily an improvement in the state of the environment but, in several cases, the reconfiguration of the entire system of governance.

In the Asia Pacific region, environmental activists also became closely linked with democracy activists and agitated for broader political reform. In these instances, environmental issues did not serve as a catalyst for regime change but did permanently enlarge the political space for social action.

Political Change and the Environment in China

Whether NGOs in China will play a role similar to those of Eastern Europe, the former Soviet Union, and Asia in advancing broader political change remains an open question. In some of the former republics of the Soviet Union and countries of Eastern Europe, forces for political change were galvanized around a single environmental issue, like the Danube dam in Hungary or the Chernobyl nuclear plant in Russia and Ukraine. In addition, disparate religious, human rights, labor, and environmental interests were able to coalesce around political change because they had developed means of communication and a formal organizational structure with clear goals and committed leaders. At least three necessary factors were present in these other countries that enabled NGOs to engage in advancing broader political reform: (1) an ability to tap into existing broader societal discontent; (2) links with other types of NGOs and an ability to communicate within the NGO community; and (3) coalescence around a particular environmental challenge, often involving governmental corruption or lack of transparency.

In China, societal discontent is evident everywhere. It is expressed in forms as diverse as labor unrest, mounting peasant protest, and increased ethnic violence. As the government has diminished its role in guiding the economy, its role in managing society has decreased as well. For this reason, it retains few levers to shape public opinion and action, with the exception of suppression or media and Internet censorship. It is this discontent, if mobilized throughout the country and more specifically directed at the Communist Party, that Chinese authorities fear.

Chinese leaders are especially wary of the potential for religious organizations to become conduits for broader social discontent. In general, the Chinese government has permitted religion to flourish during the past two decades. However, the reform process is now fostering conditions for the politicization of religious organizations. The current political and economic uncertainty, the public perception of a lack of virtue and integrity among Chinese officials, and the role of religious groups in meeting social welfare needs such as education and medical care, all suggest that religious organizations might become a vehicle through which Chinese society is mobilized for political change. Moreover, China's pre-1949 history is replete with examples of challenges to political authority by religious movements and secret societies. Hence, Beijing's full-scale attack against practitioners of Falun Gong, the spiritual and exercise movement, after ten thousand adherents gathered around the leadership compound Zhongnanhai in Beijing in April 1999.

The widespread discontent in China's countryside is another worry for the Party leaders. In Hunan Province in January 1999, for example, more than ten thousand peasants, organized by a two-year-old illegal organization of local farmers (Volunteers for Publicity of Policies and Regulations) rallied to protest excessive taxes and the corruption of local CCP officials. They were met by hundreds of police and a riot squad from the provincial capital. The leaders of the organization fled to Beijing to try to appeal to the central party leadership, where they were later arrested.[142]

Cities, especially in China's northeastern rustbelt, have also become sites for frequent protests. In March 2002, between thirty to fifty thousand oil workers in Daching protested the giant oil company PetroChina's failure to fulfill its pension obligations to its retired workers. In another city in Liaoning Province, Liaoyang, labor leaders organized tens of thousands of Chinese workers and pensioners in March 2002 to protest low retirement pay. Although the organizers of the protests were quickly arrested—indeed swift reprisals are the rule whenever a protest appears to be well planned and organized—the workers continued to demonstrate, calling for their leaders' release.

Such protests are not likely to abate in the foreseeable future, as Beijing continues to have difficulty in meeting the social demands of its citizens.

Based on the experience of other countries, what would it take for China's nascent environmental movement to become a real political force, tapping into this broader societal discontent? Three elements would be essential: (1) a unifying aspiration, (2) a means of communicating, and (3) an issue or event that would serve as a catalyst for action.

First, there would need to be a broad goal that unifies disparate interests. The Charter 08 movement that began in December 2008, for example, accomplished this goal in an important way. The Charter 08 manifesto, which first appeared online on December 10, 2008, calls for the fundamental reform of China's political framework, as well as amendments to the constitution to strengthen the protection of civil rights in China. The list of demands in Charter 08 include the separation of powers and an independent judiciary, direct elections open to multiple political parties, freedoms of religion, assembly and expression, the environmental protection, protection of private property, and social security.

Upon publication, Charter 08 carried 303 signatures of support from political dissidents, midlevel government officials, and Communist Party academics. As the Charter spread over the Internet over the next month or so, it gained broader support, receiving some 8,100 signatories by the end of January 2009. Though initial support for the Charter came from China's political and academic elite, it later drew together support from a diversity of backgrounds, including students, peasants, journalists and lawyers.

The Chinese leadership learned about Charter 08 prior to its release. Two days before the document was released on the Internet, on December 8, 2008, authorities detained one of Charter 08's primary drafters, Liu Xiaobo. Liu was detained on suspicions of "inciting subversion of state power."[143] A total of seventy additional signatories were interrogated by authorities within the first month of Charter 08's release. Liu, who had previously spent two years in jail for his involvement in the 1989 Tiananmen Square protests, quickly became the focus of international media. In January 2009 Liu and the original 303 signatories were awarded the Homo Homini prize by Vaclav Havel, one of the signatories of Charter 77, the document that Charter 08 was based on. Liu was sentenced to eleven years in jail on December 25, 2009. Chinese web censors have since blocked access to Charter 08.

The plight of He Qinglian, the acclaimed Chinese journalist and author of *China's Pitfall* (1998), however, suggests the precarious position of those who link environmental protection to broader social, political, and economic challenges. While He is not an environmentalist per se, her work includes discussions of environmental degradation in the broader context of the failings of the CCP, such as corruption, lack of accountability, and lack of transparency. During 2000, He lost her job as an editor at the *Shenzhen Legal Daily* for her outspokenness, and in June 2001, fearing imminent arrest, she fled to the United States.

Second, there would need to be a means of communication among NGOS. One possibility is the Internet. The Charter 08 movement, for example, used the Internet to communicate both within and across provincial boundaries, demonstrating that this vehicle is a potent force for organizing subversive activity. The SARS (severe acute respiratory syndrome) crisis in spring 2003 also demonstrated the potential of instant messaging as a means of communicating within society.

The Internet has added a powerful new dimension to China's environmental movement. In 2008, there were an estimated 298 million Chinese people trafficking the web, the highest number of users in the world.[144] Chinese bloggers are growing in number, broadening in their range of political viewpoints, and criticizing government policies more boldly. Part of this growth is due to Beijing's increased tolerance for disparate opinion—and its recognition that the Internet can serve as a useful barometer for public sentiment. Chinese Internet users have demonstrated the ability to maneuver around censors and post commentaries openly questioning government policies, from Tibet to the economy, and to organize environmental protests. In the case of the environment, the Internet has not only empowered China's citizens to raise awareness about local pollution cases and related official corruption, but it has also enabled linkages to form between local environmental protest and a broader political movement.

One incident in 2007 is particularly renowned for the role that mobile phones and the Internet played in mobilizing a massive antipollution demonstration. For several days in the coastal city of Xiamen, after months of mounting opposition to the planned construction of a $1.4 billion petrochemical plant nearby, students and professors at Xiamen University, among others, are said to have sent out a million text messages calling on their fellow citizens to take to the streets on June 1. That day, and the following, protesters reportedly numbering between 7,000 and 20,000 marched peacefully through the city, some defying threats of expulsion from school or from the Communist Party. Live accounts of the demonstration, in the form of blog posts, photos, and videos, proliferated across the Internet on sites such as YouTube and Twitter. One video featured a haunting voice-over that linked the Xiamen demonstration to a concurrent environmental crisis near Tai Lake, some four hundred miles away, where a large bloom of blue-green algae caused by industrial wastewater and sewage dumped in the lake had contaminated the water supply of Wuxi city. The video also referred to the Tiananmen

Square protest of 1989. The Xiamen march, the narrator said, was perhaps "the first genuine parade since Tiananmen."

In the immediate aftermath of the 2007 protests in Xiamen, local authorities also launched an all-out campaign to discredit the protesters and their videos. Still, more comments about the protest and calls not to forget Tiananmen appeared on various Web sites. Such messages, posted openly and accessible to all Chinese, represented the Chinese leadership's greatest fear, namely, that its failure to protect the environment may be linked to broad-based demands for political change.

The Xiamen march led to the suspension of the petrochemical project for almost two years. The project re-emerged in the public spotlight in February 2008 when rumors spread that the plant would be moved to the neighboring town of Zhangzhou, fifty miles west of Xiamen. As a result, up to ten thousand local residents staged a demonstration that lasted almost five days and was ultimately quelled by the police. One year later, on January 12, 2009, the Ministry of Environmental Protection announced that it had approved the environmental impact assessment for the plant in Zhangzhou.[145] Officials insist that the project is safe, but public skepticism remains. One newspaper, *Eastern China Morning News*, ran an article saying, "When the cost of satisfying the public is decreased, the value and efficiency of a public decision is increased greatly. Therefore, when the paraxylene project left Xiamen and moved to Zhangzhou, the relevant departments should be courageous enough to hold public hearings and disclose information, providing sufficient opportunities for public participation."[146]

In May 2009, a similar incident in Shandong province drew attention from China's top leadership. In Dongming county, a group of residents posted an online petition calling for an investigation of four cyclohexanone chemical plants that they believed were polluting local air and water, causing an unusually high number of thyroid cancer cases since the factories began operating in 2008.[147] Initially, the county government ignored the petition. Previous complaints about the thyroid cancer incidents had received little response from county officials, who maintained that the factories, which were not allowed to drain waste water until it met provincial standards, had passed official water quality tests. Over the next month, the petition circulated on high-traffic web portals such as Baidu and Tianya, collecting an estimated 1,400 signatures.[148] In an open letter published on Internet forums, one resident even called for a broader "uprising" that might not be successful but "marks the start of a revolution against a crude regime," and even called for the killing of the Communist Party chief and county director. The author later told the *South China Morning Post* that more than five thousand residents had signed up for the protest. In June 2009 China's premier Wen Jiabao saw the petition and ordered the Shandong officials to investigate the claims and respond to the public.

There might well have to be a catalytic event or disaster to tap into and ignite the widespread but often latent dissatisfaction that many in China feel concerning the CCP and the current social and economic situation. The Chinese leadership, however, has proved adept in handling such situations (for example, the 2008 Sichuan earthquake, where despite initial outcries over government corruption and a lack of transparency, the government effectively silenced its most outspoken critics).

Without such a catalytic event, a more likely future path for China may well be that taken by some of its Asian neighbors, with environmental NGOs serving as a constant force for reform, exposing corruption, demanding political transparency, and contributing to the gradual evolution of the political system.

For China's leaders, the message of history is clear. While involving citizen participation in environmental protection, encouraging regional initiatives, and supporting the efforts of private business may yield some important gains in improving specific environmental problems, these strategies are not sufficient. Moreover, an environmental protection apparatus that is weak and undermined by corruption or by more powerful industrial interests only fans the flames of environmental protest. In extreme cases, once the door has been opened to the formation of social groups, like environmental NGOs, other social interest groups focused directly on advancing political change can be expected to join the cause. Few countries have managed to retain an authoritarian government while permitting nongovernmental action to thrive.

CHAPTER EIGHT

AVERTING THE CRISIS

China's leaders face a daunting task. With one-quarter of the world's population, centuries of grand-scale campaigns to transform the natural environment for man's benefit, intensive and unfettered economic development, and, most recently, its entry into the global economy, China has laid waste to its resources. The results are evident everywhere. Water scarcity is an increasingly prevalent problem. Over one-quarter of China's land is now desert. China has lost twice as much forested land over the centuries as it now possesses. And air quality in many major cities ranks among the worst in the world.

Of equal, if not greater, concern than the immediate environmental costs of China's economic development practices, however, are the mounting social, political, and economic problems that this clash between development and environment has engendered. China's leaders must now contend with growing public health problems. Rising rates of cancer, birth defects, and other pollution-related illnesses have been documented throughout the country. The public health crisis also contributes to growing numbers of protests, some peaceful and some violent, as the government, either through incompetence, corruption, or lack of capacity, proves incapable of taking appropriate action to address the people's concerns.

The economic costs of China's environmental degradation are rising sharply. Most immediately, poor air and water quality has direct costs in terms of crop loss, missed days of work from respiratory diseases, and factory shutdowns from lack of water. Even greater challenges are on the horizon. Several of China's major river systems are running dry in places, necessitating huge and costly river diversion schemes. Much of China's north is under increasing threat of desertification, prompting vast afforestation schemes, with only mixed results.

These depleted land and water resources, coupled with the river diversions, will contribute to migration on the scale of tens of millions over the next decades. While this will relieve population pressure on some of China's most overgrazed and intensively farmed land, it will increase the strain on many urban areas. Chinese officials are greatly concerned about the growing water demand by China's wealthier, urbanized citizens.

At the same time as the reforms have exacerbated old (as well as introduced new) environmental challenges, they have not managed to break free of other aspects of China's environmental legacy. Particularly damaging has been Beijing's continued reliance on campaigns to address vast, often complex environmental problems. History has demonstrated repeatedly that the challenges of deforestation, pollution, and scarcity of natural resources are poorly addressed by grand-scale campaigns that attend little to the complex social, economic, environmental, and scientific issues that underpin these challenges. Moreover, even as China assumes a leadership position in the global economy and the international community, its leaders struggle to move beyond traditional notions of security that contribute to large-scale development programs with potentially highly deleterious environmental consequences, such as the grain self-reliance, South-to-North Water Transfer Project and Go West campaigns.

Yet there are signs of hope.

China's post-Mao leaders have developed a far more institutionalized system of governance, with a codified system of laws. This is a critical step forward for environmental protection. In the 1970s and

1980s, the leaders established an environmental protection bureaucracy, held a series of important meetings related to the environment, and issued laws and regulations to strengthen environmental protection throughout the country. Official investment in environmental protection by the central government—practically nonexistent in the 1970s—increased to 1.3 percent of the country's gross domestic product (GDP) at the turn of the century.

Over time, Chinese environmental protection officials have become increasingly adept at developing new policy approaches, drafting laws, and, to a lesser extent, enforcing them. In many instances, they have taken advantage of other aspects of the reform process—utilizing expertise and funding from abroad and relying on growing grassroots and media pressure for better enforcement at the local level.

Still, by most measures, the central environmental protection bureaucracy in China remains weak. With roughly five times the population of the United States, China possesses a central environmental protection bureaucracy only one-sixth as large. Central government funding for environmental protection, while increasing steadily over the course of the reform period, is still well under the level that Chinese experts claim is necessary to prevent further deterioration. Since 1998, there exists no central environmental agency or commission capable of convening the full range of ministries necessary to resolve many complex environmental challenges that cross bureaucratic boundaries. Even as laws are passed, administrative decrees issued, and regulations set, the politics of resource use conspire to undermine environmental efforts; and the lack of a strong legal infrastructure has enhanced opportunities for corruption and resulted in a systemic crisis for environmental protection enforcement.

Yet, it seems plausible that the small central environmental protection apparatus and its relatively weak reach are at least partly by design. Through the reform process, the central government evidences the belief that, as with the economy, reliance on local authorities and the nonstate sector will yield a better outcome than strong central governance.

Devolution of significant authority for environmental protection to local officials represents one critical element of this process. It has resulted in significant variability in China's environmental situation from one region to the next, with some regions and localities aggressively pursuing stronger environmental protection efforts while others fall further behind.

Cities such as Dalian, Shanghai, and Xiamen routinely invest a significant percentage of their local government revenues in environmental protection; reach out to the international community for extensive technical and financial support for environmental concerns; and have developed relatively well-staffed, well-funded, and well-supported local environmental protection bureaus (EPBs). In all these cases, the driving force was a mayor who perceived his personal advancement and/or the reputation of his city as linked to an improved environment, although economic development clearly provided the wherewithal to address the region's environmental challenges.

As was the case centuries ago, however, only those regions with enlightened local officials and substantial local resources—whether derived domestically or from the international community—have managed to control, if not abate, environmental pollution and degradation. In many other instances, this devolution of authority has contributed to poor efficacy in responding to local environmental challenges. Many local EPBs are grossly understaffed and underfunded and, most important, beholden to local governments for their livelihood. Not surprisingly, they generally lack the political clout within the local bureaucracy to monitor, much less to respond effectively to, local environmental problems. The weak financial and enforcement links between Beijing and provincial and local governments compound the problem: central directives are rarely, if ever, well executed. In poorer regions, such as Sichuan Province, even when the officials recognize the necessity of improving their environmental protection efforts, they are stymied by a lack of resources.

A third aspect of the reform process, China's decision to join the international economy and the international community writ large, has also equipped China's leaders with a vastly different set of political and economic tools than their predecessors possessed. China has opened its arms to embrace technological assistance, policy advice, and financial support from the international community to help improve its environmental situation.

Environmental governance in China increasingly incorporates not only technologies but also norms from abroad. China's participation in the United Nations (UN) Conference on the Human Environment in 1972 and the UN Conference on Environment and Development in 1992 sparked enormous change in the environmental attitudes and orientations of Chinese elites, which have begun to trickle down through education to the wider society. The 2002 UN World Summit on Sustainable Development in Johannesburg had a similar impact, having served as the occasion for China to announce its decision to ratify the Kyoto Protocol to address the challenge of global climate change. The Olympics in 2008 have helped raise awareness of environmental technologies, encouraging, for example, the introduction of natural gas into Beijing as a replacement for coal and the purchase of a range of alternative fuel vehicles by the local government. As China's economy has skyrocketed, too, China's leaders have begun to invest significant resources in new technologies such as electric cars and wind power.

Outside actors have also taken advantage of China's economic reforms to introduce new policy approaches to environmental protection. International governmental organizations, such as the World Bank and Asian Development Bank, individual countries such as Japan, Germany, the United States, and international nongovernmental organizations have been instrumental in persuading their Chinese colleagues to experiment with market-based mechanisms such as price reform for natural resources, tradable permits, and energy service companies. In some cases, such as pricing reform for water, resource scarcity and population pressure provided the opening for the reform to be initiated, giving credence to the more optimistic view of how population affects the environment.

Further, China's accession to the World Trade Organization (WTO) has placed new strictures on its some of its production practices, particularly in agriculture. Several Chinese products have already been deemed insufficiently green, resulting in a sharp drop in those exports to WTO member countries. Yet, the WTO also has offered some highly polluting industries such as textiles the opportunity to ratchet up significantly their exports.

And there are concerns over the implications of China's burgeoning levels of foreign trade and investment for the environment more broadly. Many multinationals bring only their best environmental practices and most advanced technologies to China. Royal Dutch Shell's broad engagement in China's environmental protection efforts—funding environmental nongovernmental organizations (NGOs), insisting on top-quality environmental and socioeconomic impact assessments for its pipeline venture, and bringing natural gas to the coastal provinces—offers a good example of the ways in which international firms can shape China's environmental trajectory in a constructive manner. Many others, however, offload their most polluting enterprises on regions desperate for foreign investment.

China's weak enforcement of its own environmental protection laws also undermines the potential environmental advantages of foreign direct investment. Many multinationals complain that despite their best efforts, local officials and enterprise managers prefer not to use the pollution control technologies they provide in order to decrease the costs of operating the plants. Or, in other instances, foreign firms simply cannot compete against domestic firms that do not abide by the country's environmental regulations.

China's weak domestic enforcement regime is also having a profound impact on the rest of the world. As Chinese multinationals go abroad in search of natural resources, they are exporting their own poor environmental practices throughout much of the developing world.

China's leaders have also placed the future of environmental protection in the hands of the Chinese people, opening the door to grassroots activities, NGOs, and the media. This has produced an exciting and vibrant—if still nascent—source of policy approaches and enforcement capabilities. Environmental NGOs, independent environmental lawyers, and an aggressive media all have injected new ideas and methods into China's environmental protection efforts, reflecting a gradual evolution in the traditional belief of the Chinese people that it is the role of the government to safeguard the environment. Moreover, NGOs and the media have begun to reshape the environmental and political consciousness of the public and some government officials in ways that are important not only for environmental protection but also potentially for broader social and political purposes. The Internet has emerged as a particularly important forum for communication among environmental activists, the Chinese government, and the local populace.

Yet, even as the NGO sector and media have become highly valued adjuncts to China's environmental protection work, restrictions governing their work still remain. The Chinese government is wary of the potential for NGOs and the media to move beyond issues of local enforcement to criticize central government policy or potentially serve as a force for broader social change. Thus, in many respects, China's environmental NGOs have developed far more slowly over the past decade—both in terms of the absolute number of such NGOs, their membership, and the scope of their work—than might have been anticipated.

Finally, this is a circular process: Even as political and economic reform shape China's environment, the environment, too, is influencing China's reform process. Environmental pollution and degradation are costly to Chinese economic productivity, contribute to tens of millions of environmental migrants, damage public health, and engender social unrest. In addition, the environment may serve as a locus for broader political discontent and calls for political reform, as it has in other countries. Thus, China's reform process has brought an extraordinary dynamism and energy to both the nature of China's environmental challenges and its environmental protection efforts; yet it also increases the uncertainty in attempting to chart China's future environmental path.

Scenarios for the Future

Given the dynamic nature of both China's economy and its evolving political system, assessing China's environmental future and its broader implications for the country and the world is no easy task. Integrating centuries of historical attitudes and approaches with the current infusion of new ideas and technologies into this interplay of economic development and environmental governance demands consideration of a range of potential outcomes.

Using China's economy as a starting point, three scenarios suggest themselves for China's environmental future, with significantly different implications for both the country and the world.

China Goes Green

In the first scenario, China's economy continues to grow, producing more challenges for the environment but simultaneously spurring greater investment in environmental protection at both the local and national levels. Not only the economy and the environment benefit but China's political system is also enhanced through more effective application of the rule of law, greater citizen participation in the political process, and the strengthening of civil society.

In this scenario, China's most vibrant cities such as Shanghai and Dalian serve as genuine models for other coastal and inland cities interested in attracting greater foreign investment and recognition for their livability. As urbanization continues, satellite cities replicate the better environmental practices of the major urban centers rather than becoming dumping grounds for the cities' most polluting enterprises. Shanghai becomes a center for the most advanced environmental thinking and cleaner production, prompting a booming industry in environmental technologies. Beautification campaigns clean up the city streets, and Shanghai develops a high-speed transit system to its satellite cities, thereby sharply slowing the growth rate in car use in the city and surrounding environs. The continued increasing wealth of the city and environmental education opportunities in schools spawn a highly energized green movement, which promotes recycling, water-saving measures, and other grassroots efforts to protect the environment and the city's natural resources. In ten years, the water in the Huangpu River is once again safe for recreation and drinking, leading to a lively riverfront community.

At the same time, Premier Wen Jiabao's successor ensures the effective coordination of government ministries on policy initiatives such as the Green GDP. The political success of environmentally proactive officials encourages others to follow suit, using the environment as a stepping stone to positions of greater political prominence. Throughout the country, tens of thousands of model environmental or eco-cities sprout, providing China's citizens with unprecedented access to a better future for themselves and their children.

China's position in the global trade regime reinforces positive trends in the quality of goods produced, the development of a legal infrastructure, and stronger enforcement capability. Chinese companies such as SunTech become global leaders in the production of renewable energy technologies for use at home as well as abroad. Others such as Haier or Vanion become global leaders in energy-efficient appliances and buildings, respectively. Coal use decreases as the desire for efficiency, clean environment, and higher quality of life becomes paramount. Environment-related public health concerns diminish as China is forced to rethink its rural development and agricultural strategies to accommodate WTO-mandated levels of food safety. As China moves away from intensive farming and toward other, more environmentally sustainable and lucrative crops, the country also becomes world-renowned for the quality and quantity of its organic produce, particularly fruits and vegetables. In the automobile sector, Chinese car manufacturers become leaders in producing fuel-efficient cars. Alternative fuel vehicles dominate the roads, encouraged by the desire of Beijing to match consumer interests with the country's desire for energy security.

On the governance front, China's NGOs continue to flourish, supported not only by the international community but also increasingly by Chinese citizens who value a clean environment and are willing to contribute both financially and personally to ensure its sustainability. China's top entrepreneurs become an important new source of funding for environmental NGOs, helped by new tax laws and a growing base of wealthy Chinese citizens. Small mass-based environmental NGOs emerge, and the well-established NGOs expand their membership and their mission as the next generation of environmental NGO leaders, led by Wen Bo, Ma Jun, and others, increasingly incorporates international practices of lobbying and lawsuits to protect the environment.

For the Chinese leadership, the environment may change from a political liability into a source of political strength as the people are able to realize both economic prosperity and improved quality of life. Environmental issues become increasingly important in local elections as people's concerns broaden past basic living conditions. Rooting out violations of environmental laws and corruption becomes a source of political credibility for aspiring leaders and community spirit for mobilized citizens. A formal and organized environmental movement evolves across provincial boundaries assisted by the media and the growing political strength of environmental NGOs. They advocate a political platform that encompasses a broad range of social and political interests tied to the environment, including population planning, environmental protection, rule of law, and economic development ideals. This scenario lends itself to a deepening or broadening of political reform, as Chinese citizens increasingly demand that their voices be heard on the full range of social, political, and economic issues. At the same time, the increasing confidence of the Chinese Communist Party (CCP) leads it, on its own initiative, to open the door to greater political diversity and political reform of its own accord. By 2020 the CCP is recast as the Chinese Socialist Democratic Union and is one of two or three parties competing for political power.

The international community—business, government, and NGOs—joins forces with domestic NGOs and environmentally proactive government leaders to increase dramatically China's technological and policy capacity to protect the environment. This partnership also transforms China's urbanization process into a vast experiment in sustainable development. Urban planners, conservationists, and business leaders join forces to develop China in a model environmental fashion, implementing cleaner production, ensuring public hearings for new development projects, and establishing local best practices with solar-powered office buildings, recycling centers, and state-of-the-art public transportation. The media, together with the public, serves as a watchdog to ensure that the new cities do not become new centers for resource exploitation and polluting industry.

For the international community, this scenario offers the potential for improved implementation of international environmental agreements, declining or stable levels of China's greenhouse gas emissions, and improvement in China's contribution to transboundary air problems such as acid rain. More broadly, it suggests a China that is more likely to be both willing and able to participate fully in international environmental, as well as other, agreements and institutions. Environmental advocates both within and outside the Chinese government will become important members of the international environmental movement supporting China's participation in the full range of regional and global environmental regimes. And they will use international regimes to hold the central government accountable for its environmental commitments.

Inertia Sets In

This second scenario extends today's status quo. The Chinese economy continues to grow, but greater economic wealth translates only slowly into enhanced environmental protection. The environment continues to be a drag on the Chinese economy, and both at home and abroad people complain about the worsening condition of China's air and water quality.

In this scenario, the growing use of automobiles, for example, is not matched by the rapid deployment of alternative energy vehicles. Automobile use increases dramatically as expected, and low-cost, low-end cars that do not employ the most advanced technologies are favored. Rather than embracing the fuel-efficient, compact cars that populate Europe and Japan, wealthier Chinese follow in the footsteps of Americans, desiring gas-guzzling luxury cars and sport utility vehicles. Public transportation becomes a least-desired mode of transport. Despite the spur of the 2008 Olympics, hybrid or electric vehicles do not spread in popularity. Air quality continues to suffer, as Chinese officials miss their targets and the number of cars continues to increase.

Top authorities rely on their traditional ineffectual use of campaigns to address nationwide problems, and the Go West campaign confirms the worst fears of local environmentalists: It leads to greater devastation of the natural resources of the interior provinces in the name of development. Political tensions in Xinjiang and Tibet heighten as the two strata of society—the wealthy Han settlers and the indigenous poorer minorities—diverge further.

The devolution of authority to local levels continues to produce a patchwork of environmental protection practices, in which only the wealthiest cities with environmentally inclined mayors use their growing economic capacity to fund improvements in their local environment. There is little transfer of environmental know-how—either technological or policy—to other regions of the country. The northeast continues to suffer the environmental impacts of declining rust-belt industries, and the interior provinces are transformed into a haven for environmentally exploitative practices to lure both domestic and international investment. The costs of remediation projects, massive river diversions, and afforestation campaigns steadily increase as China's leaders continue to favor cleanup rather than prevention. These campaigns serve primarily as public works projects to stimulate the economy and provide work to otherwise unemployed farmers and migrant workers, but simultaneously drain the coffers of the state banks.

The WTO produces improved enforcement capacity in areas such as intellectual property protection, but this enhanced capability remains narrowly trained on business and does not translate readily into other arenas. Large-scale transfer of environmental technologies continues to be hampered by weak incentives and enforcement. Even when technologies are deployed, they are not employed. China remains unable to develop and sustain a domestically driven environmental technology industry.

With little reinforcement from the central government, NGOs remain constrained in number and in the range of their activities. The next generation of environmental activists becomes frustrated by the political limitations of their work and instead turns more to media and other outlets to express their environmental and political interests. Interest in environmental law develops only slowly because it is viewed as an area with poor future growth prospects.

International actors remain engaged in environmental protection work in China, but are stymied by recalcitrant local actors, weak incentives for adopting new approaches or technologies, and few opportunities for replication of their work beyond single demonstration projects. For the international community, China remains a partner in international environmental accords, but not necessarily a reliable one. Driven overwhelmingly by their continued desire to grow economically and maintain political stability, China's leaders continue to resist what they perceive as onerous environmental commitments to address problems such as climate change. At the same time, China's contribution to climate change and other transboundary air pollution problems increases as the country continues to develop with enterprises fueled primarily by coal and as automobiles proliferate.

Environmental Meltdown

There is no guarantee, of course, that China's economy will continue to grow at the 7 percent that some analysts predict necessary to maintain social stability. If indeed there were a prolonged economic slowdown, there might be some environmental benefits. Declining industrial production, for example, could lead to decreasing emissions of greenhouse gases. Overall, however, the environment would likely be an early victim, as was the case in the early stages of the global financial crisis.

In the third scenario, China's economy experiences a prolonged downturn. Local officials continue to favor economic development at the expense of the environment in an effort to preserve social stability. As a result, China's air quality does not improve, as the country continues to rely on older, more inefficient polluting technologies and automobiles. Water pollution increases throughout the major river systems. And, most important, investment in waste treatment or new conservation efforts diminishes as a short-term outlook prevails.

Massive layoffs and growing problems with environmentally and economically induced migration would also challenge the ability of local governments to provide work for the people. The social welfare system is overwhelmed as continued corruption drains local coffers and impairs the development of a functioning pension and healthcare system. There are frequent demonstrations, which often turn violent. The outlook for improved quality of life is bleak. Positive environmental trends in forestry and agricultural practices are reversed as logging bans are ignored and farmers attempt to eke out a living on increasingly degraded land.

In China's west, environmental and economic exploitation prompt not only growing political disaffection but also increased violence and protests against domestic and international businesses perceived to support such policies. International business stops investing and withdraws from the west, which is now viewed as politically unstable. Weaknesses in the banking infrastructure and law enforcement deepen as Chinese officials seek any means to keep local industry afloat. After making small gains in the rule of law, courts are increasingly reluctant to press enterprises to adhere to environmental protection laws for fear of promoting further social unrest. Corruption continues to erode economic institutions and leadership credibility as Chinese citizens believe they have no recourse for justice.

Unwilling to risk massive layoffs, Chinese officials backtrack on WTO commitments in an effort to preserve Chinese industries. Bureaucracies are given greater latitude to develop regulations that impede the access of foreign companies to China's market. Foreign investors respond by denouncing Chinese practices, further contributing to international friction and trade disruptions. Fewer environmental benefits are also felt due to a slowdown in the influx of foreign technology and increasing acceptance of poorer environmental practices. Gains for China's industry come largely in the highly polluting manufacturing or heavy industries; few benefits are reaped in the expected area of agriculture, as China resists opening its market to large-scale grain imports promised in its WTO accession agreement.

Climate change exacerbates the challenges of water scarcity and land degradation. Agricultural output falls significantly. In the coastal areas, rising sea levels force tens of millions of Chinese to flee their homes.

In the political realm, this kind of economic downturn could produce at least three different scenarios. The first and most predictable would be a reversal in even modest gains in openness over the past decade, exacerbating the tension within the Chinese leadership between its relatively newfound belief that there is much to gain from embracing forces of local political action and integration with the international community and its traditional fear that such processes will undermine the security of the state and their capacity to govern. In such a time of domestic stress and leadership vulnerability, the environment is not likely to receive much positive attention. More likely, the public security apparatus would increasingly scrutinize the work of NGOs and independent lawyers for the political content of their work. Peasant and worker unrest would be managed through repression and, perhaps, through the projection of an external threat to rally nationalist sentiment and deflect attention from the country's economic woes.

Although the CCP has proved remarkably adept at harnessing nationalistic sentiment for its own legitimizing purposes, the wave of anti-Party sentiment expressed during the confrontation with the United States over the EP3 spy plane during spring 2001 (when a Chinese fighter jet crashed and a U.S. spy plane was forced to land on Hainan Island) suggests that such views could spiral out of the government's control, producing a new challenge to the stability of the regime.

A second possible outcome would be for China's leaders to pursue a path akin to that of former Soviet general secretary Gorbachev in the mid-to-late 1980s. Gorbachev responded to economic malaise and his inability to reform the Soviet economy by opening up the political system as a means of diffusing popular discontent and channeling it into institutions such as political parties. This is a less obvious option. Many reform-oriented Chinese leaders have explicitly rejected such an approach. But scholarly studies revisiting the lessons of the Soviet experience, as well as visits by senior Chinese officials to Europe to study social democratic parties, suggest that discussion has not been closed completely. Reform-minded leaders might well ally with labor, environment, and women's NGOs to explore alternative formulations for restructuring the government to involve greater public participation.

In this scenario, China's environmental NGOs would be a logical locus of political action, drawing on both the intellectual and political skills of the NGO leadership as well as the innate attractiveness of their message and mission for many Chinese. The role played in effective environmental protection by transparency, rule of law, and public participation suggest a natural synergy between movement toward greater political openness and the work of the environmental community in China. Potential alternatives to the CCP might include a green party or a broader "democracy" party that would embrace many of the social issues of greatest concern—labor, the environment, and education among them—that CCP-led development has brought to the Chinese people.

Third is the scenario that many China watchers have previously described: that China might collapse or be riven by wide-scale civil strife. Regime-threatening protests emanating from China's minorities, especially the Uighurs in Xinjiang and Tibetan independence advocates, or from a combination of striking laborers, peasants, and urban intellectuals, are all within the realm of possibility. In this scenario, the environment could be one of many causes espoused by the protesters. An environmental disaster of significant magnitude, like a collapse of the Three Gorges Dam, could serve as the trigger for such protests—a giant symbol of the corruption, lack of transparency, and limited political participation of China's current system.

Which Way? The Role of the United States

Millions of people concerned with the environment, both in China and elsewhere, are hoping that the first scenario of growing prosperity, democracy, and environmental protection becomes reality. But this is by no means assured. Both China's domestic reforms and its deeper integration into the international system require a fundamental change in values. The nationalistic and occasionally violent demonstrations in the wake of the U.S. accidental bombing of the Chinese embassy in Belgrade and the EP3 collision demonstrated that within at least some sectors of Chinese society and the Chinese leadership, the commitment to this kind of change is a tenuous one.

The world community has an opportunity to assist in the process of developing China's approach to environmental protection. The impact of the international community on China's environmental practices has already been substantial. In every regard—technology transfer, governance, and policy development—the international community has helped to shape the evolution of China's environmental protection effort. Fortunately, this involvement shows no evidence of abating and, indeed, seems likely to grow in the future.

Yet much more remains to be done. Technology transfer and adoption of new policy approaches await the development of a stronger legal and enforcement apparatus. Here, the international community, in particular the United States with its strong environmental enforcement apparatus and history of public participation in environmental protection, could be far more active in contributing to the development of China's environmental future.[1]

The environment provides a natural and nonthreatening vehicle to advance U.S. interests not only in China's environmental protection efforts but also in its basic human rights practices and trade opportunities.[2] Climate change has already engendered a number of public-private partnerships under the auspices of the U.S.–China Strategic and Economic Dialogue, and more will undoubtedly be forthcoming. U.S. multinationals and venture capitalists are also eagerly seeking opportunities in China in the fields of clean energy and environmental technologies. Yet for these efforts to bear real fruit, more will have to be done to assist China in creating a favorable policy environment at home. Several simple steps could be taken to help shape China's future environmental, political, and economic development. Chief among these is removing restrictions on the Overseas Private Investment Corporation and other foreign-aid related restrictions. In part, these restrictions have been kept in place for political reasons. Congress has required, for example, that U.S. representatives to international financial institutions vote in favor of projects in Tibet only when it is evident that the projects do not encourage Han Chinese to migrate to or own property in Tibet, which raises fears of eroding Tibetan culture and identity.[3] These restrictions, which date to the 1989 Tiananmen Square protests and before, severely limit U.S. influence in China. The United States Agency for International Development (USAID), with its broad emphasis on governance, public health, rule of law, and poverty alleviation could be especially valuable in addressing China's most pressing needs and the United States' most direct interests. Although USAID money flows through the Department of State, for USAID to become actively and directly involved in such activities would require the United States to remove either the prohibition on USAID funding of communist states or the label of communist state from China.

The United States has the chance not only to benefit more significantly from China's current reform process but also to aid in the future evolution of that process in ways that serve broader U.S. political, economic, and environmental interests. This will require the U.S. leadership to develop both an understanding of the opportunities to influence China's future path and a newfound commitment to take the bold steps necessary to do so. It is a challenge that the United States cannot afford to ignore. Deep U.S. engagement involving both trade and substantial support for political development has been an essential component in the development of our close relations with many nations in Asia, including Japan, Taiwan, and South Korea. As the United States considers the importance of mainland China to regional stability, to the world economy, and to the global environment, it need look no further than its past successes in the region to understand that it has a substantial opportunity at a critical juncture in China's development to play a similarly catalytic role. No matter how extensive China's interaction with the United States and the rest of the world, China itself bears the brunt of the challenge. A future in which China fully embraces environmental protection will require new approaches to integrating economic development with environmental protection. Equally if not more important will be a commitment by China's leaders to develop the political institutions necessary to ensure such a future, to bring true transparency and accountability to the system of environmental protection. Speculation remains as to the boldness of China's Fifth Generation leaders, who will assume power in 2012. Yet change will require nothing short of boldness. This is a system thousands of years in the making, one in which the greatness of leaders has often been achieved at the expense of nature, through grand-scale development campaigns to control and exploit the environment for man's benefit. But today, greatness may well depend on resisting this tradition and instead developing a new relationship between man and nature.

NOTES

Chapter 1. The Death of the Huai River

1. "Huaihe River Avoids Pollution Disaster—SEPA," Xinhua News Agency, August 7, 2001.
2. Michael Ma, "River Flooding Sets off Pollution Alarm," *South China Morning Post*, August 4, 2001, p. 8.
3. Information for Anhui: "Annual Review of Anhui Economic Performance (2007)," Anhui China: The Official Website of Anhui Government, August 20, 2008, apps.ah.gov.cn/showcontent.asp?newsid= 1595. Information for Jiangsu: Song Hongmei, "Jiangsu Strives to Build on Decades of Success," *China Daily*, November 6, 2008, www.chinadaily.com.cn/bizchina/2008-11/06/content_7181596.htm.
4. *2002 Nian Zhongguo Huanjing Zhuangkuang Gongbao* [2002 Report on the State of the Environment in China] (Beijing: State Environmental Protection Administration, 2003).
5. Jasper Becker, "River Gives Way—to Pollution," *South China Morning Post*, January 13, 2001, p. 10.
6. Hugo Restall, "Examining Asia: A Top-Down Coverup," *Asian Wall Street Journal*, March 14, 2001, p. 6.
7. "China Calls for Rational Exploitation of Major River," Xinhua News Agency, April 19, 2001.

8. Jiusheng Zhang, "Water Resource Protection and Water Pollution Control for the Huai River Basin," World Bank Huai River Basin Pollution Control Project Report, pp. 2–3, www.wb.home.by/nipr/china/pids/huai.htm.

9. Becker, "River Gives Way," p. 10.

10. Mark Hertsgaard, "Our Real China Problem," *The Atlantic Monthly*, November 1997, www.theatlantic.com/issues/97nov/ china.htm.

11. Abigail Jahiel, "The Organization of Environmental Protection in China," *China Quarterly* 156 (December 1998): 781.

12. *China Environment News*, July 1993, p. 4.

13. Hertsgaard, "Our Real China Problem."

14. Patrick Tyler, "A Tide of Pollution Threatens China's Prosperity," *New York Times*, September 25, 1994, p. A3.

15. Hertsgaard, "Our Real China Problem."

16. Ibid.

17. Notes provided by Chinese scientist to author, June 1996.

18. "China's Huai River Cleanup Lagging," Kyodo News Service Japan Economic Newswire, November 21, 1997.

19. Joseph Kahn, "China's Greens Win Rare Battle on River," *Wall Street Journal*, August 2, 1996, p. A8.

20. "China Takes Action to Huaihe Polluters," Xinhua News Agency, January 1, 1998.

21. Jasper Becker, "Cracking Down on the Chemical Waste Outlaws," *South China Morning Post*, May 21, 1999, p. 15.

22. *Newsprobe* reporter and producer, interview by author, Beijing, April 2000.

23. Mary Kay Magistad, Robert Siegel, and Noah Adams, "Cleaning Up the Huai," *All Things Considered*, National Public Radio, April 7, 1998.

24. Ibid.

25. "Families Seek Truth over Deaths Near Notorious Polluted Overflow," *South China Morning Post*, June 16, 2000, p. 7.

26. Ibid.

27. "Exploitation Exhausts the Dwindling Huai," *South China Morning Post*, January 14, 2001, p. 6.

28. "Central China Hit by Severe Drought," Associated Press Newswire, August 26, 1999.

29. "Exploitation Exhausts the Dwindling Huai," p. 6.

30. Ibid.

31. Jasper Becker, "Steps for Cleaning up Act on Pollution Announced," *South China Morning Post*, January 1, 2001, p. 4.

32. Jasper Becker, "Clean up of River a Sham," *South China Morning Post*, February 26, 2001, p. 8.
33. "Intelligence," *Far Eastern Economic Review*, March 1, 2001, p. 10.
34. "Firms Ordered to Curb, Stop Operation to Prevent Pollution Disaster," fpeng.peopledaily.com.cn/200108/02/eng200110802_76373.html.
35. "China: Huai River Pollution Control Project," World Bank Group, March 22, 2001, www.worldbank.org/sprojects/Project.asp ?pid=PO47345.
36. Hua Shen and Luisetta Mudie, "Activists Defend China's Huai River," Agence-France Presse, July 20, 2009.
37. "Local Gov't Project Delays 'Hamper Efforts to Clean up China's Huai River,' " Xinhua News Agency, June 24, 2009.
38. "Three Provinces Fail on River Targets," *China Daily*, April 22, 2008.
39. Becker, "River Gives Way," p. 10.
40. Wenjun Cai, "Baby Boom Urgently Required," *Shanghai Daily*, July 24, 2009, shanghaidaily.com/sp/article/2009/200907/20090724/art icle_408480.htm.
41. Karl Polanyi, *The Great Transformation* (New York: Rinehart, 1944), 184.
42. See, for example, Vaclav Smil, *China's Environmental Crisis* (Armonk, N.Y.: M. E. Sharpe, 1993); Abigail Jahiel, "The Environmental Impact of China's Entry into the WTO," draft article, 2002.
43. Yok-shiu F. Lee and Alvin Y. So, *Asia's Environmental Movements* (Armonk, N.Y.: M. E. Sharpe, 1999), 4.
44. Asayehgn Desta, *Environmentally Sustainable Economic Development* (Westport, Conn.: Praeger, 1994), 122–23.
45. Jose I. dos R. Furtado and Tamara Belt, eds., *Economic Development and Environmental Sustainability: Policies and Principles for a Durable Equilibrium* (Washington, D.C.: World Bank, 2000), 75.
46. Ronald Inglehart, "Globalization and Postmodern Values," *The Washington Quarterly*, 23, no. 1 (2000): 219.
47. Jagdish Bhagwati, "The Case for Free Trade," in John J. Audley, *Green Politics and Global Trade: NAFTA and the Future of Environmental Politics* (Washington, D.C.: Georgetown University Press, 1997), 34.
48. Vaclav Smil, *China's Environmental Crisis* (Armonk, N.Y.: M. E. Sharpe, 1993), 192–93.
49. Furtado and Belt, eds. *Economic Development and Environmental Sustainability*, 75.
50. Jahiel, "Environmental Impact," p. 5.
51. Lee and So, *Asia's Environmental Movements*, 4.

52. *Environment and Trade: A Handbook* (Winnipeg, Manitoba: United Nations Environment Programme and International Institute for Sustainable Development, 2000), 3–4.

53. Furtado and Belt, *Economic Development and Environmental Sustainability*, 75–80.

54. Audley, *Green Politics and Global Trade*, 34.

55. John Carey, "Will Saving People Save Our Planet?" in Desta, *Environmentally Sustainable Economic Development*, 85.

56. Desta, *Environmentally Sustainable Economic Development*, 84.

57. See, for example, Geping Qu and Jinchang Li, *Population and the Environment in China* (Boulder, Colo.: Lynne Rienner Publishers, 1994); Angang Hu and Ping Zou, *China's Population Development* (Beijing: China's Science and Technology Press, 1991).

58. Hu and Zou, *China's Population Development*, 191.

59. E. Boserup, *The Conditions of Agricultural Growth* (London: Allen and Unwin, 1965).

60. Carey, "Will Saving People Save Our Planet?" 85.

61. Desta, *Environmentally Sustainable Economic Development*, 80.

62. See David W. Pearce and Jeremy J. Warford, *World Without End: Economics, Environment, and Sustainable Development* (New York: Oxford University Press, 1993), 149; *Environment and Trade: A Handbook* (Winnipeg, Manitoba: United Nations Environment Programme and International Institute for Sustainable Development, 2000).

63. Only in the arena of population policy did the government exert significantly greater rather than lesser control, in an effort to reverse the population explosion that had occurred during Mao's tenure.

64. "China Quick Facts," World Bank, 2008, web.worldbank.org/WB SITE/EXTERNAL/COUNTRIES/EASTASIAPACIFICEXT/CHINAEX TN/0,,contentMDK:20680895~pagePK:1497618~piPK:217854~theSi tePK:318950,00.html.

65. Yan Tan and Fei Guo, "Environmental Concerns and Population Displacement in West China," presented at the eighth Asian Pacific Migration Research Network Conference, May 26–29, 2007, Fujian, China, apmrn.anu.edu/conferences/8thAPMRNconference/26.Tan %20Guo.pdf.

66. Jonathan Woetzel et al., "Preparing for China's Urban Billion," McKinsey & Company, March 2009.

67. Richard McGregor, "750,000 a Year Killed by Chinese Pollution," *Financial Times*, July 2, 2007.

68. Adam Segal and Eric Thun, "Thinking Globally, Acting Locally: Local Governments, Industrial Sectors, and Development in China," *Politics and Society* 29, no. 4 (2001): 557–88.

Chapter 2. A Legacy of Exploitation

1. See, for example, Richard Baum, "Science and Culture in Contemporary China: The Roots of Retarded Modernization," *Asian Survey* 22, no. 12 (1982): 1166–86; Joseph Needham, *Science and Civilisation in China*, vol. 2 (London: Cambridge University Press, 1956).

2. Baum, "Science and Culture," 1168–76.

3. Derek Wall, *Green History* (London: Routledge, 1994), 2.

4. Samuel P. Hays, *Beauty, Health, and Permanence* (Cambridge: Cambridge University Press, 1987), 13–22.

5. Ibid.

6. Yushi Mao, "Evolution of Environmental Ethics," in *Ethics and Environmental Policy: Theory Meets Practice*, ed. Frederick Ferre and Peter Hartell (Athens: University of Georgia Press, 1994), 45.

7. Ibid.

8. Xiaoshan Yang, "Idealizing Wilderness in Medieval Chinese Poetry," in *Landscapes and Communities on the Pacific Rim*, ed. Karen K. Gaul and Jackie Hiltz (Armonk, N.Y.: M. E. Sharpe, 2000), 104.

9. Rhoads Murphey, "Man and Nature in China," *Modern Asian Studies* 1, no. 4 (1967): 316.

10. Vaclav Smil, *The Bad Earth* (Armonk, N.Y.: M. E. Sharpe, 1984), 6.

11. Yang, "Idealizing Wilderness in Medieval Chinese Poetry," 92.

12. Wenhui Hou, "Reflections on Chinese Traditional Ideas of Nature," *Environmental History* 8, no. 4 (1997): 482–93.

13. Among historical records, different dates are frequently provided for the beginning and end of dynasties. In this book, the dates are taken from William Theodore de Bary, *Sources of Chinese Tradition*, vol. 1 (New York: Columbia University Press, 1960). This book will use C.E. ("of the common era") and B.C.E. ("before the common era") for abbreviation of eras.

14. Geping Qu and Jinchang Li, *Population and the Environment in China* (Boulder, Colo.: Lynne Rienner Publishers, 1994), 16.

15. Mao, "Evolution of Environmental Ethics," 43.

16. Ibid.

17. Carol Stepanchuk and Charles Wong, *Mooncakes and Hungry Ghosts* (San Francisco: China Books and Periodicals, 1991), 53.

18. Wenhui Hou, "The Environmental Crisis in China and the Case for Environmental History Studies," *Environmental History Review* 14, no. 1–2 (1990): 152–53.

19. Charles O. Hucker, *China's Imperial Past* (Stanford: Stanford University Press, 1975), 69.

20. Ibid., 55–56.

21. Richard Edmonds, *Patterns of China's Lost Harmony: A Survey of the Country's Environmental Degradation and Protection* (London: Routledge, 1994), 24–25, quoted in Hong Fang, "Chinese Perceptions of the Environment" (master's thesis, University of Oregon, June 1997), 44.

22. Fang, "Chinese Perceptions," 66.

23. The Tao is "the process by which the cosmos operates. It functions through the interaction of two opposed but complementary and inseparable forces, Yang and Yin, which are perhaps most usefully compared to the positive and negative poles of an electrical system. Yang is associated with the sun, light, and warmth; Yin with the moon, dark, and cold. . . . When the natural alternation of Yang and Yin is aborted, the result is inappropriate and might be harmful or otherwise disadvantageous; but no question of good or bad arises in any absolute, abstract sense." Hucker, *China's Imperial Past*, 70–71.

24. Ibid., 84.

25. Kenneth E. Wilkening, "A Framework for Analyzing Culture-Environment Security Linkages, and Its Application to Confucianism in Northeast Asia," draft paper prepared for the University of Washington and Pacific Northwest Conference Series on Environmental Security conference "Cultural Attitudes and the Environment and Ecology, and Their Connection to Regional Political Stability," University of Washington, Seattle, January 16–17, 1998, www.nautilus.org/esena.

26. Hucker, *China's Imperial Past*, 79.

27. Deshu Xu, *Construction of Safety Culture in China* (Chengdu: Sichuan Science and Technology Press, 1994), 255, quoted in Fang, "Chinese Perceptions," 63.

28. Xu, *Construction of Safety Culture*, 255, quoted in Fang, "Chinese Perceptions," 65.

29. Ibid.

30. Hou, "Environmental Crisis in China," 153.

31. Xu, *Construction of Safety Culture*, 255, quoted in Fang, "Chinese Perceptions," 65.

32. De Bary, *Sources of Chinese Tradition*, 207.

33. Ibid.

34. *Tian*, again signifying the sky, God, and nature, and *zi* meaning the son of *tian*.

35. De Bary, *Sources of Chinese Tradition*, 207.

36. Fang, "Chinese Perceptions," 67.

37. Mao, "Evolution in Environmental Ethics," 43.

38. Helen Dunstan, "Official Thinking on Environmental Issues and the State's Environmental Roles in Eighteenth-Century China," in *Sediments of Time: Environment and Society in Chinese History*, ed. Mark Elvin and Ts'ui-jung Liu (Cambridge: Cambridge University Press, 1998), 587.
39. Ibid.
40. Murphey, "Man and Nature," 314.
41. Hucker, *China's Imperial Past*, 90.
42. Ibid.
43. Mao, "Evolution of Environmental Ethics," 46.
44. Hucker, *China's Imperial Past*, 91.
45. Ray Huang, *China: A Macro History* (Armonk, N.Y.: M. E. Sharpe, 1997), 20–21.
46. Mao, "Evolution of Environmental Ethics," 46.
47. Weiming Tu, "The Continuity of Being: Chinese Visions of Nature," in *Confucianism and Ecology: The Interrelation of Heaven, Earth, and Humans*, ed. Mary Evelyn Tucker and John Berthrong (Cambridge: Harvard University Press: 1998), 113.
48. Ibid.
49. Robert P. Weller and Peter K. Bol, "From Heaven-and-Earth to Nature: Chinese Concepts of the Environment and Their Influence on Policy Implementation," in *Confucianism and Ecology*, ed. Tucker and Berthrong, 322.
50. Ibid., 323.
51. Ibid.
52. Hucker, *China's Imperial Past*, 93.
53. Ibid., 94–95.
54. Ibid., 164.
55. Mao, "Evolution of Environmental Ethics," 45.
56. Ibid., 45–46.
57. Chang-Qun Duan, Xue-chun Gan, Jeanny Wang, and Paul K. Chien, "Relocation of Civilization Centers in Ancient China: Environmental Factors," *Ambio* 27, no. 7 (1998): 575.
58. Mark Elvin, "The Environmental Legacy of Imperial China," *China Quarterly* 156 (1998): 738–39.
59. De Bary does not provide any dates for the Xia dynasty; however, Hucker offers unverified dates of 2205–1766 B.C.E.
60. Duan, Gan, Wang, and Chien, "Relocation of Civilization Centers," 572.
61. Ibid., 573.
62. Elvin, "Environmental Legacy of Imperial China," 743.

63. Ibid., 742–43.

64. Jinxiong Xu, *Zhongguo Gudai Shehui* [Society in Ancient China] (Taipei: Taiwan shangwu, 1988), 408–11, data cited in Elvin, "Environmental Legacy of Imperial China," 740.

65. Huang, *China: A Macro History*, 25.

66. Ibid., 24.

67. Ibid., 25–26.

68. Fang, "Chinese Perceptions," 46.

69. Qu and Li, *Population and the Environment*, 17.

70. Archaeologists in Gansu Province in 2002 discovered an imperial order dating to the Han that banned felling trees and hunting young animals in spring, burning wood in summer, and mining in autumn. "China Finds Oldest Environmental Protection Rule," *People's Daily*, April 24, 2002, fpeng.peopledaily.com.cn/ 200204/24/ print20020424_94647.html.

71. Qu and Li, *Population and the Environment*, 17.

72. Elvin, "Environmental Legacy of Imperial China," 736–37.

73. Fang, "Chinese Perceptions," 69.

74. Qu and Li, *Population and the Environment*, 21.

75. Ibid., 22.

76. Ibid., 24–25.

77. Yuqing Wang, "Natural Conservation Regions in China," *Ambio* 16, no. 6 (1987): 326.

78. Elvin, "Environmental Legacy of Imperial China," 736.

79. Ibid., 747.

80. Jasper Becker, *Hungry Ghosts* (New York: Henry Holt, 1996), 11.

81. Angang Hu and Ping Zou, *China's Population Development* (Beijing: China's Science and Technology Press, 1991), 60.

82. Elvin, "Environmental Legacy of Imperial China," 753.

83. Dunstan, "Official Thinking on Environmental Issues," 592.

84. Ibid., 592.

85. Hu and Zou, *China's Population Development*, 60.

86. Qu and Li, *Population and the Environment*, 16.

87. Ibid.

88. Ibid., 24–25.

89. Ibid., 23.

90. Dunstan, "Official Thinking on Environmental Issues," 592.

91. Ibid.

92. T'ung Tsu Chu, *Local Government in China under the Ch'ing* (Cambridge: Harvard University Press, 1988), 116–67.

93. Ch'ing hui-tien shih-li, chüan 927 in *Local Government in China under the Ch'ing*, 167.

94. Dunstan, "Official Thinking on Environmental Issues," 591.

95. Ibid., 602.

96. Sen Yu, "On the Growing of Trees," in *Statecraft Anthology*, j.37, p. 11a–b, quoted in Dunstan, "Official Thinking on Environmental Issues," 602.

97. Dunstan, "Official Thinking on Environmental Issues," 603–5.

98. Ibid., 605–6.

99. Ibid., 595.

100. Ibid., 609.

101. Ibid., 609–10.

102. Mary B. Rankin, John K. Fairbank, and Albert Feuerwerker, "Introduction: Perspectives on Modern China's History," in *The Cambridge History of China*, ed. Denis Twitchett and John K. Fairbank, vol. 13, *Republican China 1912–1949*, part 2, ed. John K. Fairbank and Albert Feurerwerker (Cambridge: Cambridge University Press, 1986), 6–7, 15.

103. Ibid., 7.

104. Ramon H. Myers, "The Agrarian System," in *Cambridge History of China*, 13:257.

105. Ibid., 13:256.

106. Lloyd E. Eastman, "Nationalist China during the Nanking Decade 1927–1937," in *Cambridge History of China*, 13:152.

107. Ibid., 13:151.

108. Lester Ross, *Environmental Policy in China* (Bloomington: Indiana University Press, 1988), 37.

109. In formulating his strategy to restore China to its previous greatness, Mao also drew inspiration from the experience of his imperial predecessors, especially Emperor Zhou of the Shang dynasty and Qin Shihuangdi, first emperor of the Qin dynasty. Both were notable for their success in expanding the territory of China and for their ruthless consolidation of power. (Zhisui Li, *The Private Life of Chairman Mao* [New York: Random House, 1994], 122.)

110. Mao Zedong, "Essay on How Shang Yang Established Confidence by the Moving of the Pole," in Stuart R. Schram, *Mao's Road to Power: Revolutionary Writings 1912–1949* (Armonk, N.Y.: M. E. Sharpe, 1992), 5.

111. Mao, "Essay on How Shang Yang Established Confidence," 6.

112. Judith Shapiro, *Mao's War against Nature* (Cambridge: Cambridge University Press, 2001), 8.

113. Mao Tse-tung [Mao Zedong], "Speech at the Inaugural Meeting of the National Science Research Society of the Border Region,"

February 5, 1940, in *Quotations from Mao Tse-tung* (Peking: Foreign Languages Press, 1966), 204–5.

114. Murphey, "Man and Nature," 319.

115. Ibid., 319.

116. Ibid., 320.

117. "Communique of the 11th Session of the Eighth Party Central Committee, August 14, 1966," in Hu and Zou, *China's Population Development*, 103.

118. *People's Daily*, January 1, 1973, in Hu and Zou, *China's Population Development*, 103.

119. Murphey, "Man and Nature," 323.

120. Hu and Zou, *China's Population Development*, 67.

121. Mao Tse-tung, "The Bankruptcy of the Idealist Conception of History," in *Selected Works of Mao Tse-tung* (Peking: Foreign Languages Press, 1967), 4:453.

122. Hu and Zou, *China's Population Development*, 104.

123. Ibid., 68 (1950 population); Yingling Liu, "China Releases Latest Census Results," Worldwatch Institute, March 21, 2006. www.worldwatch.org/node/3899.

124. Shapiro, *Mao's War against Nature*, 33.

125. Hu and Zou, *China's Population Development*, 88.

126. Ibid.

127. Shapiro, *Mao's War Against Nature*, 45.

128. Hu and Zou, *China's Population Development*, 105.

129. Qu, *Environmental Management in China*, 211–12.

130. Mao Zedong, "Request for Opinions on the Seventeen-Article Document Concerning Agriculture," *Selected Works of Mao Tse-Tung* (Beijing: Foreign Languages Press, 1977): 5:279.

131. Becker, *Hungry Ghosts*, 70–82.

132. Vaclav Smil, *The Bad Earth: Environmental Degradation in China*, quoted in Becker, Hungry Ghosts, 77.

133. Becker, *Hungry Ghosts*, 77.

134. Mao Zedong, "Speech at the Fifteenth Meeting of the Supreme State Council, 8 September 1958 [excerpt]," Cold War International History Project, Woodrow Wilson International Center for Scholars, wwics.si.edu.

135. Becker, *Hungry Ghosts*, 63–64.

136. Antoaneta Bezlova, "Environment-China: Beijing Gasps for Clean Air," Inter Press Service, January 3, 2000.

137. Qu, *Environmental Management in China*, 212.

138. Shapiro, *Man's War against Nature*, 82–83.

139. Qu, *Environmental Management in China*, 212.
140. Shapiro, *Mao's War against Nature*, 89.
141. Hu and Zou, *China's Population Development*, 13.
142. Qu and Li, *Population and the Environment*, 28.
143. Qu, *Environmental Management in China*, 213.
144. Ibid.
145. Murphey, "Man and Nature," 330.
146. Smil, *The Bad Earth*, 16.
147. Qu, *Environmental Management in China*, 213.

Chapter 3. The Economic Explosion and Its Environmental Cost

1. Susan Shirk, *The Political Logic of Economic Reform in China* (Berkeley: University of California Press, 1993), 176–81.
2. Ibid., 181–82.
3. International Monetary Fund, World Economic Outlook Database, October 2009, imf.org.
4. Kate Xiao Zhou, *How the Farmers Changed China* (Boulder, Colo.: Westview Press, 1996), 46–71.
5. "Zhongguo Wai Shang Zhi Jie Touzi 2008 Nian Chuang Xin Gao" [China's Foreign Direct Investment in 2008 Reaches New Heights], *International Business Times*, January 16, 2009, china.ibtimes.com /articles/2009116/zhongguowaimao.htm.
6. Ron Duncan and Xiaowen Tian, "China's Interprovincial Disparities: An Explanation," China Center for Economic Research, Working Paper Series, no. 1999012, table 2.
7. "Shanghai," U.S. Commercial Service China, 2009, www.buyusa .gov/china/en/shanghai.html.
8. Joshua Muldavin, "The Paradoxes of Environmental Policy and Resource Management in Reform-era China," *Economic Geography* 76, no. 3 (2000): 255.
9. *China Daily*, July 18, 1994.
10. Vaclav Smil, *China's Environmental Crisis: An Inquiry into the Limits of National Development* (Armonk, N.Y.: M. E. Sharpe: 1993), 61.
11. *World Resources 1994–1995* (New York: Oxford University Press, 1994), 131.
12. John Pomfret, "China's Lumbering Economy Ravages Border Forests; Logging Industry Taps Unregulated Markets for Wood," *Washington Post*, March 26, 2001, p. A19.

13. Jason (Guangyu) Wang, "The Development of China's Forestry Sector and Its Implications for Canada," *Canadian International* Council, July 2008, www.canadianinternationalcouncil.org/download/resourcece/archives/foreignpol/cic_wang_e; and Mike Davis, "Illegal Timber Exports Could Cost China Dear," *The Guardian*, March 22, 2006.

14. The official estimate of total forestland in China is 16.55 percent (*2003 Nian Zhongguo Huanjing Zhuangkuang Gongbao* [2003 Report on the State of the Environment in China] [Beijing: State Environmental Protection Administration, 2004]) or approximately 159 million hectares. According to the 1998 and 2000 *State of the Environment* reports from SEPA, the amount of forested land expanded from 13.92 percent to 16.55 percent in those two years (SEPA, *State of the Environment Report*, 1998, 2000, www.zhb.gov.cn/english/SOE/index.htm.) Since the beginning of China's history, China has lost approximately twice that amount—about 290 million hectares of forest or an area three times the size of Alaska. ("Tougher Measures Urged to Enforce Law," *China Daily*, August 30, 1999, p. 2).

15. "Developments in China's Forestry Sector," Xinhua News Agency, March 20, 2009, www.china.org.cn/environment/report_review/2009-03/20/content_17473108.htm.

16. "Global Forest Resources Assessment 2005," Food and Agriculture Organization of the United Nations, 2006, www.fao.org/forestry/static/data/fra2005/global_tables/FRA_2005_Global_Tables_EN.xls.

17. Bochuan He, *China on the Edge* (San Francisco: China Books and Periodicals, 1991), 25–26.

18. Sichuan Environmental Protection Bureau official, taped interview with author's research associate, June 14, 2000, transcript on deposit with author.

19. Ma Tianjie, "Interconnected Forests: Global and Domestic Impacts of China's Forestry Conservation," Wilson Center China Environment Forum, August 2008, www.wilsoncenter.org/topics/docs/forestry_aug08.pdf.

20. "Key Indicators for Asia and the Pacific 2008," Asian Development Bank, 2008, www.adb.org/documents/books/key_indicators/2008/pdf/Key-Indicators-2008.pdf.

21. Jim Yardley, "China's Turtles, Emblems of a Crisis," *New York Times*, December 5, 2007, www.nytimes.com/2007/12/05/world/asia/05turtle.html.

22. "2007 Zhongguo Huanjing Zhuangkang Gongbao: Cao Yuan" [2007 Report on the State of the Environment in China: Grassland], Min-

istry of Environmental Protection, November 17, 2008, www.zhb
.gov.cn/plan/zkgb/2007zkgb/200811/t20081117_131277.htm.

23. *State of the Environment Reports*, 1996, 1997, 1998, 1999, 2000, 2001, 2002.

24. World Bank, *China: Air, Land, and Water* (Washington, D.C.: World Bank, 2001), 23, lnweb18.worldbank.org/eap/eap.nsf/Attachments/China+Env+Report/$File/China+Env+Report.pdf.

25. Zijun Lee, "Deserts Swallowing Up China's Grasslands and Cities," Worldwatch Institute, June 1, 2006, www.worldwatch.org/node/3963.

26. Geping Qu and Jinchang Li, *Population and the Environment in China* (Boulder, Colo.: Lynne Rienner Publishers, 1994), 61–62.

27. Ron Gluckman, "The Desert Storm," *AsiaWeek*, October 13, 2000, www.asiaweek.com/asiaweek/magazine/2000/1013/is.china.html.

28. Shi Yuanchun, "Reflections on Twenty Years' Desertification-control," www.china.com.cn/english/2002/May/32353.htm.

29. Yan Tan and Fei Guo, "Environmental Concerns and Population Displacement in West China," presented at the eighth Asian Pacific Migration Research Network Conference, May 26–29, 2007, Fujian, China, apmrn.anu.edu/conferences/8thAPMRNconference/26.Tan%20Guo.pdf.

30. "Developments in China's Forestry Sector," Xinhua News Agency, March 20, 2009.

31. Qu and Li, *Population and the Environment*, 76.

32. David Murphy, "Desertification—To Heal a Barren Land," *Far Eastern Economic Review*, July 19, 2001, p. 30.

33. Lester R. Brown, "Dust Bowl Threatening China's Future," *Earth Policy Alert*, May 23, 2001, p. 1.

34. John Copeland Nagle, "The Missing Chinese Environmental Law Statutory Interpretation Cases," *New York University Environmental Law Journal* (1996): 520.

35. Ee Lyn Tan, "China Dust Cloud Circled Globe in 13 Days, Study," Reuters, July 20, 2009.

36. Zijun Lee, "Sandstorms Affect Air Quality in Northern China, Beijing," Worldwatch Institute, May 23, 2006.

37. Jim Yardley, "China's Turtles, Emblems of a Crisis."

38. Ibid.

39. "2007 Zhongguo Huanjing Zhuangkang Gongbao: Ziran Shengtai" [2007 Report on the State of the Environment in China: Natural Ecology], Ministry of Environmental Protection, November 17, 2008.

40. Li Xiaohua, "Lack of Funding Causes Dilemma for Nature Reserves," China.org.cn, November 19, 2006, china.org.cn/English/material/189447.htm.
41. World Bank, *China: Air, Land, and Water*, 32–35.
42. "PRC to Build Nature Reserves on Qinghai-Tibet Plateau," Xinhua News Agency, March 9, 2000.
43. Linden Ellis, "Desertification and Environmental Health Trends in China," Woodrow Wilson Center China Environment Forum, April 2, 2007.
44. Sean Gallagher, "Desertification: On the Trail of Abandoned Cities," *The Digital Journalist*, June 2009, www.digitaljournalist.org/issue0906/desertification-on-the-trail-of-abandoned-cities.html.
45. Tian Lei, "Water Crisis in North China," *Southern Window (Nan Feng Chuang)*, June 21, 2008, translated by Three Gorges Probe, - www.probeinternational.org/index.php?g=Beijing-water-crisis/news-and-opinion/water-crisis-north-china.
46. Chris Buckley, "Olympic City's Water in State of Crisis—Report," Reuters, June 26, 2008.
47. "Official: Beijing's Major Water Supplier Faces Serious Water Shortage," Xinhua News Agency, March 21, 2009.
48. Jian Xie, "Addressing China's Water Scarcity: Recommendations for Selected Water Resources Management Issues," World Bank, January 1, 2009.
49. As defined by the World Bank in its *1992 World Development Report* (New York: Oxford University Press, 1992, p. 48), water scarcity is a severe constraint when annual renewable water resource supply is less than 1,000 m³ per capita. Water scarcity exists, however, when there is less than 2,000 m³ per capita.
50. Molly DeSalle et al., "China's South-to-North Water Diversion Project," Columbia University Water Center, August 14, 2008.
51. "Cost of Pollution in China: Economic Estimates of Physical Damages," World Bank and State Environmental Protection Administration of China, 2007, p. 9.
52. "Ground-Water Depletion across the Nation," U.S. Geological Survey, November 2003, pubs.usgs.gov/fs/fs-103-03.
53. "China's Water Shortage to Hit Danger Limit in 2030," Xinhua News Agency, November 16, 2001.
54. Jian Xie, "Addressing China's Water Scarcity," p. 1.
55. Jenny Lieu, "China's Power in Wastewater," Wilson Center China Environment Forum, January 2009, www.wilsoncenter.org/topics/docs/wastewater_jan09.pdf.

56. "Cost of Pollution in China," p. 33.
57. "Poor Pay Most for Water Corruption, Says Anti-Graft Watchdog," Agence-France Presse, June 25, 2008.
58. Ling Li, "Irrigated Area Stays Stable," Worldwatch Institute, November 8, 2007, www.worldwatch.org/node/5445.
59. "Agriculture and Water," *Water Encyclopedia*, www.water encyclopedia.com/A-Bi/Agriculture-and-Water.html.
60. "Frequently Asked Questions," California Farm Water Coalition, 2008, www.farmwater.org/FAQs/Frequently-Asked-Questions.html.
61. *China Statistical Yearbook 2008*, "Water Supply and Water Use."
62. *China Statistical Yearbook 2008, 2007, 2006, 2005, 2004*, "Basic Statistics on Tap Water Supply in Cities by Region."
63. Chen Hong, "Guangdong Water Woes 'To Worsen,'" *China Daily*, November 28, 2007.
64. Philip P. Pan, "Wetlands Running Dry in China; Drought Erodes an Ancient Way of Life in Mythic Marshes," *Washington Post*, July 1, 2001, p. A14.
65. Jian Xie, "Addressing China's Water Scarcity," p. 11.
66. Chris Buckley, "Olympic City's Water in State of Crisis."
67. "Beijing's Water Crisis: 1949–2008 Olympics," Probe International, June 26, 2008.
68. "5.9 Million Chinese Short of Drinking Water: Report," Agence-France Presse, March 1, 2008.
69. "2003 Nian Zhongguo Huanjing Zhuangkuang Gongbao" [2003 Report on the State of the Environment in China].
70. "2007 Zhongguo Huanjing Zhuangkang Gongbao: Dan Shui" [2007 Report on the State of the Environment in China: Water Environment], Ministry of Environmental Protection, November 17, 2008.
71. "Cost of Pollution in China," p. 82.
72. "Report on the State of the Environment in China 2006: Water Environment," Ministry of Environmental Protection, November 5, 2007.
73. "2007 Report on the State of the Environment in China: Water Environment."
74. The main sources of China's water pollution are industrial and municipal wastewater discharges, agricultural runoff from chemical fertilizers, pesticides and animal manure, and the leaching of solid waste. (World Bank, *Clear Water, Blue Skies*, 90.)
75. Mark Wang et al., "Rural Industries and Water Pollution in China," *Journal of Environmental Management* 86, no. 4 (March 2008): 648–59.

76. *China Environment News*, October 4, 1994, p. 4.

77. In one early 1990s case, for example, in a rural village in Hebei Province, farmers established a tannery that earned them revenues of 300 million yuan ($36.6 million). However, in 1993, this tannery discharged 11.3 million m^3 of wastewater with a high content of sulfides and chromium directly into sewage pits. This wastewater seriously damaged surface and groundwater, reduced crop yields, and produced "sour" fruit. However, the farmers claimed they were indifferent to the poor yield because the tannery was far more important to their economic well-being. (*China Environment News*, October 4, 1994, p. 4.)

78. Ryan Hodum, "China's Need for Wastewater Treatment, Clean Energy Grows," Worldwatch Institute, February 1, 2007. www.worldwatch .org/node/4889.

79. *China Human Development Report*, 25.

80. "Research Report on China's Chemical Fertilizer Industry, 2008–2010," Yahoo Business Wire, March 5, 2009, finance.yahoo.com/ news/Research-Report-on-Chinas-bw-14551440.html.

81. World Bank, *China: Air, Land, and Water*, 58.

82. Jian Xie, "Addressing China's Water Scarcity," p. 14.

83. Joseph Kahn, "In China, a Lake's Champion Imperils Himself," *New York Times*, October 14, 2007, www.nytimes.com/2007/10/14/world/ asia/14china.htm.

84. Chris Buckley, "China Says Water Supplies Exploited by 2030," Reuters, December 14, 2007.

85. "Beijing Air Quality Improves in 1999," Zhongguo Xinwen She News Agency [in Chinese] (Beijing: December 28, 1999), translated in *BBC Worldwide Monitoring* (February 2, 2000).

86. Frank Langfitt, "China Struggles to Clear Its Air," *Baltimore Sun*, January 17, 2000, p. 2A.

87. "Cost of Pollution in China," p. 2.

88. "China Quick Facts," World Bank 2008.

89. "Cost of Pollution in China," p. 3.

90. Joseph Kahn and Jim Yardley, "As China Roars, Pollution Reaches Deadly Extremes," *New York Times*, August 25, 2007.

91. "Third of China 'Hit by Acid Rain,'" BBC News, August 27, 2006.

92. "Cost of Pollution in China," p. xvii.

93. U.S. Energy Information Administration.

94. "Japan Energy Data, Statistics and Analysis," Energy Information Administration, www.eia.doe.gov/cabs/Japan/Background .html.

95. Daniel Rosen and Trevor Houser, "China Energy: A Guide for the Perplexed," *China Balance Sheet*, May 2007, p. 17, www.iie.com/publications/papers/rosen0507.pdf,

96. *China Statistical Yearbook 2002*, 28–29.

97. Mao Yushi et al., "The True Cost of Coal," Greenpeace, October 27, 2008, 2.

98. "China: Coal and Mining Equipment," U.S. Commercial Service, 2009, www.buyusa.gov/china/en/coal.html.

99. Coal combustion in industrial boilers and small household stoves (most households still burn solid fuels such as raw coal and wood for cooking and heating) account for up to two-thirds of ambient levels of fine and ultrafine particles, which are the most damaging to human health. These boilers—which are usually inefficient and emit through low smokestacks (*World Resources 1998–1999* [New York: Oxford University Press, 1998], 117)—and stoves are also responsible for most sulfur dioxide and nitrogen oxide emissions. Over time, China has been replacing these boilers with more efficient ones, however, the less efficient boilers are often maintained in service by industry outside the major cities.

100. H. Dean Hosgood III, "Environmental Health and Indoor Air Pollution in China," Woodrow Wilson Center China Environment Forum, May 2007.

101. "Polluting Power: Ranking China's Power Companies," Greenpeace, July 28, 2009, 5.

102. Edward S. Steinfeld et al., "Greener Plants, Grayers Skies?" China Energy Group at the Massachusetts Institute of Technology Industrial Performance Center, August 2008.

103. Hilary French, "Can Globalization Survive the Export of HAZARD," *USA Today*, May 1, 2001, p. 23.

104. Yulanda Chung "Now You See It . . . Now You Don't," *Asiaweek*, October 1, 1999, www.asiaweek.com/asiaweek/magazine/99/1001/hongkong.html.

105. "Sulfur Dioxide Emissions—Guangdong Halts Ten-Year Rise," Xinhua News Agency, January 7, 2007.

106. "Clear Objectives for Cleaner Air," Hong Kong Environmental Protection Department, 2008, www.epd.gov.hk/epd/misc/ehk08/en/air/index.html.

107. Chung, "Now You See It."

108. *Exporting Harm: The High-Tech Trashing of Asia*, ed. Jim Puckett and Ted Smith (Basel Action Network and Silicon Valley Toxics

Coalition, February 25, 2002), 22, www.svtc.org/cleancc/pubs/technotrash.pdf.

109. Cheung Chi-fai, "Greens Fear Impact of Cross-Border Bridge Project," *South China Morning Post*, October 2, 2001, p. 4.

110. "168 mln Motor Vehicles on China's Roads, Up 5% Year-On-Year," Xinhua News Agency, October 8, 2008.

111. Joe McDonald, "China Surpasses U.S. in 2009 Auto Sales," Associated Press, January 9, 2010.

112. Ted C. Fisherman, "The New Great Walls," *National Geographic* 213, no. 5 (May 2008): 142.

113. Xie Chuanjiao, "Beijing Moves to Curb Car Growth," *China Daily*, October 10, 2008, www.chinadaily.com.cn/china/2008-10/10/content_7092425.htm.

114. Jasper Becker, "Car-Crazy Mainland Risks a Wrong Turn," *South China Morning Post*, December 28, 2001, p. 12.

115. Peter Gorrie, "China's Green Leap Forward," *The Star*, March 8, 2008, www.thestar.com/News/Ideas/article/32694.

116. "New Fuel Standards Take Effect in Beijing in Drive for Clean, Green Olympics," Xinhua News Agency, January 1, 2008.

117. Jim Bai, "Beijing to Switch to Cleaner Fuel: Report," Reuters, December 25, 2007.

118. "China's Top Economic Players Explain Economic Stimulus Measures," Xinhua News Agency, December 9, 2008.

119. "Green Watchdog Grants Approval to 153 Projects," *China Daily*, January 10, 2009.

120. Jonathan Ansfield, "Slump Tilts Priorities of Industry in China," *New York Times*, April 18, 2009.

121. Hu and Zou, *China's Population Development*, 92.

122. Ibid., 92–93.

123. "Premier's 'Math' Underscores Scientific Development," Xinhua News Agency, March 4, 2004.

124. "Chinese Population Would be 1.7 Bln Without Family Planning," National Population and Family Planning Commission of China website, April 1, 2009, www.npfpc.gov.cn.

125. July 2009 estimate, *CIA World Factbook*.

126. "Survey Hints China in Face of Possible Baby Boom," National Population and Family Planning Commission of China website, January 16, 2009, www.npfpc.gov.cn.

127. "Chinese Population May Swell to 1.5B," National Population and Family Planning Commission of China website, October 24, 2008, www.npfpc.gov.cn.

128. "China to Stick with One-Child Policy," Agence-France Presse, March 9, 2008.

129. Sharon LaFraniere, "Chinese Bias for Baby Boys Creates a Gap of 32 Million," *New York Times*, April 10, 2009.

130. Sarah Marie Harmon, "China's Missing Women," United Press International, August 6, 2009.

131. Joseph Kahn, "China's Time Bomb; the Most Populous Nation Faces a Population Crisis," *New York Times*, May 30, 2004.

132. In 1994, China bought 34 percent more grain—including wheat, corn, and rice—than in 1993, an increase of 16 million tons. In 1994–95, Chinese wheat buying increased by 13 percent to 17.9 million tons; and in 1995–96, imports dropped only slightly to 16.25 million tons. (Lester Brown, *Who Will Feed China?* [New York: W.W. Norton, 1995], 100.) By 1995, China had become the world's second largest grain importer, second only to Japan.

133. Xie was echoing the title of Lester Brown's article, which was expanded into a full-length book. Brown, *Who Will Feed China?* 17.

134. Guangdong, in particular, was criticized for neglecting its agricultural base; it routinely suffered a shortfall of 2 million tons. ("Commentary Views Agricultural Problem," Xinhua News Agency, February 25, 1995, in Foreign Broadcast Information Service [hereafter FBIS], China Daily Report, March 6, 1995, p. 81.)

135. "Party Chief Discusses Importance of Agriculture," Xinhua News Agency, February 27, 1995.

136. "Renmin Ribao on Conference," *People's Daily*, February 28, 1995, in FBIS, China Daily Report, March 1, 1995, p. 64.

137. *China Statistical Yearbook 1999*, 378.

138. "Severe Drought in Northern China Threatens Agricultural Output for 2nd Year," *Dow Jones International News*, May 30, 2001.

139. "Drought-Hit Chinese Farmers Protest over Fees Policy," *Kyodo News*, June 13, 2001.

140. Zhang Wenjie, "Grain Safety," cctv.com, February 4, 2004, www .cctv.com/english/special/chinatoday/20040204/100699.shtml.

141. "Provincial Agriculture Officials on Investment," *People's Daily*, February 26, 1995, in FBIS, China Daily Report, February 26, 1995, p. 60.

142. Joseph Kahn, "Feeding the Masses: China's Industrial Surge Squeezes Grain Farms, Spurs Needs for Imports," *Wall Street Journal* (Europe), March 13, 1995, p. A6.

143. Lester Brown, "Dust Bowl Threatening China's Future," 2.

144. Ibid.

145. "China Agriculture: Cultivated Land Area, Grain Projections, and Implications," MEDEA summary report, November 1997.

146. Tania Branigan, "Soil Erosion Threatens Land of 100M Chinese, Survey Finds," *The Guardian*, November 21, 2008, www.guardian .co.uk/world/2008/nov/21/china-soil-erosion-population.

147. "Soil Erosion Threatens China," Xinhua News Agency, November 20, 2008, news.xinhuanet.com/english/2008-11/20/content_10389313.htm.

148. "China Reports Erosion Reducing Black Soil in Heilongjiang Province," Xinhua News Agency, January 25, 2000, collected by *BBC Worldwide Monitoring*.

149. Zhong Ma, "China's Past Speaks to Sustainable Future," *Forum for Applied Research and Public Policy* 10 (winter 1995): 53–54.

150. Antoaneta Bezlova, "China: Buying Farmland Abroad, Ensuring Food Security," Inter Press Service, May 9, 2008, ipsnews.net/news/asp?idnews=42301.

151. Jing Ulrich, "China's Grain Security: A Rising Challenge," *Hands-On China Series*, J.P. Morgan, July 2007.

152. Ibid.

153. Bezlova, "China: Buying Farmland Abroad."

154. Rüdiger Falksohn et al., "The Struggle to Satisfy China and India's Hunger," *Der Spiegel*, April 28, 2008.

155. Ulrich, "China's Grain Security."

156. China's migrant worker population was 115 million in 2006. ("China's Migrant Workers Rise in Number to 115mln," website of the Embassy of the People's Republic of China in the United States of America, November 22, 2006, www.china-embassy.org.) These include both those who have registered as temporary residents and those who have not. The size of the latter has been expanding since the early 1980s. (Laurence J. C. Ma and Biao Xiang, "Native Place, Migration, and the Emergence of Peasant Enclaves in Beijing," *China Quarterly* 155 [September 1998]: 556–87.)

157. Ma and Xiang, "Native Place, Migration, and the Emergence of Peasant Enclaves," 554–55.

158. "Financial Crisis Forces China's Migrants Back Home for Work," *People's Daily*, December 9, 2009, english.peopledaily.com.cn/90001/90776/90882/6550129.html.

159. "206,000 People to Move in NW China Relocation Project," Xinhua News Agency, May 7, 2008.

160. Vaclav Smil, "China's Environmental Refugees: Causes, Dimensions, and Risks of an Emerging Problem," in *Environmental Cri-*

sis: Regional Conflicts and Ways of Cooperation, Report of the International Conference at Monte Verita Ascona, Switzerland, 3–7 October 1994 (Center for Security Studies, 1995), 86.

161. "Desertification Causes Yearly Loss of 54 Billion Yuan in China," *People's Daily*, November 26, 2008.

162. Branigan, "Soil Erosion Threatens Land of 100M Chinese."

163. Jonathan Woetzel et al., "Preparing for China's Urban Billion: Summary of Findings," McKinsey Global Institute, March 2008.

164. Chen Jia, "Birth Defects Soar Due to Pollution," *China Daily*, January 31, 2009, www.chinadaily.com.cn/china/2009-01/31/content _7433211.htm.

165. Zhang Ming'ai, "Irong Mine Brings Sickness to Villagers," China .org.cn, December 18, 2008, www.china.org.cn/environment/ news/2008-12/18/content_16973405.htm.

166. Emma Graham-Harrison and Vivi Lin, "China 'Cancer Village' Pays Ultimate Price for Growth," Reuters, December 11, 2008, www.reuters.com/article/worldnews/idustre4ba0kz20081211.

167. Cui Xiaohuo and Gong Zhengzheng, "Polluting Smelters Shut Down After Damaging Farmers' Skin," *China Daily*, October 15, 2008.

168. "Tainted China Water Sickens 450," BBC News, October 11, 2008.

169. Yang Yang, "A China Environmental Health Project Factsheet: Pesticides and Environmental Health Trends in China," Woodrow Wilson Center China Environment Forum, February 28, 2007.

170. Particulates and sulfur dioxide contribute to chronic obstructive pulmonary disease, lung cancer, heart disease, and stroke; increased risk of respiratory infection; and impaired lung functioning. A study of the health effects of air pollution in Shenyang and Shanghai indicated that indoor air pollution, primarily from coal burning stoves, was responsible for 15 to 18 percent of lung cancers and outdoor pollution contributed to another 8 percent.

171. "Cost of Pollution in China."

172. Ivan Tang, "Mainland Air Deadly for Children," *South China Morning Post*, May 6, 1999.

173. While China has begun to phase out leaded gasoline, in Beijing "30% of the gas used is estimated to fall short of the government's environmental standards." Henry Chu, "China Is Passing Pollution to a New Generation, Study Finds," *Los Angeles Times*, June 19, 2002.

174. "Statistic: 10.45%—One in Ten Children in China Has Lead Poisoning," *Beijing Youth Daily*, March 19, 2005, www.pressinterpreter .org/node/84.

175. Ling Li, "Beijing's Auto Emissions Threaten Children's Health," Worldwatch Institute, May 22, 2007, www.worldwatch.org/node/5084.

176. "Pollution Fuelling Social Unrest—Chinese Official," Reuters, April 21, 2006.

177. Ma Tianjie, "Environmental Mass Incidents in Rural China: Examining Large-Scale Unrest in Dongyang, Zhejiang," in *China Environment Series*, no. 10 (2008/2009), ed. Jennifer L. Turner, 33–49.

178. "China Villages Battle Lead, Zinc Poisoning," Radio Free Asia, November 29, 2006.

179. Luisetta Mudie, "Violence in Chongqing Water Dispute," Radio Free Asia, November 25, 2008.

180. "Hundreds Storm Smelter Over Lead Poisoning of Children," Reuters, August 17, 2009.

181. Shi Jiangtao, "Order Restored After Factory Protest," *South China Morning Post*, August 18, 2009.

182. Jim Yardley, "Thousands of Chinese Villagers Protest Factory Pollution," *New York Times*, April 13, 2005.

183. "Hundreds Protest Shanghai Maglev Rail Extension," Reuters, January 12, 2008.

184. Elaine Kurtenbach, "Shanghai Residents Protest Train Line Construction," Associated Press, August 27, 2009.

185. Erik Eckholm, "China's Inner Circle Reveals Big Unrest, and Lists Causes," *New York Times*, June 3, 2001, p. 14.

186. Ma, "Environmental Mass Incidents in Rural China."

187. The real numbers are likely much higher once the damage from large-scale disasters such as the 1998 Yangtze River floods or the 2001 drought are included.

188. Liu Jianqiang, "China Releases Green GDP Index, Tests New Development Path," Worldwatch Institute, September 28, 2006, www.worldwatch.org/node/4626.

189. "Pollution Costs Equal 10% of China's GDP," *Shanghai Daily*, June 6, 2006.

190. Steven Q. Andrews, "Seeing Through the Smog: Understanding the Limits of Chinese Air Pollution Reporting," in *China Environment Series*, no. 10 (2008/2009), ed. Jennifer L. Turner, 5–29.

191. "Cost of Pollution in China," p. 105.

192. Ibid., p. xvii.

193. "Cost of Pollution in China," p. xvii.

194. "China Reels from Worst Drought in a Decade," Reuters, December 21, 2007.

195. Environment, Science, and Technology Section, U.S. Embassy Beijing, "Issues Surrounding China's South-North Water Transfer Project," April 2001, www.usembassy-china.org.cn/english/sandt/SOUTH-NORTH.html.
196. Tamar Hahn, "China Dealing with a Wealth of Environmental Challenges," *The Earth Times*, March 27, 2001.

Chapter 4. The Challenge of Greening China

1. Geping Qu, *Environmental Management in China* (Beijing: China Environmental Sciences Press, 1999), 214.
2. Ibid.
3. United Nations, "Report of the United Nations Conference on the Human Environment" [hereafter UNCHE], paper presented in Stockholm, 1972, www.unep.org/Documents/Default.asp?Document ID=97.
4. "Chinese Delegation Makes Statement on 'Declaration on Human Environment,'" *Peking Review*, June 23, 1972, pp. 9–11.
5. UNCHE, "Report of the United Nations Conference on the Human Environment," UN Document A, conf.48/14/Rev.1.
6. This leading group included officials from the ministries of planning, industry, agriculture, communications, water conservancy, and public health.
7. Qu, *Environmental Management in China*, 214–16.
8. Ibid., 219.
9. Ibid., 219.
10. Ibid., 222.
11. Abigail Jahiel, "The Organization of Environmental Protection in China," *China Quarterly* 156 (December 1998): 769.
12. Ibid., 150.
13. Xiaoying Ma and Leonard Ortolano, *Environmental Regulation in China* (Lanham, Md.: Rowman & Littlefield, 2000), 16.
14. Qu, *Environmental Management in China*, 113–14.
15. State Science and Technology Commission official, interview with author, Beijing, April 1992.
16. During the UNCED, countries engaged in the final negotiations for a framework convention on climate change to control the emissions of greenhouse gases. One of the top emitters of these gases, along with the United States and Russia, China categorically refused to consider any targets or timetables for limiting its emissions, arguing that, as a newly industrializing country, it bore little

historical responsibility for the problem of climate change and that given its status as a developing country, it should not be expected to take action unless fully compensated by the advanced industrialized nations.

17. A commonly accepted definition of sustainable development is provided by the World Commission on Environment and Development in *Our Common Future* (Oxford: Oxford University Press, 1987), 43: "The ability of humanity to ensure that it meets the needs of the present without compromising the ability of future generations to meet their own needs. Sustainable development is not a fixed state of harmony but rather a process of change in which the exploitation of resources, the direction of investments, the orientation of technological development and institutional changes are made consistent with future as well as present needs."

18. In the aftermath of the UNCED, for example, China became the first country to develop an action plan embodying the ideal of sustainable development. China's Agenda 21, modeled on the UNCED's global Agenda 21, was a call to action on every environmental issue from local air pollution to biodiversity. The program incorporated input from over 300 Chinese ministries, commission and local governments, and totaled 128 projects. (SEPA official, interview with author, Beijing, April 2000.) Within the Priority Program for China's Agenda 21, for example, there was also a call to enhance the legal system in order to attain sustainable development. This led to revisions in laws such as the Air Pollution Prevention and Control Law in 1995 (ibid.).

19. This was stated in the "Notice on strengthening management of environmental impact assessments in construction projects undertaken with loans from international financial organizations." Qing Dai and Eduard B. Vermeer, "Do Good Work, But Do Not Offend the 'Old Communists,'" in *China's Economic Security*, ed. Robert Ash and Werner Draugh (New York: St. Martins, 1999), 143.

20. Ibid.

21. In the wake of the UNCED, international environmental NGOs began to flood into China with much-needed technical expertise and funds. International business, too, became more directly involved in elevating the environmental awareness of their Chinese counterparts and in contributing to development projects under the rubric of sustainable development.

22. *World Resources 1998–1999* (Oxford: Oxford University Press, 1998), 124.

23. "White Paper: China's Policies and Actions on Climate Change," State Council Information Office, October 29, 2008, www.china environmentallaw.com/wp-content/uploads/2008/10/china-white-paper-climate-change.doc.

24. "West Told to Keep Its Promises on Tech Transfer," *China Daily*, October 29, 2008, china.org.cn/environment/news/2008-10/29/content_16682184.htm.

25. "Guoji Huanjing Gongyue" [International Environmental Conventions], Ministry of Environmental Protection, www.zhb.gov.cn/inte/gjgy.

26. Shi Jiangtao, "Beijing Gets Flak for Pollution of Waterways," *South China Morning Post*, September 17, 2007.

27. According to Alford and Liebman, "The NPC's power includes the authority to enact all 'basic laws' (*jiben fa*), to supervise the implementation of such laws, and to make amendments to the Constitution. The full NPC meets only once a year. . . . Most law-making activity is instead conducted by its [roughly 155-member] Standing Committee, [which] is authorized to interpret the Constitution, pass laws (*fa*) other than basic laws, which are the domain of the full NPC, interpret laws, and supervise the work of the other principal organs of government." (William P. Alford and Benjamin L. Liebman, "Clean Air, Clear Processes? The Struggle over Air Pollution Law in the People's Republic of China," *Hastings Law Journal* 52 [March 2001]: 706–7.)

28. The name of the National Environmental Protection Agency was changed to the State Environmental Protection Administration in 1998, marking an elevation in the agency's status to the level of a ministry. In 2008, SEPA was elevated to cabinet-level status and renamed the Ministry of Environmental Protection.

29. See, for example, Frank Ching, "Rough Justice: The Law Is No Longer an Ass, but Many Judges Still Are," *Far Eastern Economic Review*, August 20, 1998, p. 13; Jerome A. Cohen and John Lange, "The Chinese Legal System: A Primer for Investors," *New York School of International and Comparative Law* 17 (1997): 345–77; Sam Hanson, "The Chinese Century: An American Judge's Observation of the Chinese Legal System," *William Mitchell Law Review* 28 (2001): 243–52.

30. Hongjun Zhang and Richard Ferris, "Shaping an Environmental Protection Regime for the New Century: China's Environmental Legal Framework," *Sinosphere* 1, no. 1 (1998): 6.

31. For a discussion of all the responsibilities of the EPNRC, see ibid.

32. Wang Jiaquan, "China to Give 'Green' Legislation More Teeth," Worldwatch, August 28, 2007, www.worldwatch.org/node/5328.

33. Wang Canfa, "Chinese Environmental Law Enforcement: Current Deficiencies and Suggested Reforms," *Vermont Journal of Environmental Law* 8, no. 2 (spring 2007): 164, www.vjel.org/journal/pdf/VJEL10051.pdf.

34. Ibid., 171.

35. Kimberly Go, Mayu Suzuki, and Quo Xiaoxia, "Trial by Fire: A Chinese NGO's Work on Environmental Health Litigation in China," Wilson Center China Environment Forum, July 2008, www.wilsoncenter.org/topics/docs/clapv_jul08.pdf.

36. Xin Qiu and Honglin Li, "China's Environmental Super Ministry Reform: Background, Challenges, and the Future," *Environmental Law Reporter*, February 2009, www.epa.gov/ogc/china/xin.pdf.

37. Ma and Ortolano, *Environmental Regulation in China*, 92–93.

38. "An Assessment of Environmental Regulation of the Steel Industry in China," Alliance for American Manufacturing, March 2009, www.americanmanufacturing.org/wordpress/wp-content/uploads/2009/03/chinaenvironmental-report-march-2009.pdf, p. 33.

39. Ma and Ortolano, *Environmental Regulation in China*, 92.

40. "Recent Environmental Law and Public Participation News," Greenlaw, April 13, 2009, www.greenlaw.org.cn/enblog?p=1020.

41. "China to Levy Tax on Polluting Firms," Xinhua News Agency, June 6, 2009, www.shanghaidaily.com/sp/article/2009/200906/20090606/article_403213.htm.

42. EPNRC official, interview with author, Cambridge, Mass., January 1999.

43. Ibid.

44. Jingyun Li and Jingjing Liu, "Quest for Clean Water: China's Newly Amended Water Pollution Control Law," Wilson Center China Environment Forum, January 2009, www.wilsoncenter.org/topics/docs/water_pollution_law_jan09.pdf.

45. "Toxic Leak Threat to Chinese City," BBC News, November 23, 2005, news.bbc.co.uk/2/hi/asia-pacific/4462760.stm.

46. Li and Liu, "Quest for Clean Water."

47. Ibid.

48. Krzysztof Michalak, "Environmental Governance in China," *Governance in China*, report for the Organisation for Economic Co-Operation and Development, September 7, 2005, www.oecd.org/dataoecd/60/37/34617750.pdf, p. 18.

49. In contrast, the U.S. EPA headquarters boasts six thousand employees (Zhang and Ferris, "Shaping an Environmental Protection Regime").

50. Gang He, "China's New Ministry of Environmental Protection Begins to Bark, but Still Lacks in Bite," World Resources Institute EarthTrends, July 17, 2008, earthtrends.wri.org/updates/node/321.

51. "China Improves Enforcement of Environmental Laws," Xinhua News Agency, October 9, 2005, en.chinacourt.org/public/detail .php?id=3957.

52. Qu, *Environmental Management in China*, 221.

53. Hua Guo, "Nation's Plan to Protect Environment Outlined," *China Daily*, May 29, 2001.

54. "China Promises 1.35% of GDP as Annual Environmental Protection Investment," Xinhua News Agency, November 27, 2007, en.chinagate.cn/economics/2007-11/27/content_9302259.htm.

55. Austin Ramzy, "China's Green Spending Falls Short," *Time*, November 28, 2007, www.time.com/time/world/article/0,8599 ,1688554,00.html.

56. Elizabeth Economy, "The Great Leap Backward?" *Foreign Affairs*, September/October 2007, 38–59.

57. Jonathan Watts, "China's Green Champion Sidelined," *The Guardian*, March 12, 2009, www.guardian.co.uk/environment/2009/mar/12/ activism-china.

58. Organisation for Economic Co-Operation and Development (OECD), *"Environmental Compliance and Enforcement in China,"* 2006, www .oecd.org/dataoecd/33/5/37867511.pdf, p. 25.

59. Jahiel, "Organization of Environmental Protection," 759.

60. OECD, "Environmental Compliance and Enforcement in China," p. 6.

61. Qiu and Li, "China's Environmental Super Ministry Reform."

62. Jens Kolhammar, "The Open Government Information Regulation: Obstacles and Challenges," China Elections and Governance, June 7, 2008, en.chinaelections.org/newsinfo.asp?newsid=17891.

63. Charlie McElwee, "Public Disclosure of Environmental Information," China Environmental Law Blog, April 30, 2008, www .chinaenvironmentallaw.com/2009/04/30/public-disclosureofenvir onmental-information.

64. Charlie McElwee, "Blacklist Blacked Out by Black Dragon River Province," China Environmental Law Blog, April 27, 2009, www .chinaenvironmentallaw.com/2009/04/27/blacklist-blacked-out-by -black-dragon-river-province.

65. Ibid.

66. OECD, "Environmental Compliance and Enforcement in China," p. 18.

67. Any entity that discharges pollutants is required to pay a fee to the local government to do so. A polluting entity must register with the local EPB the type, quantity, and concentration of pollutants it will discharge, and then the EPB calculates the fee based on the volume and concentration of pollutants discharged. "Enforcement Trends under Chinese Environmental Law," O'Melveny & Myers LLP, April 16, 2008, www.omm.com/newsroom/publication.aspx?pub=615.

68. Wanxin Li and Hon S. Chan, "Pollution Discharge and Treatment in China: Implications for Environmental Governance," paper presented at the Urban China Research Network Conference, International Conference on Contemporary Urban China Research, January 1–2, 2009, mumford.albany.edu/chinanet/events/guangzhou09/paper/Li_2008_IncomeCapacityEnvironment_draft%206%20tables%20included.pdf.

69. Thomas V. Skinner, "Modifications to EPA Penalty Policies to Implement the Civil Monetary Penalty Inflation Adjustment Rule," Environmental Protection Agency of the United States of America, September 21, 2004, www.epa.gov/compliance/resources/policies/civil/penalty/penaltymod-memo.pdf.

70. Between 1985 and 1994, the number of firms that had charges levied against them grew from approximately 80,000 to over 300,000, and the total amount of fines levied reached approximately 3 billion yuan ($365 million) for pollution discharges. *China Environment News*, February 1995, p. 1.

71. OECD, "Environmental Compliance and Enforcement in China," p. 26.

72. Alex Wang, "View from China: The Yunnan Arsenic Spill Criminal Trial," NRDC Switchboard Blog, April 24, 2009, switchboard.nrdc.org/blogs/awang/view_from_china_the_yunnan_ars.html.

73. Wang Canfa, "Chinese Environmental Law Enforcement: Current Deficiencies and Suggested Reforms," *Vermont Journal of Environmental Law* 8, no. 2 (spring 2007): 167, www.vjel.org/journal/pdf/VJEL10051.pdf.

74. "Gov't Protection of Polluting Factories Causes Concern," Xinhua News Agency, November 28, 2006, www.china.org.cn/english/government/190419.htm.

75. OECD, "Environmental Compliance and Enforcement in China," p. 29.

76. Congressional-Executive Commission on China, "2007 Annual Report of the Congressional-Executive Commission on China: the Environment," October 10, 2007, p. 3.

77. Wang, "View from China."

78. Hua Wang, Susmita Dasgupta, Nlandu Mamingi, and Benoît Laplante, "Incomplete Enforcement of Pollution Regulation: Bargaining Power of Chinese Companies," World Bank Policy Research Working Paper No. 2756, January 18, 2002, p. 6.

79. Qu, *Environmental Management in China*, 318–19.

80. OECD, "Environmental Compliance and Enforcement in China," p. 27.

81. Ibid., p. 6.

82. Jennifer Wu, "Public Participation in the Enforcement of China's Anti-Pollution Laws," *Law, Environment and Development Journal* 4, no. 1 (2008), www.lead-journal.org/content/08035.pdf.

83. "China Intensifies Regional Environmental Supervision," China .org.cn, December 19, 2008, www.pacificenvironment.org/article .php?id=2943.

84. Tod Kaiser and Rongkun Liu, "Taking the Pulse: The One-Year Anniversary of China's Open Government Information Measures," Wilson Center China Environment Forum, August 2009, www .wilsoncenter.org/index.cfm?topic_id=1421&fuseaction=topics .documents&doc_id=549155&group_id=233293.

85. John Copeland Nagle, "The Missing Chinese Environmental Law Statutory Interpretation Cases," *New York University Environmental Law Journal* (1996): 523–24.

86. Jerome Cohen and John E. Lange, "The Chinese Legal System: A Primer for Investors," *New York Law School Journal of International and Comparative Law* 17 (1997): 350.

87. William P. Alford, "Limits of the Law in Addressing China's Environmental Dilemma," *Stanford Environmental Law Journal* 16 (January 1997): 141.

88. Phyllis L. Chang, "Deciding Disputes—Factors That Guide Chinese Courts in the Adjudication of Rival Responsibility Conduct Disputes," *Law and Contemporary Problems* 52, no. 3, in Ma and Ortolano, *Environmental Regulation in China*, 91.

89. Nagle, "Missing Chinese Environmental Law," 537.

90. Ted Plafker, "Chinese Activists Take to the Courts," *International Herald Tribune*, August 28, 2002, p. 20.

91. Violence sometimes accompanies court rulings. In one 1994 case, after a county People's court in Hubei ordered a chemical plant to pay

a fine it had avoided for two years, the workers became enraged, ha-
rassing local EPB officials and destroying their offices. (*China Environment News*, November 1994, p. 1.)

92. Nagle, "Missing Chinese Environmental Law," 530.

93. Chinese environmental lawyer, Council on Foreign Relations, interview with author, New York, January 1999.

94. Julie Chao, "More and More Chinese Saying 'I'll Sue' to Settle Disputes," Cox Newspapers, October 8, 2000, www.coxnews.com/
washingtonbureau/staff/chao/10-08-00CHINALAWSUISADV081SCOX
.html.

95. Ching, "China: Rough Justice," 13.

96. C. David Lee, "Legal Reform in China: A Role for Nongovernmental Organizations," *Yale Journal of International Law* 25 (summer
2000): 367–68.

97. "Court in Foshan Rules in Waste Dumping Case," China Radio
International, March 21, 2008, english.cri.cn/2946/03/21/1321@
335476.htm.

98. "Three Executives Jailed over Toxic Lake," *China Daily*, June 3,
2009, english.sina.com/china/p/2009/0602/245577.html.

99. Gao Jie, "Environmental Protection Courts: Incubator of Environmental Public Interest Litigation or Just A Decoration?" GreenLaw,
October 5, 2008, www.greenlaw.org.cn/enblog/?p=4.

100. Lindon Ellis, "Giving the Courts Green Teeth," Wilson Center
China Environment Forum, October 2008, www.wilsoncenter.org/
index.cfm?topic_id=1421&fuseaction=topics.event_summary&
event_id=477342.

101. Ibid.

102. Gao, "Environmental Protection Courts."

103. "Yunnan Jiang Zai Jiu Hu Liuyu Sheli Huanbao Fanting" [Yunnan
Will Establish Environmental Court in the Nine Lakes and River
Basins Region], Sina, May 31, 2009, news.sina.com.cn/c/2009-05-
31/143117920501.shtml.

104. Gao, "Environmental Protection Courts."

105. Ellis, "Giving the Courts Green Teeth."

106. Wang Canfa, Council on Foreign Relations, interview with author,
New York, May 18, 2001.

107. "Chemical Plant Pollution Case," GreenLaw, March 26, 2009,
www.greenlaw.org.cn/enblog/?p=$912.

108. Go, Suzuki, and Quo, "Trial by Fire."

109. The China Construction Bank, one of the four largest state-owned
commercial banks, for example, reportedly raised $5.11 million in
overseas funds for air pollution monitoring projects in eleven

cities. These projects were the first concrete programs developed by China and the United States following President Clinton's 1998 visit to China. Eighty-five percent of the $5.11 million in funds came from a preferential loan from the Bank of America. ("Bank Clears Air with Help from US Loans," *China Daily*, August 19, 1999, p. 5.)

110. *China Environment News*, January 1995, p. 1.
111. Richard McGregor, "China's Green Credit Move Faces Obstacles," *Financial Times*, February 13, 2008, www.ft.com/cms/s/0/ 03d1ba80-da23-11dc-9bb9-0000779fd2ac.html.
112. Skye Gilbert, "Victory: A Grassroots NGO Empowers a 'Cancer Village' to Take Action," Wilson Center China Environment Forum, January 2009, www.wilsoncenter.org/topics/docs/green _anhui_jan09.pdf.
113. McGregor, "China's Green Credit Move."
114. Zhang Xiya, "Green Securities Policy Presses Forward in China," GreenLaw, March 3, 2009, www.greenlaw.org.cn/enblog/?p=726.
115. The officials must sign contracts with local EPBs outlining specific environmental goals and pledging to work together to achieve these targets. Environmental protection is also, on paper, a criterion for future political advancement for these officials.
116. *China Statistical Yearbook 2008*.
117. Susmita Dasgupta and David Wheeler, "Citizen Complaints as Environmental Indicators: Evidence from China," unpublished manuscript, Environment, Infrastructure and Agriculture Division, Policy Research Department, World Bank, Washington, D.C., 1996, in Ma and Ortolano, *Environmental Regulation in China*, 71.
118. EPB official, interview with author, Dalian, April 2000.
119. "Hotline to Help Settle Environmental Problems," Xinhua News Agency, July 30, 2001, www.xinhuanet.com/english/20010730/ 434912.htm.
120. OECD, "Environmental Compliance and Enforcement in China," p. 33.
121. "Hotline Receives More Complaints about Pollution," Xinhua News Agency, December 6, 2006, www.china.org.cn/english/ environment/191379.htm.
122. "China's Environment Watchdog Warns Leaders of Penalties over Pollution Failures," Xinhua News Agency, September 11, 2008, news.xinhuanet.com/english/2008-09/11/content_9922169.htm.
123. Chen Huiman, "Beijing Shui Jia Tiaozheng Jiang Ting Zheng Nanshui Bei Diao Tuichi Jin Jing Yin Caice" [Changes in Beijing Water Prices Will Be in Accordance With the Delay of the South-North

Water Transfer Project] Nanhai Wang (Nanhai Web), May 12, 2009, www.hinews.cn/news/system/2009/05/12/010476270.shtml.

124. Cui Xiaohuo, "Beijing Looks to Dampen Demand for Scarce Water," *China Daily*, May 12, 2009, www.chinadaily.com.cn/china/2009-05/12/content_7765925.htm.

125. "Beijing to Raise Water Prices This Year—Report," Reuters, May 10, 2009, uk.reuters.com/article/idUKPEK25802.

126. Alex Wang, "The Role of Law in Environmental Protection in China: Recent Developments," *Vermont Journal of Environmental Law* 8, no. 2 (spring 2007): 214–15, www.vjel.org/journal/pdf/VJEL10051.pdf.

127. EPB official, interview with author, Dalian, April 2000.

128. "Jingji De Gao Fenzhi Yu Shengtai Huanbao Ye Bu Xun Se" [The Economy's Large Extra Proportion Given to Environmental Protection], *Yangcheng Xinwen* (Yangcheng Evening News), August 25, 2007, news.163.com/07/0825/14/3MOGJH3A0001124J.html.

129. Robert W. Mead and Victor Brajer, "Environmental Cleanup and Health Gains from Beijing's Green Olympics, *China Quarterly* 194 (June 2008): 275–93.

130. EPB officials, interview with author, Zhongshan, April 2000.

131. Economy, "The Great Leap Backward?"

132. Elizabeth Economy, "Accounting for the Environment in China," PBS, 2006, www.pbs.org/kqed/chinainside/nature/greengdp.html.

133. Ibid.

134. "Yunnan Lake Pollution Controls Detailed," Xinhua News Agency, January 15, 1999.

135. EPB official, interview with author's research associate, Kunming, June 2000.

136. "2007 Zhongguo Huanjing Zhuangkuang Gongbao: Dan Shui Huanjing" [2007 Report on the State of the Environment in China: Water Environment], Ministry of Environmental Protection, November 17, 2008, www.zhb.gov.cn/plan/zkgb/2007zkgb/200811/t20081117_131335.htm.

137. "Water Pollution Controls at Dianchi Lake Pay Off," Xinhua News Agency, November 11, 2002.

138. "China's South-to-North Water Diversion Project," Xinhua News Agency, August 14, 2003.

139. U.S. Embassy in Beijing, "Update on China's South-North Water Transfer Project," June 2003, www.usembassy-china.org.cn/sandt/SNWT-East-Route.htm.

140. Patrick Tyler, "Huge Water Projects Supply Beijing by 860-Mile Aqueduct," *New York Times*, July 19, 1994, p. A8.

141. "Update on China's South-North Water Transfer Project," June 2003.

142. Ibid.

143. Carter Brandon and Ramash Ramankutty, "Toward an Environmental Strategy for Asia," World Bank discussion group paper, Washington, D.C., 1993.

144. Shai Oster, "China Slows Water Project," *Wall Street Journal*, December 31, 2008, online.wsj.com/article/SB1230642759448 42277.html.

145. Christina Larson, "On Chinese Water Project, a Struggle Over Sound Science," *Yale Environment* 360, January 8, 2009, e360.yale.edu /content/feature.msp?id=2103.

146. Chris Buckley, "China Delays Finishing Mammoth Water Project: Report," Reuters, December 5, 2008, www.reuters.com/article/ latestCrisis/idUSPEK345711.

147. Larson, "On Chinese Water Project, a Struggle Over Sound Science."

Chapter 5. The New Politics of the Environment

1. NGOs in China are not the same as their western counterparts. They must be sponsored by a government institution, which has nominal oversight for the NGOs' activities and membership. Still, they represent a substantial advance in independence from the government-organized NGOs that continue to predominate in Chinese society.

2. Minxin Pei, "Democratization in the Greater China Region," *Access Asia Review* 1, no. 2 (1998): 5–40.

3. "Environment Fourth among Chinese Top Concerns: Survey," *China Daily*, April 8, 2008.

4. Guan Xiaofeng, "NGOs Have More Room to Develop," *China Daily*, May 25, 2007.

5. "Paul Mooney, "How to Deal with NGOs—Part I, China," Yale-Global Online, August 1, 2006, yaleglobal.yale.edu/content/how-deal-ngos—part-1-china.

6. Anna Brettell, "Environmental NGOs in the People's Republic of China: Innocents in a Co-opted Environmental Movement?" *Journal of Pacific Asia* 6 (2000): 34.

7. Ibid., 35.

8. Falun Dafa is the spiritual movement that practices Falun Gong (Practice of the Wheel of the Dharma), a set of exercises and

guiding principles that are said to lead its adherents to a higher dimension. The Chinese government, however, has labeled Falun Dafa a cult, and the practice of Falun Gong is forbidden in China.

9. Zhigang Xing, "NGOs Can Become Key Gov't 'Partner,'" *China Daily*, March 13, 2004.

10. "Chinese government praises NGOs' role in making environment-friendly policies," *People's Daily*, October 31, 2007.

11. State Council of the People's Republic of China, *Regulations for Registration and Management of Social Organizations*, People's Republic of China State Council Order No. 250, translated from *People's Daily*, April 11, 1998, in *China Development Brief*, www.chinadevelopmentbrief.com/page.asp?sec=2&sub=1&pg=1.

12. Elizabeth Knup, *Environmental NGOs in China: An Overview*, China Environment Series, no. 1 (Washington, D.C.: Woodrow Wilson Center Press, 1997), 10.

13. John Pomfret, "Chinese Crackdown Mixes Repression with Freedom," *Washington Post*, December 19, 1998, p. A14.

14. Jasper Becker, "Tightening the Noose on Parties," *South China Morning Post*, December 5, 1998, p. 2.

15. State Council, *Regulations for Registration and Management*.

16. Becker, "Tightening the Noose," p. 2

17. "China: Freedom of Association Regulated Away," www.threefreedoms.org/finalreport2/1-cfoa.htm.

18. Congressional-Executive Commission on China, "Development of the Rule of Law," *2008 Annual Report*, 145.

19. Tony Saich, "Negotiating the State: The Development of Social Organizations in China," *The China Quarterly*, March 2000, 133.

20. Ibid., 126.

21. Mooney, "How to Deal with NGOs."

22. Guan, "NGOs Have More Room to Develop."

23. Carl Minzner, "Chinese Civil Society in Transition," *China Review*, no. 47 (summer 2009): 10.

24. Fangqiang Yu, "Challenges for NGOs in China," Asia Catalyst, June 26, 2009. www.asiacatalyst.org.

25. Minzner, "Chinese Civil Society in Transition," 10.

26. Ibid.

27. *2008 Annual Report*, Congressional-Executive Commission on China, 145.

28. Simon Montlake, "China Snares NGOs with Foreign Funding," *Christian Science Monitor*, August 4, 2009.

29. U.S. Embassy official, interview with author, Beijing, March 2000.
30. Brettell, "Environmental NGOs in the PRC," 47.
31. Agenda 21 official, interview with author, Beijing, March 21, 2000.
32. Fengshi Wu, *New Partners or Old Brothers? GONGOs in Transnational Environmental Advocacy in China*, China Environment Series, no. 5 (Washington, D.C.: Woodrow Wilson Center Press, 2002), 56–57.
33. This discussion excludes the many research-oriented environmental NGOs. Their work is discussed in chapter 6, in the context of the international community's involvement in China's environmental situation.
34. Brady Yauch, "Environmentalists Cheer Premier Wen Jiabao's Call to Stop Construction on Liuku Dam," *Probe International*, May 22, 2009.
35. Chinese environmental activist, interview with author, Beijing, July 6, 2000.
36. Ibid.
37. Tang Xiyang and Marcia Marks, *A Green World Tour* (New World Press: Beijing, 1999), insert for p. 240.
38. Ibid., insert for p. 221.
39. Ibid., insert for p. 240.
40. Chinese environmental activist, interview with author, Beijing, July 6, 2000.
41. Andy Cheng, "Wild at Heart," *South China Morning Post*, September 30, 2005.
42. Bochuan He, *China on the Edge* (San Francisco: China Books and Periodicals, 1991), 209.
43. Mark Hertsgaard, "What We Need to Survive," *Boston Globe*, January 24, 1999, p. F1.
44. Bochuan He, *China on the Edge*, 43–49.
45. Ibid., 50–51.
46. Hertsgaard, "What We Need to Survive," p. F1.
47. Ai Wang, "Chinese Environmentalist Dai Quing [*sic*] Speaks Out on Three Gorges Dam," Environment News Service, May 26, 1999, www.threegorgesprobe.org/tgp/print.cfm?contentID=2808.
48. Ibid.
49. The English-language version of the book includes several essays not in the 1989 Chinese version, including a letter by Li Rui, Mao Zedong's secretary for industrial affairs and a vice minister of the Ministry of Water Resources and Electric Power, to Jiang Zemin urging that the project be canceled.

50. Qing Dai, *Yangtze! Yangtze!*, ed. Patricia Adams and John Thibodeau, trans. Nancy Liu, Mei Wu, Yougeng Sun, and Xiaogang Zhang (Toronto: Earthscan Publications, 1994), 136.
51. Ibid., xxiii.
52. Mark Levine, "And Old Views Shall Be Replaced By New," *Outside*, October 1997, www.outsidemag.com/magazine/1097/9710oldviews.html.
53. John Pomfret, "Dissidents Back China's WTO Entry: Trade Status Said Essential for Improved Human Rights," *Washington Post*, May 11, 2000, p. A01.
54. Brady Yauch, "Chinese Officials Still Angry over the Appearance of Dissident Writers at Last Weekend's Symposium," *Probe International*, September 16, 2009.
55. "China Bans Author from the Frankfurt Book Fair," *Probe International*, September 24, 2009.
56. Chinese environmental activist, interview with author's research associate, Beijing, July 6, 2000.
57. In addition to the formally approved name, Liang wrote Friend of Nature (later changed to Friends) under the Chinese name on his seal. Friends of Nature then became the name by which the organization was known.
58. Chinese environmental activist, interview with author, Beijing, April 2000.
59. Qing Dai and Eduard B. Vermeer, "Do Good Work, But Do Not Offend the 'Old Communists,'" in *China's Economic Security*, ed. Robert Ash and Werner Draugh (New York: St. Martins, 1999), 147.
60. Chinese environmental activist, interview with author, Beijing, April 2000.
61. "About Friends of Nature," *Friends of Nature News* 2 (1999): 8.
62. Chinese environmental activist, interview with author, New York, 1998.
63. "Activist Writer Wang Lixiong Dismissed from Environmental Group," iso.hrichina.org/iso/news.
64. George Wehrfritz, "Green Heat," *Newsweek*, October 7, 1996, 13.
65. Martin Williams, "The Year of the Monkey," *BBC Wildlife* (January 2000): 72.
66. Ibid., 73.
67. Chinese environmental activist, interview with author, New York, June 2000.
68. Williams, "Year of the Monkey," 74.

69. Chinese environmental activist, interview with author, Beijing, April 2000.

70. Wehrfritz, "Green Heat," 13.

71. Chinese environmental activist, interview with author, Beijing, April 2000.

72. Chinese environmental activist, interview with author, New York, June 2000.

73. The Chinese name, *Beijing Zhinong Shengtai Baohu Fazhan Yanjiu Zhongxin*, translates into Beijing Zhinong Research Center for Ecological Conservation and Development. This name includes Xi Zhinong's given name—Zhinong—and has remained the same even as the English name has changed.

74. Lihong Shi, co-founder, Green Plateau Institute, talk at Woodrow Wilson Center, Washington, D.C., December 8, 2000.

75. Ibid.

76. Lihong Shi, interview with author, New York, February 2002.

77. Guy Trebay, "Dead Chic," *Village Voice*, May 26–June 1, 1999.

78. "About Friends of Nature," 2.

79. Peter Popham, "These Animals Are Dying Out, and All Because the Lady Loves Shahtoosh," *The Independent*, June 20, 1998, reprinted in "About Friends of Nature," 7.

80. "Wild Yak Brigade Rides to the Rescue of the Rare Chiru," U.S. News and World Report, November 22, 1999, 38.

81. Congjie Liang, "Many Successes—But Much More Still Needs to Be Done," *Friends of Nature News* 2 (1999), www.fon.org.cn/ newsletter /99–2e/4.html.

82. Chinese NGO leaders, interview with author, Woodrow Wilson Center, Washington, D.C., December 8, 2000.

83. "Plans For the Establishment of the Second NGO Sponsored Nature Protection Station in China," Green River website, www.green-river .org/english.

84. "The Main Awards Acquired by the Green River," Green River website, www.green-river.org/english.

85. Chinese environmental activists, interview with author's research associate, Kunming, June 2000.

86. John Pomfret, "Environmentalists Keep Up Fight over Chinese Dam," *Washington Post*, June 22, 2003.

87. Ma. Ceres P. Doyo, "RM Award for China's Water Guardians," *Philippine Daily Inquirer*, August 30, 2009.

88. "The 2009 Ramon Magsaysay Award: Response of Yu Xiaogang," Ramon Magsaysay Award Foundation.

89. Chinese environmental activist, interview with author, New York, March 2000.

90. "Individuals Changing the World," *Beijing Review*, August 14, 2000, p. 20.

91. Ibid., 16.

92. Ibid., 17.

93. Chinese Academy of Social Sciences, "2007 Nian Quan Guo Gongzhong Huanjing Diaocha Baogao" [2007 China General Public Environmental Survey], China Environmental Awareness Program, April 3, 2008, pp. 3–4.

94. Ibid.

95. Wang Yongchen, interview with author, New York, February 2002; Kelly Haggart and Mu Lan, "People Power Sinks a Dam," *Three Gorges Probe News Service*, October 16, 2003.

96. Xiaowei Chen, "The Multiple Roles of Media in Today's Chinese Society," paper presented at the "Memory and Media in and of Contemporary China" conference, University of California, Berkeley, in Xiaoping Li, *Significant Changes in the Chinese Television Industry and Their Impact in the PRC—An Insider's Perspective* (Washington, D.C.: Center for Northeast Asian Policy Studies, Brookings Institution, August 2001), 13, www.brookings.org /dybdocroot/fp/ cnaps/papers/li_01.pdf.

97. Xiaoping Li, *Significant Changes*, 8.

98. Joel Martinsen, "Everybody Loves CCTV," *Danwei*, December 21, 2007.

99. Ibid., 10.

100. "Cases of Citizens Defending Environmental Rights: 'Cancer Village' Residents Petition for Clean Water," Greenlaw, February 25, 2009, greenlaw.org.cn/enblog/?p=1407.

101. Chinese environmental activist, interview with author, Beijing, April 2000.

102. Ying Wang, "Re-energizing Battery Recycling Efforts," *China Daily*, August 7, 2000.

103. Jun Liu and Qian Zeng, "Public Take Recycling into Their Own Hands," *China Daily*, September 8, 2000.

104. Ibid.

105. For a discussion of such activities, see Dai and Vermeer, "Do Good Work," 154.

106. Kanping Hu, talk at Woodrow Wilson Center, Washington, D.C., December 8, 2000.

107. Joseph Kahn, "In China, a Lake's Champion Imperils Himself," *New York Times*, October 13, 2007.

108. Environmental activist, talk in Washington, D.C., December 8, 2000.
109. Chinese environmental activist, interview with author, Beijing, June 2002.
110. "Environmental Groups Join Beijing's Bid for Green Olympics," *People's Daily*, August 25, 2000, fpeng.peopledaily.com.cn/ 200008/24/eng20000824_48957.html.
111. "Beijing Relocates Steel-Making Capacity to Hebei Province," *New China News Agency*, January 20, 2003, as reported in BBC Monitoring International Reports.
112. Dai and Vermeer, "Do Good Work," 147.
113. Amanda Bower, "Not Everyone in China Is Cheering," *Time*, July 23, 2001, 10.
114. Hannah Beech, "China's Turn," *Time*, August 9, 2004.
115. Kenji Hall, "China's Commuter Olympics," *BusinessWeek*, February 12, 2008.
116. *China after the Olympics: Lessons from Beijing*, Greenpeace China, July 28, 2008.

Chapter 6. The Devil at the Doorstep

1. This is discussed at length in chapter 4.
2. For an in-depth examination of China's process of accession to international environmental treaties and its record on implementation of those treaties, see Michel Oksenberg and Elizabeth Economy, "China's Accession to and Implementation of International Environmental Accords 1978–1995," occasional paper, Asia/Pacific Research Center, Stanford University, February 1998.
3. Ibid., 13.
4. For the extraordinary story of World Wildlife Fund's first, tumultuous cooperative venture in China, see George Schaller, *The Last Panda* (Chicago: University of Chicago Press, 1993).
5. UN Environment Programme [hereafter UNEP], "China Closes Ozone Depleting Chemical Plants," press release, July 1, 2007.
6. "Data Access Centre," UNEP, Ozone Secretariat, updated March 23, 2009.
7. Oksenberg and Economy, "China's Accession," 29–30.
8. "China Closes Ozone Depleting Chemical Plants," UNEP, press release, July 1, 2007.
9. Elizabeth Economy, "Negotiating the Terrain of Global Climate Policy in the Soviet Union and China: Linking International and

Domestic Decisionmaking Pathways" (Ph.D. diss., University of Michigan, 1994), 159.

10. Ibid., 179.

11. State Science and Technology Commission officials, interviews with author, Beijing, June 1994 and May 1996.

12. State Planning Commission official, interview with author, Beijing, June 1992.

13. Joint implementation was a scheme proposed by the advanced industrialized countries whereby they would receive credit toward achieving their targets for greenhouse gas reduction by undertaking projects in developing countries (e.g., a U.S. power company could pursue a reforestation effort in Brazil) where the cost of taking action would be substantially lower than the domestic cost.

14. The rules governing CDM have yet to be fully worked out.

15. Registered Project Activities by Host Party, Clean Development Mechanism Statistics, United Nations Framework Convention on Climate Change, www.dm.unfccc.int.

16. "China Per-unit Energy Consumption Falls 3.35% in H1," Xinhua News Agency, August 2, 2009.

17. "China to Increase Renewable Energy," United Press International, July 6, 2009.

18. Eadie Chen and Tom Miles, "China to Hike Fuel Taxes, Float Prices in Major Reform," Reuters, December 5, 2008.

19. "Developments in China's Forestry Sector," Xinhua News Agency, March 20, 2009.

20. Norihiko Shirouzu, "China Uses Green Cars to Bolster Auto Sector," *Wall Street Journal*, March 23, 2009, online.wsj.com/article /SB123773108089706101.html.

21. Martin Lees, "China and the World in the Nineties" (conference summary report, Beijing, January 25, 1991), 30–31.

22. Ibid., 9–19.

23. Ibid., 22.

24. Foreign Broadcast Information Service [hereafter FBIS], China Daily Report, December 27, 1990, p. 31.

25. The sponsoring entities for CCICED later expanded to include the United Kingdom, Germany, the Netherlands, and the World Bank in the wake of the UNCED. The CCICED has anywhere from five to seven short-term task forces focusing on issues such as resource accounting and pricing, biodiversity, trade and environment, and energy. It consists of fifty Chinese and foreign environment and economics experts, as well as Chinese officials and scientists. The group meets annually and issues reports that provide concrete rec-

ommendations for the government. November 2002 recommendations included enhancing the role of private organizations in environmental enforcement and employing eco-taxes. Recommendations are often directly delivered to top-level Chinese officials because some Chinese participants themselves are vice ministers or even ministers. (They also run seminars and workshops to disseminate key information.)

26. These included protection of sovereignty over natural resources, free transfer of technology from the more to the less advanced industrialized countries, and the responsibility of the advanced industrialized countries to bear the cost of addressing the global environmental problems to which it contributed so heavily.

27. See chapter 3 for a full discussion of UNCED's impact on Chinese domestic environmental practices.

28. Correspondence with U.S.–based NGO leader on file with author, November 2001.

29. FBIS, China Daily Report, June 29, 1994, p. 22.

30. FBIS, China Daily Report, July 11, 1994, p. 31. Officially, in 1996, the Chinese claimed that one-third of the $4 billion necessary to fund these projects had been raised. One SSTC official, however, suggested that this figure was likely inflated.

31. Not all Chinese officials welcome the deeper integration of international environmental protection values, attitudes, and approaches with those of China. Despite now widespread acceptance of the ideals of sustainable development, for example, the term's western roots became problematic in 1995–1997. There was increasing discussion in the Chinese media suggesting that sustainable development was part of a master plan by advanced industrialized countries (and especially the United States) to contain China by forcing it to slow the pace of economic growth in order to protect the environment. While this period appears to have been a temporary aberration in an overall trend toward accepting the ideals embraced by the concept of sustainable development, it suggests that environmental protection, like many other multilateral issues, has the potential to be easily politicized.

32. Agenda 21 Center official, interview with author, Beijing, April 2000.

33. Notably, SEPA is the secretariat for CCICED and co-sponsor of the World Bank report.

34. UNEP, "Summary of Information Publicly Available on Relevant Elements of the Operation of Clean Development Mechanism and the Amounts of HCFC-22 Production Available for Credits," Executive

Committee for the Multilateral Fund for the Implementation of the Montreal Protocol, April 3, 2009, www.multilateralfund.org/files/57/5762.pdf.

35. Chris Wright, "Green Finance: Cleaning Up in China," *Euromoney*, October 3, 2007.

36. Jeffrey Ball, John D. McKinnon and Shai Oster, "China Cashes In on Global Warming," *Wall Street Journal*, January 8, 2007, p. A11.

37. Daniel Esty and Seth Dunn, "Greening U.S. Aid to China," *China Business Review* (January–February 1997): 41–45.

38. World Bank, "Country Lending Summaries—China," 2009, go.world bank.org/J7TULWEO00.

39. Asian Development Bank, *Annual Report 2007*, April 8, 2008, 45.

40. OECD, ODA by Recipient by Country, stats.oecd.org/Index.aspx ?DataSetCode=ODA_RECIPIENT.

41. Ministry of Foreign Affairs of Japan, "Japan's International Cooperation: Japan's ODA White Paper 2008," March 2009, 179.

42. "Japan to Promote Environmental Tech Transfer in China," *People's Daily*, December 29, 2007, english.people.com.cn/90001/90776 /90883/6330165.html, and "Japan PM Calls for 'Creative Partnership,'" *China Daily*, December 29, 2007, chinadaily.com.cn/china /2007-12/29/content_6357675.htm.

43. United States Department of the Treasury, "U.S. Fact Sheet: Energy and Environment Accomplishments," press release, December 4, 2008.

44. Conversation and email exchange (April 22, 2009) with U.S. embassy in Beijing officials Brent Christianson and Clark T. Randt.

45. Elizabeth Economy, "China: The Great Leap Backward?" in *Environmental Policy*, ed. Norman J. Vig and Michael E. Kraft (Washington, D.C.: CQ Press, forthcoming).

46. U.S. Department of Energy, "U.S.–China Clean Energy Research Center Announced," press release, July 15, 2009.

47. Duncan Clark, "West Blamed for Rapid Increase in China's CO_2," *The Guardian* (UK), February 23, 2009.

48. Geoffrey York, "Beijing's Footprint," *The Globe and Mail* (Canada), January 3, 2009.

49. York, "Beijing's Footprint."

50. "FOCUS—China's Sinopec Provokes Conservation Uproar in Gabon," Xinhua Financial Network News, October 1, 2006, accessed on Nexis; and Lydia Polgreen, "Pristine African Park Faces Development," *New York Times*, February 21, 2009.

51. U.S. Department of the Treasury, "HP 417: Fact Sheet: Second Meeting of the U.S.–China Strategic Economic Dialogue," press release,

May 23, 2007; Wan Zhihong, "Westinghouse Helps Develop China's Nuclear Sector," *China Daily*, March 2, 2009; Alex Pasternack, "Hillary Clinton Hearts Beijing's Super Efficient Trigeneration Power Plant," Treehugger.com, February 23, 2009; BP, "BP Reinforces Its Commitment to China," press release, January 18, 2008.

52. NRDC official, phone interview with author, February 2002.

53. Shanghai EPB official, interview with author, Shanghai, September 1999.

54. "Water Crisis, Part I," www.websiteasaboutchina.com/envi/ envi ronment_1_1.htm.

55. William P. Alford and Yuan Yuan Shu, "Limits of the Law in Addressing China's Environmental Dilemma," *Stanford Environmental Law Journal* (January 1997): 136.

56. Arthur Cheung, "Nation's First Emissions Exchange Likely to Start Trading by End of Year," Clear the Air News Blog (online, via Reuters), February 20, 2009.

57. Julian Wong, "Tianjin to Win the Environmental Exchange Race?" The Green Leap Forward, October 7, 2008, greenleapforward .com/2008/10/07/Tianjin-to-win-the-environmental-exchange-race.

58. Aminul Huq, Bindu N. Lohani, Kazi F. Jalal, and Ely A. R. Ouano, "The Asian Development Bank's Role in Promoting Cleaner Production in the People's Republic of China," *Environmental Impact Assessment Review* 19 (1999): 550–51.

59. Huq et al., "Asian Development Bank's Role," 542.

60. Some corporations, such as BP, have moved well beyond supporting only capacity building directly related to their immediate needs and are also focusing on China's long-term environmental outlook. BP has been working for seven years with the World Wide Fund for Nature to support the inclusion of environmental education in a range of subjects at three teaching universities. After a three-year trial run, the program is now being expanded to ten universities and developing certificate and masters degree courses in environmental education. On a much smaller scale, Shell has supported renewable energy projects such as the development of biogas in Yunnan and gasified straw in Zhejiang. "Multinationals Meet to Explore 'Corporate Social Responsibility in China,'" *China Development Brief* 4, no. 1 (2001).

61. United Nations Environment Programme, "Promoting Chemical Safety and Emergency Preparedness in Chemical Industry in China," September 16, 2008.

62. The international demand for partnership has far outpaced the capabilities of the limited number of qualified Chinese counterparts.

Venturing outside the major cities and well-known Chinese institutions greatly increases the start-up costs for the international partner. The top Chinese research institutes, universities, and think tanks, however, are full, if not over-subscribed, with international cooperative ventures. This produces its own challenges. In one case, for example, a U.S.–based think tank expended several years and almost $120,000 in travel and research expenses before its prominent, well-respected Chinese partner admitted that he would not be able to undertake the research project he had promised because his time was occupied with several other substantial international projects.

63. Director, Beijing-based U.K. multinational, email correspondence on file with author, March 2002.

64. Huq et al., "Asian Development Bank's Role," 551.

65. World Bank, *China: Air, Land, and Water* (Washington, D.C.: World Bank, 2001), 2.

66. PRC Ministry of Environmental Protection, "Premier Calls for Closer Cooperation in Environmental Protection with Germany," press release, January 30, 2009.

67. Cleaner production is also a central element of China's Agenda 21 action plan.

68. International Organization for Standardization, "The ISO Survey—2007," 2008, www.iso.org/iso/survey2007.pdf.

69. Environmental Defense Fund, "The Wal-Mart Effect," November 5, 2008, www.edf.org/page.cfm?tagID=2101.

70. "Yutong Building Eco-Friendly Buses for 2008 Beijing Olympics," ChinaCSR.com, September 24, 2007, www.chinacsr.com/en/2007/09/24/1710-yutong-building-eco-friendly-buses-for-2008-beijing-olympics/.

71. "Alcoa to Work with China's Henan Province on Sustainable Aluminum Production," ChinaCSR.com, February 18, 2009, www.chinacsr.com/en/2009/02/18/4522-alcoa-to-work-with-chinas-henan-province-on-sustainable-aluminum-production/.

72. Zhao Ming, "EMCA and ESCO Industry Development in China," China ESCO Association (EMCA), presentation at CTI Industry Joint Seminar, New Delhi, India, March 7–8, 2007; and EMCA homepage, March 2009, www.emca.cn.

73. John Copeland Nagle, "The Missing Chinese Environmental Law Statutory Interpretation Cases," *New York University Environmental Law Journal* (1996): 537.

74. Ibid.

75. Robert C. G. Varley, "The World Bank and China's Environment 1993–2003," World Bank Operations Evaluation Department, 2003, 2.

76. "Polluters Told to Clean Up Their Act," *China Daily*, April 15, 2009.
77. Ibid.
78. The case of the U.S. firm Combustion Engineering has become part of the lore of multinationals' experience in China. After Combustion Engineering licensed its designs to the Ministry of Electric Power, the Ministry shared the designs with all of China's large boiler makers, failing to compensate Combustion Engineering appropriately in the process. Even the Global Environmental Facility, whose Chinese counterpart is the powerful Ministry of Finance, has encountered serious problems in this regard. A large-scale project to "subsidise the acquisition of technology licenses for new industrial boiler technologies by Chinese firms" failed to attract top multinationals in part because of their concern that their intellectual property would not be respected by their Chinese partner (Jim Watson, Xue Liu, Geoffrey Oldham, Gordon Mackerron, and Steven Thomas, "International Perspectives on Clean Coal Technology Transfer to China: Final Report to the Working Group on Trade and Environment," China Council for International Cooperation on Environment and Development, August 2000, 55). The experience of Combustion Engineering has chastened other companies, such as Mitsui Babcock, which has resisted licensing its technology. Some multinationals attempt to protect themselves by identifying some parts of a technology or process that they are willing to transfer and some that they are not. Shell, for example, transfers the know-how embodied in its gasification process but retains the design of key components to preserve the company's technological and market advantage. Others, such as General Motors, may not only share the technology but also work jointly with Chinese partners on basic R&D, investing Chinese managers, scientists, and experts in the long-term future of the joint venture. GM's venture with Shanghai Automotive, for example, includes basic research and collaboration on engineering, software, and biomechanics, among other areas of technology development. Chinese managers and technicians are also sent to GM plants in the rest of the world, and GM places foreign managers and technicians in its Chinese venture. Still, GM does not share some of its most advanced technology, for example, with regard to fuel cells, for national security reasons.
79. Watson et al., "International Perspectives," 36.
80. Ibid., 29.
81. A joint effort among the Massachusetts Institute of Technology, Qinghua University, and the Swiss Federal Institutes of Technology

to improve boiler efficiency in 256 sites in Henan, Jiangsu, and Shanxi provinces initially failed, despite developing a number of well-tailored and inexpensive measures for the various boiler sites. The MIT-led team discovered that the SOE directors had no immediate incentive to upgrade the technologies in their plants. The team is now researching the linkage between pollution and local health costs to help persuade local officials and enterprise directors of the importance of the project as well as searching out mechanisms for funding to implement the upgrades. (At the same time, the team is confronting resistance from local public health officials, who do not want to share information.) Watson et al., "International Perspectives," 50.

82. World Bank, *China: Air, Land, and Water*, 102–4.

83. Terence Tsai, Stefan Eghbalian, and Hans Tsai, "China's Green Challenge," *Harvard China Review* 2, no. 1 (2000): 85.

84. Ibid.

85. Ibid.

86. World Bank, *China: Air, Land, and Water*, xxii.

87. Peter Morici, *Reconciling Trade and the Environment in the World Trade Organization* (Washington, D.C.: Economic Strategy Institute, 2002), 8.

88. Changhua Wu, "Trade and Sustainability—A China Perspective," *Sinosphere* 3, no. 3 (2000): 29.

89. Li Zijun, "EU 'Green' Directives Cast Challenge to China's Electronics Industry," WorldWatch Institute, February 22, 2006, www .worldwatch.org/node/3883.

90. Jieqiong Yu, Peter Hills, and Richard Welford, "Extended Producer Responsibility and Eco-design Changes: Perspectives from China," *Corporate Social Responsibility and Environmental Management* 15, no. 2 (2007): 111–24.

91. "China to Keep General Tariff Level at 9.8% in 2009," Xinhua News Agency, December 18, 2008.

92. Daniel Rosen and Trevor Houser, *China Energy: A Guide for the Perplexed*, Center for Strategic and International Studies and Peterson Institute for International Economics, May 2007, 8–10; and Flora Kan, "TOP-1000 Enterprises Energy Saving Project in China," UNDP, presentation for UN Energy conference, September 22–23, 2008, www.unido.org/fileadmin/user_media/Services/Energy_and _Climate_Change/EPU/TOP1000_UN_Energy_FloraKan.pdf.

93. Trevor Houser, "Green and Mean: Can the New U.S. Economy be Both Climate-Friendly and Competitive?" testimony before the

Commission on Security and Cooperation in Europe, U.S. Congress, March 10, 2009.

94. "UPDATE 1-China Energy Intensity Fell 4.59 Pct in 2008," Reuters, February 25, 2009.

95. Flora Kan, "Top-1000 Enterprises Energy Saving Project in China," UNDP, presentation for UN Energy conference, September 222–3, 2008, www.unido.org/fileadmin/user_media/Services/ Energy_and_Climate_Change/EPU/TOP1000_UN_Energy_FloraKan .pdf.

96. Li Jing, "Green Light Given to 153 New Projects," *China Daily*, January 10, 2009, chinadaily.com.cn/china/2009-01/10/content _7384689.htm.

97. "Tianjin Reduces EIA Approval Process to Seven Days," *Tianjin Daily*, February 9, 2009, news.sina.com.cn/o/2009-02-09/07381 5132565s.shtml.

98. United States Trade Representative, "World Trade Organization Adopts Panel Report in *China–Intellectual Property Rights* Dispute," press release, March 20, 2009.

99. General Electric, "Intellectual Property in China," 2009, www.ge .com/citizenship/performance_areas/public_policy_china.jsp.

100. "Ministry: No Surge Expected in China's Textile Exports," *People's Daily*, January 22, 2009, English.peopledaily.com.cn/90001 /90776/90884/6579775.html.

101. Ibid., 6.

102. Ibid., 5–8.

103. Asia-Pacific Economic Cooperation [APEC], "Summary: APEC in Sustainable Development 1999," 203.127.220.67/apec_ groups /other_apec_groups/sustainable_development.downloadlinks.0002 .linkURL.download.ver5.1.9.

104. Asia-Pacific Economic Cooperation [APEC], "APEC Energy Ministers Joint Statement on Clean Energy and Sustainable Development" May 12, 2000, 203.127.220.67/apec/ministerial_statements/ sectoral_ministerial/energy/00energy/00cleanenergy.html.

105. Asia-Pacific Economic Cooperation [APEC] homepage, 2009, www .apec.org.

106. Ibid.

107. Michael Richardson, "Sharing the Mekong: An Asia Challenge," *International Herald Tribune*, October 30, 2002, p. 2.

108. For an informative and insightful look at the historical and contemporary issues surrounding the Three Gorges Dam, see Qing Dai, *Yangtze! Yangtze!*, ed. Patricia Adams and John Thibodeau,

trans. Nancy Liu, We Mei, Sun Yongeng, Zhang Xiaogang (London: Earthscan, 1994).

109. Former president of the World Bank James Wolfenson has increased the range of "safeguards" accounted for in any project assessment. Gender, resettlement, minority populations, environment, and public participation are all factors that must be considered before the Bank will fund a project. In China, such considerations have hampered several potential collaborations.

110. Karen Cook, "Dam Shame," *Village Voice*, March 29–April 4, 2000, p. 48, www.villagevoice.com/issues/0013/cook.php.

111. International Rivers Network, "Three Gorges Dam: The Cost of Power," fact sheet, October 2008, internationalrivers.org/files /3Gorges_factsheet.lorez_.pdf; and Chang Hongxiao and Ouyang Hongliang, "Three Fragile Gorges," *Caijing*, January 21, 2008, www .caijing.com.cn. The *Caijing* article says RMB 40 billion has been allocated for resettlement, a figure roughly confirmed by a 2007 *China Daily* article that puts the figure at RMB 34 billion.

112. "Three Gorges Work 'Shoddy,'" *Financial Times*, June 8, 1999, www.irn.org/programs/threeg/990608.ft.html410A.

113. Kelly Haggart, "SARS and Falun Gong Provide Pretexts for Three Gorges Arrests," Three Gorges Probe News Service, August 14, 2003, www.threegorgesprobe.org/tgp/index.cfm?DSP=Content& ContentID=8122.

114. "China Spent 26.5 Bln U.S. Dollars on Three Gorges Project," *China Daily*, March 26, 2009; and "4 Million More People to be Moved from Gorges Area," *China Daily*, October 12, 2007.

115. Jim Yardley, "Chinese Dam Projects Criticized for Their Human Costs," *New York Times*, November 19, 2007, nytimes.com/2007 /11/19/world/asia/19dam.html.

116. International Rivers Network, "Three Gorges Dam."

117. Peter H. Gleick, "Water Brief 3: Three Gorges Dam Project, Yangtze River, China," *The World's Water 2008–2009: The Biennial Report on Freshwater Resources* (Washington, D.C.: Island Press and Pacific Institute for Studies in Development, Environment and Security, 2009), 145.

118. Chang and Ouyang, "Three Fragile Gorges."

119. Ryan Hodum, "China's Need for Wastewater Treatment, Clean Energy Grows," Worldwatch Institute, February 1, 2007, www .worldwatch.org/node/4889.

120. John Pomfret, "China's Giant Dam Faces Huge Problems," *Washington Post*, January 7, 2001, p. A1.

121. Hodum, "China's Need for Wastewater Treatment."

122. "China Warns of Environmental 'Catastrophe' from Three Gorges Dam," Xinhua News Agency, September 26, 2007.

123. "China Spent 26.5 Bln U.S. Dollars," *China Daily*.

124. National Bureau of Statistics of China, *China Statistical Yearbook 2008* (Beijing: China Statistical Press, 2008), 87.

125. Ibid., 328, 341.

126. "China Sets Route for Second West-East Natural Gas Pipeline," Xinhua News Agency, August 27, 2007, news.xinhuanet.com /English/2007-08/27/content_6612538.htm.

127. GE, "China's Milestone West-to-East Pipeline, One of the World's Largest Gas Transmission Projects, Again Turns to GE Oil & Gas Technology," press release, March 25, 2009, www.genewscenter .com/Content/Detail.asp?ReleaseID=6376&NewsAreaID=2&Menu SearchCategoryID=.

128. Jiang Gaoming, "Stopping the Sandstorms," *China Dialogue*, April 13, 2007, chinadialogue.net/article/show/single/en/920-Stopping-the-sandstorms.

129. Shaun Tandon, "Tibetans Rally 50 Years after Uprising," *Washington Post*, March 9, 2009, washingtonpost.com/wp-dyn/content /article/2009/03/09/AR2009030902106.html.

130. Barbara Demick, "Chinese Riot Police, Muslims Clash in Northwestern City," *Los Angeles Times*, July 6, 2009.

131. "Top Chinese Leaders Discuss Policy, Development of Western Regions," Xinhua News Agency, January 23, 2000.

132. Luke Harding, "BP Caught in Tibet Crossfire," *The Guardian*, October 2, 2000.

133. "BP to sell 2 percent stake in PetroChina," *China Daily*, January 13, 2004.

134. World Bank, "Country Lending Summaries—China," 2009, go.worldbank.org/J7TULWEO00.

135. Douglas McGray, "Pop-Up Cities: China Builds a Bright Green Metropolis," *Wired Magazine*, April 24, 2007.

136. Malcolm Moore, "China's Pioneering Eco-city of Dongtan Stalls," *Telegraph* (UK), October 19, 2008, telegraph.co.uk /news/worldnews/asia/china/3223969/Chinas-pioneering-eco-city-of-Dongtan-stalls.html.

137. Moore, "China's Pioneering Eco-city."

138. "Weekly Update," *Access Asia* newsletter, April 16, 2007, excerpted in the *China Economic Review*, www.chinaeconomicreview.com/ editors/2007/04/19/dongtan-eco-potemkin/.

139. McGray, "Pop-Up Cities."

140. Steven Cherry, "How to Build a Green City," Institute of Electronics and Electrical Engineers website, June 2007, www.spectrum .ieee.org/jun07/5128/3.

141. Paul French, "Dongtan: China's Eco-Potemkin Village and Arup's Political Connections," *Ethical Corporation*, podcast, June 4, 2007.

142. Christina Larson, "Cities Grand Plans for Eco-cities Now Lie Abandoned," *Yale Environment 360*, April 6, 2009, e360 .yale.edu/content/feature.msp?id=2138.

143. Paul French, "Dongtan—The line Changes on the Greenwash Eco-city in China," *Ethical Corporation*, February 18, 2008, ethicalcorp .com/content.asp?ContentID=5722.

144. "Asia: City of Dreams; A Chinese Eco-City," *The Economist*, March 21, 2009, 43.

145. Melinda Liu, "All Form, No People," *Newsweek*, March 28, 2009, www.newsweek.com/id/191492.

146. William McDonough & Partners, "Huangbaiyu," www .mcdonoughpartners.com.

147. William McDonough, "The Wisdom of Designing Cradle to Cradle," TED (recorded lecture), Monterey CA, February 2005, www .ted.com/index.php/talks/william_mcdonough_on_cradle_to_cradle _design.html.

148. William McDonough & Partners, "Huangbaiyu."

149. Sarah Schafer and Anne Underwood, "Building in Green," *Newsweek*, September 26, 2005, www.newsweek.com/id/104598/ page/1.

150. Ibid.

151. Singapore Government, "Sino-Singapore Tianjing Eco-city," June 24, 2008, www.tianjinecocity.gov.sg/.

152. Julian Wong, "Creating a Better Life: A Closer Look at the Sino-Singapore Tianjing Eco-city Project," The Green Leap Forward, November 16, 2008, greenleapforward.com/2008/11/16/creating-a-better-life-a-closer-look-at-the-sino-singapore-tianjin-eco-city-proje ct/; and Singapore Government, "Sino-Singapore Tianjing Eco-city."

153. Gu Xiaosong and Li Mingjiang, "Beibu Bay a Good Eco-city Prospect," *Straits Times*, January 6, 2009.

154. Cezar Tigno, "Country Water Action: People's Republic of China Rising Eco-Town Boasts 'No-Flush Toilets,'" Asian Development Bank, March 2008, www.adb.org/water/actions/PRC/Rising-Eco -Town.asp.

155. Berkeley Institute of the Environment, "Bus Rapid Transit in China," University of California Berkeley, 2007, bie.berkeley .edu/brtchina.

Chapter 7. Lessons from Abroad

1. Susan Baker and Bernd Baumgartl, "Bulgaria: Managing the Environment in an Unstable Transition," in *Dilemmas of Transition: The Environment, Democracy, and Economic Reform in East Central Europe,* ed. Susan Baker and Petr Jehlicka, special issue, *Environmental Politics* 7, no. 1 (1998): 189.
2. Fred Singleton, "Czechoslovakia: Greens versus Reds," in *Environmental Problems in the Soviet Union and Eastern Europe,* ed. Fred Singleton (Boulder, Colo.: Lynne Rienner Publishers, 1987), 175–76.
3. Singleton, "Czechoslovakia: Greens versus Reds," 176.
4. Joan DeBardeleben, "The Future Has Already Begun: Environmental Damage and Protection in the GDR," in *To Breathe Free: Eastern Europe's Environmental Crisis,* ed. Joan DeBardeleben (Washington, D.C.: Woodrow Wilson Center Press, 1991), 179.
5. Ibid., 177–78.
6. Joanne Landy and Brian Morton, "Perestroika May Be Both Good and Bad for Eastern Europe's Severe Ecological Crisis," *Utne Reader,* January/February 1989, 86.
7. Miklós Persányi, "Social Support for Environmental Protection in Hungary," in DeBardeleben, *To Breathe Free,* 213–14.
8. Michael Waller, "Geopolitics and the Environment in Eastern Studies," *Environmental Politics* 7, no. 1 (1998): 32.
9. Frances Millard, "Environmental Policy in Poland," *Environmental Politics,* 7, no. 1 (1998): 145.
10. In some cases the functions of environmental protection were merely grafted on to previously existing ministries of agriculture, forestry, or water management. In others, such as Poland, the GDR, and Hungary, in the mid-1980s, environmental protection agencies were granted ministerial status (Barbara Jancar-Webster, "Environmental Politics in Eastern Europe in the 1980s," in DeBardeleben, *To Breathe Free,* 29).
11. DeBardeleben, "The Future Has Already Begun," 185.
12. Susan Baker and Peter Jehlicka, "Dilemmas of Transition: The Environment, Democracy, and Economic Reform in East Central Europe—An Introduction," *Environmental Politics,* 7, no. 1 (1998): 8.

13. Jancar-Webster, "Environmental Politics in Eastern Europe, 25.
14. Michael Waller and Frances Millard, "Environmental Politics in Eastern Europe," *Environmental Politics* 1, no. 2 (1992): 164.
15. Singleton, "Czechoslovakia: Greens versus Reds," 180.
16. Waller and Millard, "Environmental Politics in Eastern Europe," 164.
17. Millard, "Environmental Policy in Poland," 146.
18. Jancar-Webster, "Environmental Politics in Eastern Europe," 38.
19. Singleton, "Czechoslovakia: Greens versus Reds," 180.
20. Christine Zvosec, "Environmental Deterioration: Eastern Europe," *Survey* 28, no. 4 (1984): 135.
21. DeBardeleben, "The Future Has Already Begun," 176.
22. Baker and Jehlicka, "Dilemmas of Transition," 9.
23. Persányi, "Social Support for Environmental Protection in Hungary," 216.
24. Zvosec, "Environmental Deterioration," 138–39.
25. Jancar-Webster, "Environmental Politics in Eastern Europe," 40.
26. Zvosec, "Environmental Deterioration," 136.
27. Millard, "Environmental Policy in Poland," 147–48.
28. Zvosec, "Environmental Deterioration," 136.
29. Persányi, "Social Support for Environmental Protection in Hungary," 218.
30. DeBardeleben, "The Future Has Already Begun," 176.
31. Zvosec, "Environmental Deterioration," 137.
32. Jancar-Webster, "Environmental Politics in Eastern Europe," 44.
33. Robert Peter Gale and Thomas Hauser, *Final Warning: The Legacy of Chernobyl* (New York: Warner Books, 1988), 27, cited in Murray Feshbach and Alfred Friendly Jr., *Ecocide in the USSR* (New York: Basic Books, 1992), 12.
34. Zhores Medvedev, *The Legacy of Chernobyl* (New York: W.W. Norton, 1990), 57, quoted in Feshbach and Friendly, *Ecocide in the USSR.*
35. Feshbach and Friendly, *Ecocide in the USSR,* 83.
36. D. J. Peterson, *Troubled Lands: The Legacy of Soviet Environmental Destruction* (Boulder, Colo.: Westview Press, 1993), 200.
37. Ibid., 197.
38. Feshbach and Friendly, *Ecocide in the USSR,* 22.
39. Jancar-Webster, "Environmental Politics in Eastern Europe," 44.
40. Zvosec, "Environmental Deterioration," 139.
41. Ibid.
42. Jancar-Webster, "Environmental Politics in Eastern Europe," 41.

43. Baker and Jehlicka, "Dilemmas of Transition," 9.
44. Feshbach and Friendly, *Ecocide in the USSR*, 232.
45. Ibid., 223.
46. Ibid., 22.
47. Ibid., 232.
48. Jeffrey Glueck, "Subversive Environmentalism: Green Protest and the Development of Democratic Oppositions in Eastern Europe, Latvia, the Czech Lands, and Slovakia" (B.A. honors essay, Harvard University, 1991), 23–24.
49. Amanda Sebestyen, "Balkan Utopias," *Catalyst* (November 1990/January 1991), 28, in Waller and Millard, "Environmental Politics in Eastern Europe," 161.
50. Glueck, "Subversive Environmentalism," 26.
51. Ibid., 23.
52. Singleton, "Czechoslovakia: Greens versus Reds," 175.
53. Ibid., 179.
54. Jancar-Webster, "Environmental Politics in Eastern Europe," 43.
55. Zvosec, "Environmental Deterioration," 136.
56. Liliana Botcheva, "Focus and Effectiveness of Environmental Activism in Eastern Europe: A Comparative Study of Environmental Movements," *Journal of Environment and Development* (September 1996): 295–96.
57. Jancar-Webster, "Environmental Politics in Eastern Europe," 44–45.
58. Persányi, "Social Support for Environmental Protection in Hungary," 218–19.
59. Helsinki Watch Committee, "Independent Peace and Environmental Movements in Eastern Europe" (Helsinki Watch report, 1992), in Botcheva, "Focus and Effectiveness," 296–97.
60. Jancar-Webster, "Environmental Politics in Eastern Europe," 45–46.
61. Ronnie D. Lipschutz, "Damming Troubled Waters: Conflict over the Danube, 1950–2000," *Intermarium* 1, no. 2 (1997): 7, www.columbia.edu/cu/sipa/REGIONAL/ECE/dam.html.
62. Botcheva, "Focus and Effectiveness," 297.
63. Jancar-Webster, "Environmental Politics in Eastern Europe," 48.
64. Waller and Millard, "Environmental Politics in Eastern Europe," 165–66.
65. Botcheva, "Focus and Effectiveness," 299–300.
66. Peterson, *Troubled Lands*, 216.
67. Ibid., 216–17.
68. Ibid., 216.
69. Baker and Jehlicka, "Dilemmas of Transition," 10.

70. C. Thomassen, "Romania's Black Town," *World Press Review* 40, no. 9 (1993): 43, in Botcheva, "Focus and Effectiveness," 304.

71. Ibid.

72. Ibid., 304–5.

73. Peter Havlicek, "The Czech Republic: First Steps toward a Cleaner Future," *Environment* 39 (April 1997): 18.

74. "Environmental Trends in Transition Economies," Organisation of Economic Co-operation and Development (OECD) Policy Brief, *OECD Observer* (October 1999): 3.

75. Gusztav Kosztolanyi, "Where There's Much There's Brass," *Central Europe Review* 1, no. 12 (September 13, 1999), www.ce-review.org/99/12/csardas12.html.

76. Gerald Fancoj, ed., *The Emerging Environmental Market: A Survey in Bulgaria, Croatia, Romania, and Slovenia* (Szentendre, Hungary: Regional and Environmental Center for Central and Eastern Europe, September 1997), 24, 49–50, www.rec.org/REC/publications/EmEnvMarket2/EmEnvMarket2.pdf.

77. "Europe: Clean Up or Clear Out," *The Economist*, December 11, 1999, 47.

78. Laura A. Henry, "Two Paths to a Greener Future: Environmentalism and Civil Society Development in Russia," *Democratizatsiya*, spring 2002, 184–206.

79. Paul Brown, "US Backs Plan for Russia to Import Nuclear Waste," *The Guardian*, February 19, 2001, in Henry, "Two Paths to a Greener Future," 205.

80. Asian Development Bank, *Asia Water Development Outlook 2007: The Philippines*, 4.

81. Tetsuro Agusa, Takashi Kunito, and Agus Sudaryanto, "Exposure Assessment for Trace Elements from Consumption of Marine Fish in Southeast Asia," *Environmental Pollution* 145 (2007).

82. "Cholera Kills 172 in Indonesia's Papua: Church," Agence-France Presse, July 30, 2008.

83. Chao-Chan Cheng, "A Comparative Study of the Formation and Development of Air and Water Pollution Control Laws in Taiwan and Japan," *Pacific Rim Law and Policy Journal* 3 (1993): S62.

84. *Newsreview*, May 21, 1994, p. 7.

85. Takanori Ohashi, "The State of Fisheries and Aquaculture in Japan," paper presented at the UNITAR Series on Sea and Human Security's Workshop on Food Security, October 1–6, 2006, Hiroshima, Japan.

86. Uma Langkulsen, Wanida Jinsart, and Kanae Karita, "Respiratory Symptoms and Lung Function in Bangkok School Children," *European Journal of Public Health* 16, no. 6 (2006): 676–81.

87. T. J. Burgonio, "Air Pollution Kills Nearly 5,000 Metro Residents Yearly," *The Inquirer* (Manila), September 4, 2007, newsinfo .inquirer.net/breakingnews/nation/view/20070904-86654/air_pollution_kills_nearly_5%.

88. Carter Brandon, "Confronting the Growing Problem of Pollution in Asia," *The Journal of Social, Political and Economic Studies* 21, no. 2 (summer 1996): 199.

89. *The Future of Population in Asia: Population, Natural Resources, and Environment,* East-West Center, 2002.

90. Thailand Forest Figures, Mongabay.com, rainforests.mongabay .com/20thailand.htm.

91. Francisco A. Magno, "Environmental Movements in the Philippines," in Yok-shiu F. Lee and Alvin Y. So, ed., *Environmental Movements in Asia: Comparative Perspectives* (Armonk, NY: M.E. Sharpe 1999), 143.

92. *Key Indicators for Asia and the Pacific,* 2009, Asian Development Bank, 123.

93. Bob Flynn, "Forestry from a Global Perspective: Present and Future," presentation for the Oregon Society of American Foresters, April 2009, www.forestry.org/pdf/osaf_2009/flynn.pdf.

94. Michael Vatikiotis, "Malaysian Forests: Clearcut Mandate," *Far Eastern Economic Review,* October 28, 1993, p. 54.

95. "Was Illegal Logging Responsible for the Flash Flood in North Sumatra?" Indonesian Mediawatch, November 7, 2003, www.rsi.com.sg/english/indonesiamediawatch/view/2003110718209/1/.html.

96. Magno, "Environmental Movements in the Philippines," 149.

97. Yok-shiu F. Lee and Alvin Y. So, "Environmental Movements in Thailand," in *Environmental Movements in Asia,* ed. Lee and So, 120.

98. Hidefumi Imura, "Japan's Environmental Balancing Act: Accommodating Sustained Development," *Asian Survey* 34, no. 4 (1994): 356–57.

99. *Newsreview,* May 21, 1994, p. 7.

100. "Environmental Moves on Right Path," *Yomiuri Shimbun,* October 22, 2000.

101. Procurement Activities—for Suppliers—Green Procurement, Sony Group website, www.sony.net/SonyInfo/procurementinfo/green .html.

102. Law Concerning Environmental Management, Law No. 23, 1997, Asia-Pacific Centre for Environmental Law, National University of Singapore. www.law.nus.edu.sg/apcel/dbase/indonesia/primary/inaem.html.

103. "Government Leader Appreciates NGOs' Cooperation with VN," Embassy of Vietnam in the United States website, November 19, 2003, www.vietnamembassy-usa.org/news/story.php?d=2003111 9162130.

104. Jenny Tan Suat Eam, "Networking for Education for Sustainable Development—A Local and Regional Perspective," presentation for the Regional Centre of Expertise Education for Sustainable Development, Penang, Malaysia, June 19–22, 2006.

105. "News Update: Malaysian Indigenous Leaders Released on Bail," Bruno Manser Fonds press release, September 2009.

106. Jeremy Hance, "Fifteen Indigenous Leaders Arrested in Borneo for Protesting Dams That Would Flood Their Lands," September 16, 2009, mongabay.com.

107. "Protest Against Represive and Intimidative Action of Police Apparatus to Menado Alliance. Indonesian Police Action in Menado is," *Sarekat Hijau Indonesia*, May 11, 2009, sarekathijauindonesia.org/id/content/protest-against-represive-and-intimidative.

108. "Editor Fired over 'Sensitive' Articles," Radio Free Asia, May 15, 2009.

109. Bruno Manser Fonds press release, "News Update: Malaysian Indigenous Leaders Released on Bail," and Sarekat Hijau Indonesia news update, "Protest Against Represive and Intimidative Action of Police."

110. Lee and So, "Environmental Movements in Thailand," 123–24.

111. Ibid., 124–25.

112. *1992 World Development Report* (New York: Oxford University Press, 1992), 88.

113. Magno, "Environmental Movements in the Philippines," 150.

114. Ibid., 152.

115. Takamine Tsukasa, "Asia's Environmental NGOs: Emerging Powers?" *Jakarta Post*, June 14, 1999.

116. Su-Hoon Lee, Hsin-Huang Michael Hsiao, Hua-Jen Liu, On-Kwok Lai, Francisco A. Magno, and Alvin Y. So, "The Impact of Democratization on Environmental Movements," in *Environmental Movements in Asia*, ed. Lee and So, 233.

117. Ibid., 233.

118. Ibid., 234.

119. "Green Korea United Launches Legal Campaign to Save Environment," *Korea Times*, March 31, 2000.

120. Ibid.

121. "Environmental NGOs Have Lost Their Soul," *Nation*, May 18, 2000.

122. Ibid.
123. Hsin-Huang Michael Hsiao, On-Kwok Lai, Hwa-Jen Liu, Francisco A. Magno, Lara Edles, and Alvin Y. So, "Culture and Asian Styles of Environmental Movements," in *Environmental Movements in Asia*, ed. Lee and So, 215.
124. Ibid., 214.
125. EuiSuok Han and Haruhiko Furumura, "Weak Environmental Movements in Japan? Study on Japanese Environmental Groups," paper presented at the Southern Political Science Association Annual Meeting, January 8, 2005, www.allacademic.com//meta/p _mla_apa_research_citation/0/6/6/9/2/pages66926-1.php.
126. Robert Mason, "Whither Japan's Environmental Movement? An Assessment of Problems and Prospects at the National Level," *Pacific Affairs*, July 1, 1999, 193.
127. Ibid., 197.
128. Ibid., 199.
129. Ibid., 198.
130. Lee and So, "Environmental Movements in Thailand," 128–29.
131. Ibid., 139.
132. Takamine Tsukasa, "Asia's Environmental NGOs: Emerging Powers?" *Jakarta Post*, June 14, 1999.
133. Mason, "Whither Japan's Environmental Movement?" 196.
134. Glueck, "Subversive Environmentalism," 30.
135. Feshbach and Friendly, *Ecocide in the USSR*, 232.
136. Ibid., 233.
137. Glueck, "Subversive Environmentalism," 2.
138. Ibid., 6.
139. Ibid., 22.
140. Ibid., 2–3.
141. Ibid., 28.
142. Eric Eckholm, "Spreading Protests by China's Farmers Meet with Violence," *New York Times*, February 1, 1999, p. A1; "Farmers Arrested: Police Arrest Nine Farmers Suspected of Leading a Rural Tax Protest," *South China Morning Post*, February 1, 1999, p. 8.
143. Human Rights in China, "Independent Scholars Detained: Start of 2009 Crackdown?" press release, December 9, 2008. www.hrichina .org/public/contents/press?revision_id=147962&item_id=85186.
144. "China Tops World in Internet Users," CNN.com, January 14, 2009. edition.cnn.com/2009/TECH/01/14/china.internet/index.html.
145. Zhang Xin and Hu Meidong, "PX Plant Cleared, to Shift to Zhangzhou," *China Daily*, January 14, 2009, www2.chinadaily .com.cn/bizchina/2009-01/14/content_7394755.htm.

146. Joan Hu, "Mixed Chinese Reactions Towards Approved PX plant in Zhangzhou," Greenlaw, January 19, 2009, www.greenlaw.org.cn/enblog/?p=378.
147. Al Guo, "Internet Petition Catches the Eye of Premier Wen; Pollution Investigation Fast-Tracked," *South China Morning Post*, June 29, 2009.
148. Ibid.

Chapter 8. Averting the Crisis

1. While U.S. NGOs, business, and universities have become active players in cooperative ventures to strengthen China's legal infrastructure, increase the capacity of China's environmental NGOs, and develop new market-based approaches to environmental protection, the U.S. government remains far behind the curve. Not for lack of trying but rather for lack of funding and opportunity, the central U.S. government agencies, including the Department of Commerce, the Department of State, the Environmental Protection Agency, and the Department of Agriculture, among others, remain hamstrung in their efforts to promote U.S. interests in China. The U.S. Department of Energy appears able to move ahead in areas such as clean coal technologies and research cooperation on nuclear energy, perhaps because these efforts directly benefit U.S. commercial interests.
2. The Department of State's Democracy, Human Rights, and Rule of Law program has embraced the environment as one of its targets of assistance in China. And the U.S. embassy in Beijing has thrown all of its (limited) economic weight behind supporting environmental governance in China.
3. Thomas Lum, "U.S.–Funded Assistance Programs in China," Congressional Research Service Report for Congress, May 18, 2007, 4.

INDEX